Writing the Scen

*Theories of Di
Late Italian F*

Writing the Scene of Speaking

Theories of Dialogue in the
Late Italian Renaissance

JON R. SNYDER

STANFORD UNIVERSITY PRESS 1989
STANFORD, CALIFORNIA

Stanford University Press
Stanford, California
© 1989 by the Board of Trustees of the
Leland Stanford Junior University
Printed in the United States of America

CIP data appear at the end of the book

In memory of Michel de Certeau

... datur hora quieti.
pone caput fessosque oculos furare labori.
—*Aeneid* 5.844–45

Preface

THE IDEA for this book first occurred to me while preparing
a study on Renaissance utopian fiction. The fact that so many
major and minor utopian texts were written in dialogue form
aroused my curiosity, and, in the course of my research, I eventually started looking for works on the theory of dialogue in
the Renaissance. But I discovered little of interest until one day
I came by chance across Speroni's *Apologia dei Dialoghi*. From
there, further reading led me to the other Italian theories of dialogue of the late sixteenth and seventeenth centuries, and ultimately to the question of their place in the history of Renaissance
and Baroque poetics, rhetoric, and esthetics. Once I saw that, despite their creaking conceptual framework, these theoretical texts
offered major—and mostly forgotten—insights into the nature
of dialogical writing, the present work began irresistibly to take
shape until, ironically, my study on utopian fiction had to be
deferred.

Like the late twentieth century, the late sixteenth century was
a time of renewed interest in literary theory. Today we may identify many reasons—historical, political, philosophical—for the
contemporary return to theory in the West. To do the same for
the late Italian Renaissance is more problematic, for the zone that
it occupies is forbidding and remote, and there are few maps
to guide those who venture into it. Still, as Pompey observed,
navigare necesse est: to navigate is necessary. Through a study of
the principal theories of dialogue of the period, this book charts
one aspect of the general trend toward literary theory in the
second half of the sixteenth century in Italy. Yet my purpose is
really a dual one, for the pages that follow are also about the

meaning and design of dialogue as it was perceived by some of the leading literary thinkers of the late Renaissance: Carlo Sigonio, Sperone Speroni degli Alvarotti, Lodovico Castelvetro, and Torquato Tasso.

Dialogue was an important genre in the Renaissance literary system, popular with readers and writers alike, and these theories of dialogue are concerned primarily with the textual procedures that produce—in the sense of Aristotle's "productive" or "poietic" art, in which an object (whether a house or a statue) is made through human labor—dialogical writing. Such writing always represents a scene of speaking; it is a representation *of* words as well as *in* words. However, although this fact was fundamental to the late Renaissance theorists' reflections on dialogue, the implications of their work reach far beyond it. These texts on dialogue provide a window onto a network of other interrelated issues (the conflicting claims of philosophy and literature, reason and imagination, truth and fiction) that much of late Renaissance literary theory was compelled to confront. Dialogue, in other words, spoke directly to some of the most pressing literary *and* theoretical concerns of the age, and this unique quality of dialogue unites the different aspects of this book.

Like many other kinds of literature popular in the Renaissance, however, dialogue did not survive the advent of modernity. The Earl of Shaftesbury, in his "Advice to an Author" (1710), already felt quite sure of himself in bluntly remarking that "dialogue is at an end"; and, notwithstanding some notable exceptions (such as Paul Valéry), the status of dialogue as a part of the literary system did not further improve with the passage of time. Yet in the twentieth century the term 'dialogue' has become a catchword across a broad spectrum of disciplines, from anthropology to hermeneutics to literary theory to psychoanalysis, that together constitute the Western human sciences. Dialogue has come to serve as a metaphor and a model of intersubjective relations or of language itself (as it does, for instance, in the work of Mikhail Bakhtin and Hans-Georg Gadamer). Dialogue was not taken in sixteenth-century Italy, as it so often is today, as an image encompassing the whole of human life, but the common ground of the sixteenth and twentieth centuries may be traced to the divided nature of an enterprise—namely, that of thinking about dialogue—that since antiquity has always brought the same powerfully conflicting set of beliefs and concepts into play and that continues to be cogent for the agenda of theory.

"Every past is worth condemning," Nietzsche remarked in *On the Uses and Disadvantages of History for Life*, but he was quick to add that "though we condemn the errors [of the past] and think we have escaped them, we cannot escape the fact that we spring from them." One may today reject the way the theorists of the late Italian Renaissance thought about dialogue, but not escape the fact that our own discourse on dialogue derives from it and its errors. This recognition does not diminish the standing of dialogue as a metaphor and a model for life in the contemporary world, but rightly recalls it to the genealogical scene in which it is inscribed. This scene—and the perspective that it opens up onto the abyss of the past—may be ignored only if we refuse to think historically, willfully blinding ourselves to the way(s) in which dialogue has come to stand for what it does, four centuries after the Italian Renaissance ceased to wonder about the same thing.

I wish to offer a few caveats to my readers. First, given the complexity of the issues involved, I have made the focus of the book the theories of dialogue themselves, and consequently I do not claim to address in detail here the whole of late Renaissance literary culture in Italy. Nor do I discuss at any length the major twentieth-century theories with a significant ideological investment in the concept of dialogue, such as Bakhtin's dialogics or Gadamer's hermeneutics. Although I am indebted to these and other contemporary approaches to dialogue (Bakhtin in particular serves throughout as an invisible—but invaluable—sparring partner), I am fully convinced that an open engagement with them would have detracted from the specific historical set of literary and esthetic problems that had to be the book's focus.

Among the difficulties that arose in the writing of this book was the choice of terminology. The term 'poetry' (*poesia*) was commonly used in the Renaissance to refer to all of what is now called 'literature,' including every variety of imaginative prose. For contemporary readers, however, this is often a source of confusion—as it often was both in antiquity (*vide* Chapter 1 of Aristotle's *Poetics*) and in the Renaissance (*vide* Castelvetro's theory of dialogue). I have therefore opted to employ the terminology of today's theory and criticism, even though terms such as 'literature,' 'theory,' 'system,' and so on, first gained currency only well after the Renaissance had come to a close and are not used by any of the Italian theorists of dialogue. One final caveat might best be expressed by the Italian maxim *traduttore/traditore* (translator/traitor). Consistent with one of the chief tenets of this book —that critical and theoretical writing is not free of figuration and is never a neutral medium for ideas—I supply the original version of every translated text either in the main body of the text or in the notes. I have used published translations wherever possible; all other translations are my own and are intended only to convey the basic sense of passages in languages other than English. I do not pretend to have captured the elegance of the originals.

The National Endowment for the Humanities generously supported the writing of this book; I received an NEH Summer Stipend in 1985 and an NEH Fellowship for Independent Study and Research in 1986–87. A University of California Regents' Summer Faculty Fellowship in 1984 funded my initial research, and the Committee on Research of the Academic Senate of the University of California at San Diego provided further funding over a number of years. The Department of Literature and the administration of UCSD cheerfully granted me the leaves of absence needed for the completion of my manuscript. I am most grateful to all of the above for their assistance.

Thanks go to Cristina Mazzoni, Christopher Fox, Rand Johnson, James Draznin, and Gail Suber for their help in the preparation of the manuscript. Lawrence d'Almeida, Renzo Bragantini, Jean-Jacques Courtine, Anthony Edwards, Luce Giard, Ed Lee, Allen Mandelbaum, Jean-Luc Nancy, and Daria Perocco gave willingly of their time and expertise as I worked on the various drafts. The staffs of the Bibliothèque Nationale in Paris, the Biblioteca Nazionale Marciana in Venice, the Biblioteca del Seminario Vescovile in Padua, the Beinecke Library, the UCLA Research Library, and the UCSD Central Library all assisted me time and again in my research. The reader for Stanford University Press, Giuseppe Mazzotta, provided helpful comments on the penultimate version of the book. At Stanford University Press itself, John Ziemer skillfully edited the text, John Feneron offered invaluable editorial advice, and Helen Tartar guided the process from start to finish with magnanimity.

My intellectual debts are many, as will be obvious to any reader of this book. One deserves mention more than any other: Michel de Certeau gave me guidance and assistance from the start of my work on the manuscript until his untimely death in Paris in January 1986. Although he would certainly have disagreed with many of the methods and conclusions of this volume, it nonetheless remains marked, as I do, by my encounter with his knowledge and compassion. Finally, a very special thanks to Lucia Re, who watched the manuscript first take shape in Paris and grow day by day in the chestnut-clad hills of the Veneto, who patiently read and commented on every page of the text, and who taught me what dialogue—as an *entre/tien*, or reciprocal "keeping together"—really is.

J. R. S.

Contents

Writing the Scene of Speaking

Theories of Dialogue in the
Late Italian Renaissance

ONE

The Problem of Dialogue in the Late Italian Renaissance

THE SUBJECT OF THIS BOOK is the critical dialogue on dialogue that took place in Italy between 1561 and 1585, toward the end—or certainly the autumn—of the Italian Renaissance.[1] Four works written in this period investigate dialogue in a systematic manner for the first time in Western thought, and in fact signal the only moment in which dialogue appeared as a genuine problem for literary theory anywhere in Europe before the Romantic period. A handful of treatises on dialogue were subsequently published over the course of the seventeenth and early eighteenth centuries, such as G. B. Manso's *Del dialogo* (1628), Sforza Pallavicino's *Trattato dello stile e del dialogo* (1646), and Rémond de Saint-Mard's *Discours sur la nature du dialogue* (1713), but they were few and far between, and did not venture into new or original theoretical territory.[2] Saint-Mard, for instance, writing in 1713 as if the sixteenth-century explorations of dialogue were completely unknown to him, observed that "the nature of dialogue has never been recognized; this is the destiny of simple things."[3] There is more than a grain of truth in this remark, for Renaissance theorists and critics never did arrive—in spite of an intensive effort—at a definitive understanding of dialogue. Even a cursory reading of Saint-Mard's treatise nevertheless shows, beyond any doubt, that his own ideas on dialogue depended heavily on the theories of dialogue of the late Italian Renaissance. It is not surprising that an eighteenth-century French critic such as Saint-Mard would wish to avoid acknowledging any debt to sixteenth-century Italian thought, but the fact is that he could scarcely have looked elsewhere in the Western tradition for a point of departure for his own theory of dialogue. Only in that period and in that place did literary critics or theorists recognize the full extent of the problem of dialogue and treat it as an urgent one for literary studies. Representing three generations of Renaissance intellectual achievement, the four informed and influential Italian writers and their texts—Carlo Sigonio (ca. 1520–84), *De dialogo liber* (1561); Lodovico Castelvetro (1505–71), *La "Poetica" d'Aristotele vulgarizzata et sposta* (1567); Sperone Speroni (1500–1588), *Apologia dei Dialoghi* (1574); and Torquato Tasso (1544–95), *Discorso dell'arte del dialogo* (1585)—that are the subject of the present study provide a unique perspective on attitudes toward dialogue in the second half of the sixteenth century both in Italy and in a Europe still looking to Italian art and thought as a vital ground of past and present culture.[4]

This inquiry begins, then, by acknowledging that to study the theory of dialogue in this light means to focus on the discourse on dialogue of the late Italian Renaissance rather than on dialogue itself. There is a pressing need for a study of the corpus of dialogues produced in the *secondo* Cinquecento, but a historical analysis of the genre of dialogue either in the sixteenth century or in general constitutes a fundamentally different project from the one undertaken here.[5] The ubiquity of dialogue in sixteenth-century Italian and European literature was unquestionably a factor in the emergence of a general theory, even though of the four works studied here only Speroni's discusses any contemporary dialogues in detail. The development of a new attitude toward dialogue in the late Renaissance, however, was marked by the appearance of a highly formalized metadiscourse differing significantly from dialogical writing itself. Rarely is it recognized that "the sixteenth century was as seminal for the theory of dialogue as it was for the writing of dialogues," but that recognition is the basis of this book.[6] This way of thinking and discoursing about dialogue, for better or for worse, represented a sharp reversal of the earlier Renaissance humanists' distrust of theory and insistence instead on "intersubjective dialogue or rhetoric *in utramque partem* as the model of human cognition."[7] Rather than choose between theory and dialogue, the late Italian Renaissance opted for a theory of dialogue, and this brings into bold relief a significant shift in the direction of literary culture and thought on the peninsula.

In their respective treatises, Sigonio, Castelvetro, Tasso, and (to a lesser extent) Speroni searched for a theory and a method with which to analyze as systematically as possible dialogical texts and their *ratio*, and the way of writing about dialogical writing that they invented is the chief focus of this book. Not all four of these theories speak about dialogue in the same way, nor do they share the same general principles and aims. On the contrary, the sharp divisions and disagreements among them, so typical of the critics and theorists of the second half of the Cinquecento, are precisely what make these theories into a "dialogue" on dialogue, rather than a series of works conveying a unified theoretical perspective or representing the position of a single school of critical thought. Whereas Sigonio and Tasso both subscribed to the dominant late-sixteenth-century esthetic principles of order and organicity, Castelvetro developed a highly idiosyncratic theory of literature, and Speroni was concerned more with mapping out the ruses than with analyzing the reasons of dialogue. Sigonio sought to regulate dialogue, Castelvetro to abolish it, Speroni to defend it, and Tasso to exalt it. Whatever their differences, though, all four strove to establish a theoretical *model* of the dialogical text, a project that defines the distance between them and the humanists of the early and high Renaissance. The insistent recurrence of certain characteristic questions in these four works—despite the divergent answers that each provides—defines the common discursive site on which they stand and offers an invaluable empirical basis for understanding what dialogue represented for the *letterati* of the late Italian Renaissance.

These characteristic questions are, by and large, questions of *poetics*, the critical discipline that studies "the systematic functioning of the basic [textual] units and relations that define the production of meaning" in literary discourses.[8] The system of devices, functions, and operations that constitutes the formal representational structure of the literary work has been the object of poetics ever since Aristotle. Both Italian Renaissance poeticians and twentieth-century poeticians (who are found working in various branches of semiotics, structuralism, narratology, text-linguistics, and so forth) seek not "the description of the particular work . . . but the establishment of the general laws of which the particular text is the product," even if their respective methodologies, terminologies, and esthetics are radically dissimilar.[9] All poetics aims at producing a general theory of literary representation rather than a theory of persuasion (rhetoric) or interpretation (hermeneutics), although in practice this distinction between poetics, rhetoric, and hermeneutics is often difficult to maintain.[10] Although the once-appealing structuralist project for a universal science of literature that could take its place alongside the other human sciences—such as linguistics and anthropology—has lost much of its allure in recent times, a similar project for the "establishment of the general laws of which the particular text is the product" was very much a part of late Italian Renaissance theory and criticism, and our view of it ought not to be obscured by the shifting currents of contemporary taste. If one thing besides a common interest in dialogue connects the works of Sigonio, Castelvetro, Speroni, and Tasso, it is that all four set out to define a theory of dialogue precisely in terms of its function as a part of the general literary system, that is, in terms of a poetics. In this respect, the *lignée* that runs from sixteenth- to twentieth-century poetics is not difficult to see. Tzvetan Todorov points out, for instance, that although all twentieth-century formalisms "have their common point of departure in Romantic esthetics, which leads them to assert the autonomy of literature and consequently of its theory," these same twentieth-century formalisms return to the undertaking of the *Poetics* "at the point where Aristotle left off," and in this sense they can more usefully be compared to their sixteenth- rather than to their nineteenth-century counterparts.[11]

In making this comparison, however, Todorov offers only the most perfunctory portrayal of Italian Renaissance literary theory. Of the sixteenth century, he remarks that "Aristotle's *Poetics* is exhumed and made to play a role comparable to that of holy writ: works of poetics will now be nothing more, so to speak, than commentaries on the *Poetics!* But in truth this book is rather betrayed by its glory, which functions as no more than a screen between itself and its readers: the text is so celebrated that no one dares contest or even, finally, to read it at all. Instead it is reduced to a few formulas quickly transformed into clichés that, removed from their context, betray their author's thought altogether."[12] Prone to inconsistency, anachronism, and mistakes of fact, Renaissance readings of the *Poetics* were indeed often profoundly flawed, as Todorov observes. In an age of transition, where the idea of method was not yet fully a part of literary culture, the *methodos* presented in the *Poetics* challenged—and often eluded—the powers of understanding of Renaissance critics and theorists. Todorov's own account of Italian Renaissance poetics is, nevertheless, inadequate. He quite rightly recognizes the genealogical link between sixteenth- and twentieth-century poetics, and his assessment of the superior scientific value of the latter is accurate enough ("the various formalists of the twentieth century are . . . closer to the spirit of the *Poetics* than were its sixteenth-century admirers").[13] However, the notion of sixteenth-century poetics as "a few formulas quickly transformed into clichés" is itself clichéd and stereotypical. Was poetics in the late Italian Renaissance simply one overblown commentary on the *Poetics*, as Todorov claims? Is there nothing to be found in these theories of literature except ritual formulas and commonplace notions that betray Aristotle's ideas on a general theory of literature? Was Aristotle's project for a poetics accepted uncritically throughout the Renaissance and then indifferently recycled over and over again until well into the seventeenth century? Did no one in the Renaissance really read the *Poetics* or contest the theory of poetics itself? The present work, through a case study of the theory of dialogue, tries to offer another, and I hope more balanced, view of Renaissance poetics and all its inherent complexities, contradictions, powers, and limits, a view that bears little resemblance to Todorov's. If he, or anyone else, wants to situate the developments of twentieth-century poetics, from Russian formalism to structuralism to narratology, as part of a genealogical descent from Aristotle's seminal work, a more accurate and a more detailed analysis of the range of resources of its half-forgotten predecessor—Renaissance poetics—is required.

Before asking "why a theory of dialogue?" one might first legitimately ask "why *dialogue*?" Why focus on the Renaissance theory of this particular literary form rather than on theories of the tragedy, lyric, novella, or masque? The reason has to do, first of all, with the double nature of dialogue itself since its inception. From its origins in ancient Greece through its Hellenistic, Roman, Alexandrine, Byzantine, and medieval phases and, finally, to its recovery in the Italian Renaissance and subsequent adoption by writers all across Europe, dialogue stood as an ideal of a casual, conversational prose that was also a "representation of the life of thought."[14] The irony of Plato's Socrates, the urbanity of Cicero and his circle of friends, the trenchant satirical wit of Lucian, the *asolare* of Bembo's courtiers and the *sprezzatura* of Castiglione's, the gentle raillery of More and the fierce mockery of Erasmus, the cunning of Aretino and the cleverness of Machiavelli, have represented for generations of readers —both during and since the Renaissance—unique and enduring qualities of the dialogical style of writing. Whether set as an encounter between friends, casual acquaintances, or adversaries, dialogue always represents a "scene of speaking" that is an intersubjective exchange not only of conversational phrases (for example, standard or scripted questions and answers) but of contrasting ideas and intellectual perspectives as well.

There were, needless to say, many different kinds of dialogues and dialogical styles in the Renaissance; the expository, the courtly, the didactic, and the satiric were simply among the most prominent of the different subgenres. More than any other, though, the *philosophical* dialogue stood out as the most significant of the various dialogical styles of the Italian Renaissance for the theory of dialogue. Although in the fifteenth century the works of Cicero were far and away the single most influential model for writers of dialogue in Italy, for much of the sixteenth century Plato's philosophical dialogues enjoyed unparalleled prestige up and down the peninsula, for in them the art of conversation as an art of thinking aloud is developed to the highest degree.[15] Socrates and his interlocutors—whether his companions or adversaries—lead their talk into an investigation of, or *inter-view* on, a question of ethical or philosophical importance, in which Socrates usually either draws an acceptable answer out of the other speaker(s) or forces him or them into a paralyzing contradiction, although occasionally the conversation is left suspended in an *aporia*. Many if not most important sixteenth-century Italian dialogues, ranging from Aretino's ferocious satires to Tasso's suave conversations, took Plato—sometimes in tandem with Cicero—as their chief discursive model or chief polemical target. And the sixteenth-century theorists of dialogue followed suit. In the pages that follow, 'dialogue' serves as an umbrella term to designate full-length literary or philosophical dialogues like Cicero's and Plato's, in which issues are raised and discussed extensively, if not always exhaustively, to the exclusion of virtually all else, rather than dramatic dialogue or narrative prose dialogue of the sort found in novels, novellas, and the like.

From Petrarch to Galileo, dialogue permeated the literary space and system of the Italian Renaissance. Especially in the sixteenth century, few if any other prose forms commanded the recognition afforded to dialogue. Charles S. Baldwin remarks that "perhaps the most popular of the ancient prose forms in the Renaissance was dialogue; for it was used even oftener in the vernaculars than in Latin, and became a favorite form of exposition. The Middle Ages, of course, had many dialogues, but not of this sort. *Débat, estrif, conflictus*, amoeban eclogue were often allegorical and generally forms of poetry. Renaissance dialogue is typically prose discussion."[16] In an age before the essay and the novel were readily available as prose forms, dialogue functioned predominantly as a means of performing analysis, exposition, narration, and the like in a prose discussion without the constraints of the more formalized genres of writing such as the demonstrative treatise or the history. Writing in 1632, Galileo noted in his preface to the *Dialogo sopra i due massimi sistemi del mondo* that "I have thought it most appropriate to explain these concepts in the form of dialogues, which, not being restricted to the rigorous observance of mathematical laws, make room also for digressions which are sometimes no less interesting than the principal argument."[17] The protean nature of dialogue, which allows for a limited number of different formal configurations and a seemingly infinite number of possible themes, certainly helps to account for its prominence and popularity in the Renaissance: in the sixteenth century in particular, everything from rhetorical handbooks to medical treatises to travel narratives to manuals on dueling to erotic fiction to utopias can be found in dialogue form. Dialogue became a convention, even an institution, for representing the margins of what could be represented in the Renaissance literary system of generic codes and forms. That dialogue would also gain greatly in prestige in the eyes of the Renaissance from its origins in ancient Greek and Roman philosophy is not difficult to understand. (Raphael's *School of Athens* fresco in the Vatican, 1510–11—perhaps one of the most famous works of art of the age—portrays Plato and Aristotle engaged in a dialogue, for instance, and similar images abound in sixteenth-century Italian painting.) The diffusion of dialogue throughout all levels of literary endeavor in the Cinquecento, however, was a phenomenon that went beyond dialogue's links to antiquity alone.

The Platonic-Ciceronian model of reasoned prose discussion was so congenial to sixteenth-century writers because it is so unusually eclectic a model of expository and narrative prose. Dialogue's appeal to those writers lay, first of all, in the rapid shifts in the direction of the conversation that it permits, and even encourages: speakers may move, or drift at times, from one topic to the next. As Galileo noted, dialogue is not "restricted to the rigorous observance of mathematical laws" in the form of its discourse; its narrative logic is not strictly linear and not always predictable for the reader. Although dialectic often plays an important role in the scene of speaking in Renaissance dialogues and limits the topical drift of the discussion, dialogue in general offers prose writers the opportunity to pursue the investigation of a given issue *laterally*. This lateral direction of dialogical conversation—as opposed to the vertical logical steps required in a demonstration—provides for a far more flexible and open arrangement of a sequence of topics, narrative *loci*, and other elements than that found in the various kinds of nonfictional prose treatises.

At the same time, the restricted literary nature of the dialogical model—its reduction of the speaking situation to a basic set of variables and to a more or less minimal degree of narrativity —contributed greatly to making dialogue so popular and utilizable for Renaissance writers in many different fields. Dialogue does not test the writer's technical skill in manipulating a highly encoded set of formal conventions to the same degree as, say, a romance in *ottava rima* or a Petrarchan sonnet. Although embellishment and ornamentation are possible, even desirable, in dialogue, the structural elements of its narrative can, if necessary, be reduced to the briefest of formulas—"X said . . . Y answered" —which does not require characterization of the speakers (even their names may at times be omitted). If so desired, the energy and creativity of the dialogist may be spent almost entirely on the text's *inventio* rather than on its *elocutio*. This helps to explain the often utilitarian nature of the form in the sixteenth century and the low level of literarization that it achieved in many manuals, travel narratives, or works of utopian fiction, in which the emphasis is on the novelty of what is being reported by the speakers rather than on how they say it. With its restricted narrative structure that mimics real-life conversation and its marked tendency toward an expository prose bordering on documentary fiction, dialogue appears as the polar opposite of allegory in the sixteenth-century literary system. Dialogue, in fact, resists complete literarization even in the case of works that are most often considered representative of the literary potential of the genre in the Renaissance, such as Castiglione's *Il Cortegiano*, More's *Utopia*, or Tasso's *Minturno*. Even in its most sophisticated form, dialogue shuttles between the literary and the extra-literary, disrupts the boundaries between fiction and nonfiction, and explores the tension between figure and statement. How and why this should occur are the main concerns of the late Renaissance theories of dialogue in Italy.

The process by which the writing of dialogue came to be seen, for a relatively brief period in the second half of the sixteenth century, as an important object of literary theory may be called its "problematization."[18] Almost as soon as critics and theorists in Italy began to consider the possibility of a general theory of literary discourse, dialogue appeared to them as an obvious problem for that theory. When Pietro Angeli wrote to the Florentine *letterato* Benedetto Varchi, in letters of November and December 1553, that Varchi was wrong to argue in *Della Poetica* (1553) that dialogue is in any way a literary genre, the problematization of dialogue was still in its prehistory in Italy.[19] By the time Torquato

Tasso completed the *Discorso dell'arte del dialogo* in 1585, however, this process of thinking about dialogue as a problem had already reached the outer limits of its trajectory. In between these two moments, the Renaissance theories of dialogue came into existence and proposed a multiplicity of possible answers to the questions raised by dialogical writing about the relationship between fiction and cognition, or, to put it another way, between fiction and statement. As Hans-Georg Gadamer observes in regard to the activity of understanding and interpreting in general works that have come down to us from the past, "We can understand a text only when we have understood that question to which it is an answer."[20] And nowhere is this more the case than in understanding the questions that dialogue posed for sixteenth-century theorists and critics, and the answer(s) that it demanded.

The present work, as a study of the rise and eclipse of the activity of theorizing about dialogue at the threshold of early modern Europe, takes as its subject "the history of an answer—the original, specific, and singular answer of thought—to a certain situation";[21] the series of texts by Sigonio, Castelvetro, Speroni, and Tasso forms that history of an answer, and the situation that they answer is the problem (the set of questions) presented by dialogue itself for literary theory in the late Italian Renaissance. This brief description does not do justice, though, to the full complexity of the motivations for the different theories of dialogue. Ranging from the orthodox to the eccentric, from the predictable to the unlikely, these texts and their arguments are writerly inventions, not coldly mechanical, quasi-anonymous responses to a merely academic matter. Only Sigonio wrote his treatise while holding a university chair; Castelvetro composed his work while in exile, a fugitive with a death sentence hanging over his head at home; Speroni produced his theory out of a face-to-face confrontation with the Roman Inquisition; Tasso completed his text in the solitude of his prison chamber in Ferrara.

Moreover, the history that these four texts form—even though focused on the problem of dialogue—cannot be described as an effect of a single identifiable cause, just as no critical or theoretical discourse, no matter how sharp its contours and how

clearly visible its agenda, is ever the product of a single intention or cause. The emergence of a discourse on dialogue in the
Cinquecento was caught up in a multitude of larger literary and
historical processes as well. These included the contemporary
sixteenth-century debate over critical methodologies, the *questione della lingua* that so concerned Italian humanists and *letterati*
as a vernacular literature took hold throughout the peninsula,
the continued efforts of humanism to recuperate ancient thought
and art for the benefit of present cultural life, the widespread
practice of writing and reading dialogues of every conceivable
kind, the rise of a print culture, the growth of censorship with
the development of the Counter-Reformation, the shift in the
institutional locus of criticism and theory from the courts to
the universities and academies, and so on; this brief list barely
scratches the surface of all the possibilities.[22] The four theories of
dialogue of concern here are, in short, implicated in some of the
most significant developments of literary discourse in Italy in
the Cinquecento. However, it is not my purpose here to examine
these texts on dialogue in terms of such a vast literary and historical framework, which is still itself imperfectly understood.[23]
The governing premise of the present work is that the conditions
of thinking and writing about—or problematizing—dialogue in
the sixteenth century in Italy are most effectively analyzed by
reading theoretical texts as elaborate fictions involving an interplay of philosophical concepts and performative elements, strategic moves and rhetorical subterfuges, elements of logic and
elements of persuasion, that map out the position of dialogue
and the theory of dialogue for the late Renaissance in Italy and
in Europe.

The possibility of a value-free, neutral, and descriptive science
of poetics was as much of a chimera in the sixteenth century
as it is in the twentieth. The late Renaissance discourse on dialogue took the form of a theoretical poetics of dialogue, but these
theories were inevitably also readings of dialogues, and reading—no matter how theoretical or descriptive—always involves
valuation, estimation, and assessment. This in turn means that
the task of reading the texts of sixteenth-century theorists of dialogue, as with other Renaissance theoretical works, is to make
explicit the *value* of a given theory for any given theorist and

thus to reveal the position of its discourse. The exploration in the present study of the original, singular, and specific answer to the problem of dialogue of each of these four late Renaissance works takes the form of an analysis of the textual procedures that provide a "field of operations within which theory is itself produced . . . a theory which is the literary gesture of those procedures themselves."[24] Each of these four theories of dialogue is a literary gesture or textual locus of the procedures implemented and inscribed in a discourse by an individual theorist, who must select a set of discursive strategies from the pool of available Renaissance methods and procedures for the analysis of literature, ranging from the various versions of Aristotelian poetics to rhetorical criticism to Neoplatonic allegorical interpretation and so on. The answer supplied by each theory to the problem of dialogue is understandable chiefly in terms of the field of operations within which it is configured, just as thinking is itself always performed from within an order that is already in place and is understandable in terms of that order. Sigonio, for instance, brings together the methodologies of rhetoric and poetics in *De dialogo liber* and marshals as much philological support as possible from the body of dialogical literature for his theory; Castelvetro, on the other hand, employs procedures of logic as well as rhetoric and poetics in *La "Poetica" d'Aristotele* but is largely indifferent to philological evidence concerning the tradition of dialogical writing. Within each of these choices many other choices (whose definition of rhetoric? what version of poetics? which tradition of dialogue?) influence, each in its own way, the production of the theoretical text. The relationship of theory to those procedures that produce it, as well as to those that are its object of study, therefore necessarily forms a part of this inquiry.[25]

The analysis performed in the chapters that follow is fundamentally two-pronged. The definition of the procedures of dialogical writing formulated by each respective discourse on dialogue is examined, naturally enough, since each theoretical text defines dialogue as having its own separate and distinct logic of representation unlike that of any other kind of writing. But although they have much to tell us about their object of study, these theories are not simply keys to reading and interpreting

Renaissance dialogue; they are themselves always figural as well as analytical in nature and demand to be read and interpreted as literary gestures in their own right. The logic of the practice that produces each theoretical text has a figural aspect that is irreducible and that is essential to that practice; and this too is crucial to understanding the problem that dialogue presents for literary theory in the late Italian Renaissance. In the most general sense, if the present work subscribes to a methodological principle, it is that these four treatises on dialogue elude the grasp of traditional literary history and instead demand to be studied as the textual products—or literary gestures—of specific discursive practices of late Renaissance culture in Italy.

One of the most important lessons of post-structuralist thought is that what is literary can no longer be confined to a narrowly defined canon of masterpieces: it is axiomatic for this study that these theoretical texts belong to a Renaissance literature about literature that still has value for us today as readers, even if it is not a part of the traditional canon. In reducing them to a single idea or set of ideas and in depriving them (through paraphrase) of their complex relationship to a given field of operations, however, we lose sight of the inherent literary and figural qualities of each of these theories. And with the loss of these qualities, all sense of the contours of the problem of dialogue for late Renaissance thought vanishes as well, for we are left with a stripped-down and highly oversimplified end result of the critical process that mocks the complexity of the process itself.[26] To localize the strategies of theorizing about dialogue in the late Italian Renaissance in the interplay between text and theory means to designate their historicity as practices of writing and to probe the problematic nature of dialogue for Renaissance poetics.

One of the interesting things about late Renaissance theories of dialogue is that, in quite different ways, they portray dialogue as making almost impossible demands on any conventional understanding of literature. Common to Sigonio, Castelvetro, and Tasso (Speroni's case is somewhat different) is the perception that dialogue differs from other kinds of writing because of its close connection—above all in antiquity—with philosophy itself and with dialectic in particular (see Chapters 2 and 3 for detailed treatments of dialectic). Each of their theoretical works examines the problem of dialogue in terms of the special bond that unites it to dialectical thought; but this bond is a deeply troubling one for late Renaissance literary theory. What guarantees the primacy of extra-literary elements in a dialogical text and makes its fiction subordinate to its dialectical topic? And if in dialogue all fictional elements hold the rank of *ancilla* (handmaiden) in relation to dialectic, then what is to be made of the specificity of dialogical representation or, as it were, its irreducible literariness?[27] Innumerable problems in poetics and esthetics characterize the Italian literary culture of the *secondo* Cinquecento, but this problem of the literariness of dialogue is one of the most imposing.[28] A heightened critical awareness after 1550 in Italy of the intricacy and ubiquity of fiction—presaging the appearance of Baroque literary culture—helps to make an encounter with the problem of dialogue, as the intersection of logic and literature, a potentially explosive one. For the four late Renaissance theorists studied here, no satisfactory understanding of the positions of dialectic and fiction in a general system of discourse is possible without a theory of dialogue, since dialogue is the common place that lies in between them. The importance of this perception in the sixteenth century can scarcely be overemphasized. Of course, many hundreds of theoretical works about dozens of literary genres appeared in the later stages of the Renaissance in Italy; not all of them are of equal quality or equal interest to us today. What makes these four particular works on dialogue worth investigating is the direct way in which they confront the relationship between the laws of fiction and a certain kind of dialectical—even, at times, philosophical—writing, or textuality. The poetics of dialogue in the late Italian Renaissance is an exploration, in essence, of one of the most fundamental questions of all theory and criticism, whether ancient or modern: What is literature?

The very possibility of a theoretical poetics of dialogue in the sixteenth century hinged on the premise of a general system of genres of discourse. Dialogue appeared as the kind of writing that, perhaps more than any other, put into question for sixteenth-century criticism and theory the notion of a fixed, predetermined, hierarchical order of discursive genres or kinds, challenging the conventional Renaissance understanding of the difference between literature and dialectical discourse or, at another level, the difference between the discourses of fiction and cognition.[29] Thinking about the poetics of dialogue thus inevitably entailed thinking about the larger system of discourses to which literature itself belongs.

More than two centuries later, and in another context, the nature of the generic distinction between literature and philosophy itself was to become a major concern of Continental Romanticism; it re-emerged once again in the post-structuralist period as the problematic of an undifferentiated universe of writing (or *écriture*), perhaps best exemplified by Jacques Derrida's programmatic remark "Il n'y a pas de hors-texte." The players change over time, of course, as do the rules of the game, but the stakes remain just as high in the passage from the sixteenth to the twentieth century. If dialogue is a fiction, late Renaissance theorists ask, then how can it also be a "kind" of dialectical/philosophical writing, and, conversely, how can dialectical/philosophical dialogue ever be considered a "kind" of literature? Despite powerful constraints, the sixteenth-century theories of dialogue interrogate the boundaries between the literary and philosophical traditions in their search for an answer to these and other related questions. The textuality of dialectic and the epistemological function of literature, as issues for late Renaissance theory, are intertwined with this notion of a generic difference between the discourses of fiction and cognition. The debate today about the reflexivity of the genres of literature and philosophy finds an important, and neglected, segment of its own prehistory in sixteenth-century theorizing about dialogue.

Perhaps there is another way of putting this point in perspective. In the early years of the seventeenth century, the results of Galileo's research in astronomy and physics suggested for the first time that to study the stars and planets scientifically also meant to accept that one is oneself an object of rational inquiry, an object of science, since in displacing the earth from its privileged position at the center of the universe one acknowledges being determined by and enclosed in the same system as that which is under study. Both of these procedures were equally challenging to the dominant *epistēmē* of Counter-Reformation culture in Italy (as Galileo's trial and conviction so eloquently demonstrate). The search, in the second half of the sixteenth century in Italy, for a philosophy of literature in the form of a theory—a poetics—of dialogue became a search for the place of dialectical discourse in relation to literature. Although in the accepted view, this place was wholly or partly outside the literary system, the problematization of dialogue led to the discovery that a philosophy of literature raised the question of the writing of (a certain kind of) philosophy as well. Although no one would claim that these texts generated the kind of revolutionary paradigmatic shift in Western thought marked by Galileo's work, they did confront one of the problems of an emergent modernity, for any answer that they proposed had either to defend or to refute the belief that the system of definite and probable knowledge is not determined and enclosed by the system of writing that it studies. The impossibility of resolving this problem in the Italian Renaissance in the same fashion as it has been in modern esthetic theory is obvious, but the resolution sixteenth-century theorists finally arrived at for the problem that dialogue presents is still anything but obvious.

From the vantage point of today, the late Renaissance theories of dialogue appear as studies of the related themes of speaking and thinking, themes that are privileged ones for both dialectic and dialogical representation (just as Socratic dialogues are often considered an exercise in thinking aloud). The relationship between thought and speech was a vital concern in the sixteenth century, whether it was formulated in terms of a theory of dialogue, a theory of conversation such as Stefano Guazzo's *La civil conversatione* (sic; 1574), or a theory of simulation such as Lucio Paolo Rosello's *De la vita de' cortigiani, intitolato la patientia* (1549).[30] More generally, this same theoretical matrix includes all of the abundant *trattatistica* of the period concerning rhetoric, dialectic, mystical discourse, and the other "arts" and practices in which speaking and thinking are inseparable. A note of caution, however, needs to be interjected here. It would be an error (although an infinitely seductive one) to see dialogue as reflecting the norms of conversation itself in the sixteenth century or to see the theory of dialogue as the literary equivalent of a theory of conversation.[31] Nothing could be further from the case. Each of these theories of dialogue aims to show how fundamentally different the rules (or codified strategies) governing writing are from the rules governing conversation or even formal debate. Dialogues are never transcriptions of conversations or debates that actually occurred (although this is one of their enabling fictions); no unmediated traces of orality can be discovered in dialogue, except in the form of a carefully constructed illusion. This point was, however, so self-evident to sixteenth-century Italian theorists of dialogue that they rarely made much of it. Instead, their concern was the art of constructing a simulated conversation in a text, and in their eyes this art was defined principally by poetics rather than by the theory of conversation itself. Although all dialogue plays on the resemblance between the spoken and the written, a clear sense of the difference between spoken and written dialogue informs all the theories examined here; the late Renaissance theorists refer to the texts of Plato, Aristotle, and other ancient thinkers, not to the practice of speaking and listening in everyday life, as the basis of their ideas on dialogue. If anything, in fact, the appearance of a chain of theories of dialogue in Italy in the years between 1561 and 1585 suggests an increasing awareness of the distance between social life and its representations or, in other words, between everyday speech acts and dialogues, which were seen as being compelled to operate according to the laws of fiction and of the literary system. The discourse on dialogue, with its awareness of the autonomy of writing from speech, appears as but one among many symptoms of the growing gap between literature and social life as the sixteenth century drew to a close in Italy.

The organization of the present study follows a fairly straight-forward chronology from Sigonio to Tasso, but more as a matter of expediency than anything else. No inexorable logic of progressive development of a discourse on dialogue leads from the former to the latter; Tasso is, in the last analysis, no closer to finding an answer to the problem of dialogue than is Sigonio. This is not, however, to be taken as the sign of a deficiency on their part. No one could have been more aware of the discontinuous nature of the development of criticism and theory than the *letterati* of the Renaissance, who devoted themselves to interpreting the enigmatic traces and restoring the ruins of a remote culture that lay more than a millennium and a half away from them (if not further), while scorning the interference of the intervening centuries. Sigonio's text serves as my point of incision into the problem of dialogue simply because it is, historically speaking, the first of the chain of sixteenth-century theories. Speroni's theory of dialogue was not published until 1596, more than two decades after it was written; although it circulated in manuscript form like so many other works of the period, it could have had relatively little direct effect on the subsequent direction of the debate about dialogue in Italy (only Pallavicino, writing in the mid-seventeenth century, took the *Apologia dei Dialoghi* into account in constructing a theory of dialogue). Despite the fact that it was published in distant Vienna, and not easily available in Italy, Castelvetro's work was so important for Tasso's that it is practical to combine the study of the two in one chapter, even though this flouts the historical order of composition of the four theories. This series of texts, in short, may best be understood not in chronological but in dialogical terms; they are contrasting and opposing voices that may address each other and engage in a dialogue with each other in these pages. The reader is invited to consider the reappearance of certain key questions from one chapter to the next as defining the link between these authors, without supposing that Speroni's ideas on dialogue necessarily represent an improvement on Sigonio's, or that Tasso's theory should be superior to all the others simply because it is the most recent one. These four theories of dialogue are all contained within the same paradigmatic discursive space of the waning phases of the Italian Renaissance, and they do not participate in a process of progressive enlightenment and critical overcoming of error, as modern thought is generally expected to do.

The literary criticism and the literary theory of the second half of the sixteenth century are, in point of fact, still largely a terra incognita. Most modern scholars would agree that this immense body of work stands "at a crucial point in the history of Western criticism, that point at which the doctrines of classical antiquity were transformed into something new and different, which in its turn became the basis of modern literary criticism" and the basis of modern esthetics as well.[32] This commonly accepted truth of literary history has, however, stimulated surprisingly little serious modern research into the texts of the period. Over the course of the nineteenth and twentieth centuries, under the influence of Romantic literary historiography and, later, of neo-Romantic stylistics and philology, the Age of Criticism has generally been treated with disdain by critics and intellectual historians alike. The many accusations made against the criticism and theory of the *secondo* Cinquecento may be summed up as follows: its discourse is excessively elaborate and labyrinthine; its insistence that no literary practice of writing is conceivable without an accompanying theory of writing stifles true creativity; its academic concern for genres and for a hierarchical literary order chills and hardens the experience of reading poetry and fiction; and its lack of true philosophical and critical rigor (as Todorov, for instance, asserts) is lamentable. The formalism of the late Italian Renaissance is, in this modern perspective, symptomatic of the general decadence of Italian culture in the late sixteenth century, a servile culture largely under foreign domination and in the iron grip of the Inquisition, no longer capable of producing great minds and great works like those of the high Renaissance humanists and courtiers.[33]

Such a view of the latter half of the Cinquecento as a period of unchecked cultural decline in Italy that has filled our libraries with forgotten, or forgettable, works is by now badly out-of-date and is already in the process of revision, but it still lingers on in many quarters.[34] Yet it would be impossible to imagine a Renaissance theory of dialogue without the vital and multiform presence of Italian Aristotelianism, for instance, which "attained its greatest development in the sixteenth and early seventeenth centuries" even as humanism began to lose its position of prominence in Italy.[35] Sigonio, Castelvetro, Speroni, and Tasso all either studied or taught at the University of Padua, which was one of the leading centers of Aristotelianism on the peninsula in the second half of the century. The literary critics and theorists associated with Padua between the 1550's and the 1580's sought to participate in the continuing development of this Aristotelian current, but by scrutinizing the *Poetics* rather than the *Physics* or the *Metaphysics*. A careful reading of late Renaissance theoretical works reveals this Aristotelianism not to be an unquestioned and unquestionable item of faith, but a flexible and composite system of thought, often combined with elements of other systems of thought (Neoplatonism, among others) in a freely individual way. In light of this, the present study explores the routes taken by the various discourses on dialogue without subscribing to the modern resistance to the theories of the late Italian Renaissance.[36] The process of transformation of the doctrines of antiquity into something new and different—into a Renaissance poetics or, in this instance, into a poetics of dialogue—is an integral component of the literary history of the sixteenth century, even if the place of theory in that history has yet to be fully defined. My aim is to trace the itinerary of the poetics of dialogue—as a *dis-cursus*, a discourse traveling in a number of different directions at once—as a part of the literary history of the sixteenth century, in order to discover what the poetics and esthetics of Sigonio, Castelvetro, Speroni, and Tasso have to do with the basis of modern criticism and theory.

The extensive—and sometimes indiscriminate—use of authorities from antiquity is a common feature of virtually all Renaissance critical and theoretical discourse in Italy. Arguments among sixteenth-century critics about contemporary literature (such as that between the advocates of Ariosto and the supporters of Tasso) were often set in a framework of "truths" and well-known *sententiae* taken from the ancient authors; and, of course, debates over ancient literature (such as that between the partisans of Homer and the enthusiasts of Virgil) almost inevitably were. The florilegia of sixteenth-century rhetorical criticism exemplify this widespread tendency to collect and accumulate *sententiae* and authorities from antiquity. This same tendency, however, also strongly reflects "a desire to find in these ancient . . . materials a new critical apparatus: what results from this desire operating on these materials" generally assumes the form of a literary theory quite unlike anything found in antiquity.[37] In late Renaissance criticism and theory, there is a constant give-and-take between concern for precedent and desire for innovation.[38] Anyone wanting to write a theory of dialogue in the Cinquecento, however, had to contend with a limited field of possible authorities from antiquity, for what the ancient world thought about writing dialogue was known only in fragmentary form; anyone wishing to arrive at an understanding of the various theories of dialogue in antiquity was obliged to seek out widely scattered statements and brief asides in philosophical and historical works, rhetorical treatises, letters, and so on.[39]

More than a little of what is now known of ancient thought is quite naturally the result of an accident of survival. Still, on the balance of all available evidence, it seems likely that no treatise on the writing of dialogue was ever produced in antiquity, even though dialogue was an important part of the canon of literary forms. Critics in the ancient world tended not to write treatises dealing exclusively with single genres: even Aristotle's *Poetics*, for example, originally existed in two parts, and dealt with both tragedy and comedy. Although the remaining traces of reflection on the dialogical *lex operis* are spread throughout the extant body of ancient criticism and philosophy, there is no sense of a fully formed *question* of dialogue—or a desire to question dialogue—in the way in which dialogical writing is discussed. Although such philosophers, rhetoricians, and critics as Xenophon, Cicero, Quintilian, Diogenes Laertius, Demetrius, Longinus, and Athenaeus addressed at least a few words to the art of writing dialogue, nowhere in the residue of ancient culture is the desire to produce a total theory—or a poetics—of dialogical writing detectable. What can be found instead are fairly general remarks on the "conversational style" of dialogue, on the rhetorical figure of dialogism (the figure of question and answer), or on the sense of one or more of Plato's own dialogues. Nevertheless, some of these fragments had a significant impact on the direction of the Renaissance discourse on dialogue, serving as touchstones for the effort to develop a poetics of dialogical writing in the sixteenth century.

Although the scattered and discrete fragments of ancient thought on dialogue represent different moments in the history of reflection on dialogue, it would be pointless to pretend to narrate here the genesis of the theory of dialogue in antiquity, for there is no story of its origins to tell. Like the theories of Sigonio, Castelvetro, Speroni, and Tasso in the sixteenth century, there is no development of ancient thought on dialogue for us to discover, and no sense that one fragment of theory is somehow closer to describing the essence of dialogical writing than any other. The differences among these texts cannot be explained in terms of a linear model of progress toward an ever-clearer sense of the meaning of dialogue, as any careful examination of those differences shows. To this extent, these fragments from antiquity do not constitute a foundation (*fundamentum absolutum et inconcussum*) for later theories of dialogue, any more than they themselves form a unified body of theory, or any more than there exists an unbroken continuity stretching from classical Greek culture to the culture of the Renaissance that would legitimate such a claim to a foundational knowledge. The affiliations between ancient thought on dialogue and late Renaissance thought on dialogue are to be understood, in other words, not as evolutionary links in the history of a theory, but as relationships traversed by resistances and reversals that escape any easy determination.[40] In antiquity, as in the Renaissance, the theme of the theory of dialogue divides and dissociates the texts examined here as much as it binds them together.

Plato and his dialogues occupy a commanding position of influence in the history of both sixteenth-century dialogue and thought about dialogue in Italy.[41] From Bembo and Castiglione to Tasso and Bruno, one of the principal reasons that sixteenth-century Italian writers chose to compose dialogues—in either the vernacular or in Latin—is that the form is so intimately associated with the venerated name of Plato. Not only did Platonic philosophy constitute one of the chief intellectual currents of the Cinquecento, but, since nearly all of Plato's works are dialogues, dialogue also enjoyed an unparalleled prestige in the period as a model textual vehicle for the representation of philosophical conversation and the (re)discovery of truth.[42] Dialogue, with its seemingly unsystematic conversational style, so different from the scholastic *altercatio*, colloquy, *sophismata*, or *quaestiones*, was seen in the Renaissance as one of the most legitimate of all ancient textual forms because of its proximity to the origin of classical Greek philosophy.[43] And since even in antiquity Plato's dialogues were imitated by Cicero and others, the practice of dialogical *imitatio* acquired validity for Renaissance writers as well. The sixteenth-century theories of dialogue were certainly, in one regard, an attempt to answer the problem posed by Plato's dialogues as one of the most authoritative of all models of writing from antiquity still without a theory to accompany it. Sigonio, Castelvetro, Speroni, and Tasso were all acutely aware of this lacuna in the late Renaissance encyclopedia of theory and sought to correct it by returning to the original Platonic model and its offshoots in antiquity for the basis of their own respective discussions of dialogue.

The lack in antiquity of an authentic metalanguage of dialogue is highly evident in the oeuvre of Plato. Although writing almost exclusively in dialogue form, Plato addresses only the briefest of comments in his work—which has survived the ravages of time virtually intact—to the question of dialogical representation. Today it is often forgotten that Plato was not the first Greek to write dialogues, although his own writings eventually became the benchmark against which to measure all other dialogues.[44] The terms *dialogos* (dialogue) and *dialektikos* (discourse, conversation), however, first appear in written Greek, as we know it today, in the *Sōkratikoi logoi*.[45] Plato may well have derived these terms from his teacher, Socrates, whom he represents in the *Sōkratikoi logoi* as a master of both the art of conversation and the art of dialectic; since Socrates himself never wrote a word, however, there is no definite proof that he could have coined these terms. Xenophon—a contemporary of Plato's—does tell us that Socrates used the verb *dialegesthai* (literally, "to discourse," "to speak alternately," "to converse") to define "a deliberation carried out by a group of men (agreed to do so), discerning things according to their kind."[46] Although it has no exact English equivalent in this context, *dialegesthai*—judging from Xenophon's remark—suggests at once a dialogical discussion aimed at arriving at an answer to a problem of common concern *and* a mutually satisfactory result of the discussion that takes the participants beyond their original points of view.[47] The term 'dialogue,' which derives from *dialegesthai*, similarly contains for Socratic and Platonic thought the sense of a specific goal and a specific formal discursive structure that neither rhetorical debate nor everyday conversation can be said to possess. Dialogue is a textual strategy for discovery, or, better still, it is a textual strategy for embodying dialectical discovery in discourse; as the textual body of dialectic, dialogue sharply differs from the representation of random conversation or the procedures of public oratory.

The appearance of dialogue in classical Greece is inseparable not only from the works of Plato, but also from the development of rhetoric and philosophy between the fifth and fourth centuries B.C. Platonic dialogue is, as Jean-Pierre Vernant argues, symptomatic of a major shift in the discursive practices of Greek culture. Vernant observes that the paradoxical, enigmatic, and highly poetic language of the pre-Socratic philosophers strongly resembles the sacred utterances of the oracle. Both pre-Socratic philosopher and oracle speak a language whose legitimacy is measured not in terms of its persuasiveness for the listener, but rather in terms of a hidden meaning contained in it that requires a privileged interpreter/initiate (an *inter-prêtre*) in order to be recovered and brought into the open. Plato's dialogues, Vernant contends, break sharply with this practice, not only through Plato's use of a lucid Attic prose (at times highly charged, to be sure, with poetic figures), but also through his use of dialectic to explore the positions of different speakers in the dialogical scene. Platonic dialogue seeks its legitimation in the (re)presentation of an exchange of points of view between partners in a dialogue. This exchange offers the possibility of arriving through a process of dialogue—with its dialectical spiral—at a discovery, whether that takes the form of an *aporia* or of a position that is generally accepted by all. In turn, this suggests the possibility of thinking itself as a kind of questioning, as an activity that occurs *between* speakers. Dialogue subverts the discursive power of the oracular and the sacred and affirms the ability of the individual mind to make informed decisions in the life of the *polis*.[48]

The first concrete indications of a way of thinking about dialogue that accompanies this kind of writing are to be found in the Socratic/Platonic terminology of *dialegesthai, dialogos,* and *dialektikos*.[49] Since these terms designate specific acts that occur between speakers, such as "dialogue" or "alternating conversation," acts concerned with testing beliefs and opinions and with searching for possible truths, they constitute the very condition of possibility for a future metalanguage of dialogue. Plato's silence on his art of dialogue is in itself not unexpected, given his express methodological preference for embedding his own ideas and precepts within the constantly shifting, changing discursive context of his dialogues. In the *Republic* (3.392C–395A), however, Socrates discusses dialogue without narration (or mimesis) as part of his general theory of literary imitation. Socrates's words are vitally important not only for subsequent thought on dialogue in antiquity, but for sixteenth-century literary theory as well:

You know then that up to the lines "and he begged all the Achaeans,/ But especially the two sons of Atreus, commanders of the host," the poet himself [Homer] is speaking and does not attempt to turn our attention elsewhere as if the speaker were someone other than himself. After this, however, he speaks as if he were Chryses and tries as far as possible to make us think that the speaker is not Homer but the priest, an old man. . . . Now is it narrative both when he makes speeches and also the parts between the speeches?
—Of course.
—But when he makes a speech as if he were someone else, shall we not say that he makes his language as like as possible to that of whatever person he has told us is about to speak?
—We shall say that.
—Now to make oneself like somebody else in voice or form is to imitate or impersonate the person one makes oneself resemble?
—Certainly.
—In these passages, it seems, he and the other poets tell their narrative through impersonation.
—Quite so.
—If the poet nowhere hid himself, the whole of his poem would be narration without impersonation . . . [but] the opposite occurs when one leaves out the words between the speeches and leaves the dialogue. . . . One kind of poetry and story-telling is wholly through impersonation . . . [whereas] another kind is through narration by the poet himself . . . and a third kind uses both, as in epic poetry and frequently elsewhere.[50]

Many modern commentators see in this passage a Platonic critique of the power of poetry to imitate human actions; one critic, for instance, observes that "the poet can make men believe that they see and hear his characters. This constitutes his real power—he enchants men so that they live the experiences he wishes to present. The poet hides himself behind his work, and the audience forgets, for the moment, that the world into which they enter is not the real one."[51] Socrates's remarks, although not specifically addressed at dialogue as practiced by Plato himself, suggest that the device of mimetic dialogue ("making a speech as if . . . someone else") allows the narrator to impersonate others, even while hiding behind the facade that they provide. This kind of dialogue dissimulates its own narrativity ("he tries as far as possible to make us think that the speaker is not Homer but the priest, an old man"); the narrative act still occurs, but the impersonation that it performs blinds readers to that fact. The disguise of mimetic dialogue—"writing wholly through imper- sonation"—makes its readers forget what is artifice, fabrication, or fiction, since no narrative openly appears in the text. The rea- sons that Socrates disapproves of this poetic power of making oneself "like somebody else in voice or form" are not difficult to surmise and do not bear repeating in full here.[52] Renaissance crit- ics, however, do not always read Socrates's words as a critique of "impersonation"; rather, they see them as a description of Plato's own dialogical practice. Speroni, for example, who never hesitates to make revisionary readings of the classics, transforms this passage from the *Republic* into the lynchpin of his defense of dialogical writing. From its origin here, the problem of the value of impersonation and of speaking as if "someone else" figures prominently in nearly all future theoretical work on dialogue.

Only in the *Letters*, where Plato is without the benefit of the fiction of dialogue, are any specific statements to be found re- garding the *writing* of dialogue itself. Although some or most of these letters are almost certainly apocryphal and do not supply a key to Plato's ideas on dialogue, they do provide us with a useful Platonistic perspective into the development of thinking about dialogue in antiquity.[53] In the Second Letter (314B–C)—ad- dressed to Dionysius, the tyrant of Syracuse—Plato professes his distrust of writing: "The greatest safeguard is to avoid writing [*graphein*] and to learn by heart; for it is not possible that what is written down should not get divulged. For this reason *I my- self have never yet written anything on these subjects, and no* [*writing —sungramma*] *by Plato exists or will exist, but that which now bears his name belongs to a Socrates become fair and young.* And now, to begin with, read this letter over repeatedly and then burn it up" [my italics].[54] Plato's remarks here evoke Socrates's critique of writing in the *Phaedrus* (257C–279C). They are echoed, furthermore, in Plato's statement to Dion in the Seventh Letter (341C–E) that "there does not exist, nor will there ever exist, any writing [*sungramma*] of mine dealing with this subject."[55]

What directly concerns the theory of dialogue here is the question raised in the Second and Seventh letters about the *authorship* of the Platonic writings. In these two letters, Plato states paradoxically that he has never written down his doctrines and will never do so in the future. At the same time, neither is the authorship of the so-called Platonic texts to be attributed to the quasi-historical character of Socrates that appears as the leading figure in them. Their author is instead "a Socrates become fair and young," which is another way of saying a wholly fictional personage, given the literal impossibility that a fair and young Socrates could have written, or would have wanted to write (considering his notorious aversion to writing), any of these dialogues. Not only is a semi-fictional Socrates represented in the *Sōkratikoi logoi*, but—Plato hints—there is also another, quite different and entirely imaginary Socrates to whom they are to be attributed. Plato's dialogues are not memoirs or transcriptions of remembered conversations, as he himself suggests in the Second Letter; nor are they chronicles or histories of Socrates's life.[56] Instead, they serve as a textual device for distancing Plato from his own scene of writing, since both speakers and author are but a fiction in these dialogues. A chief poetic stratagem of Platonic dialogue is that its author is as much of a fiction as are its characters. Plato is not to be found where he is sought, for he is never "there" in the scene of dialogue, and this elusive disappearing act is not an attribute of dialogue as much as it is its definition.[57]

Plato can freely disown his own work because at no point in his dialogues is he ever named as either their author or narrator; nor does he even once openly figure as a character in any dialogue, except in the *persona* of Socrates himself. Any narration in Plato's dialogues is always performed by one of the characters; otherwise, direct discourse—the mode of impersonation of which Socrates speaks in the *Republic*—is used to represent the dialogical scene of speaking between Socrates and his interlocutors. The dialogist leaves no signature within the work itself;

its writing belongs, in a sense, to no one. This fiction is what saves Plato from an open contradiction between his theory of writing (most eloquently stated in the *Phaedrus*) and his practice of writing; the fictional or feigned is an essential and enabling element of Plato's dialogical poetics. That Plato—or the Platonist who forged the *Letters*—sees his works as being to some degree literary is subtly underscored by the use of the term *sungramma* (literally, a "writing" or "prose work") in both the Second and Seventh letters to describe his practice of dialogue, for in antiquity the term commonly denotes a specifically literary work or a literary style of writing.[58] Since dialogues are at once a kind of prose writing (*sungramma*) and a kind of fiction—as any work of art is a fiction (according to Socrates's argument in the *Republic*) —then, the text of the Second Letter implies, they are themselves a kind of prose fiction or prose poetry. Although this may not appear to be a particularly novel idea to today's readers, the fact remains that—in context of the emergence of a theory of dialogue—it is exactly that. The controversies and quarrels of the sixteenth century regarding the literary status of Plato's dialogues are evidence enough that this idea of dialogue as a kind of fictional prose writing posed a tremendous challenge to both ancient and Renaissance literary theory. And it could not fail to have ramifications for Plato's most brilliant pupil, Aristotle, when he turned his attention to the elaboration of a theory of literature in the *Poetics*.

Aristotle's *Poetics* represented for sixteenth-century criticism and theory in Italy what Freud's *Interpretation of Dreams* does for twentieth-century criticism and theory; namely, a text provoking advanced reflection on narrative, on the theory of representation, on the work of writing, and on other related issues. This analogy goes only so far, of course, but it effectively stresses the momentous importance of the rediscovery of the *Poetics* by sixteenth-century Italian thought. Few theorists of the period could avoid confronting the ground-breaking ideas of the *Poetics* regarding a "practical science" of poetry, ideas that seem to have had almost no currency in antiquity, but whose impact on the direction of sixteenth-century literary studies in Italy was nothing short of revolutionary.[59]

The text of the *Poetics* had been available to Renaissance readers for some time before any critic in Italy evinced more than a passing interest in it. By the end of the 1470's (or, at the latest, the early 1480's), Ermolao Barbaro seems to have known the text of the *Poetics*, and he introduced the poet and philologist Angelo Poliziano to it at around this same time. Giorgio Valla translated it into Latin (1498), and the work was published in Greek some ten years later; Valla's translation was reprinted in 1515. Erasmus's Greek text appeared in 1532, followed by Alessandro Pazzi's text and Latin translation in 1536 (reprinted in 1537 and 1538), and finally by Bernardo Segni's translation into Italian in 1549, the first translation of the *Poetics* into any European vernacular. Francesco Robortello's *In librum Aristotelis de arte poetica explicationes* (1548) was the first published commentary on the *Poetics* and was followed soon afterward by the joint work of Bartolomeo Lombardi and Vincenzo Maggi, *In Aristotelis librum de poetica communes explanationes* (1550).[60] From that point on, an irregular flow of commentaries, translations, and new editions continued to make the *Poetics* a text to be reckoned with—in many different ways—for later sixteenth-century Italian critics and theorists alike. Other signal events of the century contributed to the resurgent interest in poetics in Italy, such as the first translations into the vernacular of Horace's *Ars poetica* (Lodovico Dolce's Italian version appeared in 1535), but none can be said to equal the effect of the *Poetics*.[61]

Often, to be sure, sixteenth-century writers simply synthesized Aristotle's ideas with those of other authorities from antiquity (such as Horace and Cicero), using them in a piecemeal fashion to support every conceivable argument. However, it is not surprising that practically no one in the Cinquecento can be said to be an orthodox disciple of Aristotle's in literary matters, given the provisional and uncertain nature of both the meaning and the text of the *Poetics* in the period. Three of the four theorists with whom this book is chiefly concerned—Sigonio, Castelvetro, and Tasso—dealt principally with problems raised by the *Poetics* and by Aristotelian thought in general, even if each took a highly individual approach to resolving those problems. If between 1548 and the end of the sixteenth century in Italy, "perhaps more than in any other time and place, the problem of criticism was essentially a theoretical problem . . . [and if] perhaps nowhere else in the intellectual history of the West can one find so continual, so abundant, and so diverse a centering of attention upon problems of literary theory," this unusual state of affairs largely reflects the powerful impact of the *Poetics* on the nascent literature about literature.[62]

Aristotle, a member of Plato's school from 367 to 348/7 B.C., wrote a large number of dialogues (his so-called exoteric works), none of which is extant. Little is known about these dialogues except for the *testimonia* provided by later authors in antiquity, chief among them Cicero.[63] We do know, however, that some of Aristotle's dialogues were not only modeled on Plato's dialogues, but in at least three cases even had the same titles as dialogues by Plato.[64] We also know that in the lost *logoi exōterikoi* Aristotle always appeared as himself; in eschewing any strategy of impersonation and in having questions put to him by disciples so that he could expound answers, Aristotle was the first writer in antiquity to become the visible center of his own dialogues.

In both the *Poetics* and the (lost) *On Poets*, Aristotle offers some significant if fragmentary reflections on the poetics of dialogue that both expand on and revise Plato's ideas. Early in the *Poetics* (1, 1447a28–b11), he observes that "the art which employs words either in bare prose or in meters, either in one kind of meter or combining several, happens up to the present day to have no name. For we can find no common term to apply to the mimes of Sophron and Xenarchus and to the Socratic dialogues."[65] There is no certain understanding of the sense of this passage, no more than there is a definitive text of the *Poetics* with which to work. It would be safe to say, however, that these few words are the most crucial of all antiquity for Renaissance theories of dialogue. Gerald Else has rightly remarked that here "interpretations have spread out in all directions" in an attempt to fathom the cryptic meaning of Aristotle's words: most Renaissance editors, for instance, conjectured that this art had to be the epic, although Aristotle nowhere says so, and they inserted the term in the text at this point.[66] Aristotle's argument, as it stands in the text of the *Poetics* as we currently have it, centers around the questions of whether dialogue belongs to the general literary system and whether indeed there is a term that can designate literature itself ("we can find no common term to apply to the mimes of Sophron and Xenarchus and to the Socratic dialogues") over and beyond the different species of poetry. All too often dialogue is not considered a kind of literary writing, Aristotle remarks, simply because—unlike epic, tragic, comic, or dithyrambic poetry—it has no meter but is written in "bare prose" (or *i parlari ignudi*, as the term was often translated into the vernacular in the Cinquecento), unaccompanied by music.[67] There is, Aristotle notes, "no name" (*anōnymos*) and no "common term" (*koinon onoma*) that can be applied to dialogue and to related literary prose forms like the mimes of Sophron and Xenarchus, long thought to have served as a model for Plato's dialogues.

This results from the tendency of most readers to decide whether a given work is or is not "poetry" solely on the basis of the presence or absence of meter (what the *Poetics* calls the "means of representation"). Aristotle remarks in this regard that both Homer and Empedocles are often called poets when in point of fact they "have nothing in common except the meter, so that it would be proper to call the one a poet and the other not a poet but a scientist" (1, 1447b17–20).[68] But if both write in meter, how is it that one is a poet and the other a scientist? And conversely, if dialogue has no meter and does not seem to be poetry, then how can it be said to belong to the same class of texts as the *Iliad* or *Oedipus Rex*, which nearly everyone acknowledges are poetic works of the highest order? Dialogue potentially provides the *Poetics* with a test case for Aristotle's theory that there is such a genus of discourse as *literature* (mimesis), of which works in meter are but a species. What makes Homer a poet as opposed to Empedocles is not his use of meter but his use of mimesis, that is, the representation—in the form of a story—of human experience and, above all else, human action (*mimēsis praxeōs*). Poets employ plot or *mythos* to organize the events of the story into an organic whole (*holos*); the emplotment determines whether a written work is truly mimetic, according to Aristotle, and thus truly a work of fiction.[69]

Mimesis is that common term or umbrella term for all fiction that Aristotle calls for in the first chapter of the *Poetics*. And the class of mimetic texts described by him is apparently intended to include dialogue; Plato's writings can therefore be grouped together with Homer's as products of the same universal art (although Aristotle himself does not say this in the *Poetics*). So-cratic dialogues are no longer nameless and unclassifiable, then, if they are viewed in terms of the object as well as the means of representation, for they are scenes of human experience and human action, even though they are written in prose. In this fashion, a theory of the definitive difference between spoken dialogue and written (fictional) dialogue is for the first time for-mally introduced by Aristotle in the *Poetics*.[70] A fragment of *On Poets* indirectly confirms Aristotle's view that dialogue does in-deed have a fictional and literary basis: "Are we then to deny," he asks, speaking of Plato's possible precursors, "that the so-called mimes of Sophron, which are not even in meter, are stories and imitations, or [that] the dialogues of Alexamenos of Teos [are not either]?"[71] Judging from this fragment, there would seem to be no question that, for Aristotle, both mime and dialogue are definitely works of mimesis and are therefore analyzable—as is any member of this same class of texts—in terms of a *poetics*.[72]

There is only one tantalizing clue to what Aristotle's own poet-ics of dialogue might have been. In Diogenes Laertius's *Lives of the Eminent Philosophers*, it is recorded that Aristotle once said that "the style of Plato's dialogues is half-way between poetry and prose."[73] Contrary to the *Poetics*, this statement (if it is in-deed Aristotle's) suggests that the means of representation of Socratic/Platonic dialogue is not "bare prose," but rather a hy-brid of different elements of *poiēsis* and prose. To study the style —or the *lexis*, in the terminology of the *Poetics*—of Plato's dia-logues would consequently mean to examine the similarities and differences between poetry and prose at their point of intersec-tion in dialogue: the poetics of dialogue maps out the liminal zone or threshold between these two means of literary repre-sentation. This notion of dialogical style as a crossing-over from poetry to prose, and from prose back to poetry, is of great in-terest and great concern for Renaissance theorists of dialogue. Some, such as Tasso, favor a hybrid prose-poetry for dialogue, whereas others, such as Castelvetro, fiercely condemn it as "im-pure" and "monstrous."

Any Aristotelian poetics would be fundamentally incomplete, however, if it did not consider the most critically important qualitative part of the literary work, namely, the *plot*. And this is where Renaissance thinkers are left wondering what sort of poetics, if any, can be formulated for dialogue within the theoretical framework of the *Poetics*. The plot always supplies the writer's fictional argument, as it were, in the form of an organically interrelated sequence of events.[74] But what sort of plot do any of Plato's dialogues have, or, to put it another way, what sort of story does any one of them tell? What kind of action can possibly be represented by a dialogue between speakers sitting in the shade of a tree or at a banquet table? How can a discussion, a talk, or a conversation of the kind that occurs in dialogue ever be said to have a plot with an identifiable structure of events? How Aristotle himself would have set about answering these questions is, for late Renaissance *letterati*, anything but clear, and this lends impetus—if not theoretical rigor—to the search for a poetics of dialogue. Today such questions may seem marginal, but to the sixteenth-century discourse on dialogue they pose a major problem for the project of a fully elaborated and codified science of the literary system, especially one that attempts to transpose the theory of the *Poetics* into the contemporary critical arena in Italy.

Although a mine of ideas for sixteenth-century theorists, the *Poetics* says—as we have just seen—little about dialogue itself. The door is thus left wide open in the second half of the Cinquecento, after an initial assessment of the *Poetics* in the first wave of commentaries, for an exploration in greater depth of what Aristotle's text does not discuss. Indeed, a whole class of sixteenth-century treatises sets out a theory of a single major or minor genre not treated in the *Poetics*, such as the romance, precisely because Aristotle's mutilated text ignores it.[75] The theories of dialogue belong to this class of works that attempt to extend the project of a science of literature in new directions and thus make the *Poetics* "more immediate and more contemporary" while going beyond its limits.[76] Since there are so few ancient authorities on the composition of dialogue, dialogue provides (as does, for instance, the romance) a golden opportunity for Aristotelian critics in the Cinquecento to reinterpret the text of the *Poetics*. The usual procedure is to look in it for hints of a latent or fragmentary line of thought on a genre such as the dialogue and then to create an essentially modern theory that incorporates the insights of Aristotle while seeking to surpass them. In his *De dialogo liber*, Sigonio provides a set of precepts for present and future writers of dialogue in the form of a reading of the *Poetics*, and Tasso's *Discorso dell'arte del dialogo*, which is a response to a request by a contemporary author for instruction on writing dialogue, alludes to a wide range of Aristotle's works. Of course, such projects do not always succeed, but they do show that this practice of critical imitation, with its concern for precedent, need not be slavishly repetitive; even in the Renaissance, true theories do not just duplicate what already exists, but claim the right to be able to criticize it as well. For writers like Sigonio or Tasso, the theory of dialogue is a privileged discursive space for testing the hypothesis of a Renaissance science of poetics that does not merely rephrase the text of the *Poetics*, but discovers in it the principles of a universal theory of Renaissance literary representation.

Other discussions of dialogue can be found in ancient criticism and rhetoric, although the majority of these are concerned with the rhetorical figure of dialogism rather than with the literary-philosophical form of dialogue itself.[77] Most do not advance far, in any event, beyond the points raised by Plato and Aristotle. The number of ancient analyses of particular Platonic dialogues is much greater, but once again these do not (generally speaking) break new ground for poetics.[78] A brief look at two of the most insightful of the surviving traces of ancient thought on dialogue may serve to conclude this survey of the origins of the theory of dialogue. These come from the hands of two of the most famous and imitated of ancient dialogists, Cicero and Lucian.

Cicero, by all accounts the preeminent Latin dialogist and probably the single greatest influence on Renaissance rhetorical theory, left only a few fragmentary observations about writing dialogue.[79] Like Plato before him, Cicero wrote both maiuetic and aporetic dialogues in which the two sides of an argument are developed by a *disputatio in utramque partem*; the difference is that Cicero's dialogical style—under the influence of Aristotle's protreptic dialogues—is "less conversation than debate with definite argument, rebuttal, and progress to a conclusion.

Cicero's dialogue is not a quest; it is an exposition of something already determined, and it unfolds that by logical stages."[80] (The differences between Plato's and Cicero's dialogues are discussed in detail in later chapters.) Like Plato before him, Cicero never reflected at any length on the representational issues raised by dialogical writing, even though rhetoric is always for him the art of speech and writing in general, and oratory itself the highest form of literature.[81] Although the treatise *Ad Herennium* (traditionally if erroneously attributed to Cicero in the Renaissance) does make some specific remarks on the figure of thought called *sermocinatio* or "interior dialogue" (4.43.55, 4.52.65), most of its ideas on dialogue are directed toward the specialized techniques of public oratory, such as the preservation of decorum or the use of oratorical dialogue in the form of a sequence of questions and answers (what the Greek rhetoricians call *cheirotēma*).[82]

In the *Orator* (19.63–64), Cicero does discuss the difference between the conversational style of the Greek philosophers such as Plato, Xenophon, and Aristotle, on the one hand, and public oratory (*itaque sermo potius quam oratio dicitur*) on the other hand. He notes that such philosophers, in their writings, "converse with scholars, whose minds they prefer to soothe rather than arouse; they converse in this way about unexciting and noncontroversial subjects, for the purpose of instructing rather than captivating; and some think they exceed due bounds in aiming to give some little pleasure by their style." The disadvantages of dialogue for the orator are clear enough, then, for philosophical writing "is gentle and academic; it has no equipment of words or phrases that catch the popular fancy; it is not arranged in rhythmical periods, but is loose in structure; there is no anger in it, no hatred, no ferocity, no pathos, no shrewdness. . . . Consequently it is called conversation rather than oratory."[83]

Oratory has a far different purpose and power, since it must be used in the public forum to stir and to sway (*movere*) the emotions of the crowd. The conversational style is the antithesis of public eloquence, Cicero argues, because the style of dialogue is by its very nature designed to appeal to the intellect rather than to the emotions and can never effectively persuade the crowd in the forum. These remarks are suggestive ones from the perspective of a poetics of dialogue, since they assign dialogue a particular stylistic tone (which Cicero calls "gentle and academic conversation"), a specific means of representation (the "loose" structure of bare prose—*nec vincta numeris sed soluta liberius*), an object of representation ("unexciting and non-controversial subjects"), and a precise philosophical purpose ("instructing rather than captivating"). Cicero, while seeking a fusion of oratory (*oratio*) and philosophy(*ratio*) through his theory of eloquence, nevertheless does not generally think in terms of any constitutive difference between writing and the techniques of oratory. Even the poet, in his point of view, simply "seeks to attain the virtues of the orator while limited by the verse-form."[84] Motivated primarily by concerns of a pragmatic nature, that is, by the relations between signs and interpreters, Cicero shows little direct interest in the kind of technical esthetic analysis performed by Plato and especially by Aristotle.

The other fragment of ancient reflection on dialogue is found in Lucian's *The Double Indictment* (33–34), written in Athens in the second century A.D., which mercilessly satirizes Plato's dialogues and boldly defends Lucian's own brand of comic/satirical dialogue.[85] Lucian's metadialogue provides some of the wittier statements from antiquity regarding dialogical writing, and, although it has few if any overt theoretical pretensions, it nonetheless makes some astute observations about the form. In *The Double Indictment*, a suit is brought before an Athenian jury by the personified figure of Dialogue, charging that a certain "Syrian" (Lucian) has wronged and insulted him. Dialogue complains to the jury that he used to ponder "upon the gods and nature and the cycle of the universe," but the Syrian has instead placed him "on the same level as the common herd" and deprived him of the "respectable tragic mask" that he used to wear (33). Moreover, Dialogue alleges, the Syrian has "unceremoniously penned me up with Jest and Satire and Cynicism and Eupolis and Aristophanes, terrible men for mocking all that is holy and scoffing at all that is right," as well as with "Menippus, a prehistoric dog" (33). In self-defense, the Syrian replies that Dialogue "had been reduced to a skeleton through continual questions . . . in that guise he seemed awe-inspiring, to be sure, but not in any way attractive or agreeable to the public" (34). The remedy for Dialogue's problems, he maintains, is to get him to walk "on the ground like a human being" without "penetrating speculations about 'ideas,' " to force him to "smile," and to pair him "with Comedy" instead of with Tragedy (34). Not surprisingly, after hearing the arguments on both sides, the jury votes overwhelmingly in favor of the Syrian and against Dialogue.

In *The Double Indictment*, Lucian means not only to mock Plato's dialogues—particularly the *Timaeus* and the *Gorgias*—and to offer a description of his own irreverent dialogical practice. He also gives us a glimpse of what he thinks of Plato's writings as *philosophical* dialogues or, in other words, as the antithesis of his own. Lucian observes that Plato's dialogues consist of "continual questions" requiring both "reflection" and "speculation" on the part of those engaged in the discussion. What happens in a philosophical dialogue—despite the apparent similarity in its structure of speaking—is thus vastly different from what happens in a comedy or a tragedy (and Lucian certainly did not need Aristotle's *Poetics* to discover this). And this activity of inquiring, asking questions, speculating, and reflecting on possible answers is what properly distinguishes philosophical dialogue from Lucian's own comic/satirical dialogues. Lucian's works inquire and question, but not toward either speculative or reflective ends; they do so only in order to provoke laughter through satire and farce. He further notes that Plato's dialogues wear a "respectable tragic mask," which would imply that they are written in an elevated poetic style not suited for comedy or satire. Although not an entirely accurate description of Plato's dialogical style (see, for example, parts of the *Symposium*, or the links between dialogue and mime), there is evident in Lucian's treatment of Plato a principle of genre new to ancient thought on dialogue. There are, Lucian suggests, two incompatible and mutually exclusive models of dialogue, one geared toward speculation and the other toward laughter, as different in their own way as are tragedy and comedy. These two models are opposed to each other, like the Syrian (Lucian) and Dialogue (Plato) themselves, and beyond the possibility of reconciliation. The speculative model of dialogue is aimed toward an elite audience, whereas the comic model of dialogue appeals to the public at large (which is why the Syrian easily wins the favor of the Athenian jury). These two versions of dialogue—one oriented toward the philosophical, and the other toward the strictly literary—necessarily accompany each other, for the latter operates as a remedy for the former. By raising his own dialogues to the same level of value as Plato's through this antinomy, Lucian sets in place an alternative model of literary dialogue whose consequences for Renaissance thought on dialogue are of a magnitude only slightly less great than those that derive from the theoretical fragments of Plato and Aristotle.

Clearly it is not feasible to piece together the fragments of ancient thought on dialogue into a unified discourse without violating the different contexts and traditions (Greek, Roman, Hellenistic) out of which they come. And it seems equally evident that the notion of such a unified theory of dialogue is in any event alien to all the ancient writers that have been mentioned except Aristotle. Nor is there any apparent cause-and-effect relation to be found among these various fragments that would validate a chronologically based notion of development in the perspective of antiquity on dialogue. Cicero or Lucian are no nearer the meaning of dialogue as a kind of writing than are Plato or Aristotle. If anything, the divergent and discontinuous nature of their insights suggests the complexity of the issues facing any total theory of dialogue. The enigma of their works leaves all subsequent study of dialogue with a host of questions to consider about the structure and function of the dialogical text and about its place in the general system of discourse. The challenge to criticism and theory that these diverse questions pose, which were not to be taken up again until the second half of the sixteenth century in Italy, is that of probing the limits of the difference between fiction and exposition, persuasion and demonstration, or rhetoric and logic (dialectic). The rediscovery of this issue of difference marks the emergence of dialogue as a problem for the late Renaissance, whose answer takes the form of a poetics of dialogical writing.

TWO

Putting Questions (in)to Language:
Sigonio's Theory of Dialogue

CARLO SIGONIO (ca. 1520–1584) completed his treatise on the poetics of dialogue, entitled *De dialogo liber* (The book about dialogue), in 1561.[1] Sigonio, professor of eloquence (*umanità*) at the university in Padua at the time, was a leading Italian historian and classical philologist in the mid-sixteenth century. His *De regno Italiae libri viginti*, published between 1574 and 1580, is still considered one of the most important sixteenth-century studies of medieval Italian history (568–1286 A.D.); he also wrote extensively on Greek, Roman, Hebrew, and ecclesiastical history. Sigonio's erudite works on Livy and Cicero, together with a host of other humanistic writings, contributed to his contemporary renown as a classical scholar, although they are little known today. He held university chairs not only in Padua, but also in Venice (as *publicus professor*) and Bologna, three of the most prestigious and vital centers of intellectual activity on the Italian peninsula in the second half of the sixteenth century. Among his students in both Padua and Bologna was the young Torquato Tasso.[2] Unlike some of his less fortunate or less diplomatic contemporaries in the late Renaissance literary world, such as Sperone Speroni, Lodovico Castelvetro, or Tasso himself, Sigonio successfully coordinated most of his published work and personal career with the changing circumstances of Italian literary life and the growing demands made on intellectuals of every stripe by the Counter-Reformation (even to the point of authoring a defense of the authenticity of the "Donation of Constantine," which Lorenzo Valla had shown to be a forgery over a century before). Yet in many ways Sigonio can be called—together with Piero Vettori and a few others of the same generation— the last of the long and illustrious line of Italian humanists.[3] Philology and literary theory continued to exist as disciplines in Italy long after Sigonio, but perhaps never again were claims advanced concerning the possibility of a union of logic and eloquence like those found in his writings. In the following pages, I examine Sigonio's perception of, and answer to, the problem of dialogue in terms of his late humanist project and the irreversible crisis in which it was placed in the second half of the sixteenth century.

In the context of Sigonio's oeuvre, *De dialogo liber* appears at first to be an anomaly. Although he worked closely with various classical texts, Sigonio was not—in an era given over to literary theory—by any means regarded as a literary theorist. He did publish a commentary on Aristotle's *Rhetoric* in 1565, but Sigonio's interest in poetics itself was a relatively minor one compared with his interests in history and philology. *De dialogo liber* is, at any rate, his only study on the theory of a specific literary genre. Sigonio was nevertheless fully versed in the latest literary developments in Italy, which, despite the flourishing of the Northern Renaissance, continued to be the chief European center of literary theory in the mid-sixteenth century. The universities of Padua and Bologna were among the most important in Europe at that time, especially for the many strains of Aristotelianism then emerging, and they attracted students and scholars from every corner of the continent.[4] In Padua, Sigonio took part in often acrid and sometimes violent public debates with leading rival *letterati*, such as Antonio Riccoboni and Francesco Robortello, that tested his command of the new critical idiom.[5] The organization of the *studia humanitatis* at the Studio di Padova involved not only the study of history, but rhetoric and poetics as well, and Sigonio had to be fully conversant in all three disciplines.[6] Furthermore, a working knowledge of poetics was an essential part not only of his professional expertise but also of his own particular notion of the *studia humanitatis*. For, as one modern critic observes, the arts of discourse—including poetics —"almost acquire, in Sigonio's epistemological project, and in complete continuity with the theses of Quattrocento humanism, the status of a unitary foundation for all knowledge."[7] *De dialogo liber*, although atypical of Sigonio's work as a whole, reaffirms the extent of his commitment as a late humanist to the elaboration and defense of a comprehensive *verborum scientia*, a commitment that plays a crucial role in the development of his ideas on dialogue.

De dialogo liber is the first full-fledged theory of dialogue to appear in the sixteenth century; as such, it stands as an important moment in both the history of thought about dialogue and the history of poetics in the late Italian Renaissance.[8] Although systematic sixteenth-century reflection on dialogue begins with Sigonio's treatise, it would be misleading to pretend that his theory was ever widely read and discussed, even in its own time. However, two of the other major sixteenth-century Italian theorists and writers on dialogue—Speroni and Tasso—certainly knew of Sigonio's ground-breaking text. (Sigonio's fellow critic from Modena, Lodovico Castelvetro, was in exile when the work appeared in print, and he may not have heard of it.) *De dialogo liber* is a difficult and, at times, bewildering work for the modern reader, who may understandably find it hard to fathom the passionate nature of the critical controversies that swirled and eddied in the mid-sixteenth century in Italy, particularly around the interpretation of Aristotle's *Poetics*. Vast amounts of ephemeral criticism and theory were produced in the course of these controversies, much of it almost immediately obsolete; the theory of dialogue—as a thorny problem for sixteenth-century Italian thought—is deeply implicated in these controversies as well, but its interest is not limited to them. Sigonio's work offers an intimate, firsthand look at the full dimensions of that problem, which, seen in the context of the sixteenth-century dialogue on dialogue, are far larger than might be expected, stretching from poetics to ethics to the theory of knowledge itself. If some of the imaginative energy invested in Sigonio's treatise can be captured and conveyed in the pages that follow, then the sixteenth-century experience of theorizing about dialogue may still prove a compelling one for readers today.

The problem of the poetics of dialogue in the late Italian Renaissance is intimately linked to the problem of writing literary theory itself. In the years after the rediscovery of the *Poetics*, as the institutional locus of criticism and theory shifted away from the courts toward the universities and academies, a vast number of possible approaches to writing literary criticism and theory were available to Italian *letterati* (including treatises, dialogues, commentaries, glosses, florilegia, and so on).[9] Sigonio's choice of a strategy for the writing of his own theory is therefore a significant one, for it supplies a first signal of his approach to dialogical poetics. *De dialogo liber* is an academic work, possibly based on a series of lectures given by Sigonio between the mid-1550's and 1561, when the final draft of the treatise was completed.[10] Both its method and its structure (*dispositio*) of argumentation are designed to be distinctly Aristotelian; this is clear from the opening sentence of the text, in which Sigonio announces that the definition of dialogue will be the first thing dealt with, "which we know that the divine Aristotle especially was accustomed to do" (1*r*).[11]

The *forma tractatus* (form of the treatise) employed by Sigonio belongs to the scholastic tradition and comprises in this instance a dedication, a table of contents, a *summa quaestionum* ([i*r*–i*v*]), twenty sections of discussion and analysis, and an extensive alphabetical index. According to the *summa*, the work begins with a discussion of the universal causes of dialogue—"which causes impel philosophers to give instruction in dialogue" ([i*r*]) —and gradually descends to an examination of the particular genres of dialogue represented by the writings of Plato, Xenophon, and Cicero.[12] Sigonio openly declares his theory to be a systematic one based on the highest philosophical principles; it is a philosophy of dialogical writing. This procedure underscores not only Sigonio's professed allegiance to the *Poetics*, but also the chief methodological premise of his text, which is that there is an order (of causes, parts, and the like) and a *ratio* in both the discourse *of* dialogue and the discourse *on* dialogue. There is no place for notions of poetic frenzy, ecstasy, or even imagination in either dialogue or the theory of dialogue itself, just as these concepts are marginal at best to the theory of the *Poetics*. Sigonio's is a fundamentally analytical poetics, blending erudition, system, and doctrine; in its perspective, a given effect can always be traced back to a given cause, since texts are—as the *forma tractatus* emblematically demonstrates—always presumed to obey purely rational precepts.

The *forma tractatus*, however, reflects only one facet of Sigonio's approach to the investigation of dialogue. His is a highly syncretic rather than a doctrinaire mind, and the text of his treatise is a thick tissue of citations from and paraphrases of Plato, Aristotle, Cicero, Horace, Diogenes Laertius, Quintilian, Proclus, Solon, Demetrius, Saint Basil, and many other ancient authorities on questions of rhetoric, dialectic, or poetics. Although his argument is seldom without a rigor of its own and never approaches the level of a simple pastiche, Sigonio constantly blends any number of these ancient authorities in order to support his own claims about dialogue. If he seems unconcerned by the *bricolage* of ideas that this approach at times produces, it is because he believes that there is a good reason for doing so.[13] *De dialogo liber* eclectically combines the ancient, medieval, and Renaissance critical traditions into a single discourse on dialogue because Sigonio assumes a full and fundamental continuity between the various ancient authorities themselves (for example, Plato and Aristotle) and the different branches of the Western literary and philosophical tradition that derive from them. There is no rupture between Platonism and Aristotelianism that cannot be sutured over, no dissonance between Plato's practice of dialogue and Aristotle's theory of literature that cannot be dissolved. Their texts form a homogeneous, if fragmented, body of writing, from the study of which a poetics of dialogue may be deduced. Since Sigonio's work cannot be simply a compendium of citations about dialogue from ancient sources, given that only a few brief statements on dialogue survived the end of antiquity (and most of these figure in the treatise), he has to seek another avenue for integrating the humanist encyclopedia of philological and philosophical knowledge about antiquity with the contemporary project for a poetics of dialogue. And what text could serve this purpose more ideally than Aristotle's *Poetics*?

In the mid-sixteenth-century controversy over the question of poetics and the *Poetics*, Sigonio could have known or referred to few other previous sustained theoretical works on poetics except Aristotle's and those of a limited number of other humanists in Italy (such as his archrival Robortello). Much Renaissance work

on the *Poetics* takes the form of a textual gloss or commentary
to an edition and translation of the original version, in which
the critic comments on each line or passage from the text as if
it were a discrete unit, usually without making any attempt to
analyze Aristotle's overall argument.[14] Although Sigonio's treatise contributes little that is new to the late Renaissance reception
of the *Poetics*, it differs from many other texts in this interpretive tradition in one important way: *De dialogo liber* is not a gloss
on the *Poetics*, but rather an attempt to reproduce the method
used by Aristotle himself within the confines of a much later
(medieval-Renaissance) mode of theoretical discourse. Although
the *Poetics* contains only one enigmatic phrase concerning Socratic dialogue, Sigonio regularly invokes the authority of Aristotle and the methodological framework of the *Poetics* in making
his case ("as I was looking into the matter rather carefully, that
excellent way of investigating the definition of dialogue occurred
to me, which Aristotle pointed out in the *Poetics* "; 9*v*).[15] Sigonio's
treatise attempts to address the silence of antiquity, particularly
that of Aristotle, on the subject of dialogue without violating the
tenets of ancient art and thought. His ambition is to do for the
genre of dialogue what Aristotle did for the genre of tragedy,
that is, to develop a general theory of its poetics. Since tragedy
is not the same as dialogue, however, Sigonio cannot belatedly
proceed to formulate a poetics of dialogue by simply substitut-
ing the term 'dialogue' for the term 'tragedy' everywhere that
it occurs in the *Poetics* and making the necessary adjustments.
In order to reproduce Aristotle's method and adhere to his authority, he must in *De dialogo liber* develop an interpretation of
the theory of the *Poetics* that translates Aristotle's intentions into
the context of contemporary sixteenth-century critical language
and thought.

In the middle decades of the century, other Italian critics and
theorists did write treatises on individual literary genres using
the theoretical framework of the *Poetics*. Robortello, for instance,
included several brief treatises (such as *De elegia* and *De comoedia*) in his 1548 edition of the *Poetics*. Giovanni Battista Giraldi
Cinthio, working in Ferrara in the same period, produced treatises on tragedy, comedy, satire, and romance; the list could be
extended a good deal further.[16] Sigonio is the first, however, to

try to discover the system of text-rules that distinguishes dialogue from the other kinds of literature, even though Aristotle did not do so. He remarks of his project for a poetics of dialogue that "having been led in imitation of the ancients, I believe that nothing should prevent us from presenting the same method for the writing out of instruction and a treatise on dialogue that they employed in other matters" ([iii*r*]).[17] This is more than just an attempt to follow a literary fashion; it expresses the essence of the meaning of the *Poetics* for *De dialogo liber*. One of Aristotle's chief insights in the *Poetics* is that literary works are sets of encoded conventions inscribed in a general textual system of representation or mimesis (the genus of poetry is for Aristotle, as we saw in Chapter 1, synonymous with the general literary system itself). Since there is but a single literary system, the method of analysis employed in the *Poetics* can consequently be assumed to be applicable to the entire universe of literary texts, even though Aristotle limited himself to tragedy, epic, and comedy. Although many of Sigonio's fellow critics further restrict this literary universe of poetry to works in verse, Sigonio himself, by studying the discursive system of conventions that constitute the *forma dialogi* and distinguish it from other kinds of writing, interprets the *Poetics* as proposing a far more extensive and more radical understanding of literature. One of Sigonio's main polemical purposes is to show that an apparently *para*-literary kind of writing—dialogue, which seems to be neither verse nor drama nor straightforward narrative fiction—can in point of fact be fully situated within the general textual system of representation. The theory of dialogue is a demonstration of the universal validity of Aristotle's method in the *Poetics* and its foundation in the idea of mimesis. Dialogue belongs to the same art form as the *Odyssey*, *Antigone*, *Oedipus Rex*, the *Aeneid*, the *Divina Commedia*, and the *Orlando furioso*; the challenge that faces Sigonio in *De dialogo liber* is to provide convincing proof of this.

Paradoxically, though, Sigonio insists on discussing only "the teachings that are to be conveyed about the *ancient* practice of dialogue" (9*r*; my italics).[18] He makes no mention of medieval and Renaissance dialogue, as if dialogue simply disappeared with the decline of the civilization of antiquity. Of course, this was not the case; among all the literary genres of the Renaissance, few if any were more widely practiced—especially by Italian humanists—than dialogue. Nor was dialogue out of fashion by the 1560's, even though the Italian Renaissance had already entered its late (or, as it is sometimes called, "mannerist") phase: Tasso, for example, had not yet even begun to compose his *Dialoghi* at the time of publication of *De dialogo liber*.[19] In his other writings, Sigonio—first and foremost a historian—always shows himself to be deeply aware of the historical process at work during the Middle Ages and the Renaissance in Italy; certainly the existence of medieval and Renaissance dialogues between the collapse of Roman civilization and his age was not unknown to him. Although Sigonio highly values Latinity both in his own work and in that of others, perhaps leading him to judge the linguistic and stylistic features of medieval and Renaissance dialogues harshly, his neglect of all postclassical dialogues in his theory may most likely be ascribed instead to his own particular concept of the function of literature and literary study in the late Renaissance.

According to Sigonio, the principal aim of the sixteenth-century writer is to compose works in the manner of the ancients; the goal of the Renaissance dialogist is "to form a perfect dialogue, such as that ancient form of dialogue [was]" (18*r*).[20] By the same token, the function of literary criticism and theory is to fill in the lacunae left in the corpus of ancient criticism and philosophy.[21] As Sigonio notes in the dedication to his treatise, dialogue is devoid of "every kind of support and instrument of all of ancient literature" ([iir–iiv]), since no formal theory of dialogue can be found in antiquity.[22] He therefore proposes to remedy that gap in ancient literary culture while following the same critical principles set down in antiquity: "I should say," he notes, "that I will offer nothing that is averse to the practice of the discipline of the ancients, but instead I shall draw out all the rivers of this question from their noble monuments, just as from the most fruitful fountains" ([iiv]).[23] His theory in turn will instruct contemporary Renaissance writers in the composition of dialogues in the manner of the ancients in order "to form a perfect dialogue." Since the form of dialogue was already perfect in antiquity, presumably all postclassical dialogues should follow as closely as possible the model that can be developed from

the works of the Greek and Roman dialogists. Ancient dialogue
is the only sort of dialogue worth studying in the first place, it
would appear, since all other dialogues are always already imitations of it.[24] For Sigonio, there is essentially only one possible
model of the poetics of dialogue, which is repeated *ad infinitum*
in Western literature without significant variation; underneath
all differences between dialogues there is a single universal textual structure of representation. Thus his theory does not try to
define simply a stylistic procedure of imitation, but maps out the
structural *differentiae* that make dialogue a unique kind of writing (for without difference there would be no structure). Theory
plays a central role in the practice of writing dialogue itself: the
exemplum of an ancient writer to be imitated by the Renaissance
dialogist is replaced by a general system of rules and precepts
instead.[25] To begin to construct this model of dialogue, Sigonio
turns first to the question—perhaps the most contested one in
sixteenth-century literary criticism and theory—that is so central
to both the *Poetics* and the poetics of *De dialogo liber*: namely, the
question of imitation itself.

From the first, Sigonio insists that dialogue cannot be thought
of as a text formulated in terms of past or present conventions of
actual conversation.[26] Calling dialogue *hoc genus scribendi* (1r), he
emphasizes that—as a "kind of writing"—it must be studied as
a *fictio* or *fabula* that adheres to the conventions of literary composition set down by Aristotle.[27] The study of dialogue no longer
means, as it did for earlier generations of humanists, a borrowing of style from the ancient dialogists; it means instead to define
its innate rules and laws as a *genus scribendi*. In opposition to a
number of contemporary exegetes of the *Poetics*, Sigonio interprets the vexed passage on Socratic dialogue as an unambiguous
endorsement of dialogue as a kind of literary mimesis: "Thus
I establish," he concludes after examining Aristotle's text, "that
nothing will seem more certain than that imitation is proper in
dialogue" (12r).[28] This in turn legitimates a poetics of dialogical
representation, since philosophers "apply this instrument [imi-
tation] to those things that are discussed in philosophy, which
truly they call dialogue, since they wish it to be formed by imitation" (4r).[29] Toward the beginning of *De dialogo liber*, in his

discussion of the reasons why the ancient philosophers wrote in dialogue, Sigonio remarks that his treatise will consider the theory of "the very nature of the dialogical writings" (1*r*), not of the language of ordinary or everyday conversation, even though the condition of belief that dialogue creates may make the reader see in it the residual traces of a conversation that once occurred, as if it were an act of trans-scribing across time.[30] Great dialogues only seem to be natural; what is significant is their *seeming* to be a mirror-like reflection of a spoken exchange, not any innate natural quality that they might appear to possess.[31] In the same fashion, Titian's portraits employ the highest degree of artifice in order to produce a strikingly verisimilar visual effect, Sigonio notes (1*v*).

Why, however, should dialogical writing ever desire to disguise itself as a by-product of speech, something secondary or supplementary to it? The task of the poetics of dialogue is to discover and describe not only the textual strategy of familiarization that makes dialogue appear so disarmingly natural and unlike other kinds of fiction, but also the fundamental motivation for that strategy. Sigonio begins that task by remarking:

It was pleasing to Ammonius that this be its [dialogue's] power, that in these [dialogical writings] the author undergoes the task of disputation of his very own doctrine, and by these other introduced characters he will provide support for himself. Since it cannot be obtained without the simulation of some conversation of others, for that reason he will resort to imitation as if he were some kind of a poet: I say I mean, however, "to imitate" in this instance, just as Plato—the best author of this entire discipline—defined it in the Third Book of the *Republic*. (1*r*–1*v*)[32]

Obviously, for Sigonio, dialogue is synonymous with philosophical dialogue or, more precisely, dialectical dialogue; his theory concentrates on works of this kind, whose subject is always a problem of knowledge and judgment. This restricted definition of dialogue arises from what Sigonio, in the above passage, sees as the purpose for writing dialogue. By placing its scene directly before the eyes of the reader (*ante oculos*), dialogue serves as an instrument for philosophers seeking to obtain a greater degree of interest—and eventual consensus—from readers than a strictly technical exposition of an argument or an idea might achieve.

Dialogue operates as a fictional mise-en-scène of speaking characters, through the division of the writer's discourse into competing voices ("the simulation of some conversation of others"); this is, for Sigonio, imitation in the sense given in Book 3 of the *Republic* (392D–394D), in which the characters speak not directly to the reader but to each other instead (1*v*).

This fiction of a scene of speaking, however, is but a strategic maneuver that allows the dialogist to "provide [philosophical] support for himself," as Sigonio phrases it, while apparently subjecting a set of ideas to close scrutiny in the form of a dialogue between speakers with differing points of view. The dialogist uses the fiction of speakers engaged in dialogue, in short, as a means of disguising the fundamentally monological nature of the doctrine (or authorial intention) being presented, for in dialogue "the author undergoes the task of disputation of his very own doctrine," and not that of someone else. (Why this disguise is not only desirable but necessary in dialogue is considered later in *De dialogo liber*.) We ought not in any case, Sigonio suggests, be fooled by the double-voiced appearance of dialectical dialogue into thinking of it as the collaborative work of more than one mind or one point of view. The fiction of a scene of speaking between different voices, rather than an undisguised single narrative voice (what he calls "perpetual narration"), enables dialogue to acquire authority because it leads the reader to believe that others have tested, and ultimately affirmed, the ideas that it proposes. But although this faculty of "making believe" comprises a major part of the special power of dialogue, the theorist of dialogue ought not to fall into the same trap that it sets for readers.

From what art does this power of dialogical simulation derive? Sigonio states explicitly (1*r*–1*v*) that it comes from the imitation or mimesis—in Plato's sense of the term in Book 3 of the *Republic*—practiced by the dialogist "as if he were some kind of a poet" rather than an orator, who does not use the fiction of multiple personae (20*v*). The characters in a mimetic work of this sort always speak in the first person as if they were actors on a stage, without the intervention of a narrator. In the *Republic*, Plato opposes the lexical mode of mimesis—which he understands as a dramatic impersonation of speakers—to the mode of diegesis. In diegesis, the "I" of the narrator openly appears and dominates the scene of speaking; this mode is today known as indirect or reported speech (in which the narrative discourse is punctuated by "she said," "he said," and so on).[33] Plato, of course, has no use in his City for mimesis or for the poets who practice it, but this does not daunt Sigonio. The power of dialogical simulation, he infers, is linked to the absence of a narrative voice and the presence of a dramatic scene of speaking: Plato's negative valuation of mimesis in the *Republic*, not his technical description of it, need merely be reconsidered in the context of the *Poetics*.

When Sigonio says that dialogue is a species of textual imitation or mimesis, he generally understands the term to mean what it does for Aristotle in the *Poetics*. There mimesis is defined as the representation of human beings doing or experiencing something (*Poetics* 2, 1448a1) or as the representation of "character and experience and action" (*Poetics* 1, 1447a27–28), whether in music, poetry, or the visual arts.[34] Mimesis does not function, according to Aristotle, as an exact artistic reproduction of the phenomenal world; there is no direct ontological link between a work of art and the world of human experience. Mimesis is instead a practice that employs representational conventions of resemblance and correspondences in form in order to reproduce a recognizable image of some sphere of human activity; it is "peculiar to the processes of art" and is not found in either nature or science.[35] Although dancing, music, and painting are all mimetic and science and philosophy are not, Aristotle is concerned primarily with the technical analysis of fiction (what he calls the genus of poetry) and its means, object, and mode of representation (*Poetics* 1, 1447a16–18). The *Poetics* argues for the study of literary texts as an ensemble of rational techniques that follow a logic of representation, rather than as a point-by-point reproduction of the real, for that would lead to a theory of history rather than of literature. So specific is the theory of mimesis— or representation—for Aristotle that the term itself is limited, in the extensive corpus of his work, practically to the *Poetics* alone, except for references to poetic problems in other works.[36]

Plato employs a myriad of possible senses of the same term, and it is practically impossible to lift these different senses of mimesis out of their context in the Platonic dialogues (which would be contrary, in any case, to the very method of the dialectic in which they are embedded).[37] In the passage from Book 3 of the *Republic* cited by Sigonio (1*v*), for instance, 'mimesis' refers to a mode of fictional discourse, not to a full-fledged theory of representation. In Book 10 of the *Republic*, in contrast, the same term takes on a different and more metaphysically oriented meaning (the Three Beds). Needless to say, this varied use of the term causes no end of confusion for Renaissance readers of Plato. Sigonio himself glides back and forth between the different Aristotelian and Platonic contexts of the term: yet although the end result in *De dialogo liber* might appear at first glance to the modern reader as merely an assemblage of heterogeneous fragments, it has instead a precise rationale.

One of Sigonio's goals in his theory of dialogue and elsewhere —a project that he shares with numerous other mid-sixteenth-century Italian critics and theorists—is to reconcile the divergent positions of the ancient authorities, in particular Plato and Aristotle.[38] In *De dialogo liber*, he posits an essential continuity between the two distinctly different literary uses of the term 'mimesis' by Aristotle and Plato, a continuity that can be maintained only as long as he does not consider all the other senses of mimesis in Plato's dialogues.[39] And so the meaning—for Sigonio's poetics of dialogue—of the phrase "he will resort to imitation as if he were some kind of a poet" begins to emerge more clearly. If, in order to support a point of philosophical doctrine, a writer resorts to a dialogical scene of speaking, then that writer must rely on a literary strategy of mimesis in *both* Plato's and Aristotle's senses of the term. The dialogical text has to be studied as a work of mimesis both insofar as it is a representation of "character and experience and action," as Aristotle defined it, and insofar as it is a simulation of the conversation of others, in the restricted Platonic sense of mimesis discussed above (an impersonation of characters who speak in direct discourse).[40] Plato and Aristotle are reconciled and brought together in order to concur that dialogue is at once an instrument of cognitive inquiry for philosophers, in which "the author undergoes the task of disputation of his very own doctrine," and "some kind" of poetic fiction, unlike a treatise or any other sort of expository or argumentative prose. Once this has been established, Sigonio turns in *De dialogo liber* to a study of the discursive position of dialogue at the crossroads of cognition and representation.

Dialectic plays a fundamental role in the theoretical scheme of *De dialogo liber*. Dialogue was, Sigonio notes, originally a product of Greek philosophy rather than poetry ("dialogue was invented by philosophers"; 1*v*).[41] It was one of the two principal textual forms—the other being the Aristotelian treatise—used in antiquity for treating philosophical subjects: "And so for writing about gods, nature, virtue, and public and private affairs," he points out, "two kinds of writing existed, one of which is chiefly celebrated by Aristotle and the other by Plato" (4*r*).[42] Yet dialogue's position as an invention of philosophers, in relation to the discourse of philosophy itself, is far from clear. As an instrument of philosophers seeking to "provide support" for themselves, is dialogue a subsidiary branch of philosophy? If it is, then how can it be said to belong to "the poetic art of imitation" (4*r*), on the one hand, and yet also serve the ends of philosophy, on the other hand? If Aristotle is right in distinguishing between theory, which deals with knowledge, and the productive arts, in which an object is produced, how can dialogue serve as their intersection? This idea of a philosophical fiction would seem, in short, to be fraught with difficulty for the Renaissance theorist. Plato, after all, burned his poetic works when he first heard the voice of Socrates in front of the theater of Dionysus and turned his back forever on fiction making.[43] The threshold status of dialogue, as a textual form that is at once both mimesis and the "disputation . . . of . . . doctrine," poses a dilemma for Sigonio's poetics. Any work of dialogical mimesis must still be subject to the laws of dialectic if it is to have any special cognitive privileges beyond those ordinarily granted to fiction:

Because the disputation is a rational investigation conducted among learned men by means of question and answer (a procedure that the Greeks called *dialegesthai*), the ancients maintained that dialogues should be composed of questions and answers and thus come under the competence of dialectic, which . . . was held to be the ability to discover arguments [*inventio*] whereby we confirm or refute anything, so impelling the adversary by means of questioning that we leave him the choice of accepting one of the two parts of the opposition. (12r–12v)[44]

Dialogical discourse, with its constant flow of questions and answers, "comes under the competence" of dialectic, but it is not to be confused with dialectic. That in dialogue dialectic is governed by, and inscribed in, a framework of fiction, yet is not itself fully and completely a fiction, is a point that deserves careful investigation, for it indicates one of the central problems of poetics in *De dialogo liber* and, for that matter, in the answer of Renaissance theory on the whole to the problem posed by dialogical writing.

Sigonio seeks in his theory to find a balance between the different yet related arts of discourse in dialogue ("by the support of which arts dialogue is sustained"; [1r]):[45] "Three in fact are the arts by means of whose rules and customs dialogue is shaped, which are (naturally enough) that of the poets, that of the orators, and that of the dialecticians; it is like poetry in that the same imitation occurs in dialogue that occurs in poetry; it is like oratory in that it is not restricted by meter, but uses prose" (8r).[46] The discursive "rules and customs" of rhetoric, fiction, and dialectic (that is, its questions and answers) supply the means of representation for dialogue, in the terminology of the *Poetics*; they are all a part of the continuum of linguistic material that constitutes it, just as tune and rhythm are the means of representation for flute playing. Yet they are also much more than that, in the context of Sigonio's theory of dialogue, for dialectic, rhetoric, and fiction are all distinct arts of discourse in their own right. The characteristic feature of any art, Aristotle remarks, is that it "can be reduced to a system."[47] And since dialogue is shaped and constituted by these three arts, it appears as a *system of systems* with a structure of its own that is neither dialectic nor rhetoric nor even, strictly speaking, fiction, but is instead a synthesis of all three.[48] This synthetic, hybrid quality of dialogical discourse is the source of its appeal, and its difficulty, for Sigonio as a late humanist seeking to theorize a general relationship of interdependence between eloquence and the different forms of discoursing about ideas.

Dialectic and rhetoric, as defined by Aristotle, share several characteristics despite the obvious differences between them. Both are universal arts of discourse: they—unlike, say, logic—do not deal with the nature of any particular subject and can be assigned no specific set of *topoi*.[49] Along with literary mimesis, they are probabilistic modes of discourse that operate according to the laws of verisimilitude. Dialogue, in turn, presumably shares these same characteristics, for—as Sigonio remarks—it is only through the co-presence of dialectical, rhetorical, and fictional discourse that dialogue can indeed become perfect:

Thus the perfect kind of dialogue . . . is achieved by the institutions of poetry for undertaking imitation with the ornament of personae, [and] by the institutions of oratory for illustrating oration by the lights of eloquence. Nor is this itself enough; dialectical furnishings need to be added, without which the writer of a distinguished dialogue cannot maintain the keen and challenging function of disputation, or the suitable practice of asking and putting a question or . . . be able to recognize the method of drawing out of circumstances or of grilling an adversary or of escaping perhaps his treachery as well as his traps, which are all tools of both dialectic and dialogues. (9r)[50]

Yet the perfection that dialogue contains, theoretically speaking, as the point of intersection of these three arts or systems is not meant to subvert the differences among the three. On the contrary, Sigonio's intention in constructing his theory is to defend the boundaries of the various systems within the fictional framework of dialogue. The aim of *De dialogo liber*—as a poetics of dialogical writing—is to discover how the text employs all three arts without erasing the necessary qualitative distinctions among them.[51] Sigonio seeks to define a textual structure of dialogue that can introduce rhetoric and dialectic into literary mimesis without completely contaminating each with the other, even if at the level of the language of the text (the means of representation) they are intermingled. Any theory of the dialogical text must be based on the principle of strict differentiation, as well as integration, of its constituent codes.[52] Sigonio calls on his poetics to construct a model of dialogue that modulates between different internal discursive fields without compromising not only the integrity of any of those fields but what is proper to dialogue itself as well. His poetics is to provide a theoretical solution to the problem posed by dialogue as a testing ground for the difference(s) between discovering, persuading, and representing.

In the *Poetics*, Aristotle remarks that tragedy is divided not only into six qualitative parts (plot, character, diction, thought, spectacle, and song), but also into quantitative parts "common to all tragedies" (prologue, epilogue, exode, and choral song, which is itself divided into parode and stasimon).[53] The second group constitutes the principal structural segments of the *récit* of tragedy, which is logically and chronologically organized to begin with the beginning and to conclude with the ending, always in accordance with the requirement of a unity of action ("the plot, being a representation of a piece of action, must represent a single piece of action and the whole of it").[54] In *De dialogo liber*, Sigonio postulates a quantitative division of dialogue into a logically arranged sequence of parts, following the general procedure of the *Poetics*. These parts are the vestibule (*praeparatio*) and the contention (*contentio*), which is subdivided into the proposition (*quaestio*) and the testing of the proposition (*probatio*). The order of these quantitative parts in the structure of dialogue is invariable according to Sigonio's model, since the vestibule always precedes the contention in the sequence of dialogical events. Within this textual structure, with its prescribed temporal and spatial arrangement, are deployed the various qualitative parts, such as character, thought (*dianoia*), and so on, as well as elements of the different constituent arts of discourse. The quantified structure of dialogue—vestibule:contention (proposition:testing)—corresponds to a universal logic of dialogical narrative; it is the cornerstone of Sigonio's theory of dialogue as a metasystem of arts. Although the qualities of dialogue do vary from text to text, all may be expected to obey, to one degree or another, this same quantitative narrative logic. The closer a given dialogue is to Sigonio's model, he concludes, the closer it is to being a "perfect dialogue" (18r); this narrative logic of places and spaces is what defines dialogue as an ideal scene of speaking.

In the vestibule (*praeparatio*), the speakers meet and first engage in conversation, as in Cicero's *De oratore* (1.7.24–29) or Plato's *Phaedrus* (229A, 230B). The vestibule is the part of the dialogical text that, in its casual and circumstantial nature, is most nearly structured like a true everyday conversation. Sigonio states that the *"praeparatio,* which the Greeks call *kataskeuē,* is that whole conversation presented in the beginning of the dialogue in order to strengthen the access to the proposed dispute" (17*v*).[55] The vestibule operates in the dialogical conversation as the prologue of a drama does and corresponds even more closely to the exordium at the beginning of a speech.[56] In regard to its narrative function as a conversational frame or antechamber for the dialectical disputation, which follows after it and depends on it for detailed information about the time and place (or *locus amoenus*) of the contention and about the identity and motivation of the main characters, Sigonio remarks that "in this so-called vestibule it should be made plain who and what sort are they whom the dialogist introduces, and at what time and what place and by what reason they come to this disputation" (20*v*).[57] These five elements of information cannot be included in the *contentio* since they would only disrupt the unfolding of the dialectical debate and distract the reader from following the give-and-take of opinions between the speakers. The conversation in the vestibule serves to enhance the characterization of the speakers ("for surely we shall try to fashion character with no less care than we would express an opinion"; 53*r*) and to establish the verisimilitude—or credibility—of the circumstances of the scene of dialogue itself; these are in effect necessary preconditions for any attempt to read and understand the contention that follows.[58] Only by the inclusion of these five elements can dialogue be firmly grounded in what might or should occur and thus satisfy the requirements of internal esthetic necessity laid down in the *Poetics.*[59]

The key term in Sigonio's discussion of the vestibule is *decorum;* as he remarks in the dedication of *De dialogo liber,* all matters regarding dialogue "must obey above all else the laws of decorum and of verisimilitude; there was never anything more difficult in all the arts than to accomplish these ends, even in the judgment of the most learned men" ([i*v*]).[60] Fiction always seeks to achieve a degree of verisimilitude or the illusion of mimetic probability, and thus "all imitation [mimesis] is achieved by observing the task of decorum and verisimilitude" (18*v*).[61] Such is the significance of decorum in Sigonio's theory of dialogue, Bernard Weinberg argues, that "his total theory of dialogue is really a theory of decorum."[62] This is an overstatement, doubtless, but the virtual equivalence of decorum and verisimilitude makes decorum not only a means to an end, but an end in and of itself, for Sigonio and for the majority of sixteenth-century Italian literary critics and theorists as well. "For in fact," Sigonio states, "what else need be prescribed with respect to this form [dialogue], besides the fact that it is based at once on observation of persons, times, places, and causes, and in keeping one's attention on them?" (18*v*).[63]

Sigonio further notes that although there are different kinds of decorum to be observed (in behavior, in speech, and so forth; 18*v*–19*r*), the one that concerns the theory of dialogue is poetic or literary decorum (20*r*). Readers of Renaissance criticism, poetry, and fiction are familiar with the concept of literary decorum as due proportion and balance among the elements of the literary work; it is whatever is fitting, proper, and appropriate to the theme, characters, and language of the text. This principle of proportion, or relational analogy, is the same one that governs (for sixteenth-century thought) the structure of the natural world and of the universe itself. Decorum, so greatly valued—at least in the eyes of Renaissance critics and philosophers—in the art and thought of antiquity, is in this sense the most natural and least formalizable of all literary devices. According to Wesley Trimpi,

The term "decorum," in its most general sense, refers to criteria to be observed in judging those things in our experience whose excellence lends itself more appropriately to qualitative than to quantitative measurement. . . . Decorum itself cannot be expressed as a fixed ratio of components or produced by a fixed series of steps. It is not to be weighed out, once and for all, in specific ingredients either to be combined together at once or to be added in sequence as in a chemical experiment. It is, rather, a continuing process, an avoidance moment by moment of an imbalance.[64]

"Nothing is more difficult than to see what is becoming," as both Cicero and Sigonio remark, precisely because it is so natural, or seems to be. The careful observance of the parts of decorum in the vestibule—the time, place, and circumstances of dialogue, as well as the identity of the interlocutors—is the key to the esthetic success of any given dialogue, Sigonio assures his readers, because it establishes the naturalness and due proportion of the work.[65] But if decorum is a continuing process of balancing and adjusting, of discriminating and judging, which works in different ways in different texts, how can it be codified and integrated into a poetics of dialogue? The difficulty facing Sigonio is that of knowing precisely what the natural, the fitting, and the appropriate are and how they may be understood as a part of a rational procedure for writing dialogue.

Sigonio contends that "poetic decorum is involved both in the imitation of the characters of men and in the creation of appropriate speech" in dialogue (20*r*); it is at once a rhetorical and a literary technique.[66] Decorum in dialogue entails both *ēthopoiïa*, or description of the "characters of men," on the one hand, and rhetoric, or the "creation of appropriate speech" in the *dianoia* of the characters, on the other hand, since "it is necessary that whatever is the case in given circumstances be also expressed in the manner of speech" (18*v*).[67] The authority of dialogue is based on both the social and linguistic appropriateness of the vestibule, on the coherency of both its thematic (semantic) and formal inscription in a specific sociocultural code of doing and speaking. Each speaker in the vestibule is to be assigned, Sigonio suggests, a different complex of appropriate conventional traits in accordance with the surrounding circumstances of time, place, and setting of the conversation; these traits help to determine the character's involvement and role in the contention that follows, and they signal to the reader how to interpret the contrasting positions taken in the contention. Thus the theory of decorum, as it appears in *De dialogo liber*, corresponds at one level to a theory of types; that is, a typology in which each speaker is assigned, on the basis of certain conventional traits, a precise identity within the dialogical situation. Presumably the reader in turn does not fail to recognize that the speakers represent certain exemplary ethical positions or privileged complexes of social and cultural values.[68]

By supplying a set of ethical and social indications for dialogue —in the form of exemplary yet typical characters—the theory of decorum inevitably leads to questions about the relationship of sameness and difference between what is represented in the idealized *locus amoenus* of the dialogical scene of speaking, on the one hand, and the existing Renaissance social and cultural norms known to the reader, on the other hand.[69] Thomas More's *Utopia*—by virtue of its division into two books, one of which (its vestibule, as it were) is set in the "here and now" of sixteenth-century Europe, and the other in the "nowhere" of Utopia— exemplifies this exploration of sameness and difference in the application of literary decorum. Decorum serves in dialogue as a device to examine, measure, and evaluate the proximity or distance of the dialogical and contemporary situations. The theory of decorum is, in this sense, a theory of difference as what is fitting and appropriate to dialogue; the scene of speaking should be familiar to the reader, yet not a completely recognizable part of everyday experience.

Although literary decorum establishes that the customs and manners as well as the thoughts and words of the speakers have to be represented in dialogue, this is not the same as saying that any and all acts and words may enter into its scene. Decorum also possesses a regulative function in Sigonio's theory. He specifies that the speakers in dialogue cannot represent just any type of exemplary character; on the contrary, decorum requires that they be "the most eminent men of the republic, charged with its weightiest affairs and concerns" (26*v*).[70] Sigonio cannot imagine the presence of anyone else in a dialogue that has kept its decorum intact; "which thing we notice that Cicero did, since he would more effectively persuade men practiced in the greatest affairs of state rather than in literary studies" (29*r*).[71] Only the *selectissimi viri*—as in Cicero's dialogues, in which many of the characters are leading historical figures in the Roman Republic—are to be allowed to cross the threshold and enter into the vestibule before beginning a dialectical disputation. Obviously Socratic dialogues, in which the characters are not always decorous (as in the *Symposium* or the *Gorgias*), are not to be imitated by the aspiring Renaissance dialogist in this regard.[72] In fact, Sigonio roundly criticizes Plato for the general lack of decorum in his dialogues. Although conceding that the vestibule of the *Phaedrus* "is endowed with a certain wonderful smoothness"

(34r), for example, Sigonio points out that "the more charming it is, the less grand it is" (34r), since it does not adhere to the standards of decorum suitable for dialogue as defined in *De dialogo liber*.[73] The grandeur of dialogue can be maintained only if the speakers in its scene are also civic leaders and historical figures of recognized importance (a point that seems to owe something to Sigonio's profession as a historian).

Even further limitations are, however, to be placed on the identities of the speakers in the dialogical scene. The *selectissimi viri* ought to be not only of equivalent social rank, Sigonio observes, but of about the same age as well, so that the superiority in debate of one or the other will emerge solely on the strength of the argument put forward, rather than because of the intellectual immaturity of one of the speakers.[74] Speakers should also be characterized as "good, congruent, conventional, and consistent" (20r), since all these qualities are necessary for any complete representation of human action.[75] The set of normative constraints imposed on the object and means of dialogical representation by Sigonio's theory of decorum is thus not just technical, but at once moral, social, and psychological as well. In formulating his argument here, Sigonio chooses to ignore chapter 25 of the *Poetics*, in which Aristotle states that "the standard of what is correct is not the same in the art of poetry as it is in the art of social conduct or in any other art."[76] Aristotle understands decorum (*to prepon*) as simply the agreement between the language and behavior of a character on the one hand and that character's condition (sex, age, nationality) on the other hand. Sigonio instead shifts the grounds of decorum from "appropriateness" to "propriety" (virtuous behavior, membership in a specific class or group).[77]

The theory of decorum in *De dialogo liber* thus has relatively little to do with Aristotle's definition of the term. The vestibule is much closer to being a specialized epideictic rhetoric of literary description that serves to control the opening moves of the speakers in the disputation and sets definite limits to the coming clash of opinions. Decorum is a representational code that guarantees the dignity of dialogue by allowing difference while limiting it; since the speakers are to be portrayed as holding differing points of view, yet as belonging to essentially the same social stratum and possessing essentially the same high personal qualities (goodness, consistency), their conflict with each other will be a controlled one. Wildly divergent individual positions, languages, and beliefs, which might lead to another, more violent kind of clash and thus destabilize the decorum of dialogue, are to be excluded from the scene of speaking in the vestibule. Decorum is to provide, in dialogue, a specific and appropriately balanced answer to the question of quality (which asks for the "what" of a given thing), a question that—in the sphere of human action—is always one of ethics.[78]

Furthermore, only a fitting choice and a fitting description of time, place, and circumstance can justify the speakers' decision to conduct a conversation in the dialogical fiction. The theory of decorum in *De dialogo liber* includes a set of external places or *loci* to be used to adapt the dialogical scene to a given setting ("no less are the time and place of it to be worked out, so that we may make clear in this same vestibule of dialogue the year, the month, and if possible, the day and the place in which the disputation has been appointed"; 26r).[79] Time and space are key operative elements of the dialogical narrative as well, Sigonio argues, for they are a part of any preamble to a scene representing speaking, thinking subjects in dialogical interaction. He understands this to agree with the argument of the *Poetics*, for if "there is no action except in time and in place" (18r), then the time and place of the action—that is, the encounter and the ensuing conversation—must be specified in the vestibule if there is to be effective mimesis. Only *praxis*, which is the entire complex of human events and emotions and intentions and thoughts that we may call action, can ever be represented by mimesis. And if dialogue is to succeed as a work of mimesis, then it must represent the conversation of the speakers as a *praxis*, not just register the linguistic event of their spoken exchange. The external places of decorum are key structural elements of the vestibule; they are the integral, irreplaceable parts of an itinerary through which mimesis is founded.[80] Above all, the external places produce the necessary credibility and probability in dialogue through their consistency and congruity with the characters and their actions ("if . . . you perceive that the matter accords with persons, places, and times," Sigonio points out, "you will

concur admiringly with everything that is said and done [in it]";
26r), and thus they stand in an organic interrelationship with
the characters' actions.[81]

Moreover, these contextual places determine the initial choice
of a topic for discussion among the speakers in dialogue. Since
these leaders of the *res publica* are generally engaged in the *ne-
gotium* (business) of civic affairs rather than in the *otium* (leisure)
of dialogue, Sigonio remarks, "it would not be decorous or har-
monious that the most eminent men of the republic, charged
with its weightiest affairs and concerns, should foray out at random on any day or to any place whatever in order to engage in
discussions of subtle points in some science or skill" (26v).[82] All
conversation in the vestibule is therefore to be bracketed within
the context of the special non-quotidian event of dialogue, which
does not just take place "on any day" or in "any place," but
most often on special holidays or feast days (compare, for instance, *De oratore* 2.5.19–22). As soon as the vestibule informs us
of the time, place, and circumstance of the conversation, then,
we are to understand that the content of the discussion will be
concerned not with specific civic and political affairs and events,
but rather with "subtle points in some science or skill." Sigonio
adds that the "instituting of the conversation" in the vestibule
ought to contain "a certain wonderful charm of intellect and a
certain gaiety of character" (29r–29v), in order to emphasize that
the conversation arises in the context of an occasion of *otium*.[83]
His theory of decorum makes the conversation in the vestibule
at once the locus of investment of political and social signs in
the characterization of the speakers (*selectissimi viri*), as well as
the bracketing device that depoliticizes the subsequent dialogical disputation, which can be concerned only with subtle points
in some science or skill.

Sigonio's analysis of the vestibule represents an effort to for-
malize and rationalize the rhetorical properties of dialogue as a
kind of writing, in accordance with his vision of an undisturbed
passage from esthetics to ethics and politics. The aim of the epideictic rhetoric of description in the vestibule is to enhance the
authority and intensify the utility of the scene of speaking; in
order to accomplish this, however, the code of decorum defined

by Sigonio must determine in advance the range of possible options and responses of the interlocutors, who may differ from each other, but only to a certain degree. There can be no cranky humanists, no malevolent tyrants, no allegorical figures of Love or Charity, in dialogue if the speakers are to achieve the necessary consensus with the necessary verisimilar effect on the reader. Sigonio theorizes, in essence, that the representability of characters in dialogue must respond to a specific ideal of equilibrium (moral, social, linguistic, and psychological) as defined by his humanist-Ciceronian typology of the ideal statesman.[84] This rhetorical ideal is in turn treated in *De dialogo liber* as a natural and therefore inviolable principle (not entirely unlike the way in which the figure of the courtier is valorized in *Il Cortegiano*). In the last analysis, then, decorum is for Sigonio not only a totalizing discursive code, but a strategic means for generating and determining a specific meaning in the dialogical text.

However, the deeply problematic nature of his notion of decorum is evident, for it violates the very basis of decorum as something that is "not to be weighed out, once and for all, in specific ingredients," but should remain an intangible faculty of judgment. "The rule of decorum cannot be theorized because it is always already the application of the rule"; it is, in other words, always already a practice rather than a theory.[85] In conflating the appropriate and the proper, *De dialogo liber* shows why any attempt to convert the practice of decorum into a theory of decorum inevitably makes it into a prescriptive and regulative mechanism that is no longer a part of a "continuing process, an avoidance moment by moment of an imbalance." Nevertheless, the value of a codified decorum of description for Sigonio's poetics of dialogue is found in its ability to *disguise* the socially and culturally encoded conventions of dialogue by naturalizing them with its power of verisimilitude, by portraying them as a part of the truth itself. This power of verisimilitude makes those same conventions appear to be necessary qualities of the dialogical text:

This poetic verisimilitude is of such power and such a nature that when it is present it causes the thing which is invented not to seem so. Rather will that seem invented which is in strong contrast to the true and which achieves no resemblance to truth, that is, whatever is in disagreement with persons, times, and places and either contains no causes why it should be done as it is or contains improbable causes. (18v)[86]

Sigonio is by no means interested in codifying the properties of decorum solely for the sake of the mimetic illusion that they may generate ("when it is present it causes the thing which is invented not to seem so"); his notion of the esthetic pleasure of the text is, at best, a utilitarian one (compare 2v). The appeal for him of a rationalized rhetoric of description in the vestibule is located in the unique guarantee that it offers his theory of dialogue. The procedure of description in the opening scene, when configured in this way, requires the dialogist to represent specifically virtuous and noble characters and their words; in adhering to the decorum of description, the writer is obliged to "select from what can be said what should be said on the particular occasion."[87] Esthetic and ethical necessity thus are made to coincide in the dialogical text. The problem with this approach is that in it the difference between a poetics of dialogue and a pragmatics of decorum tends to be elided and lost altogether.

The second major quantitative part of dialogue is the contention (*contentio*). In this segment, the speakers introduced in the vestibule grapple with a particular problem (*quaestio*) by engaging in a dialectical discussion: "Contention, which is called *agōn* by the Greeks, is whatever words are spoken about the thing that was proposed for argumentation, whether for confirming or disproving it" (18r).[88] The contention is the part that is fully and completely dialogical and so forms the core of the work. As Sigonio remarks, "It is truly the place that embraces the whole dialogue by means of its own strength and power" (34v).[89] Despite its importance in establishing the coordinates of the scene of speaking, the vestibule is but an auxiliary to the contention, which contains the true essence of dialogical writing. As its name suggests, the conversation in the vestibule prepares the way for the narration of the contention to follow, but the contention alone expresses the true desideratum of dialogue, which is a conflict and contest (*agōn*) of wits and ideas. Dialogue is defined, then, by the appearance in the contention of dialectic: "We assert dialogue to be a certain kind of dialectic; for in every way, it is necessary to say that dialogue is a certain kind of disputation, if we seek the proper and celebrated power of dialogue by the most noble ancient authors; the very same *materia* can be said to be proper to dialogue, which is in turn subject to dialectic" (13*r*).[90]

The vestibule is structured as a brief and casual conversation arranged around a series of *loci* that introduce the information needed to establish decorum, but these *loci* may come up in any order, and other important descriptive details may be brought in anywhere. The vestibule ought to have at least some semblance of the apparent randomness and drift of true conversation (even if it is in fact anything but random). In contrast, the contention is always sequentially subdivided into two separate parts, the proposition (*propositio*)—in which the problem under examination is first posed—and the debate itself, or the "testing [*probatio*] of the proposition," in which opinion (*sententia*) and judgment are expressed by the speakers.[91] (Implicitly included in Sigonio's theory is a third part of the contention, the conclusion of the discussion; see, for instance, 45*v*.)[92] This entire second segment of dialogue is, unlike the vestibule, formally marked by a shift to the discourse of dialectical reasoning, centering around an examination of the proposition ("contention . . . is whatever words are spoken about the thing that was proposed for argumentation").

The use of the term *propositio* in *De dialogo liber* is probably derived from Cicero, who employs it in *De oratore* in the sense of the rhetorical term 'thesis.'[93] A proposition or thesis is an indefinite question that, as Quintilian states in the *Institutio oratoria* (3.5.5), "may be maintained or impugned without reference to persons, time or place and the like."[94] Generally speaking, the proposition or thesis is considered indefinite because it is formulated in terms of a question along the lines of "Should one do a certain thing, or not?" without necessarily referring to individual cases. Sigonio specifies that the semantic content (*materia*) of the contention may consist only of this sort of indefinite question. In dialogue, he notes, the interlocutors are to speak in dialectical terms "on God, on nature, on our souls, on virtues, on public or private affairs, on reason, on knowledge, on oratory" (13*r*) and the like, but are not to address specific contemporary issues or problems.[95] The indefinite nature of such questions confers the status of dialectic on the language of the *probatio* that tests them since, according to the classificatory division of the arts and sciences underlying *De dialogo liber*, the thesis belongs to dialectic, and the hypothesis (or definite question) belongs to rhetoric, even if the latter is always implicit in the former.[96]

The proposition plays a key role in the poetics of dialogue put forward by Sigonio, serving as the dividing line between the descriptive rhetorical system of the vestibule and the system of dialectical statements of the contention. The proposition constitutes both the end of the vestibule, since it emerges from and interrupts the flow of casual conversation, and the beginning of the contention, where that same conversation turns toward more serious matters; it marks the point of passage in the dialogue where the proposition "either in the first words (which I have shown is often done), or certainly not much later . . . stands forth and becomes visible" (34*v*), so that it is clear to every reader that the resolution of the "proposition is nothing other than the conclusion of the testing [*probatio*]" (36*r*).[97] In ancient rhetorical theory, for instance, the proposition is generally the moment of *inventio*, when the argument (or topic) is discovered and produced. In Sigonio's dialogical poetics, the proposition signals not only the end of the first part (vestibule) and the beginning of the second part (contention), but also the transition in the text from pure literary mimesis (decorum) to dialectic; it is the point in the structure of dialogue at which the discourse modulates from one of its three constituent arts to the next.[98] His poetics thus designates a logical spatio-temporal order of discourse, or *dispositio*, for the articulation of the dialogical text, since—according to this logic or order—a question must first be formally raised before it can be truly answered. The priority of question to answer is irreversible in terms of the theory of *De dialogo liber*, whose narrative logic depends on it.[99]

The proposition plays a second, equally important role in Sigonio's theory of dialogue: it functions as the equivalent of plot in the theoretical scheme of the *Poetics*. Aristotle stresses in the *Poetics* (8, 1451a15–19) that the right kind of plot provides the necessary unity of action for tragedy. Sigonio reasons that if dialogue is to be the object of a poetics, it, too, must have an organic structural principle of unity of action like that of tragedy; otherwise it would just be a conversation that could wander in any one of a number of different directions. Sigonio's reading of the *Poetics* on this point is problematic (although typical on the whole of his generation of Italian critics and theorists), since it presumes that every element in Aristotle's analysis of tragedy —the only surviving part of Aristotle's treatise—is applicable to other genres. The central action of dialogue, Sigonio argues, is to be found "in the very communication of speech of those who converse together" (36v).[100] Whereas the vestibule is also a part of the ongoing conversation, the unified action in dialogue is constituted exclusively by the dialectical give-and-take between the speakers in the contention itself. As a question, whether openly or implicitly stated, the proposition anticipates—and, to a greater or a lesser degree, determines—the possible direction of any answer. The proposition is that single unifying strand or narrative line of the contention that organizes the event of the dialogical discussion into a whole, just as the action of tragedy is unified by the plot. It is the agenda of places to which the conversation may travel in the contention; it operates as the center of the disputation, thus guaranteeing the organicity and order of the flow of statements and counterstatements. Indeed, Sigonio concludes, the proposition "is almost supposed to constitute the narrative *fabula* of the dialogue" (34v).[101] There is no talking at cross-purposes in dialogue, thanks to this controlling *fabula*; unlike some other kinds of argumentation, the contention is never allowed to become a *quodlibet* (or "question on whatever you please").[102]

The second structural part of the contention—which Sigonio calls the "testing" of the proposition—is based chiefly on dialectic, which supplies the means for the testing of a topic through systematic doubt and systematic interrogation, in the form of a series of questions and answers. Tragedy develops its plot (*mythos*) in a progressively deployed series of parts, such as reversal and recognition; dialogue develops its own drama in the same way, but through a skillfully orchestrated interplay of questions and answers instead. As the term *contentio* indicates, Sigonio takes for granted the agonistic nature of every dialogue. Dialogue depends not only on the other speaker's continued presence in the scene of speaking, but on a relationship of difference between the speakers as well. There are, however, a number of ways in which this agon may unfold in dialogue, according to the mode of questioning employed. These ways define, in effect, the system of subgenres of dialogical writing. Rather than following the procedure of the *Poetics* and looking for an inner textual logic of division, however, Sigonio develops his theory of the dialogical subgenres out of a reading of the canon of dialogues from antiquity. The reason for this is the glaring difference in the mode of questioning used by his two paragons, Plato and Cicero, a difference that a late Renaissance theorist such as Sigonio must satisfactorily explain. Plato's dialogues—since they stand at the origin of the textual tradition of dialogue—serve here as the principal point of reference for Sigonio's theory of dialogical subgenres. These are subdivided into three main kinds: *expositio*, or "expository" dialogue; *inquisitio*, or "maieutic" dialogue; and peirastic, or "testing" dialogue, which is a mixture of the first two ("one of which is *expositio*, another of which is *inquisitio*, and a third of which is mixed"; 40*v*).[103] This is not merely a classification for classification's sake, however, as is often true of Aristotelian criticism and theory in mid-sixteenth-century Italy; Sigonio intends to use this classification as a means to evaluate further the role of dialectic in his model of dialogical representation.

The different Platonic subgenres of dialogical questioning are, Sigonio observes, distinguished from each other by the role played by the main speaker in the scene of dialogical agon. The central interlocutor—Socrates or his equivalent—initiates and leads the ensuing dialectical discussion, functioning as a persona for the writer in order to bring forth that writer's doctrines in dialogue; however, this same interlocutor is not necessarily the agent of the questioning. The first of the three modes, *expositio*, is—as its name indicates—the expository mode of dialogue, dominated by the main speaker and often overtly didactic in style and content: "I call it the *expositio* when he who has the function of teaching openly shows what he thinks about the proposed question, as Socrates usually does in the works of Plato, with another person doing the questioning" (40*v*).[104] Actually this is the mode of Aristotle's lost dialogues and of a number of Cicero's dialogues (for example, *De partitione*), rather than of the *Sōkratikoi logoi*. Sigonio, however, is willing to twist the evidence of Plato's dialogues to suit the needs of his theory and to gain the support of Plato's authority for his own model of dialogue. Usually there is a teacher-student relationship (parent-child or elder-youth) between the speakers in expository dialogue; in its scene of speaking, the main interlocutor always supplies the answers rather than the questions. The leader of the participants in the scene of speaking is by necessity always, in this kind of dialogue, a designated persona of the author. Even though this seems to contradict Sigonio's theoretical model of decorum, in which the speakers in a dialogue are always to be of more or less the same age and social rank, he nevertheless prefers this mode of dialectical questioning to any other since it allows the author's position to be articulated clearly and systematically and without interference (in the form of interruptions or digressions) by other speakers. Expository dialogue provides, in short, a means of un-contested control—through the use of a dominant figure within the dialogical scene itself—over the direction of the disputation.

In contrast, the maieutic mode of dialogue employs the Socratic method par excellence, in which the doctrines of the writer emerge into view through the main interlocutor's (Socrates's) questioning of others in dialogue.[105] As Sigonio points out, "*Inquisitio* is truly that which [occurs] when that very same one, in the process of interrogating others, makes clear the innermost feeling of his own mind, although he does so somewhat obscurely" (40v–41r).[106] This is the eristic mode of dialectical dialogue, in which the protagonist pursues a line of questioning requiring a yes or no answer from the other interlocutor(s) for each question. The main speaker or Socrates-figure (like the Eleatic Stranger in the *Sophist*) controls the direction of the discussion by framing all questions in the form of antitheses that display the necessity of choice between them and eventually drive the other participant in dialogue into an *elenchos* (forcing "the person who converses with him to contradict himself"; *Sophist* 268B).[107] Sigonio is less inclined to favor the maieutic mode of dialogue since the main speaker's profession of a *docta ignorantia* is—in his view—not decorous and since the direction of the argument is somewhat more difficult for the reader to follow; in maieutic dialogue the writer's main point must be drawn out of the other speakers by a series of questions, rather than formulated as a doctrinal answer to a question.

The third mode of questioning—the peirastic mode—is a testing of ideas in dialogue, where questions may be posed by both sides (the term *peirastikos* appears in Diogenes Laertius's discussion, 3.49, of Plato's dialogues).[108] Peirastic dialogue is a dialectical combat on nearly equal terms between skilled adversaries, such as Socrates and the sophists in the *Gorgias*, or in those dialogues by Cicero that employ dialectical arguments *in utramque partem quaestionis*. Sigonio does not favor the peirastic mode, which is "experimental, tentative, and above all speculative," because of—like the maieutic mode—the difficulties in coming to a clear and uncontested conclusion posed by its rhetorical method of questioning.[109] It is an *altercation*, in the technical rhetorical sense of the term (a "period of questions and counter-questions"), that does not necessarily lead to an eventual consensus among the speakers in the dialogical scene.[110]

This description of the three modes of questioning confirms that Sigonio has a specific kind of dialectic in mind for the testing of ideas in dialogue. Categorically excluded from Sigonio's privileged theoretical model in *De dialogo liber* are the maieutic and peirastic modes of Platonic dialogue, which resist the kind of systematization that Sigonio favors. Although Plato's practice of dialogue is to be held in esteem for any number of reasons, Sigonio acknowledges, it is once again Aristotle who "discloses in the *Topics* the praise and the means by which we may most likely attain it" (37*v*) in dialogue.[111] Dialectic, according to Aristotle, does not deal with the nature of any definite subject: instead it is a faculty of furnishing arguments and discovering probabilities in the form of opinions.[112] The instruments of investigation to be used in dialectic are syllogism and induction, both real and apparent, and the probable proofs that they produce resemble demonstrative proofs, although only to a degree (for the probable is that which happens generally, but not always). Dialectic is, therefore, a particular division of logic itself, even if the testing process of dialectical dialogue explores the zone of epistemological probability (*eidos*) in argumentation without aspiring to attain the absolute degree of certitude of truly logical discourse. Sigonio states that "by these kinds of instruments [syllogism and induction] all should be ratified or eliminated [in dialogue]; the foundations of these arguments—which the art of dialectic ought to show openly to us—must be dug up" (37*v*).[113] Syllogisms and inductions, however, must always be presented in the form of systematic argumentation, or *epicheirēma* (38*v*). The only mode of dialectical questioning that permits full and systematic employment of syllogistic reasoning is *expositio*, for in it the main interlocutor can construct an argument that is bracketed at the beginning and end by questions, but not interrupted during its development either by them or by the need to ask them. If invention—the proposition—discovers evidence and argumentation, then the *probatio* tests and criticizes what has been discovered; in other words, it discovers the probabilities of the proposition itself. The dialectical exchange between the speakers operates in dialogue as a procedure of verification and judgment, not as a place for dazzling displays of verbal pyrotechnics.[114]

Dialectic—when defined in this way—represents for Sigonio much that is supremely valuable about dialogue as the representation of a scene of speaking. Since dialectic is designed to test repeatedly the validity of concepts and statements (even within the limited framework of the expository mode) through the application of a specific argumentative procedure, its use assures that dialogical debate has the status of a system. This systematicness, when combined with the unified narrative program of the proposition, guarantees that the contention differs visibly from either ordinary or literary conversation, which does not proceed through the methodical formulation of syllogisms and inductions. At the same time, since the presence of dialectic forces us to recognize that in dialogue "truly the same subtlety of truth is not sought for in all things, but in the greatest number of them it is enough if the probabilities are discovered" (39*v*–40*r*), this system is understood to lead to provisional rather than to definitive conclusions (that is, to those that do not depend on the rigor of demonstrative proof), and thus not to possess the same status as logical or scientific knowledge.[115] Knowledge (*scientia*) is "always valid" and "certain," according to *De dialogo liber*, whereas opinion is instead "unsteady" and "unstable" (38*r*). But

the important point is that the speakers in dialogue arrive at conclusions, even if in the form of unsteady and unstable opinions.
There is no such thing in Sigonio's view as half a system; either
dialectic works completely, or it does not work at all. Doubt is a
destabilizing and yet essential element of dialogue, and dialectic serves simultaneously as its means of implementation and its
means of regulation in Sigonio's theory.

Although Sigonio can hardly exclude either systematic doubt
(*si cum dubitatione, opinio [sc. dicitur]*; 39*r*) or systematic questioning from his poetics of dialogue, all the doubting, challenging,
and probing in the testing process leads in the end to either the
ratification or the elimination of an argument through the application of dialectic; the speakers are never left in a state of un-
decidability or *aporia* at the end of their agon. Just as the expository mode controls the direction of the dialogical disputation, so
the method of dialectic supplies a controlled form of testing that
produces a final consensus concerning "a certain probability of
opinion" (40*v*), rather than a suspension of judgment.[116] Dialectic
is, as it were, the decorum of thought itself. Dialectic thus justifies the presence of doubt in dialogue by giving it utility in terms
of the end result of the *probatio*; doubt functions in dialogue to
help draw out and prolong—to give duration to—the discourse
of the speakers in order that they may eventually be shown discovering what they are searching for, not in order to confound
the workings of the dialectical process itself.

It is critically important to Sigonio's theory that, since dialogue is "a certain kind of dialectic" (13*r*), or, more accurately,
"a certain kind of image of a dialectical dispute" (14*v*), the respective roles of dialectic and rhetoric in dialogue be clearly distinguished; for rhetoric, as Aristotle observes, is a "counterpart"
(*antistrophē*) or a "division" or even a "likeness" of dialectic.[117]
The chief difference between the arts of rhetoric and dialectic
is that although both are concerned with topics and both may
be reduced to systems, rhetoric seeks to discover the real and
apparent means of persuasion in reference to any given subject,
whereas dialectic instead seeks to discover the real and apparent syllogism.[118] Omnipresent in the dialogical text is, of course,
the linguistic medium of prose itself, or *oratio soluta*; Sigonio calls

this "rhetoric," as we have seen, but he means something very particular by it. Since he can find no convincing treatment in the *Poetics* of prose fiction as an art form, Sigonio incorporates into his theory the Aristotelian notion that the orator is the primary practitioner of the art of prose (just as the tragedian is the primary practitioner of the art of poetry).[119] Every dialogist is in this sense a rhetorician as well as a poet, inasmuch as all dialogues are written in prose.

A second sense of the term 'rhetoric'—as a system of persuasion—plays an even more important role in *De dialogo liber*. Rhetoric is not just the art of prose writing, but the art of discovering the available means of persuasion in any situation and therefore the most appropriate mode of discourse to achieve a particular end by operating on the beliefs, ideas, and emotions of the listener or reader. As we have seen, however, for Sigonio the contention is always a contest of dialectical rather than specifically rhetorical skills between the speakers. Although working without the "necessary things" of scientific proof and thus dealing solely in opinion, the contention is concerned with the construction of a syllogistic schema of quasi-logical argumentation, with producing *probable* opinion as opposed to rhetorically *persuasive* belief. This confers unique importance on the fiction of dialogue, for it is an intermediary between purely representational and purely logical discourse. Dialogue, because of its special relationship to dialectic (of which it is the *imago*), stands one degree closer to philosophy and analytic than either poetry or rhetoric.

The difficulty for *De dialogo liber* as a theory of dialogue—and for sixteenth-century thought in general—is distinguishing the probable and the persuasive in a fully satisfactory fashion.[120] If this is not done—and it constitutes a major challenge for everyone from Lorenzo Valla to Petrus Ramus—the difference between dialectic and rhetoric in the dialogical scene is in danger of erasure; in the case of *De dialogo liber* an admixture of the two codes would disrupt Sigonio's claims for the cognitive value of the contention itself. Although both rhetoric (as a system of persuasion) and dialectic are arts of argumentation, the agon between speakers in a dialogue concerning a given topic must remain strictly dialectical in nature or the probable opinions about it that they seek to discover will not possess that relationship of resemblance to demonstrative proof that Sigonio requires of all true dialogue. Nor will the form of reasoning developed in the disputation prove systematic enough to allow those opinions to emerge completely into view. Sigonio, following what he argues is the authority of Aristotle (*Topics* 1.1), defines the difference between probable proof and persuasion in dialogue in terms of the kind of opinion that each produces. Dialectical opinion is a rational result of the mind's examination of a universal thesis, through the use of syllogistic proofs; rhetorical opinion derives from desire (*ab appetitu*) rather than from reason, and it treats only single, specific hypotheses such as those formed in the "places" of decorum (39*r*). Dialectic leads to the discovery of probabilities, whereas rhetoric brings us under the sway of persuasion and belief (*fides*):

> Probable statements are those which are assented to by the opinion of all, or a large number, or at least by the opinion of the wise. Persuasive statements are those to which the rude and ignorant multitude generally assent. "It is nobler to receive an injury than to give one"—as many philosophers hold—would be granted in a dialectical discussion but in a speech before a popular audience, as it has no persuasive power, it would most likely be ridiculed. (39*v*)[121]

As long as the proposition ("it is nobler to receive an injury than to give one") is an indefinite one, the participants in the scene of speaking cannot in theory treat it in terms of persuasive or pragmatic purposes—that is, in order to influence the listener into making specific choices or decisions—since relatively few individuals ("popular" or otherwise) are likely ever to favor the idea of being injured. Thus stripped of all strategies of rhetorical persuasion, Sigonio implies, the strictly dialectical status of the *probatio* may be preserved.

Sigonio aims, through the structural logic of his poetics of dialogue, to isolate argumentation *ad fidem* from dialectic in the contention, confining it to the vestibule alone, in order to defend the privileged "strength and power" of this kind of dialectical fiction. The conversation in the vestibule is designed to be the chief locus of persuasive rhetoric in dialogue, for its primary function is the establishment of "decorum and verisimilitude" (18*r*). In contrast, the contention must not be governed by a rhetorical purpose. The savants who participate in a dialectical discussion in the scene of speaking do not resort to strategies of persuasion, as must be done in a "speech before a popular audience," for a consensus among them will naturally and inevitably emerge from the discovery of the probabilities of the proposition. For Sigonio, as for Cicero, dialectical thinking consists of a "conferring together of reasoned positions" (*quum philosophia ex rationum collatione constet*); where they differ is in Sigonio's belief that a reconciliation of these positions always occurs in dialogue.[122] Sigonio's argument here is, however, a far cry from the sense of either the *Topics* or the *Rhetoric*, and it goes against the prevailing sixteenth-century humanist tendency to favor a dialectic either altogether subordinate to rhetoric or complementary to it.[123] Sigonio is obliged—for the sake of his notion of the epistemological power of dialectic in dialogue—to invent a binary opposition between rhetoric (as a system of persuasion) and dialectic where for Aristotle and for many of Sigonio's own Renaissance contemporaries there exists a relationship of resemblance instead.

Undeniably Sigonio belongs to the Italian Renaissance tradition—essentially humanistic and Ciceronian in orientation—that deeply respects rhetoric, even though its value is for him on no account to be confused with the value of logic or philosophy. In *De dialogo liber*, for instance, he shows no hesitation in establishing a basis for distinguishing between probable proof and persuasion in terms of rhetoric itself, rather than on logical or philosophical grounds; for the operations of both rhetoric and dialectic, in the passage cited above (39*v*), are evaluated specifically in regard to *who is speaking* and *who is listening* in dialogue. The difference between rhetoric and dialectic in dialogue is defined in terms of two possible poles of public reception, "the wise" and "the rude and ignorant multitude," not in terms of any formal discursive properties of syllogism, enthymeme, exemplum, or the like. Sigonio's use of rhetorical criteria to prevent any overlapping between the discourses of probable proof and persuasion in dialogue preserves in his eyes the integrity of dialectic in the scene of speaking, as well as the integrity of the structure of dialogue itself, since it precludes the entrance of the values of the rude and ignorant multitude—who always require the use of persuasion, not dialectical reasoning—into the dialogical scene. We know in advance that the speakers will not seek to persuade each other (or us) through rhetorical stratagems, for they are the wise and are concerned only with discovering the probabilities of indefinite propositions; intellect, rather than belief and desire, governs the contention and the testing of the proposition. Because of this, dialogue can be considered genuinely dialectical, for the quasi-logical part of its discourse is always a disinterested search, free of rhetorical interference, for a general consensus.

Sigonio's turn to a fundamentally rhetorical theory of reception to explain why dialogues are a kind of dialectic is symptomatic of a (barely) submerged vein of rhetorical thinking that runs through the entire text of *De dialogo liber* and accompanies its poetics of dialogue. Even though he in effect argues against the importance of rhetoric in dialogue by insisting on the essentially dialectical nature of dialogical writing, he nevertheless forms his argument in terms of a theory of rhetoric at the point that his notion of the governing structure of dialogue appears weakest and most problematical. The same argumentative strategy is employed in numerous other places in *De dialogo liber*, making the procedures of poetics and rhetoric sometimes appear indistinguishable. The reasons given for the inclusion or exclusion of a given element of the contention, for example, often refer to the effect of that element on the mind of the reader, not on the internal narrative logic of dialogue itself. The proposition is placed at the beginning of the contention, Sigonio asserts, "so that *the mind of the reader* does not for long wander too far in trying to get hold of the argument" (34*v*; my italics).[124] Plato's dialogues are open to rebuke because, since the proposition is not always clearly formulated, in reading them "you will wander and float around in your mind, for a long time uncertain of the judgments and controversies that went on between [the speakers]" (35*v*).[125] Digression is to be kept out of dialogue on the grounds that it distracts the reader from following the disputation, not because it undermines the esthetic unity of the text; Sigonio calculates distraction in terms of a psychology (read: rhetoric) of reading, rather than in terms of its structural role in the unfolding of the dialogical *fabula*.[126]

In the *Poetics*, a literary text's persuasive power is proof of its esthetic efficacy in satisfying the requirements of reason. The ultimate function of poetic persuasion is to confirm the organic logic of the representation itself and to measure the success of its verisimilitude, not merely to exercise its power over a given audience.[127] In Sigonio's theory of dialogue, however, the dialogical text has to take the measure of the reader's mind because its effect must be a definite and precise one—to make the reader "get hold of the argument" and to understand in no uncertain terms the judgments and controversies and answers of those who speak in the dialogical scene. It is often difficult to tell in *De dialogo liber* if this reader-oriented definition of dialogue is motivated by an organic logic of representation or by a desire to exercise power over the audience in order to support the dialogist.

This is not the result of a banal misreading or misunderstanding on Sigonio's part of the sense of the *Poetics*.[128] His poetics of dialogue reverts to rhetorical theory not out of ingenuousness or duplicity, but rather because the idea of a poetics without a fully empowered rhetoric as its cornerstone is inconceivable to him. Although granting great significance to the art of dialectic and to the dialogical fiction in its employ, he cannot accept the idea of a methodology for the analysis of literary representation divorced from the methodological premises of rhetoric as a system of persuasion. Although Aristotle argues that poetics and rhetoric are separate, though related, arts of discourse, Sigonio is not ready to follow the *Poetics* nearly as far as he would have his readers believe.[129] He is simply not prepared to yield the privileges accorded rhetoric within the Italian humanist tradition, even though the concept of mimesis—the methodological foundation of the *Poetics*—is one basis of his own theory of dialogue. His resistance to an autonomous poetics in *De dialogo liber* is not a resistance to theory itself (far from it). It is instead a resistance to the theory of the literary text as the place of production of a disinterested esthetic pleasure (a notion at least implicit in the *Poetics*), rather than a place of production of readerly pleasure useful to the writer for explicit moral and didactic ends.

Sigonio holds fast in his work to the basically Horatian notion, prevalent in much of Italian criticism and theory in the early and mid sixteenth century, that esthetic pleasure must be accompanied by a clear-cut moral and didactic purpose (*utile dulci*); literary works should persuade and win over the minds of readers in the name of some version of the truth (whether ethical or ontological).[130] In this regard, the motto of the influential Italian critic J. C. Scaliger is equally applicable to the theory articulated in *De dialogo liber*: *imitatur ut doceat*. Given this as an axiom, we can begin to see the difficulty—for a theorist like Sigonio in a work such as *De dialogo liber*—of formulating a poetics of dialogue in terms of poetics alone. Only through recourse to pragmatic criteria can an acceptable sense of purpose be recuperated by him for dialogue. If the dialogist is, as Sigonio says, to "provide support for himself" (1r) and for a set of ideas through the use of dialogue, then this support does not take only the form of the testing and defense of one's own doctrine in the hopes that the wise reader will concur with the conclusions drawn in the contention. Despite its dialectical furnishings, dialogue, as a kind of writing, also supports the dialogist by actively persuading the reader of the probable truth of the arguments put forward. The goal of the theorist of dialogue is to find a critical language and method that can reconcile the study of the esthetic structure of dialogical representation with the principle of its persuasive purpose.

The narrative sequence, or structure, of the parts of dialogue that Sigonio theorizes in *De dialogo liber* is undoubtedly intended to adhere to the requirements of internal probability prescribed by Aristotle in the *Poetics*. Yet the seemingly necessary order of these parts strongly resembles that of another of the *formae loquendi et scribendi* known to Renaissance readers and writers, suggesting another reason behind Sigonio's dialogical design. There is a marked similarity between this structure of dialogue and the structure of rhetorical argumentation as broadly defined in antiquity by Plato, Aristotle, Cicero, and many others. In the *Phaedrus* (266D–267E), for instance, Socrates defines the structure of argumentative discourse as consisting of a proem, narrative, testimony, evidence, probabilities, and recapitulation, in that order. Aristotle, in the *Rhetoric* (3.13–19), argues that the order of parts of a speech is comprised of a proem, statement, proof, and epilogue. The *Ad Herennium* (2.28) contends that the "most complete and perfect argument" contains the following parts in the following order: *propositio, ratio, rationis confirmandis, exornatio, complexio.*[131] This list could be extended considerably, but the point should be clear. For these examples of the *dispositio* or sequential arrangement of the parts of public speech in antiquity are strikingly like the dialogical structure—*praeparatio, propositio, probatio, complexio*—that Sigonio has theorized.[132]

Even though these are two distinct discursive models, one intended primarily for public speaking and the other for the writing of dialogical texts, the similarity between the two suggests that the order of the parts in dialogue is designed to achieve essentially the same effect that it does in public oratory. The purpose of the *dispositio* in ancient rhetorical theory is, generally speaking, to construct an argument that persuades listeners either by appealing *ad fidem* to a belief in the logical probability of the argument or by operating *ad movendos animos* in the realm of affective psychology.[133] The convergence of the structure of dialogue in *De dialogo liber* with the general oratorical model of antiquity seems to suggest that its own division into quantitative parts is based as much on a reading of ancient rhetorical theory as on a consideration of the internal logic of dialogical representation. The order of the parts of dialogue formally reflects both the requirements of a narrative logic of representation and the principles of a preexisting discursive model elaborated by ancient oratorical theory, and it serves the ends of both. Dialogical writing, like a perfect argument, persuades its readers of the probable truth of the discoveries made in the scene of speaking; it is a rhetorical fiction conveying something that is neither wholly fictional nor wholly rhetorical. Yet the rhetorical organization and function of the dialogical text do not, as far as Sigonio is concerned, compromise the work of *De dialogo liber*. On the contrary, the *dispositio* of dialogue represents precisely the sought-after synthesis of rhetoric and poetics, of the gamut of ideas of Plato, Aristotle, Cicero, and other ancient authorities on the arts of discourse, on which Sigonio has staked his critical

project; *De dialogo liber* is a defense of his belief in the unity of
the entire field of ancient discourse on language and in the unity
of the entire field of discourse of the *studia humanitatis*.

The structural poetics—or poetics of the *dispositio*—of dialogue articulated in *De dialogo liber* is, in essence, a fiction of how
that field of discourse should be ordered. It is an image—or,
better still, a metaphor—of Sigonio's own desideratum, which
is to celebrate and yet at the same time control the force of the
fiction of dialogue by carefully dividing it into separate and discrete discursive units that coexist within the same text but do not
interfere with each other. The structure of dialogue with which
Sigonio tries to keep intact the boundaries between rhetoric and
dialectic functions only as a fiction in its own right; on the basis
of the argument of the treatise, there is nothing to be found in
dialogical representation itself, but rather only in Sigonio's program for dialogue, that actually requires a binary division of the
text into rhetorical and dialectical segments. The ultimate, and
self-contradictory, aim of this desire and this program—given
Sigonio's cultural stake in the late Renaissance *humanae litterae*—
is to make dialogue into a figural version of the method of dialectic itself, one that would also serve the ends of rhetoric and
fiction writing. Dialogue is for him a hybrid philosophical poem
that has a privileged relationship to logic and philosophy, while
at the same time synthesizing the arts of the poet and orator and
dialectician.

De dialogo liber attempts to state this in terms of a theory of dialogue that combines a set of conceptual elements borrowed from
various critical practices and then put together and presented as
a unique and distinct product (it should be recalled that Sigonio,
in his prefatory remarks, claims to be doing what the ancients
themselves did not do). The interest of this theory lies not in its
ability to account for all elements of the textual corpus to which
it is applied, but rather in the manner in which it makes possible the use of certain concepts that it tries to integrate.[134] In *De
dialogo liber*, dialogue serves as a system of systems by bringing
together the contiguous but discrete arts of rhetoric, dialectic,
and literary representation. Yet in the end dialogue becomes the
only possible textual system because all other so-called systems
—when placed within the dialogical frame—always reveal them-

selves to be partial and incomplete, as each one is opened up to interrogation by others.[135] Dialogue, as the metasystem that frames the testing of other systems in discourse, alone eludes the possibility of such a critique. Although his text leads to this insight, Sigonio cannot bring himself to acknowledge it, for it threatens the very idea of authentically dialectical dialogue and the discursive order that it implicates.

Finally, then, Sigonio's theory of dialogue attains synthesis and unity only at the cost of calling into question the notion of poetics itself; although tightly intertwined with rhetoric since antiquity, poetics must be allotted a degree of autonomy from it, or it ceases to be anything more than a rhetoric of fiction.[136] The closer one looks at Sigonio's dialogical poetics, the less it appears to be a poetics at all, or at least not the Aristotelian one it claims to be. *De dialogo liber* is unwilling and unable to escape the labyrinth of the classicist tradition of the late Renaissance, with its deep commitment to the principle of syncresis. Any notion of a formal division between poetics and rhetoric is alien to Sigonio's approach to literary theory, which sets them in a relationship of proximity instead. His treatise can thus be understood as a metasystem of its own, like the texts that it studies, eclectically combining rhetoric and poetics to create a late Renaissance theory of dialogical writing. This strategy of synchronizing divergent discursive elements ultimately governs every level of Sigonio's argument about dialogue. Both dialogue and the theory of dialogue are—although organically unified —equally heteroclite, composite, and heterogeneous in nature. Dialogue and *De dialogo liber* both stand at the crossroads of the different sixteenth-century arts of discourse and register the event of their coming together in a text and in a theory.

Sigonio's version of the history of dialogue as a genre is essentially one-dimensional, since in it all postclassical dialogues of the Middle Ages and the Renaissance appear as a perpetual re-turn *ad fontes*. By the same token, all readings of postclassical dialogues in reality involve a re-reading of the ancient models, which are present in the former in a diluted but still recognizable form. For Sigonio, all dialogue is represented by the legacy of Plato and Cicero ("that incredible ability of both the Platonic and

Ciceronian intellect for all things"; 57v), a legacy that consists chiefly of Cicero's use of dialectic and decorum combined with the results that Socrates obtains in his non-aporetic dialogues.[137] As we have seen, *De dialogo liber* claims to follow Aristotle's method of inquiry in the *Poetics*, while offering an amalgamated reading of Plato and Cicero that draws the principles of a universally valid theory of dialogue out of their texts. Sigonio's poetics of dialogue, however, has a much more complex origin and aim; his readings of Plato and Cicero are at best fragmentary, and his model of dialogue does not correspond to any known dialogue of antiquity. Sigonio seeks to return to the origin of dialogue, in other words, but the results of his theory cannot be identified with any of its own acknowledged sources.[138] The model of dialogue that he proposes appears instead to answer a set of contemporary sixteenth-century concerns and problems, foremost among them the accelerating drift away from humanist beliefs and the consequent strain on the unity of the field of the discursive arts and the sciences of inquiry. Rather than constituting a return to the literary principles of antiquity per se, *De dialogo liber* offers—in the form of a theory of dialogue—an interpretation of those principles from its position within the cultural horizons of the late Italian Renaissance.

All Renaissance genre theories inevitably assume the double burden of historical and immanent reading of texts, and *De dialogo liber* is no exception. On the one hand, a Renaissance genre critic-theorist such as Sigonio argues for the historical or diachronic nature of all textual understanding, since what is written "now" in dialogue must be in dynamic continuity with what was written "then," at some point in the classical past. The contemporary study of writing is, in this perspective, no more and no less than the investigation of the literary past itself.[139] Yet, on the other hand (in Sigonio's own classicizing perspective, at least), the history of dialogue comprises a set of unchanging, eternally present textual norms whose origins lie in antiquity. The genre system described by Sigonio is in principle—at least since the death of Cicero—both synchronic and homeostatic: to study ancient esthetics is to study contemporary esthetics as well. In this case, the task of the Renaissance thinker is to recover these unalterable norms for the contemporary practice of writing dialogue, without undue concern for all that may have occurred in the vast stretch of time that lies between the sixteenth century and antiquity. In short, in his theory of dialogue (as in his other work) Sigonio insistently seeks to combine system with history. The history of the genre of dialogue may correctly be understood only by applying the analytic grid of Sigonio's poetics to the corpus of dialogical texts; this poetics supplies a lens that allows us to see retrospectively (a posteriori) the recurrent presence of the form in the literary system over time. On the one hand, then, genres have no legitimate existence of their own apart from the genre theories that make them visible to us. On the other hand, however, the poetics of dialogue originates not only in other theories, according to Sigonio, but in the practice of interpretation of ancient dialogue, which assumes a priori (with the full authority of the tradition) that the genre of dialogue already has an independent empirical existence. The textual system of dialogue is thus historical in origin, and the history of dialogue is in turn inscribed in a literary system: but which one is prior to the other in the theoretical process in *De dialogo liber*?[140]

If Sigonio ultimately favors the synchronic description of a model of dialogue over the investigation of the historical body of dialogical texts, it is (once again) for a specific—if unacknowledged—pragmatic reason. The selectional constraints of his poetics represent an effort to control the formation of the Renaissance dialogical canon and to direct its development. Genre theories, whether concerned with dialogue or tragedy or epic, define the formal and semantic interrelationships among a discrete series of texts by identifying and articulating the universal elements shared by all the members of the genre. However, this discovery of the universal basis of a given genre, and the promise of totalization that it offers, can be achieved only by placing definite limits on the body of texts to be considered. Only those texts that contain the same key elements—a certain code of decorum, a certain kind of plot—will be regarded as members of the set. Since no genre theory can explain every feature of a given work, it functions by looking only for certain preselected textual features (formal or thematic), excluding from consideration all texts for which the theory cannot account (as is the case for sixteenth-century theories of the epic and the romance and the problems

posed by Ariosto's *Orlando furioso*). In Sigonio's poetics of dialogue, which claims to be an all-encompassing one, the criteria
of selection for inclusion among the canonical or most authentic
works of the genre—Plato, Xenophon, Cicero, et al.—are formulated in such a way that only a handful of texts at most can
be said to be dialogues at all. Dialogues not sanctioned by this
theory are downgraded to the status of mere fiction; *De dialogo
liber* is a study in the value of this model of dialogue for Sigonio,
or, rather, it is an attempt to solve the problem of its value.[141]

The model of dialogue that Sigonio proposes excludes, in particular, comic and satirical dialogues from the dialogical canon.
This would seem surprising at first, for both are among the principal kinds of dialogue practiced in antiquity (Lucian) and in
the Renaissance (Leon Battista Alberti, Erasmus, Pietro Aretino,
and countless others).[142] And tradition holds that the use of dialogue was first suggested to Plato by the mimes of Sophron
and Xenarchus, as Aristotle records in *On Poets* and as Sigonio
himself notes (7r–7v, 10r–10v). Yet Sigonio—in recognizing the
existence of a specifically comic and satirical vein of dialogue—
complains that "finally by Lucian it [the practice of dialogue] was
rashly transferred, for the sake of getting attention by laughter,
to the gods, to the dead, and to whores, as he himself confessed"
(12v).[143] With these disparaging words, he launches into an attack
on Lucian's dialogues and their "depravity" (12v–13r, 13v–14r).[144]
Following this attack, Lucian's and all other dialogues of laughter are effectively banished from consideration for the remain-
der of *De dialogo liber*. From the Quattrocento on, the model
established by Lucian's dialogues was regularly employed—both
in Italy and abroad—as a counterfoil to the favored humanist
model of Ciceronian dialogue, just as that model of dialogue was
used by the early Italian humanists as an effective counterfoil to
scholastic writing. Sigonio's theory of dialogue cannot account
for Lucian's use of satire, parody, and allegory to subvert his
philosophical target-texts (particularly his mocking and deliber-
ate violations of decorum), and thus Lucian's dialogues are what
must be suppressed by it.

Comic-satirical dialogue, with its sacrilegious treatment of the
tenets of the philosophical style, represents the "other" of dialogue as it is defined in *De dialogo liber*. Sigonio openly warns

all dialogists against putting "zeal and effort into eliciting laughter" in dialogue, which should only be used "as sparingly as salt" (57r).[145] (Paradoxically, the single most important work of antiquity on laughter is Cicero's *De oratore*, 2.54.216–2.71.290, which advocates that "it clearly becomes an orator to raise laughter"—*est plane oratoris movere risum*; 2.58.236.) This is a warning against the subversion of the code of decorum itself, which has no place for parodic and satiric elements. The premises of the dignity and seriousness of the speakers (and their language) must not be called into question in dialogue if decorum is to be preserved intact in the conversation and disputation. Sigonio's model of dialogue seeks to expel from the scene of speaking the ironic laughter and essential *disorder* of Lucianic dialogue, which is open to the representation of voices and social strata other than those of the *selectissimi viri*.[146] Once dialogue is no longer confined to portraying only a restricted elite of eminent men, but is open to almost anyone at all (even allegorical figures) of either sex and of any social status, then the representation of a tightly controlled dialectical discussion between intellectual and social equals becomes practically impossible to codify. The theory of this other kind of dialogue thus accompanies Sigonio's own theory of dialogue as what it represses because such a theory poses a threat to its foundations.

What is at stake in the banishment of laughter from dialogue is the validity not only of Sigonio's inflexible and somewhat frigid classicism, but of a certain notion of the language of literature itself. In the diagnostic and prescriptive framework of *De dialogo liber*, literature—in the form of dialogue—is restricted not only to the Greco-Roman tradition but to the Greek and Latin languages as well.[147] Comic-satirical dialogue in the vein of Lucian, in all of its many varieties (from the mock encomium to the erotic satire), lends itself far too readily to popular vernacular uses—as was indeed the case in Italy in the middle decades of the century. Although earlier sixteenth-century vernacular dialogues, such as Bembo's *Gli Asolani* or Castiglione's *Il Cortegiano*, often maintain a certain classical sense of decorum (even if they are on the whole more Platonic than Ciceronian), the Lucianic mode of an Aretino or an Arsiccio Intronato overthrows both the linguistic and thematic bases of Sigonio's philosophy of literature and therefore is more of a danger to it than any other. Consequently it becomes the primary target of control in *De dialogo liber*. No doubt Sigonio would prefer to keep dialogue an exclusively humanist tool for the use of a small group of *letterati* inside the university and the academy, who alone possess the learning and the code of decorum needed to practice the writing of dialectical dialogue. Ideally, for Sigonio, the classical linguistic and thematic qualities of dialogue should always implicate each other, just as the *studia humanitatis* should involve the contiguous study of all aspects of language and thought. Greek and Latin dialogues in the mode of Plato and Cicero dramatize the textuality of much of classical philosophy, vividly illustrating the strict interdependence of language and thought, whereas dialogues in the Lucianic mode and popular vernacular dialogues in general do not.

In the last analysis, Sigonio's theory of dialogue represents an effort—one of the last in the late Italian Renaissance, as Carlo Dionisotti observes—to preserve the continuity of one of the major philosophical and ideological presuppositions of much (although not all) of Italian humanism in the face of a rising vernacular culture and the growing strength of those seeking to separate philosophy once and for all from literary and rhetorical culture. Sigonio's is not simply an archaeological classicism, despite its deceptively antiquarian veneer, but rather a heuristic instrument for a specific contemporary cultural project.[148] Dialogue is an emblem for that project in *De dialogo liber*, since it is for Sigonio the textual form where the language of ideas and the ideals of language are most in evidence together, in the perfect fiction of philosophical speaking.

THREE

Writing Under Pressure: Speroni and the Dialogical Mask

Dialogue on Trial

Sperone Speroni degli Alvarotti (1500–1588) today is considered one of the seminal thinkers of the sixteenth century on issues of literary, linguistic, and rhetorical theory.[1] Speroni, who in his youth studied with Pietro Pomponazzi, held various teaching positions in philosophy in Padua during the 1520's, but spent most of his long life outside the university system, as an active participant in the civic affairs of Padua.[2] Although he possessed solid academic credentials, he was not—unlike Sigonio—a professor and certainly not a humanist; rather, he was a professional *letterato* and orator in the employ of the aristocracy, the Church, and the municipal administration of Padua. During a career spanning much of the sixteenth century, Speroni came to know many of the leading literary and critical figures of his time, from Pomponazzi, Pietro Bembo, Benedetto Varchi, Vincenzo Maggi, Giovanni Battista Giraldi Cinthio, and Alessandro Piccolomini to Bernardo Tasso and Torquato Tasso (who requested that Speroni serve as one of the censors for the revised version of the *Gerusalemme liberata*).

The list of his literary accomplishments is as lengthy, and as distinguished, as the list of his literary acquaintances. Speroni's *Dialogo delle lingue* (1542), a vigorous defense of the unfettered use of the vernacular in contemporary literature, played a central role in the *questione della lingua* in Italy and served as a major source for Joachim Du Bellay's *Deffence et illustration de la langue françoyse* (1549), the first manifesto of the new French poetics.[3]

The Accademia degli Infiammati in Padua, in which he was active for a number of years (serving as its "prince" in 1541–42), represented—with its anti-classicism—an important phase in the development of vernacular Italian literature in the Cinquecento. The controversy that erupted over his tragedy *Canace e Macareo* (1542), including Speroni's defense of the work and its daring theme of incest, constituted the century's single most sustained critical discussion of a dramatic genre and helped to popularize Aristotle's *Poetics*. Speroni contributed, moreover, to the acrid critical polemics in Italy concerning the *Aeneid*, the *Divina Commedia*, and the *Orlando furioso*. But his renown resulted principally from his widely popular dialogues (*Dialoghi*, 1542), which were reprinted repeatedly during his own lifetime and translated into French as well.[4] This volume included the famous *Dialogo delle lingue*, together with nine other dialogues on rhetoric, love (a major source for Maurice Scève's *Délie*), family life, and assorted topics. Given Speroni's international stature as both a writer and as an original critical mind, his impassioned defense of his own dialogues before the Roman Inquisition—the *Apologia dei Dialoghi* (An apology for the *Dialogues*)—is a text of exceptional significance for any analysis of the theory of dialogue in late Renaissance Italy.

The *Apologia dei Dialoghi* begins with a brief narration by Speroni, in which he recounts how, while residing in Rome in 1574, he first heard that his *Dialoghi* had been denounced to the Roman Inquisition by an anonymous "gentleman."[5] Speroni, who was to remain in Rome as a part of the papal court until 1578 (he had already sojourned there once before, from 1560 to 1564), could hardly have been unaware of the potential risks that such a denunciation carried. His anonymous accuser had "annotated and marked" (*notati e segnati*; p. 313) the passages in the *Dialoghi* that were arguably offensive to the public morality and the political and theological principles of the Counter-Reformation, and had then submitted his marked copy to the appropriate authorities.[6] The passages from the *Dialoghi* selected by Speroni's accuser are not particularly scabrous or shocking, certainly not by the standards of the mid-sixteenth century. In the case of the *Dialogo della dignità delle donne*, for instance, certain passages appear to have caught the interest of this "gentleman" and, afterwards, the censors because they are spoken by a prelate: "Love, the true lord and true God of everything that we do"; "they foolishly decided to convert that sweet name 'lover,' derived from the word 'love,' into two strange and hateful words, 'husband' and 'wife' "; "thus, woman's soul is composed of feeling and of love, that greatest and most excellent God."[7] Booksellers in Rome were immediately prohibited from either bringing new copies of the *Dialoghi* into the city or selling the copies already there. Speroni, now 74 years old, requested and obtained an unusual audience at the Holy Office with the Magister Sacri Palatii (Master of the Sacred Palace), the Dominican friar whose business it was to give or withhold the *nulla osta* necessary for the publication of books, in hopes of getting the suspension lifted and of preventing any future "expurgation" of his works.[8]

In the *Apologia dei Dialoghi*, Speroni describes the first moments of his encounter with the Master of the Sacred Palace: "When the Reverend Father began to read aloud to me some passages from my dialogues, even though he read them to me slowly and in a most charitable tone of voice, I nevertheless was left as if dumbstruck upon hearing those words, no differently than if the sound of them had come to me as a thunderbolt or a mortar shell" (p. 266).[9] Despite his distress, however, and despite the difficult position in which he found himself, Speroni defended his dialogues before the Master of the Sacred Palace, and—as he later reported in a letter—the inquisitor eventually "grew rather gentler" in regard to the *Dialoghi*.[10] In that same year (1574), Speroni composed the *Apologia dei Dialoghi* in Rome and sent copies of the manuscript to his friends Antonio Ricconi and Alvise Mocenigo in Padua to be read aloud to others in his defense and to forestall further attacks on the *Dialoghi*. Soon afterward, Speroni, still in Rome, heard that, without his permission, the first part of his treatise had been published in Venice; this proved, however, to be no more than a rumor. In a letter of October 1574 to another friend, Speroni wrote that when that friend came to read Speroni's theory of dialogue, "I do not delude myself when I tell you that you will see it fully dressed out, but in a no longer familiar fashion, even though it was taught some eighteen hundred years ago; you will see it in a style that is no longer seen and formed with such art that you will say: 'This is his.' "[11] Nevertheless, Speroni made no attempt to publish his manuscript between 1574 and his death in 1588, even though he continued to lead an active literary life.

Despite what Speroni believed to be the merits of the argument contained in the *Apologia dei Dialoghi*, his talk with the Master of the Sacred Palace seems to have had a relatively small impact on the fate of the *Dialoghi* themselves. Shortly after completing his treatise, Speroni was obliged in 1575 to correct and amend some of his earliest dialogues (*Dialogo di amore*, *Dialogo dell'usura*) and to compose an *Orazione contra le cortigiane* in order to suit the Roman censors.[12] This he did, following the instructions given to him, because he wanted to reprint the *Dialoghi* in Rome.[13] Speroni's plans for his *Dialoghi* were, however, unrealistic in the increasingly reactionary climate of Rome in the 1570's. Although he cooperated fully with the directives of the censors, not only were his dialogues not granted an imprimatur, but they were later placed on the Index of Forbidden Books. Speroni's dialogues were the product of another period in Italian literary history (most of them appear to have been composed between the late 1520's and 1542), and it would have been remarkable for them to have been accepted in their original form by the mid-1570's in Rome, given the radical redirection of Italian —and in particular Roman—cultural life in the meantime. Especially since the establishment of the Congregation of the Index in 1571, the Inquisition had begun to intervene, in the name of an ever more tightly formulated notion of orthodoxy, not only in matters of spiritual and social life, but in science and politics, philosophy and art, reaching further and further out from its original nucleus of institutional religious concerns.[14] Speroni's texts and his own intellectual autonomy were compromised by this consolidation of the role of the Inquisition, as the pall of violence that hangs over the *Apologia dei Dialoghi* amply attests: "If that [purification] cannot be done, I will be happy if the flames devour their [the *Dialoghi's*] stains" (p. 271).[15] Nonetheless his treatise, although deeply scarred by its author's encounter with power and ultimate failure to defend the *Dialoghi* against the papal bureaucracy, also offers a literary theory that is part of the ongoing sixteenth-century project of thinking about the problem of dialogue. The arguments and stratagems of the *Apologia dei*

Dialoghi approach the problem of dialogue in a way entirely different from that of Sigonio's *De dialogo liber*, and in many ways it is the most compellingly modern contribution to the theory of dialogue to appear in the entire sixteenth century.

One reason why the *Apologia dei Dialoghi* has been so little read and discussed since the Renaissance—although in the midseventeenth century, for instance, Sforza Pallavicino spoke highly of it—is that it is not on a par with much of Speroni's earlier work.[16] Its discourse tends to float from topic to topic, often seemingly at random (for instance, a set of lectures on the liberal arts simply materializes in the middle of Part 3), giving the text a fragmentary appearance. The rhizomatic disorder of the treatise—in terms of both its *inventio* and *dispositio*—is certainly a far cry from the precise topical structure of argumentation of Sigonio's *De dialogo liber*. Because of this textual disorder, I will selectively (if reductively) concentrate on only a few of the most crucial and cogent ideas and arguments. Part 1 is, relatively speaking, the most closely and carefully reasoned of the four parts of the treatise; since it is primarily concerned with articulating the basis of Speroni's poetics of dialogue, I focus principally on it, but occasionally refer to the other three parts as well, for in them Speroni returns from time to time to the theoretical issues addressed in Part 1. This fundamental disregard for the traditional decorum of composition and argumentation does not represent a deficiency on Speroni's part, but rather a precise strategic choice of a forensic and critical rhetoric. We need to recognize, in reading the *Apologia dei Dialoghi*, that its discourse is an exemplary instance, to paraphrase the late Joan Kelly, of "the agony of theory in the Counter-Reformation" in the face of the mounting demands of centralized papal power.[17] Theorists in the late sixteenth century in Italy often had to resort—as is the case here—to crafting ruses and stratagems in order to deal with writing under pressure. More than at other times or in other places in the Renaissance, perhaps, we may here openly see theory as *strategy*, rather than as a purportedly neutral practice of writing.

In choosing not to anchor his discourse to a topical bedrock and in casting its argument adrift (at least in appearance), Speroni's strategic aim is to incorporate into it the widest possible range of different defenses, rather than attempt to follow a single line of reasoning throughout, as Sigonio tries to do. He even explicitly tells his readers at one point that "I defended my dialogues" with "the precept of rhetorical exercise, so highly praised by Cicero" (p. 343).[18] Yet he does not in fact follow the Ciceronian rhetorical model; on the contrary, he rejects not only the notion of systematic argumentative procedures, but methodical or systematic thought itself. Speroni's theory of dialogue emerges in a text that is a *satura*, a mélange of many things, ranging from parable to oration to literary pastiche to dialogue itself.[19] This protean critical rhetoric or metalanguage constitutes a defensive maneuver in its own right, masking Speroni's own stake in his text. Often backtracking to an earlier point or leaping ahead over several intermediate steps in the logic of his argument, Speroni says so much about dialogue in so many ways that only with considerable difficulty can he be pinned down to a single position. All the arguments concerning dialogue and the *Dialoghi* that appear in the *Apologia dei Dialoghi* are intended as defenses, to be sure, but not all of them are compatible with each other, any more than are all the authorities that Speroni cites, ranging from the Bible to Virgil to Saint Basil to Petrarch.[20] This practice can at times be maddening for the modern reader, who is likely to perceive it simply as a symptom of intellectual weakness and superficiality. A definable set of theoretical and pragmatic concerns, however, does motivate almost everything in the treatise; to read this particular theory as a poetics means to interpret it as a delimited set of textual strategies and tactical maneuvers, rather than as a completely consistent system of thought about dialogical writing. If Speroni's practice at times seems dangerously close to sophistry, it is because he can envisage no other means to put forward his theory of dialogue in the situation in which he finds himself. From Speroni's point of view, a single systematic argument would run the risk of an equally systematic refutation; the disorder of the treatise functions as a defense of its defense, which in turn is designed to convince us of the innocence of Speroni's dialogues.

"My most innocent dialogues, *in regard to the precepts of their particular art* . . . cannot be condemned" (p. 403; my italics), Speroni protests at one point.[21] If the *Apologia dei Dialoghi* can lay claim to a single, central proposition in its array of theoretical arguments and ruses, this is it. The language of this proposition, in its use of terms such as *innocentissimi* and *condannati*, leaves no doubt—as does the title of the treatise itself—that Speroni's defense of dialogue adopts the genre of the apology. The term 'apology' "derives from a Greek word that means 'a speech in defense' (from *apo*, 'away,' and *logia*, 'speaking')" and in the Renaissance it still possesses the original Greek sense of self-justification.[22] Speroni's apology is clearly designed to justify the *Dialoghi*, but it does so in a rather singular way, as the following passage reveals:

> I will give a particular account of the goodness and the mischievousness of my youthful dialogues, with which—according to the custom of comedies—I will venture to be severe, being their father and being older than anyone else. If they are found to be innocent, without a doubt the judgment of others will graciously accept them and absolve them (which I cannot promise that I myself will do). . . . I will cure well— how I hope so!—their sickly innocence, and will purge their contested passages with the artifice of writing well as it was taught in antiquity (I call their innocence "sickly" here, which is [however] still in doubt). (p. 270)[23]

Speroni says that his goal is to defend the "goodness" (*bontà*) and the "innocence" (*innocenzia*) of his dialogues, but at the same time he promises "to cure" (*sanarò*) and "to purge" (*purgarò*) them of their "mischievousness" (*malizia*), judging them as would a "severe father" (*padre severo*). Yet in treating his own dialogues in this way, his ulterior purpose is, as he states, actually not to correct them at all, but rather to persuade the Master of the Sacred Palace to "accept them and absolve them" (*li accoglierà ed assolverà*) as they are, meaning to accept them as "most innocent" and to absolve them of any accusations of error. There would, at first glance, seem to be a contradiction here. How can the author of the *Dialoghi* establish their original—if sickly—innocence by curing and purging them? Would that not imply that they did indeed contain inexcusable errors? The answer lies in the means with which he intends to accomplish this—"the artifice of writing well, as taught in antiquity"—which is Speroni's name for a general theory, or poetics, of dialogical writing. He in fact nowhere states that, in defending his dialogues, he intends to censor them or surgically excise the contested passages. On the contrary, Speroni says that he will cure them and purge them in interpreting them in light of the principles of "writing well" and "the precepts of their particular art" of dialogue. These principles and precepts will fully account, he insists, for both the *bontà* and the *malizia* of dialogue; they will at once defend and cure the *Dialoghi*. Speroni's apology is formulated in terms of a paradox: the errors of dialogue *are* the very excuse that absolves them of all charges of error, as long as we consider dialogue in terms of its poetics. The task of the *Apologia dei Dialoghi* thus takes the form of a theory of the form of dialogue.

The encounter between Speroni and the Master of the Sacred Palace at the beginning of the *Apologia dei Dialoghi* is reported as a dialogue. This fiction of an interview thematizes the dialogical situation itself in the treatise.[24] Yet the friar makes in fact only one brief interlocution in this fictional dialogue; the rest of the text consists of Speroni's apology for his works (with the exception of an inserted dialogue among his friends in Part 3).[25] Beneath its dialogical disguise, there is no room in the treatise for a true exchange between the figure of power (the inquisitor) and Speroni himself. The silent presence of the inquisitor serves throughout to remind the reader of the continuous pressure being exerted on Speroni's apology by outside forces and, as a consequence, of the stakes involved in its argument.[26] For the authority of the friar in their conversation is absolute, and nothing he might say may be directly contested or challenged; an inquisitor does not need to apologize to anyone. For this very reason, there can be no genuine exchange between him and Speroni, for Speroni would find himself at a distinct disadvantage if accused directly by the inquisitor, who is also his judge.[27] All formal charges against the *Dialoghi* must therefore come instead from an absent third figure in the dialogical scene: namely, Speroni's anonymous accuser. The silent figure of the Master of the Sacred Palace represents the ideal audience—one that only listens patiently, without speaking—for Speroni's apology.[28] Such a prescription of silence and patience for the other alone allows Speroni to stake out "a space to defend himself" (*uno spazio a difendersi;* p. 276) in the treatise and to find the means with which to defend that space. If Speroni's theory of dialogue is also a kind of dialogue, then it is in truth a dialogue between Speroni and his own writings or, rather, between Speroni and the writing of dialogue itself.

The *Apologia dei Dialoghi* is written under the threat of material violence (the "flames" that wait to devour Speroni's dialogues) exercised by power over language and thought. It is also written under the sign of hermeneutical violence; Speroni's apology is marked throughout by a fear of misreading and misprision in the context of the current Counter-Reformation system of reception and interpretation. For him, this is far more than just the proverbial anxiety that *scripta manent, verba volant*. The danger is that of having his words deliberately ripped out of their context and semantically redirected by readers who will twist their sense to suit an alien purpose, with no chance for him to defend himself (this same fear is not entirely foreign to another writer of dialogues and the author of an apology—namely, Plato himself).[29] What intensifies Speroni's perception of this danger to the writer in the expanding print culture of the second half of the sixteenth century in Italy is the institutionalization of such a practice of misreading in the form of the Congregation of the Index, with consequences ranging from the relatively mild to the relatively serious. The only way to anticipate and forestall the threat of willful misreading of his works by others, in Speroni's eyes, is to force open a "space" for self-defense in the form of a theory of dialogue. The reasons for the *Dialoghi* ("the most general reasons that led me to write them"; p. 295), he contends, cannot be understood unless the reasons for dialogical writing itself are first understood.[30] Thus Speroni observes that, in Part 1 of his treatise, "I will not speak especially about my own dialogues; I will speak instead about the *idea* of my dialogues and others' dialogues" (p. 276; my italics).[31] This theory of dialogical representation ("the idea of my dialogues and others' dialogues") has in turn a fundamentally strategic design: its purpose is to fend off any attempts to do interpretive violence to his own dialogues, and dialogue in general, by refuting in advance all readings that fail to acknowledge dialogue's special literary status. A knowledge of the poetics of dialogue, Speroni argues, is a fundamental precondition for the interpretation of any dialogue ("and the same may be said generally in regard to the form of all dialogues"), including the *Dialoghi*. All readings of dialogue that do not take the unique structure of the dialogical scene into account are, accordingly, invalid, because that structure alone can always explain and justify any and all thematic "flaws" (*falli*) discovered in dialogue. A dialogical poetics counters any attack on the meaning of a given dialogue by canceling the very possibility of a thematic—rather than structural—reading. The defensive power of poetics, in Speroni's opinion, cuts off any attack on single "places" (*loci*) or passages in dialogical texts by convincingly showing that it is pointless to try to interpret them without first granting priority to the esthetic structure of dialogical writing, which is the textual (pre)condition that makes meaning possible in dialogue. The theory of the *Apologia dei Dialoghi* precludes any revisionary reading of dialogue that is thematic and local in orientation, rather than structural and global, by turning all analysis of meaning back toward the analysis of representation instead. Only in light of this does the claim that "my most innocent dialogues, in regard to the precepts of their particular art, cannot be condemned" reveal its full resonance. Poetics serves Speroni as a "writerly" strategy of defense against the hermeneutical pressures of the Counter-Reformation.[32]

Comedy and Truth

Speroni commences his defense of dialogue with the "truth" that "every dialogue is more than a little like a comedy" (p. 267); later on, he states outright that "dialogues are comedies" (p. 334).[33] There is no doubt, then, that a "dialogue is a poem" (p. 285), not a work of philosophy, and that both the poet and the dialogist depend equally on the "poetical or dialogical fiction" (p. 286) in their writing.[34] When he speaks of *la commedia* as a particular kind of poem or fiction that dialogue resembles, Speroni is saying that dialogue is generically related to the staged comedies of Aristophanes or Renaissance comedies such as *La Calandria* or *La Mandragola*, but not that it should be set on stage itself. Dialogue is similar to comedy in terms of the particular style of language that it uses ("comically, that is to say, in a low and not very polished style"; p. 355) and in terms of its narrative mode.[35] This differs radically from Sigonio's elitist code of decorum and his banishment of laughter from the scene of dialogue.[36] The "resemblance that exists between dialogue and comedy" (*la sembianza che è tra 'l dialogo e la commedia*; p. 278), Speroni notes, is not based simply on the fact that both are works of literary mimesis and follow the same general rules of textual representation, as Sigonio argues. Even though there are fundamental differences in their means of representation (comedies have both actors and a stage, whereas dialogues have neither), comedy and dialogue share the same end, that of producing laughter, and the same approach to characterization and narration. One of comedy's chief devices is the use of characters that are not only like the spectators, but inferior to them as well. And as in a comedy, where characters generally come from all walks of life and all levels of society and are expected to speak in a manner consistent with their social status, so in dialogue "each one speaks as what he is, or seems to be" (p. 267).[37] When the figure of a sophist or a dunce appears in dialogue, that character's remarks should appear to be "true to life" or verisimilar; they should, in other words, obey a certain decorum (*il decoro delle persone*; p. 278) by conforming to what the reader expects the sophist or the dunce to be.[38] This means, however, that if there are all sorts of speakers in dialogue, as there are in comedy, and if each one speaks "as what he is, or seems to be," then not every statement uttered in dialogue can possibly be free from the falsehoods and errors to which inferior characters are prone. Not everything that is said in dialogue can be true, even though—or precisely because—its decorum has been preserved.

This similarity between comedy and dialogue would appear to place Speroni's theory in an unsustainable position in regard to philosophical dialogue. Even if possessed of a certain number of comic elements and devices, how could true philosophical dialogue be legitimately considered a comedy? Although the works of Lucian may arguably fit Speroni's definition of the comic style of dialogue, what about those of Plato, who publicly burned his writings for the theater and turned to philosophical dialogue instead? Even though "it does no honor to Plato that dialogue is comedy," Speroni admits, one must still wonder why "if he was first a tragedian who became a philosopher almost out of his disdain [for tragedy], then what reason must have led him, since he was a philosopher, to have to write in a comic style . . . the refinement of his high and worthy concepts?" (pp. 354–55).[39] It might at first seem puzzling in this regard that throughout the *Apologia dei Dialoghi* Speroni refers to Plato as the fountainhead of the tradition of dialogue and as its principal exponent.[40] His solution to the problem posed by Plato's dialogues for his own theory of dialogue as comedy is in essence a solution to the problem of dialogue itself. The reader of the treatise must remain aware at all times that Speroni's approach to Plato's dialogues is never analytic or systematic; he does not offer a firsthand reading of the corpus of Platonic writings or a balanced look at the evidence that they supply in support of his claims concerning dialogical writing. Moreover, although he reduces the art of Plato's dialogues to a single textual logic, Speroni does not formulate this logic in terms of the kind of comprehensive rationalist poetics favored by sixteenth-century Aristotelians (and he nowhere mentions the *Poetics* in his treatise). He instead seeks to legitimate his own strategy for writing dialogue through the discovery of an identical practice of Plato's, which can then pass as a universal, and a universally valid, structure of dialogical representation on the grounds of Plato's authority and prestige. Plato is the example (*exemplum*) that becomes the rule for Speroni; and this transformation of the species into the genus is, as will shortly become clear, a crucially important maneuver in his defense of dialogue.

Speroni's reading of Plato takes the form of a collage of fragments of Plato's own practice of dialogue-writing that have been reassembled and reshaped to serve the specific pragmatic needs of the *Apologia dei Dialoghi*. For instance, Plato's dialogues are linked to comedy not only by their use of a certain kind of language, Speroni notes, but by their use of a multiplicity of speakers representing a cross-section of the social order, as would be the case in comedy. Comedy "has many and various interlocutors that speak according to the social customs and the way of life that each of them represents to us" (p. 267).[41] Plato's dialogues have *molti e varii interlocutori*, since these are so essential to Plato's fiction of a participatory philosophy; thus they are also comedies of a sort. However—and this is typical of the procedure employed in the *Apologia dei Dialoghi*—Speroni's reasoning goes against the grain of Plato's dialogues. For a number of Plato's non-narrative dialogues have only two speaking characters, such as the *Phaedrus*, the *Phaedo* (opening scene), the *Euthydemus* (opening scene), the *Menexenus*, the *Ion*, the *Alcibiades* I, the *Euthyphron*, the *Greater Hippias*, and the *Crito*.[42] Other non-narrative dialogues do have more than two speakers—including the *Meno*, the *Timaeus*, the *Critias*, the *Sophist*, the *Gorgias*, the *Laches*, and others—but no matter how many characters appear in the course of these dialogues, Plato rarely has more than four speakers active in a discussion at a time. In contrast, if one looks at Plato's narrative dialogues, the number of possible speaking characters is much greater: in the *Protagoras*, for instance, Socrates's *récit* includes eight interlocutors, and in the *Symposium* eleven characters speak out at different points. Others in this group include the *Charmides* (four), the *Lysis* (five), the *Republic* (six), and the *Parmenides* (eight, counting the prologue).[43] Speroni is not interested in Plato's narrative dialogues, however, and flatly discounts the evidence that they provide (we will shortly see why). For him, there is no question that Plato employed only one approach to writing dialogue: Plato's fiction of dialogue *always* operates as comic and dramatic fiction do, and a wide variety of speakers (and of positions that they represent) constitutes an important feature of all dialogical form.[44] Here as elsewhere Speroni's argument is governed wholly by pragmatic concerns, rather than by the textual analysis of Plato's corpus, but as long as his statements about ancient literature and philosophy in the *Apologia dei Dialoghi* are not taken at face value, it may be possible to see them as what they are—namely, as a means to the end of discoursing about and defending dialogue and the *Dialoghi*.

It is the privilege of dialogue "to make men and women of differing ranks and manners speak in a probable fashion about any subject and to dispute it in their own way" (p. 294).[45] The fiction of dialogue figures forth the play of a plurality of languages and a plurality of perspectives in a conversation that may concern "any subject" (*ogni materia*) at all, as long as the characters speak of that subject "in a probable manner" (*probabilmente*). This differs radically (once again) from Sigonio's definition of dialogue in *De dialogo liber*. With the notion of *il parlare probabilmente* at its basis, Speroni's theory does employ the concept of dialectic, but does not make it into the foundation of dialogical representation. In Part 1 of the *Apologia dei Dialoghi*, in point of fact, Speroni limits himself to this single remark about dialectic, most likely derived from the widely known definition given in Rodolphus Agricola's *De inventione dialectica* (in which it is considered a kind of speaking "in a probable way on any matter"). He makes no attempt to distinguish Platonic dialectic—that is, the *praxis* of Plato's dialogues—from Aristotelian dialectic, and he does not mention the anomaly of making Plato's work the principal point of reference for his theory, when in fact what he calls "dialectic" is far more Aristotelian than Platonic (as the term *probabilmente* indicates).[46]

Like many other Italian critics and theorists of the mid-to-late sixteenth century, Speroni uses the term 'dialectic' to refer to a mode of argumentation that is "a rational structure, more or less involved in dialogue between persons, made up of probabilities only, so that it never arrives at full certainty, but argues from probable premises to probable conclusions," without much evident concern for the complex philosophical origins of the term in antiquity.[47] For Speroni's defense of dialogue, however, this rather vague shorthand definition of dialectic as a process of interrogation through which the speakers proceed from a state of doubt to a state of probable opinion, but still may remain in error at the end of their conversation, is the appropriate one. Unlike Platonic dialectic, where doubt is an intermediate state or stepping-stone on the way toward a more absolute (and more absolutely certain) state of knowledge, for Speroni dialectic—and hence dialogue—is no more and no less than a way of searching for what is generally, but not always, true. In this process, truth may perhaps be discovered in dialogue, but it will always necessarily remain a relativized truth; it will simply be the final meaning of one particular dialogical event.

Equally significant is Speroni's tacit recognition that dialectic cannot be isolated from the art of persuasion, or rhetoric, in the conversation among the speakers. In its process of testing, dialogue uses praise and blame in paradoxical ways that are identical to those of rhetoric itself (pp. 267–68). A professional rhetor in his own right, Speroni notes that not only were "orators and philosophers . . . the seed that led to the birth of my dialogues" (p. 272), but that Plato himself was both a philosopher and a rhetorician, for "he also eloquently damns philosophy and rhetoric, which were his own professions, without which his glory would not exist today" (p. 269).[48] Discounting Plato's claim for the innate superiority of dialectic over rhetoric, Speroni instead defines rhetoric as a fitting counterpart of dialectic: "Dialectic and rhetoric are two arts fit to test the true and the false, the 'yes' and the 'no' of every thing, and to persuade" (p. 267).[49] Dialectic is always compromised with rhetoric in the dialogical scene of speaking (only later, in his discussion of dialogue as a "speaking painting," does Speroni try to draw a firm distinction between the two). In order for characters to speak *probabilmente* or dialectically, they always have to speak *a lor modo*, with richly ironic and comic language, with feinting, dissembling, and simulation and falsehood, as well as with syllogism and induction. There can be no framing of dialectic in the fictional scene of dialogue.

In this regard, dialogue is the staging of a scene of mutual recognition between dialectic and rhetoric, between speaking *probabilmente* and speaking for a persuasive or epideictic effect. All that is said in dialogue (all that is written by the dialogist in the scene of speaking) is part of this scene, where "the 'yes' and the 'no' of every thing" are tested and tried in the encounter between speakers, and where discoveries of what is plausible, persuasive, and probable can be made only through the support of both arts. The composite quality of dialogical discourse —its constant switching and commingling of codes in the scene of speaking—has an entirely different value for Speroni than it does for Sigonio. This quality could not be achieved by the dialogist without the fiction of a comic dialogue freed from the constraints of philosophical decorum: dialectic and rhetoric both belong in the dialogical scene because those who speak in it are not just the wise, or even the good, but also those who may not ever be able to understand each other.

Given the variety and number of speakers in dialogue (*molti e varii interlocutori*) and the gamut of positions that they represent, then, dialogue must contain arguments and ideas that are

—or may eventually prove to be—"incorrect," for the sake of maintaining a structure of difference of opinion. Otherwise, if all speakers were in equal possession of the same probable opinions, there would be no need for dialogue or for the supporting arts of dialectic and rhetoric. To deprive dialogue of its oppositional nature in order to purge its discourse of all possible errors, as his anonymous accuser wants Speroni to do, "would damage generally the art and the form of every dialogue" (p. 293).[50] In Platonic dialogue, for instance, one of the speakers often takes up a philosophically unacceptable position that is only gradually disproved or dismantled by Socrates "as a dialectician" (*come dialettico*; p. 269); this process of dismantling and discovery constitutes its central drama. Such "thorny twigs" and "spines" (*le spine*; p. 293) in the text are simply a necessary prelude to the discovery or recovery of whatever probable truth may eventually emerge in the characters' conversation. It is, Speroni grants, inevitable that the dialogical text will appear to be a tissue of deceit for readers who do not understand the demands of the form, for the conversation does not evolve in a single, always clear direction: "In dialogue many times the good things are usually censured, and the not-so-good things are praised" (p. 267).[51] Yet the praising of what is not praiseworthy and the blaming of what is blameless inevitably figure as a part of all dialogical encounters, and do not degrade dialogue as long as they are understood to belong to the process that Speroni calls "dialoguing" (*[il] dialogizzare*; p. 267). Error is an operational condition of possibility for dialogue, but the presence of error must always be understood in dynamic terms, as a part of a process of testing and searching for something probable in discourse. Error is never to be interpreted literally as representing what the writer means to say in dialogue, but only as a provisional point of passage in discourse on the way toward another, still-concealed meaning, lying somewhere beyond the next question and the next response.

Error and Eros

Speroni's defense of his *Dialogo di amore*, perhaps the earliest of all his dialogues, and of two other brief dialogues on love included in the collected *Dialoghi* develops at greater length this notion of the structural necessity of error in the dialogical scene of speaking. The surface of these dialogues, Speroni contends, is a "pleasant labyrinth" (*un piacevole labirinto*; p. 286), a tangled textual maze that stands in diametrical opposition to the "lofty and serious" (*alta e grave*; p. 285) discourse of true philosophy. Dialogue is not just a discourse of error; it is also one of *erranza*, that is to say, of both "erring" and "wandering," of both error and the errant. Dialogical writing is a labyrinth of detours in which writer, characters, and reader all wander in turn: "Dialogue speaks in vain, while it wanders [*erra*] from game to game without getting closer to the truth; but to wander in such a way is neither wicked nor dishonest" (p. 285).[52] The erring and drifting of dialogical discourse is by definition aimless, since there is no center, no absolute truth (*senza appressare alla verità*), to approach in dialogue. The play of the text is forever lateral in direction, structuring the conversation as a passage through a series of games (*egli erra di giuoco in giuoco*) that is potentially infinite, since no truth is guaranteed to emerge in dialogue and put an end to its erring.

The "pleasant labyrinth" of dialogue described by Speroni is not, then, modeled on the classic figure of the labyrinth of Knossos, where there is a center toward which all who enter are inevitably led by whatever path is chosen; for there is a hidden order in the apparent disorder of this kind of labyrinth.[53] Nor is the dialogical labyrinth an *Irrweg* in which all possible paths into or out of the labyrinth—except for one—turn out to be blind alleys or dead ends, and in which all who are inside are constantly forced to retrace their steps as they err.[54] "The delight of reading" (*il diletto della lettura*) instead derives, in the maze of dialogical writing, from the reader's discovery that s/he is completely lost in the perpetual lateral play of the conversation, since there is no center to it and no certain exit from it (except to stop reading altogether). Dialogue, in Speroni's model textual labyrinth, is a network of fully reversible relations, a system of equivalence (*di giuoco in giuoco*) as well as of equivocation. And the theory of dialogue is a map without fixed coordinates, charting the errant play of pleasure, delight, and desire itself along "the path of dialogues" (*il sentiero delli dialogi*; p. 274).

Once more comparing dialogue to comedy, Speroni observes that if "there is no comedy that is not amorous," then "speaking about love . . . is not unbecoming to dialogue [either]" (p. 276).[55] The object of dialogical representation is not only the questioning subject, but the questing and desiring subject as well: Speroni in fact states that "my dialogues are mirrors of lovers" (p. 289).[56] Dialogue is a comic imitation of lovers' discourse, whose model labyrinth is the mirror, a place where the mobile images of desire multiply infinitely: "I call a 'pleasant labyrinth' not love for love's sake and our getting entangled in its delights, but rather the discourse of lovers, and the imitation of them in words, [but] without feeling" (p. 286).[57] Dialogue is not an imitation of love per se but of the *discourse* of lovers, which is entwined with and inhabited by desire. Rather than represent the sensual delights of love, dialogue imitates the scene of speaking between lovers with all the "flattery, jealousy, stupidity, and vanity" (p. 293) that it contains, but without reproducing its full emotional force (*senza lo affetto*).[58]

The number of sixteenth-century dialogues devoted to the theme of love is immense, reflecting in part the prevalent Neoplatonic belief that dialogue was particularly well-suited for discoursing about the many facets of love (especially courtly love).[59] In interpreting his own Neoplatonic *Dialoghi*, however, Speroni does not say that they discuss the topic of love itself, as a treatise would, but only that they are an erotic fiction of the twists and turns of lovers' discourse, a series of "paintings and playful comedies" (p. 293).[60] What is spoken in this scene by the desiring subjects, "being naturally full of qualities that are contrary to each other" (*pieno essendo naturalmente di qualitadi tra se contrarie;* p. 286), resembles the same dialogical fiction that reflects it, since the latter is equally based on contrast and equivocation between speakers. Dialogue is an apt mirror of the scene of desire as the latter emerges in discourse, for both lovers and speakers in dialogue misunderstand and contradict each other in innumerable ways; both desire and dialogue, which mirrors it, are accidental rather than essential, and they are thus forever destined to err (in both senses of the term). All dialogue is therefore erotic to the extent that it is structured like the scene of speaking between lovers. And both writer and reader, lost in this labyrinth along with all other lovers and speakers, will be delighted—Speroni concludes—to wander along through its linguistic games of error and eros.[61]

This notion of the necessity of error in dialogue is, Speroni notes, "the point from which my defense derives, as the circumference derives from the center" (p. 289). It is, paradoxically, the imperfect nature of lovers' discourse that makes perfect the discourse of his dialogues: "Such words, if they are written in my dialogues," he affirms, "not only do . . . not make dialogue wicked, but they make it complete and perfect" (pp. 288–89).[62] The appearance of imperfection in the dialogical text—that is, the tangled and contradictory nature of the discourse of desire— is in fact compelling proof of the perfection of its form. Dialogue is as troubled and as troubling, as perplexing and as "fallen," as the scene of speaking between desiring subjects that it mirrors. Thus the supposed errors of the *Dialoghi* may be understood and justified as merely the necessary result of the rules of dialogical representation. Speroni complains that to censor any dialogical "roses" (pp. 290–91) on the basis of their "thorny twigs" of error and to purge the text of them, as the Roman "gentleman" wishes to do, is to misunderstand completely the nature of dialogue's perfection as a kind of writing.[63] The anonymous accuser of the *Dialoghi* "says that he wants only to select the spines and eradicate them"; but what if, Speroni asks, a dialogist by definition "only knows how to discourse of thorny twigs and spines" (p. 293)?[64] The organicity of the dialogical text is founded on the representation of error, and any attempt to strip it of its spines leads to the "tearing apart and divorce" (*cotal strazio e divorzio*; p. 293) of the voices of dialogue itself.

The desires of lovers never completely coincide, and so their discourse is a comedy of continually renewed error and misunderstanding; speakers in dialogue, even if they do reach an eventual consensus, can arrive at it only by coming down the same path taken by lovers. This *alē*, or wandering (as Plato calls it in the *Cratylus*), is also dialogue's *alētheia*, or truth.[65] Rather than rip apart the body of dialogue in order to purify it, we should realize "that the pricking of these thorny twigs does [not] arouse many irrational thoughts in whoever reads my dialogues . . . rather, great benefit can be derived from the thorny twigs, and not only from the flowers, of my dialogues" (p. 291).[66] This theory of the organicity of the form of dialogue (the perfection of its textual body) remains for Speroni the most legitimate defense against any mode of thematic interpretation that would separate out each word uttered by the speakers in the scene of speaking and interpret it as a statement of the writer's own opinion or belief. In dialogical discourse, meaning can be finalized only through a violation of the very basis of dialogical representation —that is, its process of testing error as well as probable truth.[67] To rend asunder and mutilate its textual body, and to silence its discourse of error in the name of decorum or ideological orthodoxy, would be tantamount to destroying dialogue itself. The flaws of the mirror, the dead ends of the labyrinth, and the spines of the rose of dialogue alone allow the text to become what it really is—a "comedy of errors."

Mimesis versus Diegesis

How does the writer represent this comic scene of speaking in dialogue, if, as Speroni claims, in it "there is a variety both of things that are spoken about and of ways of narrating [them]" (p. 274)?[68] The possible options are the same as for Sigonio in *De dialogo liber*, but the ends are entirely different. Turning to the famous Platonic distinction between mimesis and diegesis (*Republic* 3.392–94), Speroni observes that in diegetic dialogue the writer inevitably figures as one of the speaking characters in the conversation, even if only by implication: "the author himself courteously seems to lead them with him in his dialogue, almost as if he were their host" (p. 275).[69] Because diegetic dialogue is narrated dialogue, the voice of the narrator is always represented in the scene of speaking to a greater or a lesser extent. As Speroni points out, "he writes . . . 'this one said' and 'that one answered' " (p. 275).[70] Such dialogue is reported (*riferito*) speech because it is referred to the reader through the mediating voice of the narrator, which filters and focalizes it. Furthermore, narration is an inherent quality in reported dialogue, because—as Socrates makes clear in the *Republic*—no dialogist can ever imitate himself/herself; mimesis, in Plato's sense of the term, cannot include the voice of the writer, since the latter is by definition an instrument of narrative (or diegesis). In appearing as a voice in the dialogical text, then, the writer of diegetic dialogue assumes to a degree the roles of both character and narrator, and thus diegetic dialogue "is not pure, but a mixture of characters and the writer, who does not imitate himself" (p. 275).[71]

Diegetic dialogue is, for Speroni, a technically impure or mixed mode of representing speech, and this mixture is a highly volatile one in the optic of the *Apologia dei Dialoghi*. Diegetic dialogue is not pure not only in the technical sense that it is a mixture of characters and narrator, but in a more figurative sense as well, because the presence of the dialogist as a speaker in the text *contaminates* the conversational scene as well. One reason for this contamination is that the intrusion of the narrator detracts from the text's realism, making diegetic dialogue seem less natural and more contrived than its counterpart. This is, however, ultimately less compelling than a second reason, which is tied to the fundamental value for Speroni of dialogue as a practice of writing. Diegetic dialogue appears contaminated by the inclusion of a narrative voice precisely because dialogue should be the textual model of a discourse of dissimulation and impersonation, in which authorial intention and intervention are impossible for the reader to discover. Speroni must, then, find a way to displace diegesis from his dialogical poetics. The strategic use of Plato in the *Apologia dei Dialoghi* begins in earnest at this point, for Plato's ruses for staying out of the scene of his own dialogues are decisive for the formulation of Speroni's self-defense.

The privileged mode of dialogical writing is, according to Speroni, the mimetic one (*il modo imitante*; p. 275), for in it there is no direct authorial presence with which to reckon in the scene of speaking. Direct mimetic dialogue is "similar to comedy" (*simile alla commedia*; p. 275), since in comedy the actors speak on stage without any apparent interference by a narrator. Such is also the case in first-degree dialogue, Speroni observes, because it "is the mode of imitating our alternating arguments, neither introduced nor interrupted by the writer, but rather in the manner of comedy, which form Plato and Lucian liked, and which Plutarch did not dislike" (p. 275).[72] Although this description is not altogether accurate in the case of Plato, as has already been pointed out (or in the case of, say, *The Double Indictment*, where Lucian—

"the Syrian"—is also a character in his own text), for Speroni the single most important feature of mimetic dialogue is that it allows no narrator to represent the action of the conversation (*li imitati ragionamenti*; p. 283) to us. Thus, it more successfully disguises its own fiction than does diegetic dialogue. Only because the narrative presence of the dialogist has been suppressed and erased from the text ("his voice, and his voice alone, is silenced"; p. 274) is this effect possible.[73] Mimetic dialogue seems more natural and less conventional than its counterpart because it presents no mediating voice of author-ity in the scene of speaking.

Needless to say, this is only an effect, for although mimetic dialogue seems to be a direct transcription of an actual conversation, it is of course still a work of fiction. Since comedy "is a species of poetry" (*è specie di poesia*; p. 275), mimetic dialogue shares comedy's "poetic privileges" (*poetici privilegi*; p. 275) as a realistic kind of representation. Thus Speroni admits that "in Plato's dialogues neither Socrates nor Alcibiades nor Gorgias speak, but in their names—which are written and painted there —speaking takes place in that [same] way that all three of them used in arguing" (p. 280).[74] Like comedy, moreover, mimetic dialogue provides the reader with a kind of delight that is essentially lacking in diegetic dialogue: "and as servants, whores, ruffians, sycophants, soldiers, and pedagogues are both the delight and the beauty of comedies, if the words that they use in imitating are appropriate to their annoying manners, so it is when in dialogue a fool, a wicked man, a lover, a flatterer, or some arrogant sophist is portrayed from life" (p. 276).[75] The delight and beauty of mimetic dialogue arise from its uninterrupted portrayal of all the facets of life (*dal naturale*)[76]—of all the facets of life, that is, except those that can be identified with the dialogist. For Speroni, it is the invisible nature of the narrator in mimetic dialogue that allows the flow of conversation and ideas to proceed unimpeded, and so to seem inherently *naturale* or recorded from real life (which is, Aristotle notes in the *Poetics*, one of the chief fascinations of mimesis for the human mind). The pleasure of "dialoguing in prose" (*in prosa dialogizzando*; p. 286) is intimately related not only to the *decoro indecoro* of the dialogical text, but also to the absence of the narrator's voice from its scene of speaking.

On the one hand, then, Speroni disapproves of diegetic dialogue because of its sense of seriousness; because of the writer's presence in the text as the voice relating the conversation, decorum demands that the language of the conversation be consistent with the dignity of the writer. The kind of language used by ruffians and parasites, when related to the reader by the dialogist, would violate that decorum, and therefore it has to be dropped from the diegetic scene of speaking. And this, obviously, is not suited to the kind of realistic and comic mode of dialogical writing that Speroni values above all others. On the other hand, he disapproves of diegetic dialogue because in it the role of the writer as narrator is so clearly one of selection and recombination in reporting the other speakers' words. Comparing the dialogist to the historian (*pace* Aristotle), Speroni states that "just as one does not write history about every single fact, but only those that are worthy and noteworthy, likewise the dialogist must [in diegetic dialogue] relate only those remarks made by the characters that he has brought into the dialogue that do him honor to speak about, and he must silence all the rest" (p. 275).[77] All words spoken in a given diegetic dialogue are chosen before they are reported/narrated by the dialogist, and the dialogist is thus presumed, in reporting a dialogical scene, to be responsible for what the speakers say in it. One of the chief fictions of diegetic dialogue is that it is a memory (the writer's) of a prior conversational event; like any memory, this dialogical memory is an act of individual selection and recombination of details that defines a single specific point of view. The writer who narrates a reported dialogue not only has a personal stake in the scene of conversation, but also has a responsibility to narrate (*riferire*) only those statements (*detti*) worthy of attention. A major part of the work of writing diegetic dialogue therefore involves the silencing (*e dee tacer tutti gli altri*)—by the writer and for the sake of the writer—of all that is not ideologically or philosophically decorous or correct in the conversation of the characters. In mimetic dialogue, the voice of the writer is what is silenced in the scene of speaking; in reported dialogue, the writer does not silence his/her own voice, but rather those voices or statements that transgress the limits of what it is possible, or prudent, to say.

The writer of diegetic dialogue must, in short, always pose as a censor of the characters' discourse. The poetics of diegetic dialogue assigns the onus of the task of controlling what is said in dialogue to the writer as an active presence in the scene of speaking; and this reflects the reciprocal relationship between control and *self*-control required of Counter-Reformation writers in Italy. A full-fledged realism is impossible to sustain in this kind of dialogue since the main criterion for the inclusion or exclusion of a given idea, theme, or expression is ultimately defined by the dialogist's own position in relation to the discourse of power ("the dialogist must relate only those remarks . . . that do him honor to speak about"), even if Speroni masks this over with a reference to honor (decorum) rather than to the realities of power relations. Without this realism, however, the founding fiction of all dialogue for the *Apologia dei Dialoghi* is weakened: in conversation, (probable) truth must necessarily be accompanied by error; yet if error is to be restricted or even bracketed altogether, as it must be in diegetic dialogue, then the very process of dialogical speaking must be radically revised. Rather than do that, Speroni banishes all narrative dialogue from consideration in his poetics. Of course, the notion that censorship is performed solely by the writer of diegetic dialogue is itself a fiction of Speroni's own invention; all writing involves, at some level, an act of selection and recombination of signs by a given subject. This fiction, however, is a necessary one if the dialogist is to evade responsibility for the "comedy of errors" of the dialogical scene. Speroni's poetics and defense of dialogue together turn to the example of Plato—the originator of mimetic dialogue—for a strategy of resistance to the pressure for control over the transgressive voices of the text.

Plato and the Maladies of Dialogue

In Plato's dialogues, error is not a sign of his own ignorance or malevolence, any more than the Socratic doctrine of *docta ignorantia* is an indication that Socrates himself knew nothing:

"Whoever would come to the conclusion that the good Plato was an ignorant and wicked man, or that his dialogues are something bad," Speroni contends, "would venture an invalid syllogism and would show that he does not know what it means to 'dialogue' [*dialogizzare*]. And the same may be said generally in regard to the form of all dialogues" (p. 267).[78] Yet Speroni also argues, in a seeming non sequitur, that "if dialogue is poetry, and if the dialogist is a poet, and if the poet knows little, even if —by imitating—he seems to know a great deal, then it follows that anyone who writes dialogue ought to know little" (p. 284).[79] How can these two contrasting statements possibly be reconciled within the framework of the same theory? How can Plato not be "ignorant" and yet "know little"? Speroni offers the following solution in the form of a paradox: "Plato wrote dialogues and was [nonetheless] a wise and learned man: it seems, in fact, that *because* he was a wise and learned man, he denied that he was the author of the doctrine of his dialogues" (p. 284; my italics).[80] Plato's paradoxical wisdom consists in his denial of the authorship of his own dialogues, or rather, it consists in knowing the necessity of dissembling his own authorship and his own authority behind the fictional mask of Socrates. This is, for Speroni, precisely "what it means to 'dialogue.'" The authority of Plato's own practice of dialogue depends on its denial that Plato could possibly know anything at all, except for this one fact that denies all other knowing. Plato knows only, in other words, and in a doubly paradoxical way, that Socrates alone knows (and yet also denies) whatever wisdom is expressed in the dialogical scene. By transferring the doctrine of *docta ignorantia* to Plato's own practice of writing, Speroni is led to the conclusion that Plato is indeed able to be at once wise and yet know little in his dialogues. Although this version of Plato's practice of writing takes into account only a few of his textual strategies while ignoring many others, it nonetheless is pivotal for Speroni's defense. For Speroni, Plato's chief insight is that dialogue always represents an *unnaming* of an author, a voice, or an authority. If dialogue is to be staged as an encounter with negativity—if it is to take the textual form of true questioning and answering—then this unnaming needs to occur, as it does in the scene of speaking of *li Socratici parlamenti*. Plato sets an example for the late Renaissance dialogist, whose knowledge must paradoxically consist of a complete lack of knowledge, except for knowing the ruse of letting another voice assume all authority in the text. As we have already seen, diegesis is in point of fact present to some degree in the majority of Plato's more complex dialogues, from the *Republic* to the *Theaetetus* to the *Sophist*. In "speaking of the good kind of dialogue, such as Plato's" (p. 275), however, Speroni seeks to make mimetic dialogue alone into an enabling mode of fiction for late Renaissance writers, one whose authority is supposed to derive directly from Plato's own practice of writing.[81] Platonic mimetic dialogues not only eliminate the troubling presence of a narrative voice in the scene of speaking, but, like all of Plato's dialogues (narrative or non-narrative), they also possess another desirable quality. One of the few fictions found in all of Plato's dialogues is that Plato himself never appears in them. No Platonic dialogue, as a dialectical mise-en-scène, ever admits its own author into that same scene of speaking. Otherwise Plato would no longer be able to pose as an amanuensis, an observer and transcriber of Socrates's conversations, but instead would himself become an active participant in the scene of dialogue.[82] If this were to occur, then the reader—Speroni reasons—would always be able to identify with precision Plato's position in any dialogue (something that instead still keeps an army of scholars busy today). Neither an authorial presence nor a controlling authorial consciousness can be represented in dialogue, except at the risk of subverting the principal fiction of Platonic dialectic itself.

There is, of course, the figure of Socrates, which, within the dialogical conversation, plays the leading role in bringing knowledge and opinion out into the "light of disconcealment."[83] Yet the fiction of the *dialektikos* itself would be placed in question if dialogue were no longer to claim to be a direct reflection of a process of collectively lived thought and experience. If it were to reveal itself as a product of a single writer and a single consciousness (to whom all the fictional voices of the text are then attributable) or if Plato's own position were to be openly stated in the conversation, then its claim to represent the processes of thinking and speaking of two or more autonomous subjects would crumble. If Plato were to appear as himself in his own dialogues, rather than in the persona of Socrates, it would result in the undoing of the fiction that his dialogues are *not* altogether a fiction. Platonic dialogue thus serves as an ideal mask for the philosophical position and voice of Plato, Speroni concludes, since even Platonic thought is generally to be ascribed to the persona of Plato—that is, to the figure of Socrates—rather than to Plato himself. Dialogue is, for Plato, a process of dialectical discovery, but it is also a locus of dissimulation: there is something, or someone, hidden at the heart of the Platonic text, according to the *Apologia dei Dialoghi*. A secret such as this is not the same thing as a lie, ethically speaking, at least not in Speroni's version of Plato's poetics, and is above reproach. Whatever the validity of this interpretation, which still has its proponents in our contemporary philosophical culture, it defines the special power of the Platonic practice of writing for Speroni and authorizes his privileging of the mimetic mode of dialogue in the *Apologia dei Dialoghi*.

Dialogue is a disguise or, rather, a fiction of neutrality for the dialogist. At the end of his preliminary defense in Part 1, Speroni remarks that Plato "with just two little words of his quiets the commotion that may be born [from dialogue], writing at the end of a letter of his that the doctrine—so full of struggle and dispute —given out in his dialogues was *not his own opinion*" (p. 269; my italics).[84] This is a pointed reference to the passage in the Second Letter (314C)—already discussed in Chapter 1—in which Plato states that "I myself have never yet written anything on these subjects, and no treatise by Plato exists or will exist, but those which bear his name belong to a Socrates become young and fair."[85] For Speroni, the question of the responsibility of Plato for the content of the dialectical discussion in his dialogues is forever deferred; the suppression of the voice and figure of the writer in dialogue denies to the reader the possibility of recognizing and identifying a specific position in the conversation as the writer's own, especially if the speakers do not arrive at a consensus. Indeed, Speroni points out, "the dialogist, having stated and tested the opinions of the characters that appear in it, rarely gives a final opinion about them, but instead remains always in between them" (p. 275).[86] What is discovered in dialogue cannot be the opinion or *parti pris* of the writer, whose true position is always suspended in the interstices between the opinions of the characters. Standing *sempre intra due*, the dialogist takes no sides in the contest, and thus "each of the speakers can claim to be right in victory and to be satisfied with his own knowledge" (p. 275).[87] This, in turn, ought to make it impossible for the reader to identify the dialogist's own beliefs and opinions among those expressed by the speakers. As another late Renaissance theorist of dialogue, Torquato Tasso, wrote in a letter to a friend: "Although you want to know what I think about it, I should not venture to write what I think in dialogue, as you apparently want me to do, inasmuch as if I were to write a dialogue, you would read someone else's opinion in it rather than mine."[88]

Speroni's theory of the permanent neutrality of the dialogist is possible, ironically, only as long as there is no fully Platonic dialectic at work in the discussion between the characters; that is, as long as there is to be—as in aporetic dialogue—no clear winner in the dialogical agon. Although his theory distorts the nature of Plato's dialogical practice in this regard, Speroni is once again concerned only with borrowing certain stratagems and fictions from Plato for his own defense of dialogue, not with giving an accurate account of the whole of Plato's work. Plato the writer of dialogue is—along with all others like him—akin to the mythical figure of the blind prophet Tiresias: split into so many different voices, Speroni observes, "he comes to transform himself unhappily, not only once like a cicada, as Titan did, but many, many times, like Tiresias" (p. 334).[89] Plato and all other dialogists are engaged in a continuous process of metamorphosis, for they occupy constantly shifting positions within the conversation and can never be assigned a single, fixed, and final opinion. The poetics of dialogue depends, for Speroni, on a textual strategy of obliquity grounded in the fiction of the author's absence from, and neutrality in, the scene of the conversation. Unlike any other kind of writing, dialogue thus provides an ideal defensive shield behind which the Counter-Reformation writer may maneuver.

In the *Phaedo* (59B), Phaedo announces to Echecrates the reason why Plato was not present at the scene of Socrates's death: "There was also Ctessipus the Paeanian and Menexenos, and some other Athenians; but Plato was ill, I think."[90] Diogenes Laertius points out in the *Lives of the Eminent Philosophers* that, excluding the Letters, "nowhere in his writings does Plato mention himself by name, except in the dialogue *Phaedo* and in the *Apology* [34A and 38B]."[91] In other dialogues, however, Plato is mentioned without being named in order to excuse his absence from the scene of conversation. At the beginning of the *Timaeus*, for instance, the following exchange occurs:

> *Soc.*: "One, two, three—but where, my dear Timaeus, is the fourth of our guests of yesterday, our hosts of today?"
>
> *Tim.*: "*Some sickness has befallen him*, Socrates, for he would never have stayed away from our gathering of his own free will."
>
> *Soc.*: "Then the task of *filling the place of the absent one* falls upon you and our friends here, does it not?"[92]

Plato's 'illness' (*asthenia*) recurs in dialogues such as the *Phaedo* or the *Timaeus* as a metaphoric ploy to displace his own figure —with an elegantly ironic touch—from the scene of speaking. *Asthenia* signifies not only illness, but a lack of strength and energy, a diminution of vitality, a weakening and debilitating of the body. This metaphor of illness or debility, and its use as an excuse for Plato's failure to appear in his own dialogues, is symptomatic of a problem that afflicts Plato's writing, the problem of presence itself: dangling uneasily at the edges of his dialogues is always the fiction of the one who is absent (Plato as author) entwined with the fiction of the one who is present (Socrates). Plato never appears as a figure in his dialogues because the presence in the text of Socrates as Plato's persona precludes that possibility. There is room in the dialogical scene of speaking only for one or the other. If Plato were to enter into the scene of conversation, Socrates would have to disappear from it, or otherwise he would lose his clearly defined function as Plato's alter ego. Seen in this light, Plato's malady is that he has been weakened, drained, and debilitated precisely because he has been *doubled* by writing dialogue.[93] The figure of Socrates is the fictional double of Plato in the scene of speaking. And if Plato is ill, and missing from that scene, it is because this doubling—and the fiction on which it relies—perpetually places in question the unity of thought and language at the very basis of his dialectic and his philosophy. Since Plato's absence from the conversation is only a fiction, and yet nevertheless an essential one, it must be defended and excused at all costs, for if he were no longer to pretend not to be present, then his dialogues would explicitly point to their own fictional nature and their own pragmatic aim as the narratives of a writer seeking to convince his readers of the truth of a philosophical point of view, not as dialectical conversations between different subjects and different *formae mentis*.[94] Without the stratagem of his illness, itself a metaphor (ironically enough) for Plato's representational malady, the poetics of dialogue would openly subvert the hermeneutics of dialogue.

Plato's double bind is the following: his fiction of dialogue supplies the necessary textual foundation for his philosophical discourse, yet it is for him inadmissible that philosophical discourse could in any way hinge on the ruses of writing (mimesis, fiction, dialogue). In the *Apologia dei Dialoghi*, Speroni in contrast celebrates the fictional qualities of dialogue and foregrounds the doubling power of its poetics. Although he is no more prepared to acknowledge any split between the dialogical utterance (the scene of speaking) and the act of utterance (its composition) than Plato is, he forcefully asserts—contrary to Plato—the full priority of the utterance itself over what it signifies. The doubleness of dialogue is anything but tragic for Speroni; the fictions of authorial absence, illness, and neutrality are all essential if poetics is to govern the interpretation of the dialogical text and protect it from hermeneutical violence. The fictional design of dialogue guarantees that the final position of the dialogist can never be discovered through rational interpretive procedures; as a result, the reader must consent, in reading dialogue, to forget the question of the position of the writer. In forgetting this question, the reader must also forget that the position of the dialogist is precisely what is in question in dialogue in the first place. If Speroni paradoxically reconfigures the Platonic problematic by making the stratagem of the author's absence an integral part of the subversive doubleness of dialogue, rather than its equally paradoxical cure, it is as an answer to the problem of dialogue as it presents itself to Speroni as a late Renaissance writer and theorist working in Italy. And if Speroni, unlike Plato, seems serene about the textual demands of dialogue and the ruses of its writing, it is because for him dialogue is not—and never can be —a place for philosophical discourse. Dialogue is totally devoid of knowledge: it is the place of disintegration and dissolution of any and every absolute claim to truth, which it replaces with a discourse of error and probability. For Speroni's precursor Plato, whose shadow looms so large in the *Apologia dei Dialoghi*, however, the problematic nature of dialogue as the text of philosophy remains to the end as disturbing, and as much of a scandal, as the face of Socrates himself.

Socrates at the Vanishing Point

The study of dialogical poetics leads back to Plato, the originator of the ruses of dialogue, yet in the end there is no place in Speroni's theory for the function fulfilled by Plato's own persona of Socrates. Although Speroni has argued that the mask of Socrates is necessary to the Platonic dialectic and to the writing of Platonic dialogue, such a function cannot be theorized as a part of his own dialogical poetics. The late Renaissance dialogist, unlike Plato, must rigorously avoid the use of a persona in the dialogical scene of speaking. This reversal is logically related to Speroni's assertion that the writer's position always remains suspended in the interstices between the opinions of the speakers. Although Sigonio establishes different subgenres of dialogue, classified according to the sort of role played by Socrates or a similar figure in leading the conversation toward a conclusion, Speroni perceives that readers tend to identify, fairly or unfairly, such a figure with the dialogist, making any such figure unacceptable in his dialogical poetics. Socrates serves as a single mask for Plato in the *Sōkratikoi logoi*, and this is exactly what Speroni believes the contemporary dialogist must avoid if the text is truly to disguise his/her own point of view from the reader. Although Socratic thought and Platonic thought are by no means the same in every case, Renaissance readers generally tended to see Socrates—who is, after all, the protagonist of most of Plato's dialogues—as representing Plato's own point of view to a greater or a lesser extent. The dialogist, in Speroni's model of writing, must instead wear a multiplicity of masks and be unnamed by a multiplicity of names in order to create a perfect illusion of neutrality.

An intercalated dialogue between some of Speroni's friends at the end of Part 3 of the *Apologia dei Dialoghi* (reported by Speroni within his own "dialogue" with the inquisitor) serves as a practical exemplum of what dialogue ought to be in this regard. In their debate about the meaning of sophistry, the central question that concerns the five speakers in this dialogue—"Is everything rhetoric?"—is never given a final and definitive answer. Each speaker argues a different point of view on the question, but none yields in the end to the others' arguments. Even though the Cardinal's view is implicitly accepted as the last word in the disputation, the reader is left to contemplate a set of divergent positions, while the narrator (Speroni himself) remains silent. This model dialogue, although reported by Speroni, has no Socrates figure that can be identified with the writer's own point of view. All judgment of Speroni's position in the work is suspended and immobilized by the dissimulating figure of dialogism itself: the voice of the dialogist must be distributed in an arabesque among many voices and the true face of the dialogist must not hide behind a single recognizable mask (such as that of Socrates), if the necessary fictions of authorial neutrality and absence are to succeed.

The turn or swerve away from the figure of Socrates is indicative of the constraints operating on the discourse of the *Apologia dei Dialoghi*, and signals another reason why Plato's use of such a persona is unthinkable for Speroni. Although Speroni endorses the essentially comic or carnivalesque nature of the dialogical style and of the *molti e varii interlocutori* that appear in the scene of speaking, ranging from lovers to sophists to ruffians to pedagogues, in this carnival of voices and discourses and laughter the figure of the philosopher—as represented, in Plato's dialogues, by Socrates—cannot be allowed to participate. Even though he "mocks" and "tricks" (p. 279) the sophists and other opponents of his, making them into the butt of his own brand of comedy, Socrates does not himself figure as a fully comic type in Plato's dialogues.[95] There is, of course, a good reason for this: Socrates also plays the central role in the development of a dialectical discourse of truth in those same dialogues. There should be no gravity in genuinely comic characters, yet Socrates at times possesses both gravity and dignity. In terms of Speroni's own poetics of dialogue, however, Socrates would have to be considered simply one more comic character since dialogues are comedies and not vehicles for the discovery of authentic philosophical truths. If philosophy cannot be represented in Speroni's model of dialogue, then, one might ask, how can philosophers be represented in it? The discourse of philosophy—meaning specifically, for Speroni, Aristotelian *scienzia*—and the figure of the philosopher, which were increasingly redirected in the official Italian culture of the post-Tridentine period into the framework of the institutional doctrines and theological dogmas of the Church, must also be kept out of dialogue because in it this discourse and this figure would be exposed to the corrosive and subversive power of its laughter.[96] Dialogue always tends to call into question the characters of the speakers that it represents, and thus Socrates and all others like him who represent the authority of philosophy must now disappear from the scene of dialogical laughter.[97] In *De dialogo liber*, Sigonio banishes laughter from the scene of speaking in the name of the decorum of philosophical dialogue; in the *Apologia dei Dialoghi*, Speroni instead banishes philosophy and philosophers from the scene of speaking in the name of a dialogical comedy of errors.

Yet no one would today deny that "in the literary tradition stretching back to Socrates and Aristophanes, philosophizing is a rich source of comic material, and the philosopher, foolish and self-absorbed, is a recognizable comic type."[98] The disappearance of Socrates has an emblematic meaning in the *Apologia dei Dialoghi*, for it tacitly recognizes that in dialogue, as defined by Speroni, the figure of the philosopher ought indeed to be an exclusively comic one (although Speroni himself cannot admit this). This confirms that Speroni's version of dialogue is a legitimate heir to the second of the two mutually exclusive models described by Lucian in *The Double Indictment*—namely, the one geared toward laughter—and explains why Speroni silently reverses most of the claims made for dialogue in *De dialogo liber*. Both of Lucian's models of dialogue descend from the same source in Plato's dialogues, and both Sigonio and Speroni trace their own theories of dialogue back to Plato as well, but these two models and these two theories are fundamentally incompatible. The figure of Socrates implicitly designates the place of philosophy in dialogical writing; but there are two possible per-

spectives on the meaning of that figure and that place.[99] Given
the constraints within which Speroni worked, the comic perspective on philosophy is precisely the one that he must not raise
in the *Apologia dei Dialoghi* at any cost, although its filiation is
clearly from the Lucianic mode of thought about philosophy in
dialogue.[100] For the Church authorities that Speroni had to confront in Rome, the discourse of knowledge and truth must be as
disciplined as the body of theological doctrine itself; it is not and
cannot be a cause for irony, laughter, or *uno scherzo*. The Socratic
persona does not figure as an element in Speroni's theory, not
only because his presence disturbs Speroni's preferred scheme
of multiple personae, but also because if philosophy is to retain
at all times the upper hand over literature (that is, over the signifier itself and the privileges of signification), as Speroni is con-
strained to argue, then the possibility for dialogue of a "comedy"
of philosophy has to be suppressed.

Speroni's "idea of dialogue," as he calls it, nonetheless has an
anticipatory value in this regard, for it can be aligned genealogi-
cally with an as-yet-unformulated theory of the novel. Constituted by an original nucleus of doubt, traversed by irony, metalanguage, and error, spoken in a comedy of voices and genres
and ideas, the fiction of dialogue represents a refusal to perform
the *expositio* of an already present, already formulated truth of
the sort found in a philosophical treatise. Dialogue is instead an
experience of an uncertain and unstable way of thinking that
perpetually re-emerges as error, not truth, in the discourses of
the other speakers in the dialogical scene. The novel, too, in its
classical form, develops its narrative out of unanswered questions, puzzles, enigmas, and doubts; it, too, is constituted by the
contrasts and clashes between characters (*il contrasto delle persone*)
and points of view; it, too, is a work of prose fiction; it, too, is
driven forward, or backward, by desire—the desire to know, the
desire to possess, the desire to desire—and informed by irony.
If Speroni at times seems uncannily modern in comparison to
Sigonio, this can in part be attributed to the similarity between
his theory of dialogue and later theories of the novel, the other
genre that blurs the boundaries between genres and ultimately
disrupts the foundations of genre itself.[101]

What is missing from dialogue that is found in the novel is, among other things, a portrayal of the sheer corporality of the speakers, the physicality of their actions and experiences: dialogue is an arena of ideas and discourses, but it is limited in its power to describe the experiences and sensations of the body itself. Despite the realism with which they are depicted, speakers in dialogue are shadowy person-ideas compared with the fully embodied figures that characters may become in novels. Speroni argues that experience and sensation are always a part of dialogical characterization by virtue of the status of dialogue as mimesis. However, such characterization is present only to a limited —if not minimal—degree in dialogical writing. A century and a half later, Saint-Mard, in his theory of dialogue, sarcastically remarks about the contemporary French novel: "Might one not say that the heroes of novels are thinking beings to whom a body has been added only out of obligation, and not to serve their pleasures at all?" [102] This could more accurately be a description of the speakers in any dialectical dialogue. Socratic dialogue is part of the prehistory of the novel, and Speroni's theory belongs to the prehistory of the theory of the novel. The Romantic theorist F. W. Schlegel's aphorism "Novels are the Socratic dialogues of our time" and Mikhail Bakhtin's coy reversal of that same aphorism, "Socratic dialogues were the novels of their time," confirm—each in its own way—the link between Speroni's and more modern modes of theoretical discourse. [103]

Speaking Painting: From a Theory of Dialogue to a Theory of Discourse

No sixteenth-century theory of dialogue, not even one that insists as forcefully as Speroni's does on the fictional or literary nature of the dialogical text, would be complete without an analysis of the relationship between fiction and the other arts of discourse in dialogue. Beginning in an unlikely way, with an elaborate comparison of the art of dialogue to the art of painting, Speroni in the *Apologia dei Dialoghi* analyzes this relationship in search of further support for his defense of dialogue's innocence. The topos likening painting to poetry is an ancient and famous one whose origin is generally attributed to Simonides (Plutarch, *De gloria Atheniensium* 3).[104] In the Renaissance, this topos or commonplace was particularly prominent by virtue of its association with Horace's dictum *ut pictura poesis* (*Ars poetica* 361); later on, in the eighteenth century, the theory of the relationship between painting and poetry helped to give rise to the modern philosophy of esthetics.[105] The argument that painting is "tacit poetry" (*tacita poesia*; p. 276) whereas poetry is none other than "speaking painting" (*dipintura parlante*; p. 277)—or *ekphrasis* —does more than satisfy Speroni's taste for paradox and oxymoron in the *Apologia dei Dialoghi*. Writing paints speech and speaks to the eyes, giving color and body to thoughts; dialogical writing does this in a very specific way. Speroni remarks in Part 3 that the style of some Flemish (such as Bosch) and "grotesque" painters, which "colors the truth" for the viewer, is very similar to the prose of the *Dialoghi* ("indeed one such painting of this kind is the prose of my dialogues"; p. 304).[106] Earlier in the treatise, Speroni formulates this parallel between painting and dialogue in a similar way: "In some dialogues a fool, a wicked man, a lover, a flatterer, or some arrogant sophist is portrayed from life [*dal naturale*]; such painting by nouns and verbs, and in other parts by oration [rhetoric], ought not to be held in any less esteem than the vernacular of colors themselves" (p. 276).[107] This paradox of *la dipintura parlante*, which speaks a realistic "vernacular of colors" and vividly paints "by nouns and verbs, and in other parts by oration," leads Speroni to examine dialogue in terms of the order of representation itself. Through the figure of "speaking painting," the *Apologia dei Dialoghi* explores the problem of the epistemological and ontological grounds of dialogue in relation to other textual systems of cognition, such as philosophical and scientific writing, while shifting the focus of Speroni's apology from poetics itself to a general theory of representation.

Dialogists "like me," Speroni notes, are similar to painters because of their interest in surface rather than depth, the outside rather than the inside of things. Both painter and dialogist aim to amuse the reader or the viewer in the making of their representation, whether it be in the form of a portrait or a literary text:

It is reasonable that the writer should desire to be read, nor is he read willingly if he does not instruct or delight. For both one and the other of these ends, we read Socrates and Xenophon, Virgil, Homer, Livy, Thucydides, Cicero, and all philosophers. But as for myself, and others like me, who write but few rhymes, romances, and such things, no one reads us if not for the fun [*lo scherzo*] and the delight of it. Now there is no doubt that such writers are very similar to painters; [their] writing usually pleases us in that same way that painting delights us. (p. 303)[108]

Unlike the true philosophy or philosophical poetry of the ancients (including that of Socrates), which has a definite utility, Speroni's dialogues seek only to delight the reader in the same fashion that painting delights the viewer. Dialogue in the vein of *lo scherzo* offers no instruction, strictly speaking, but simply desires to be read, as a painting desires to be seen. A theory of dialogue as *la dipintura parlante* must, then, find a place for the pleasure of the text and its stratagems for the seduction of the reader.

Yet the pleasure and delight of the dialogical text, so similar to those of painting, point to an underlying problem in its means of representation. The words that constitute the dialogical discourse of *lo scherzo* and *il diletto* are comparable to the paint that the artist puts on the canvas, not only in their colorful nature, but also in their superficiality. "Words," Speroni says, "are the images of things"; they are but the "signs, ghosts, images, and similitudes" (p. 381) of them, as different from and discontinuous with what they arbitrarily signify as is the oil paint on a canvas.[109] The means of representation of comic dialogue is as inherently flat and two-dimensional as a painted surface, for its verbal texture is made up of ghostly simulacra and signs far removed from any direct, unmediated representation of the object. "Speaking painting" becomes a metaphor in the *Apologia dei Dialoghi* for the insurmountable distance between signifier and signified in the dialogical text:

Just as the painter shows us nothing of the whole man except the outermost surface, with certain lines and certain colors—for which reason he should be considered a mere illusionist of nature—likewise the dialogist does not truly go inside the written thing so that he might reach its essence, but instead circles around it almost as if he were dancing, in such a way that he never teaches anything. For who knows nothing teaches nothing, but [only] seems to know and to teach. (p. 285) [110]

Dialogue, like painting, is only a play of brightly colored surfaces, a game of light and shadow: it is powerless to penetrate to the essence of the thing that it represents. "Tacit poetry" and "speaking painting" are able to create a portrait of the real (*ritratti dal naturale*; p. 276) with a verisimilitude that makes the portrait appear almost as natural as the very act of seeing. They are, however, forever unable to take the reader or the viewer beneath the surface appearance of the things that they represent, Speroni concludes. A dialogical representation that does not have a primarily moral and didactic function—that is, that aims instead to produce only delight and pleasure in the reader—is condemned to be a version of the real that is always secondary or supplementary to the true cognition of things.

Even though he does not openly acknowledge it, here as elsewhere Speroni is heavily indebted to Plato (*Republic* 10.595A–608B; *Sophist* 234B–236C) in his discussion of imitation.[111] The similitude between painting and dialogue that he draws in the *Apologia dei Dialoghi* opposes their respective sign-systems (the means of representation) to the thing that they signify (the object of representation); Speroni assigns full ontological authority only to the object of representation. Truth exists in things before it exists in words, and thus things themselves completely condition every sort of formalization. Paintings and dialogues are counterfeit copies or repetitions of the real ("signs, ghosts, images, and similitudes") that at best only vaguely correspond to what they copy or repeat. Neither painting nor dialogue can by definition contain any genuine or authentic foundations for knowledge, then, "but [only] seem . . . to know and to teach" (p. 285). Speroni uses the metaphor of "speaking painting" in the *Apologia dei Dialoghi*—and exploits it in a Platonic perspective —to argue for the fundamentally derivative nature of *all* representation; the sign always stands to the signifier exactly as the shadow does to the body and as the portrait does to the face (*siccome segno a significato, o l'ombra al corpo, o alla faccia la dipintura*; p. 382). The end result is that this ontology of truth erases every possible epistemological pretense of dialogical writing.

Dialogue—like painting—is forever condemned to show only the external appearance of things (*la sua ultima superficie*; p. 285), Speroni contends, in the same way in which a portrait is a simulacrum of the face, which is itself in turn a mirror of the soul or mind (according to another Renaissance *locus communis*). As in a set of Chinese boxes, neither the dialogist nor the painter can ever succeed in prying open the center of the *res* and in arriving at the essence of the thing.[112] This failure is, however, a comic rather than a tragic one and must be understood as consistent with dialogue's essentially ludic purpose. As Speroni tells his readers, "Imitation in dialogue is a comic thing and is poetry without verse. It is therefore a game and a delight, and an idle sort of delight" (p. 276).[113] And once we see that this is the case and that no knowledge can ever appear in the scene of speaking, then dialogue can never be accused of deviance from the official discourse of philosophical and scientific authority, for it has absolutely nothing to do with philosophy and science. In its very means of representation, dialogue is denied the possibility of articulating any form of knowledge except that which paradoxically consists of playful illusion.

Speroni has nothing particularly original to say about the art of painting itself in the *Apologia dei Dialoghi*.[114] It serves him as a convenient, and reductive, means with which to theorize about dialogical representation as a kind of textual *image* ("a speaking painting") that merely copies the real without capturing its truth. As he remarks at one point, "Its writing is a jest because it paints but does not incarnate things" (p. 285).[115] In this approach to the theory of representation, Speroni is light-years away from the sense of the *Poetics*, which suggests that in a work of mimesis a writer or a painter represents a personal conception of the object of representation, never the object itself. In this regard, Speroni's Platonically inspired system of reflections is totally at odds with the Aristotelian notion of the literary text. Yet as always in his apology, Speroni's argument—however skewed—leads to the development of a theoretical line of defense of dialogue. If dialogue is but a textual image that has no closer or more privileged relationship to the real (and the truth that is coextensive with it) than painting does, he reasons, then "probabilistic debate between characters about any subject ought to be just as legitimate for dialogue to imitate as it is for the poet and the painter to portray any subject and to represent it" (p. 278).[116] Dialogical writing portrays, represents, or imitates the particular subject that it treats, just as painting does, for the same general purpose of producing an effect of realism (or verisimilitude). Yet dialogue differs from painting in one crucially important respect; it imitates not only things themselves, but also the speech acts of the characters (*il disputarsi probabilmente d'ogni materia*). Paint and canvas do not always take other paint and other canvas as objects of representation, but the written words of the dialogical text must inevitably take spoken words as one of their principal objects of representation (since the characters in dialogue are by definition always speakers as well).

This last point, Speroni infers, "can complete our reasoning about imitation in dialogue" (p. 280).[117] The idea that words reflect words in dialogue—which is the function that distinguishes it from painting itself—is a key to understanding dialogue's position in relation to other textual systems of cognition and/or representation. Although dialogue does not incarnate things or close the gap between sign and thing, we are told, "In dialogue not only are the characters that are introduced in it imitated, but in the things that are said in the debate true and certain knowledge (which can be acquired from them) is not expressed in effect as it is in the Aristotelian method, but *is itself imitated and portrayed*" (p. 280; my italics).[118] Dialogue is not merely a comic fiction of dialectical philosophy; it is an imitation of what is already an imitation of philosophy, inasmuch as dialectic ("the things that are said in the debate") is itself already a portrait of philosophy. Dialogue stands in relation to dialectic as dialectic in turn stands in relation to true and certain knowledge, or as a mirror-image stands to the thing mirrored (*lo specchiato*; p. 280). Like the work of art in Plato's example of the Three Beds (*Republic* 10.596B–621D), the discourse of dialogue is three degrees removed from the truth of things themselves, providing the reader with a portrait of a kind of speaking that is in turn "a portrait of knowledge" (*di scienza ritratto*; p. 280); even this dialectical portrait of knowledge merely resembles its subject while expressing it in an entirely different way. As the final point in a chain of reflections that leads further and further away from an original truth, dialogue is a degraded image—or better still, a *parody*—of the discourse of knowledge.[119] This parodic relationship between the discourses of mimesis and truth, or fiction and knowledge, relies on a predetermined order of the different disciplines of knowledge and arts of discourse. Such an order is, as Speroni himself says, "presupposed" (*presupposto*; p. 281) by the argument that he makes in the *Apologia dei Dialoghi*. The formal arrangement of the logical disciplines and arts of discourse into a hierarchical system is a common feature of sixteenth-century treatises on poetics.[120] Generally, however, these classificatory schemes tend to assign literature a privileged position among the other arts and sciences, and the poet a position of semidivinity. Speroni instead proposes a taxonomy of "three finely ordered ranks of our various imitations and cognitions" (p. 281), which are "either knowledge, such as Aristotle has defined it, or opinion, or persuasion" (p. 386).[121] The apodeictic method is based on the true "demonstrative syllogism" and results in "that first cognition, which is certain and invariable" (p. 280).[122] Demonstrative logic (*la somma dimostrazione*; p. 281) is but one degree less certain than the symbolic logic of mathematics itself; it is the only true and perfect discipline of discourse that both uses natural language and leads to certain knowledge, since it reflects the logic of nature itself.[123] Demonstration is formal deduction; it is a passage from a set of accepted propositions to a proposition implicitly implicated by them (and necessary to them) or, in other words, from the implicit to the explicit. The second of these imitations and cognitions is dialectic, or the system of topical logic that "generates opinion" (p. 280) through the use of "syllogism and induction" (p. 386).[124] The knowledge imparted by dialectic is of "other things not known with certainty" (p. 280) and is essentially probabilistic in nature, for, as Speroni notes, "Plato, Socrates, and Xenophon, with their dialectical arguments, give us probable opinions about our civic affairs" (p. 281).[125] The third in Speroni's taxonomy of the logical disciplines and arts of discourse is rhetoric, which is "persuasion by enthymeme or example" (p. 386).[126] Enthymemes are syllogisms in which either the major or minor premise (or the conclusion) is not stated but is instead understood, because it is easily recuperable by anyone. Both dialectic and rhetoric are, argues one of the speakers in the embedded dialogue in Part 3, "sophistical kinds of knowledge . . . not because they deceive us . . . but because of their lack of certainty" (p. 386).[127]

The hierarchical arrangement of these three kinds of *imitazioni e cognizioni* is based on descending degrees of cognitive certitude: "The rhetorical enthymeme is practically an imperfect effigy of the probable syllogism, and the probable syllogism is an image of the perfect demonstration, no different from the ape who imitates certain gestures of a man or a parrot who imitates his words. For what reason should one not infer that rhetorical persuasion is a painting and imitation of opinion [dialectic], as opinion is of science . . . ?" (p. 281).[128] The declining degree of certainty that leads from logic to dialectic to rhetoric, and the discursive order that it establishes, is understood by Speroni to constitute a representational series in its own right. Dialectic is an "image" of logic, and rhetoric is in turn "an image of images" (*è imagine delle imagini;* p. 281). The chain of images or the representational series that constitutes the order of all the arts and sciences of discourse is, as has already been suggested, an essentially parodic chain (as Speroni's metaphors of the ape and parrot seem to confirm), for all discourse is imitation except for demonstrative logic, which is its zero degree, and all representation is always only a parody of truth. Only logic is truly nonrepresentational because it is the one kind of discourse that can validate itself and the knowledge that it generates without referring to any other part of the chain of discourses. In Speroni's model, logic does not reflect—and thus depend on—another discourse, but rather incarnates in its own discourse, and coincides with, its object or *res;* it alone goes beyond the errors of figure found in all the different kinds of discursive "painting." Philosophy (demonstrative logic) is the one discipline that is autonomous of all others or, better still, that is not just another kind of writing. If Speroni does not classify poetry ("imitation") as an art of discourse among others, it is because—in his understanding of the term—the principle of imitation governs all the non-logical discourses, each of which is one step further removed from the absolute and autonomous ground of logic and its perfect epistemological certainty, and it is already included as a structural element in each of them.

Where does this finally leave dialogue, and the defense of dialogue, in the *Apologia dei Dialoghi*? Speroni's scheme eventually leads him to surmise "a most strange truth," which is that dialogue is positioned below both rhetoric and dialectic, reflecting them and imitating them in its playful and comic way; it can therefore convey only a distant glimmering image of the discursive ground (demonstrative logic) that anchors the entire epistemological system in place.[129] Speroni's classification of the arts and sciences is designed to serve as another guarantee for his theory of the "weak" nature of dialogue and a backhanded defense of the form from thematic readings that might imperil it. Dialogue is utterly devoid of any possible claim to truth, both in terms of its own specific poetics and in terms of Speroni's general semiotics of representation. The price for this defensive stratagem is a high one, needless to say, for everything that does not follow "the useful Aristotelian road in the sciences and arts, which leads to knowledge" (p. 273), simply becomes another painting, another jest, including the *Apologia dei Dialoghi* itself.[130] "If," as Speroni tells us, "to imitate is to play, then the opinion that is generated in dialogue is a game" (p. 281).[131] And if everything except logic is a kind of imitation, then everything except logic (or the Aristotelian method) is just a game and nothing more.

Speroni never shows his readers, however, what the zero degree of his system—*la somma dimostrazione*—might be; it remains, or rather it has to remain, only a metaphor in the text of the treatise. From the very first, even though he searches (sometimes wildly) for ancient authorities to uphold his argument, Speroni is extremely circumspect, and extremely evasive, in the use and citation of Aristotelian texts—the domain of much of post-Tridentine theology and philosophy—in his apology for dialogue. "If I had had definite knowledge of that which is dealt with here," he remarks, "I would not have written dialogues, but I would [instead] have written everything in the Aristotelian manner" (p. 284).[132] Yet although general references to the demonstrative method and the true syllogism abound in the *Apologia dei Dialoghi*, never once does Speroni provide an example of what he is referring to or any indication of where true knowledge might be found in Aristotle's writings.[133] Once again this leads us back to the set of constraints surrounding Speroni's theory of dialogue. Despite his insistence on its paramount importance, if the Aristotelian method figures in his theory only as a blank space or as something that can be pointed to but not included in the treatise, it is in order to protect—or, better still, to defend—Speroni's own defense of dialogue. The omission of any evidence or proof of the zero degree of discourse in the *Apologia dei Dialoghi* shows the limited, secondary, or reflective nature of Speroni's treatise as a rhetorical work in its own right, unable to follow the true path of thought and language.[134] It is not a *scienzia* of dialogue, nor does it have any means of access to Aristotelian knowledge, nor does it even know anything about Aristotle's works except that what they say is unquestionably true. Everything that the treatise argues may therefore be dismissed as only a harmless game; in this way, it may be automatically—at least in its author's eyes—excused from any charges of error (or worse). Speroni's refusal to discuss Aristotle directly in his theory of dialogue serves indirectly to confirm his own theory and to validate it, if only as something invalid and weakened.

This lacuna in the text of the treatise not only confirms but also (paradoxically) calls into question the very basis of Speroni's own classificatory scheme. If *la somma dimostrazione* is but a metaphor in the text of the *Apologia dei Dialoghi* for the absolute ground of all discourse—if it is a metaphor, in other words, for what is supposedly not metaphorical—then this poses two different and irreconcilable readings of Speroni's argument. It is difficult to imagine that this could occur by accident rather than by design, since Speroni had to be aware—as perhaps few other sixteenth-century theorists were—of exactly what he was trying to say and do at all times in presenting his apology to the inquisitor. The first reading is that discussed above: the procedures of demonstrative logic are simply not visible (except as remote reflections) within the rhetoric of the *Apologia dei Dialoghi*, just as they are not visible in the *Dialoghi*, since neither one—by Speroni's own admission—contains any definite knowledge. The second, radically divergent reading of the metaphor of *la somma dimostrazione* suggests instead that since demonstrative logic appears only as a metaphor in the text of the treatise, pointing to the place of a procedure that must remain out of sight, it is meant by Speroni to be no more and no less than a metaphor in the first place. Despite his professed belief in the absolute ground of (a certain version of) Aristotelianism, the absence in the treatise of any evidence or proof of the workings of demonstrative logic is, in this second reading, a cunning ruse of Speroni's to resist and undermine the constraints imposed on his theory. Although this might seem inconsistent with the rest of Speroni's opus or with the tendencies of late Renaissance thought in general, the possibility of double-reading the treatise cannot be excluded. This second reading would revalue dialogue, by making it no longer secondary or auxiliary to the now equally metaphorical and ungrounded discourse of demonstrative logic: both appear in this light as kinds of writing, or rather, as belonging to the same kind of writing. Such a reading would, of course, also demolish Speroni's carefully constructed classificatory scheme by depriving it of its absolute ontological foundation.

Speroni forces his readers to suspend judgment between these two incompatible interpretations of the *Apologia dei Dialoghi*; we can decide between them on the basis of belief or our faculty of judgment, but not on the basis of any statement found in the treatise.[135] If this is the case, then perhaps it is because we are asked here to see his theory as something more than an impoverished and enfeebled discourse condemned to operate as a mere reflection of philosophy. We are, Speroni suggests with his double-edged argument, to see that its assertions of its own inferiority to true philosophical discourse—and the inferiority of dialogue as well—are in the end themselves but metaphors too and therefore no more true than anything else that the treatise says. This stratagem—which relies on the rhetorical figure of paradox—defines the project for a *limited* rationality that informs all of Speroni's discourse on dialogue: pressured by power, the late Renaissance theoretical text resorts to ruses as well as to reasons (as does the fiction of dialogue itself): it makes no pretense to describing and analyzing the textual functions and devices of dialogue in a more or less logical manner, as sixteenth-century poetics generally proposes to do. Speroni's treatise denies the validity of its own theoretical claims even as it makes them; the reader is left with the difficult task of identifying the "truth" of the text. The fundamental ambiguity of the *Apologia dei Dialoghi* is founded on the circular, paradoxical, and aporetic practice of argumentation that it employs in order to figure dialogue and to give its discourse a space to defend itself from coercion.

The discourse on dialogue of the *Apologia dei Dialoghi* thus eludes finalization, just as does—in Speroni's eyes—dialogical writing itself. The preceding pages have sought to identify only one of the governing strands of Speroni's uncontrollably proliferating text, which, like a rhizome, cannot be said to have a center or a single direction of development. What is interesting about this particular literary gesture of the *Apologia dei Dialoghi* for the analysis of the problematization process is the way that it defines the position of the theory of dialogue. Not for one moment does Speroni try to dissemble the fact that he is writing under pressure; rather, he explicitly brings into play, in his theory of dialogue, the conflicting forces that bear on his text, making dramatically evident the illusory nature of any coolly rational and neutral poetics. His attempt to rationalize a certain set of textual strategies as the sole possible model of reading and writing dialogue—as, in other words, its universal narrative "dia-logic"—has to be understood as something other than purely rational. Reason itself becomes but one of an arsenal of argumentative stratagems employed in the treatise in order to present and sustain a necessary fiction of what dialogue is and of what it represents. The undermining of reason as the chief analytic means of describing and understanding the textual structure of dialogue leads Speroni far from the method of the *Poetics* or of the sixteenth-century Aristotelians, although it does not deprive his portrait of dialogue of all validity. His is, simply put, a deeply rhetorical and necessarily pragmatic vision of poetics, which constantly focuses on the structure and nature of dialogical representation, but only as the result of a prior strategic decision concerning those features in dialogue to be defined that will disrupt the possibility of a thematic reading and defer all acts of interpretive violence. For Speroni, the purpose of a dialogical poetics is to salvage the late Renaissance art of writing dialogue from the growing conflict with the institutions of the Counter-Reformation that threatens to engulf it, even if that means sacrificing the possibility of philosophical dialogue and the traditional unity of the arts of discourse. By making dialogue into a scene of speaking that is always also a scene of error, this rhetorical poetics at once speaks eloquently to us of a sixteenth-century view of dialogue (Sigonio's) that is headed for eclipse, and of its own incipient modernity.

FOUR

The Reasons for Asking: Castelvetro and Tasso on Philosophy and Fiction

Decomposing Humanism: Castelvetro's Poetics of Dialogue

Lodovico Castelvetro (1505–71) was a northern Italian thinker whose life was a long and eventful sequence of political intrigue, persecution, struggles with the reconstituted Roman Inquisition, murder trials, clandestine activity, accusations of heresy, escape *in extremis*, and exile.[1] The Counter-Reformation era, in Italy, witnessed a widespread revolt against the tenets of classical humanism and the practice of *imitatio*, in the name of a new kind of criticism and a new kind of literature; and Castelvetro was at the forefront of this revolt, even if his motives differed from those of many of his contemporaries. Nonetheless, Castelvetro's contribution as an evangelical Protestant to the intellectual ferment of his time has yet to be given the careful study that it deserves.[2] The facts of his life testify to the dramatic difficulties facing dissenting intellectuals in Italy as the sixteenth century progressed and the hegemony of the Roman Curia was gradually consolidated and reinforced. The one fact about his life and work that is most significant for the present study is his extraordinary impact as a literary theorist—despite all the obstacles in his path—throughout Italy and Europe.[3] After studying in Bologna (perhaps with Pomponazzi), Ferrara, Padua, and Siena, where he belonged to the Accademia degli Intronati, Castelvetro resided and worked in his home city of Modena from 1529 to 1560. Here, during the so-called evangelical period in Italy following the beginning of the Reformation, Castelvetro and his circle developed their radically unorthodox ideas on the relationship between reason and faith.[4] He fled into exile in 1561, following his condemnation *in absentia* as a heretic by the Roman Inquisition, and spent the last ten often tumultuous years of his life moving between France, Switzerland, and Austria.

Besides his work as a translator of, or commentator on, Melanchthon, Provençal poetry, and Cicero, Castelvetro wrote, among other works, *Giunte alle Prose di Bembo, Le rime del Petrarca brevemente sposte, Sposizione a XXIX canti dell'Inferno dantesco, Correttione d'alcune cose del dialogo delle lingue di Benedetto Varchi,* various works on religious questions, a number of brief treatises on classical and vernacular literature and on philosophical issues, grammars, and studies of orthography and etymology. Despite his prolific scholarly output, none of these works were published in Italy in Castelvetro's own lifetime; the manuscripts of some were lost in 1567 (when Castelvetro fled religious strife in Lyon), others vanished in later centuries, and those that managed to find their way posthumously into print in the sixteenth century generally were published abroad. Yet his influence on criticism and theory in Italy in the final three decades of the Cinquecento is comparable to that of few other theorists, even if his ideas were controversial and often bitterly contested. Practically all major literary theories published in Italy after the early 1570's refer to Castelvetro's work in some way. In their theories of dialogue, both Tasso and Speroni, for instance, give evidence of having felt the force of his arguments, and Sigonio (who was also from Modena) seems to have held Castelvetro in high esteem, even if he could never have agreed with most of Castelvetro's ideas.[5] The explanation for his prominence in late Renaissance Italian literary culture is to be found in the one work of his that did appear in his own lifetime and that today remains his chief claim to a place in the history of Western literary theory and criticism —namely, the famous edition, translation, and commentary *La "Poetica" d'Aristotele vulgarizzata et sposta* (Aristotle's *Poetics* translated and explained).

The *"Poetica" d'Aristotele,* completed while its author was in Lyon in 1567 and published in Vienna in 1570, beyond the reach of the Roman Inquisition, was the first commentary on the *Poetics* to appear in Italian or in any other European vernacular, as well as one of the most influential theories of poetics to appear in any

European language in the sixteenth or seventeenth centuries.[6] The "three unities" of seventeenth-century French neoclassical dramatic theory, for example, derived directly from Castelvetro's treatise. This monumental and pioneering work is not, of course, devoted to dialogue alone; in fact, Castelvetro is not even exclusively concerned in it with establishing, translating, and explaining the text of the *Poetics*, which serves as little more than a springboard for a discussion of his own theory of literature. Nevertheless, his treatise can legitimately be counted among the other sixteenth-century theoretical works on dialogue because it offers an all-encompassing theory of dialogical writing, not just a few random remarks on the genre (although the pages on dialogue are few in number, relative to the size of the treatise itself, Tasso's entire *Discorso dell'arte del dialogo* is not much longer).

A plausible case can be made for the influence of Castelvetro's theory of dialogue on the *Apologia dei Dialoghi*, even though Speroni—naturally enough, given Castelvetro's status as an Italian intellectual maverick and a convicted heretic—neither mentions Castelvetro nor (unlike Tasso) alludes to his work: Speroni's argument that all dialogue is comedy would appear to owe more than a little to the *"Poetica" d'Aristotele*. With Tasso, in contrast, the significance of Castelvetro's theory of literature is far more apparent. Not only did Tasso specifically mention Castelvetro's treatise in letters of 1575 and 1576, but the manuscript of his "Estratti" (Extracts) from the *"Poetica" d'Aristotele*, with Tasso's comments on the ideas that it contains, documents his vivid interest in—and sometimes equally vivid disagreements with—the Modenese critic's work. Tasso was originally drawn to Castelvetro by their mutual concern for the problem of the relationship between history and poetry, but he carefully studied the thought of *il Grammaticuccio* (as Castelvetro often called himself—although the epithet was coined by his hated archrival, Annibale Caro) on a number of other matters as well, as Tasso's renowned *Discorsi del poema eroico* testifies.[7] And although the *Discorso dell'arte del dialogo* does not name him openly, out of prudence, it takes Castelvetro's theory of the form and function of dialogue as its point of departure. Though brief, Castelvetro's theory of dialogue is a necessary prelude to a reading of Tasso's treatise on dialogue, because of the place that it holds in the history of thought about dialogical writing and about poetics in general in the late sixteenth century in Italy.

Castelvetro's *"Poetica" d'Aristotele* is structured, like so many other works of its kind, as a series of micro-commentaries to the successive sections of the *Poetics* (supplying the reader with an edition of the Greek text and a vernacular translation as well). Despite the discontinuous nature of its mode of analysis, which works through Aristotle's text word-by-word and section-by-section without setting them in the context of an overall argument, these nine hundred or so pages of commentary present a remarkably rationalistic poetics of the literary system (even if it is hardly the same as Aristotle's). To summarize the whole of Castelvetro's theory would be pointless; for the present analysis, the important part is the section, or *lemma* (1: 4), concerning dialogue itself.[8] The passage from the *Poetics* under examination in this section is the familiar one (1, 1447a28–1447b24) containing Aristotle's enigmatic remark on dialogue (Castelvetro observes that "this text is reputed to be rather obscure"; p. 31).[9] Castelvetro's reading of the original Greek text varies considerably from the modern reading—as did that of nearly every Renaissance critic—and allows him to formulate an almost wholly different sense for Aristotle's argument.[10] Specifically, the interpretive path that leads him to discuss dialogue, in commenting on this passage from the *Poetics*, is characterized by a series of complex if somewhat maladroit philological and rhetorical maneuvers designed to make it clear that Aristotle could not possibly have approved of Plato's dialogues, thereby fully legitimating a modern critique of them.

Unlike Sigonio, Tasso, or even Speroni, Castelvetro assumes no fundamental continuity in ancient thought and seeks no absolute foundation for his own theory in the unalterable "truths" of the Greek and Roman authorities. On the contrary, he enjoys catching them in open contradiction with each other; for he has —more than any other critic or theorist of his time—a system of his own on which to rely. In point of fact, his deep dislike of the classicizing tendencies of late Italian humanism—and of the privileges that it accords to dialogue—contributes greatly to the making of his argument about dialogue in the *"Poetica" d'Aristotele*; his hidden agenda is to dissolve the authority of the classical canon and thus challenge the very basis of the human-istic culture of the Renaissance. To simplify Castelvetro's line of reasoning as far as possible, the principal cause of Aristotle's dis-approval is that Plato's dialogues, "although they have a poetic subject (that is to say, mimesis) . . . are laid out in prose and not in verse" (p. 35).[11] Castelvetro does not go into the specifics of Plato's dialogical praxis any further than this, except to observe "that Plato in writing his *Dialogues* violated the very laws that he had laid down for his ideal commonwealth, from which he would have banished Homer and all [mimetic] poetry" (p. 34).[12] This is the case, however, not only because Plato's dialogues are themselves works of mimesis, but more specifically because they are—Castelvetro claims—*dramatic* fictions, works destined (de-spite the fact that "they are laid out in prose and not in verse") for performance on stage, like the great tragedies of Sophocles or the great comedies of Aristophanes.

Castelvetro's claim for the dramatic nature of Plato's dialogical fictions lays the cornerstone for his theory of dialogue. Turning to a fragment from the lost work *On Poets* in order to shed light on the *Poetics*, like both Sigonio and Speroni, he remarks that "to prove that Plato's dialogues are imitations, the speaker [in a passage in Athenaeus's *Deipnosophistae*] invokes the authority of Aristotle in *On Poets*."[13] But here as elsewhere in the *"Poetica" d'Aristotele*, Castelvetro's interpretation of the *Poetics* and of Aris-totle's thought in general is only a provisional moment in the de-velopment and articulation of his own theory of literature. Once he has cited Aristotle's authority on dialogue, Castelvetro freely admits that now "we will speak in general about all those dialogi-cal discussions [*ragionamenti*] that the Greeks call *dialogoi*" and abandons the task of commenting on the enigmas of the *Poet-ics* itself: the proof that Plato's dialogues are works of dramatic fiction will come from Castelvetro himself.[14] Beginning with the same tripartite distinction between the modes of dialogical rep-resentation made by Sigonio in *De dialogo liber*, Castelvetro turns a seemingly innocuous theory of these modes into the first strike in an all-out attack on the legitimacy of dialogical writing itself:

These dialogues, therefore, are divided into three modes. The first one may be set on stage and may be called "dramatic," since characters are introduced into it in order to discourse *dramatikos*, that is, in action, as is commonly done in tragedies and comedies. This is done by Plato in his *Dialogues* and by Lucian in most of his. But there is another mode of dialogue that cannot be set on stage; in this one the author, preserving his own character in dialogue, narrates as a historian what this character or that other one said. These dialogues may be called "historical" or "narrative," and most of Cicero's dialogues are of this sort. Moreover, there is a third mode of dialogue made up of those that are a mixture of the first and the second modes. Here the author at first preserves his own character and narrates as a historian; then he introduces into it the characters who speak *dramatikos*, as is done in tragedies and comedies. This mode of dialogue may and may not be set on stage: that is to say, it cannot because the author at first preserves his own character and is like a historian [narrator]; and yet it can because characters are introduced into it in order to speak dramatically. Cicero wrote some dialogues of this sort.[15]

Although this neatly arranged and not entirely unfamiliar (cf. *Republic* 3.392–394C) classificatory scheme may not seem at first glance to be a *mise en cause* of dialogue, the reader soon discovers the point of all this is that there are certain "*defects* common to all three" modes of dialogue (p. 36; my italics).[16] Castelvetro dwells at length, and with great relish, on these alleged defects of dialogue. His theory represents an effort—the opposite, strategically speaking, of Speroni's defense—to undermine the privileges of dialogue, and of the culture that produces dialogue, by discovering the logical self-contradictions of the form and illuminating them through the analytical power of his poetics.

Castelvetro sets out to expose the flawed and defective nature of dialogue through a series of deductive leaps. First, he contends, dialogues of the dramatic mode—where each character speaks in direct discourse—cannot be "perfect" unless they are performable on stage (*senza la qual montata non hanno la loro perfezione*; p. 36), insofar as they are imitations of action as well as speech. Since all characters act as well as speak, as we know from the *Poetics* (insofar as speech is a species of action), this must mean that dramatic dialogues are always to be performed on a stage *in front of an audience*, Castelvetro reasons, because that is the only place where characters may discourse *dramatikos*. The success or failure of a given dramatic dialogue as a work of mimesis can therefore be evaluated solely in terms of its impact on a specifically defined public and not in terms of the general esthetic precepts of its particular art, since no dialogue could ever be said to succeed without gaining the consensus of an audience. Following this line of reasoning, Castelvetro returns insistently—and against the dictates of both tradition and common sense (neither of which are of much value to him)—to the criterion of the stage as the sole effective means of classifying and evaluating dialogue. Even the apparent absurdity of designating Plato's dialogues as works meant principally for the stage does not faze Castelvetro, because his purpose in the treatise is not to produce a poetics that can be used to analyze and explain individual dialogues as textual representations, even if it means that he must distort and travesty the sense of those same texts in the process. Castelvetro considers all of Plato's dialogues to belong to the mimetic mode—which is the key to his fiercely negative critique of them—simply because Plato himself does not appear in them as their narrator: the fact that the *Phaedrus* and the *Timaeus* contain long narratives and are so clearly designed to be read rather than performed in front of an audience, or that many of Plato's dialogues are more diegetic than mimetic in nature, is of slight concern to him. Plato's dialogues are wrenched out of their context and stripped of their original semantic direction because the model of the text takes priority for Castelvetro over the history (canon, tradition) of texts. The logic of his argument concerning Platonic dialogue, and dialogue in general, in the *"Poetica" d'Aristotele* is strictly self-validating and does not require verification by empirical textual evidence. As he sees it, the task of a poetics such as his is to establish a normative, a priori discursive grid of conventions, functions, and representational principles that can account for the whole of the literary system; individual works can be evaluated by sifting them through this pre-established grid (direct discourse = stage, etc.), but no challenge can be made to the validity of the logic of the grid by the works that it evaluates.

One of the chief defects of dramatic dialogue for Castelvetro is that it does not consider the problem of its own reception adequately:

If, therefore, they are set (or may be set) on stage—as the first mode always is, and as the third one is in part—it necessarily follows that they have the common people as their viewer and hearer; it is for the common people, and for the delight of the coarse crowd alone, that the stage and the dramatic performance were invented . . . it similarly follows of necessity that the subject must be suitable for the people and for the crowd, who are not—and cannot be—capable of engaging in and understanding scientific or artistic disputes, but are only able to understand earthly events under fortune's sway. (pp. 36–37) [17]

Every staged dialogue must be configured for a specific audience—the "common people" and the "coarse crowd" (as opposed to Sigonio's elite readership of *letterati e potenti*)—which wholly determines the dialogist's choice of an appropriate style and subject. The means, mode, and object of representation of dramatic dialogue must belong to the conventional and thematic horizon of expectations of the general public.[18] For Castelvetro —unlike Aristotle (who was certainly concerned with the audience in his theory of tragedy, but not with any specific *kind* of audience)—the public of the dramatic work always dictates the writer's choice of an object of mimesis because of what it presumably can and cannot understand. Whereas the representation of "earthly events under fortune's sway" appeals to the public, the representation of "scientific or artistic disputes" generally does not and so should be avoided. Any dialogue that is to be performed must function with credibility and verisimilitude for the sake of producing "pleasure" (*per diletto*) in the public (*il popolo*), which is not normally interested in science or art or edification.[19] Otherwise, Castelvetro notes, its failure as a dramatic work is certain. This "coarse crowd" (*rozza moltitudine*), anxious for gratification and delight, is therefore the privileged measure of all things in dramatic/mimetic dialogue (there may also be educated persons in this same crowd, granted, but only as a distinct minority): it defines the function of the dialogical text as the production of pleasure. Every dialogist is by definition a rhetorician as well, then, for dialogues are oriented completely toward the production of a single specific effect—*il diletto*—in the mind of the spectator. Thus, Castelvetro concludes, Plato's dialogues err "gravely" (*gravemente*; p. 37) in their use of philosophical and dialectical arguments and terms that are too difficult for the coarse crowd to understand.[20] The writer must adapt dialogue to the linguistic, psychological, and intellectual capacities of the common people; a dialogue should simply and realistically represent life as it is seen and lived by them. Yet Plato, in writing his philosophical dialogues, does just the opposite, thereby committing a fatal error in Castelvetro's view, inasmuch as his texts fail to fulfill their designated function. Dialogue may become either tragedy or comedy, but not a dramatic *representation* of philosophical discourse, which is nothing if not a contradiction in terms.[21]

Castelvetro's argument, as it stands to this point, would eliminate virtually all non-narrative philosophical dialogues (with the possible exception of some written in a satiric vein) from the ranks of perfect *rassomiglianza* (mimesis) since such works rarely "contain material that any ignoramus or simple man is capable [of understanding]" (p. 39).[22] There is, however, a further—and even more serious—formal contradiction to be found in practically every dialogue, even the most satiric or comic ones. Once the nature of this second defect is grasped, Castelvetro argues, we can see why Aristotle disapproved of Plato's dialogues:

The other defect that is, or may be, common to all three modes, is that dialogues are written in prose, and prose is not suitable for dialogues whose subject is mimetic and invented by the writer's genius, a subject that in truth was never taken up by those characters that are represented in them. Similarly, no dialogue by any of the aforementioned authors [Plato, Cicero, et al.] ever actually took place. For the use of verse is a very strong argument to make us understand that the subject contained in it is imaginary and not true. . . . The use of prose ought not to be any less strong of an argument to demonstrate that its subject is the truth and not an imaginary thing. (p. 37)[23]

Although this second argument against dialogue may appear to the modern reader even more tenuous than the first, it is linked to one of the Gordian knots of Renaissance theory and criticism: namely, the question of the necessity of verse for poetic fiction.[24] Castelvetro—never one to disguise or deliberately render ambiguous his critical opinions—comes down squarely in favor of the essentiality of verse for all poetry (mimesis). The language of fiction (whose subject "is imaginary and not true") is verse, and the language of history (whose subject is instead the "truth") is prose. It follows that dialogue, since it is a fiction (*di soggetto rassomigliativo*), must necessarily be written in verse—and none of Plato's or Cicero's dialogues meet this requirement. Whereas Sigonio says specifically that dialogue is to be written in *oratio soluta* and Speroni calls dialogue *una specie di prosa*, Castelvetro condemns outright all dialogue in prose as impossibly self-contradictory. This is not because prose has a special relationship with the real that is denied to dialogue, but simply because—in Castelvetro's eyes—it is an accepted convention of writing that prose is the language of history (of things that have happened) and that verse is the language of fiction (of things that are verisimilar). The autonomy of poetry from history must be maintained at a formal as well as at a thematic level. Prose and verse openly signal to the reader/spectator the kind of subject that the writer is to discuss, and this operation is critical for the successful production of the desired effect in the mind of the reader/spectator. Dialogues of practically every variety violate this norm by pretending to be history through the use of prose, when everyone knows that they are instead fiction, since "no dialogue by any of the aforementioned authors ever actually took place."[25] And even if dramatic dialogue were to be written in verse, it would still be inappropriate as a mode of representation for *la rozza moltitudine*, which does not expect fictional characters to reason about philosophical or scientific subjects in verse on stage (*non s'usa tra gli uomini di ragionare in versi*; p. 44). There is finally no escape left for dialogue from the conceptual web of arguments that Castelvetro has spun around it.[26]

Castelvetro's arguments against dialogue, in accordance with the general theoretical procedure that he observes in his treatise, usually take the form of a categoric syllogism.[27] The use of a logically implicated proposition such as "dialogue ought therefore to be written in verse" to complete an argument ("poetry is verse; dialogue is poetry; therefore dialogue is or should be verse") in which the conclusion contradicts the major premise—even if it goes completely against the tradition of dialogical texts—is typical of the method of the *"Poetica" d'Aristotele*. This same logically implicated categoric proposition acquires the status of a demonstrative proof, in Castelvetro's view, because it is formally necessary to the other parts of the syllogism. His theory of dialogue is the product of a globally valid deductive logic of discourse that discovers a theory of dialogue as it discovers a middle term. Castelvetro's method does not attempt to explain dialogue in its irreducible historical and esthetic specificity, then, but only to obey—in its own inner discursive workings—this same syllogistic line of formal reasoning. Certainly this logic, rigged in favor of rhetoric, is suggestive of the work of Ramus (and even that of Melanchthon, whom Castelvetro translated).[28] In generating a preformed set of abstract theoretical norms—or a rigidly rationalized discursive model—for dialogue, Castelvetro is concerned with the devices and techniques (verse, verisimilitude, and the like) of the dialogist that can be verified by this same deductive logic of discourse; he is by and large indifferent, for instance, to the kind of epistemological and metaphysical problems raised by Speroni in the *Apologia dei Dialoghi*—although his call for a dialogical realism seems to have nonetheless found its way into the heart of Speroni's theory—and openly hostile to the humanists' reverence for the exemplary value of the tradition of the forms and fictions of antiquity.

Any truly literary text can be reduced to an internally consistent system of discursive devices and functions, and the work of the true poet can be described as a fully rational and systematic utilization of these devices and functions (rather than as a kind of divine frenzy, or even as a parroting of philosophical discourse) in order to delight the public through its coherence and credibility. Neither ancient nor Renaissance dialogue, needless to say, meets these standards in Castelvetro's eyes, and therefore he banishes them from the literary realm. If the Reformation is a challenge to Renaissance cultural conventions of every kind, then Castelvetro's theory of dialogue challenges one of the most widespread of all Renaissance literary conventions —namely, dialogical writing. But the *"Poetica" d'Aristotele*, despite the forceful way in which its poetics is presented, is itself a fragile work, founded on a positive procedural logic that must be accepted either in its entirety or not at all. Castelvetro, in quarreling with the tenets of a classical humanism that privileges the traces and residues of an archaic past, does not proceed in a dialectical way. He never confronts the possibility, for instance, that certain of the premises of his syllogisms (such as "dialogues can be set on stage") are themselves only rhetorical propositions without any claim to universal validity. Allowing this possibility would place the procedural logic (*methodos*) of his theory in question, a logic that must remain unchallenged because Castelvetro has burned all his other bridges behind him (the authority of the *Poetics*, the evidence of the tradition) and has no other available means of support for it. Unlike the *Apologia dei Dialoghi*, however, his text employs no defensive stratagems to disguise the vulnerability of the premises of its argument; they are openly visible, and a rejection of any one of them jeopardizes Castelvetro's reading of the classical and Renaissance literary system. Nevertheless, the sheer polemical energy of his thought—and the grounds of his dissent—survive even this. Although in the last analysis it offers only limited insight into the nature of dialogue, the *"Poetica" d'Aristotele* does tell us something—in its insistence on the autonomous logical and rhetorical organization of the literary system, rather than on either a prescriptive and classicizing procedure of writing (Sigonio) or a duplicitous strategy of control over interpretation (Speroni)—about the intensifying concern for method in the generations preceding Bacon and Descartes.[29]

Castelvetro's attack on dialogue appears at times an almost absurd reduction of the ideas of the *Poetics* concerning a rational art of poetry; at other times, it appears the result of rhetorical and pragmatic criteria that have fairly little to do with the *Poetics* at all.[30] What Castelvetro does glean from his encounter with Aristotle is the notion of an esthetic pleasure (*il diletto*) unconstrained by utility. Works of poetic fiction have nothing at all to do with a moral and ethical discourse of ideas; literary and philosophical discourse are wholly alien to each other and must not intermingle. In this sense, Castelvetro's theory of dialogue stands as a critique not only of the literary taste of late Italian humanism (such as Sigonio professed), but of the mannerist way of thinking about dialogue and about literature in general. Dialogue, in enmeshing fiction and dialectic, is far too hybrid a form for Castelvetro's brand of poetics, which condemns almost all mixtures of verse and prose—like late medieval *versiprosa*—as "monstrous" (*mostruose*; p. 35) aberrations. He has little patience for the paradoxes of dialogue, and no interest whatsoever in exploring the ambiguities of its position at the crossroads of fiction and dialectic. The notion of a philosophical fiction is just as monstrous, and just as impossible, he contends, as a centaur or a minotaur in nature. If an identity is to be maintained between prose and truth on the one hand and verse and verisimilitude on the other hand, such hybrid forms have to be expelled entirely from the literary system. If dialogue has any place at all in that system, Castelvetro implies, it is strictly as a poem written in verse, and the object of its representation is an "imagined thing." This, however, in effect eliminates dialogue altogether from his classificatory scheme, since under these conditions it would become indistinguishable from drama or even epic. The works of Plato and Cicero are therefore lost to the literary order, and with them go syncresis and synthesis as fundamental qualities of the literary-philosophical text.

In sounding the death knell of philosophical dialogue, the theory of the *"Poetica" d'Aristotele* is uncannily prophetic. Not surprisingly, though, Castelvetro's theory of literature in general and his antihumanist treatment of dialogue in particular were not universally accepted in the late sixteenth century by other Italian critics and theorists. Indeed, as one chronicler of Renaissance criticism and theory has remarked, "A large section of the critical history of the final three decades of the sixteenth century can be written in terms of the objections raised to the ideas of Castelvetro by the generation of literary critics that followed him." [31] It is in this context that I now turn to the final major theory of dialogue of the Cinquecento.

The Limits of Figure: Tasso's Crisis

In the early spring of 1585, Torquato Tasso (1544–95) was nearing the end of his long confinement, by order of Duke Alfonso II, in the Arcispedale di Sant'Anna in Ferrara. In spite of his being held prisoner, Tasso was relatively free to read and to write while in the Sant'Anna hospital; most of his *Dialoghi*, in fact, were finished there, along with many other literary works and a large number of letters. Among Tasso's correspondents during his final years of confinement was the Benedictine monk and poet Angelo Grillo, who had begun an intensive exchange of epistles and poems with Tasso in 1584. It seems that Grillo, probably during the winter of 1584–85, wrote to Tasso asking him for his advice on writing dialogue. Grillo's request was hardly an extraordinary one, for although chiefly remembered today as the author of the epic *Gerusalemme liberata*, the pastoral *Aminta*, and the *Rime*, Tasso started to compose dialogues fairly early in his career and completed his last dialogue (*Il conte*) less than a year before his death in Rome. Tasso's collected dialogues appeared in several editions in Italy during his own lifetime, were well known in both France—where they were later translated—and England, and unquestionably played a significant role in the development of his towering literary reputation in Europe in the sixteenth and seventeenth centuries.[32] To Tasso, dialogue seemed an ideal vehicle for the deeply syncretic blend of poetry and philosophy that he pursued over the final decades of his life, which even today—given Tasso's continuing fame—needs no introduction for the English-speaking reader. Thus between March and April 1585, after having spent approximately six years in the Sant'Anna hospital following his violent outburst at the Este court, Tasso composed his theory of dialogue, entitled *Discorso dell'arte del dialogo* (Discourse on the art of dialogue), and sent it to Grillo, noting that "in your letters, most reverend father, you ask that I give you some instruction. Unless I am deceived, you want to learn about writing dialogues" (p. 17).[33]

Of course, Tasso would have been interested in the theory of dialogue for other reasons, over and beyond Grillo's request for *ammaestramento* (p. 16) in the matter. Tasso was a student of Carlo Sigonio's in Padua at precisely the time that Sigonio published his *De dialogo liber*, a work Tasso knew very well, as even a cursory comparison with the *Discorso dell'arte del dialogo* reveals. When Sigonio left Padua to teach in Bologna, subsequent to his public quarrel with Robortello, Tasso loyally followed him there (although the young poet was expelled from the university in 1564 for indiscreetly satirizing some of his professors). As the preface to the *Rinaldo* testifies, Sigonio's version of late Italian humanism influenced the thought of the young Tasso. The poet also knew Speroni personally (his father, Bernardo Tasso, figures as one of the interlocutors in Speroni's *Dialogo della famiglia*) and admired him in his youth. "While I was studying in Padua," Tasso wrote of Speroni, "I was in the habit of frequenting his private rooms not less often and less willingly than I frequented the public schools, for it seemed to me to present a likeness of that Academy and that Lyceum in which the Socratics and the Platonists used to dispute."[34] Without question, Tasso was familiar with many of Speroni's critical ideas of the 1540's–70's and with Speroni's *Dialoghi* themselves. Even though by 1585, after his fiasco with the censors of the *Gerusalemme liberata*, Tasso was bitterly disenchanted with Speroni (the other censors were Scipione Gonzaga, Pier Angelio da Borga, Flaminio de' Nobili, and Silvio Antoniano), it is at least plausible that Tasso knew that Speroni had written his *Apologia dei Dialoghi* some years earlier, although there is almost no evidence in Tasso's theory of dialogue showing that he had read one of the circulating copies of Speroni's manuscript. Most important of all, Tasso had—in the 1570's—attentively read Castelvetro's *"Poetica" d'Aristotele*, the most authoritative and controversial work on the *Poetics* yet to appear, and had been both irritated and intrigued by it. Castelvetro's treatise serves as one of the chief target-texts for the *Discorso dell'arte del dialogo*, a fact not as widely recognized by scholars as it should be.[35] In short, although not an academic or a professional humanist, Tasso was throughout his life deeply interested in the philosophy of literature and in the many different theories of poetics then in vogue, as his numerous treatises and *discorsi* attest. Very much in line with the practice of his own age, Tasso was always a theorist as well as a poet, even if his treatises and *discorsi* are nowadays considered a rather minor part of his overall work.[36]

Tasso's theory of dialogue, although it first appeared in print as a part of the *Rime e prose, parte quarta* (Venice, 1586), was sent to Angelo Grillo before the end of April 1585 in manuscript form.[37] Addressing himself to Grillo at the beginning of the treatise, Tasso describes the *Discorso dell'arte del dialogo* as "a very brief work" (*una operetta assai breve*—in the *editio princeps* it takes up only twenty pages) and downplays its value as anything other than personal opinion (pp. 16, 17). Yet of all the kinds of writing practiced by Tasso, the *discorso* is one of the most recurrent and the most representative of his approach to the pressing philosophical and critical issues of the late Renaissance.[38] Within this brief and seemingly occasional work, Tasso touches on the problem of dialogue in all of its complexity and proposes his own distinctly individual theory of "writing dialogues" (*lo scrivere i dialogi*; pp. 16, 17). Despite his fluency in the critical idiom of the period and his familiarity with the more academic style of Sigonio and others like him, Tasso chooses to present his ideas concerning dialogue in an abbreviated, almost elliptical manner, sharply different from that of any of his precursors; his text is free of any hint of a scholastic apparatus, for instance, or any arid display of erudition for its own sake. Tasso's theory of dialogue does not possess the didactic authority of Sigonio's *De dialogo liber*, the dramatic urgency of Speroni's *Apologia dei Dialoghi*, or the deductive rigor of Castelvetro's *"Poetica" d'Aristotele*. It instead poses as a letter to an admired friend, an intellectual exercise in which Tasso is on equal terms with his audience (Grillo and his circle), and an invitation to a frank discussion of his ideas on dialogue: as he notes, "I ought to conceal nothing from you that might be useful to others, or even to myself" (p. 17).[39]

If anything, the form of the *Discorso dell'arte del dialogo* most resembles the essay in its understated presentation of Tasso's ideas, although it is far from either the spirit or the style of Montaigne's nearly contemporary *Essais*. His *operetta*, for all its brevity and apparent disregard for the preferred protocol of late-sixteenth-century critical and theoretical discourse, is nevertheless in many ways an encyclopedic work. It carefully and lucidly reconsiders the points of contact between major trends and tendencies in the sixteenth-century debate over dialogue, while addressing such broader but related topics as the significance of theory for literary study, the relationship between Aristotelian and Platonic philosophy, and the privileges enjoyed by tropes and figures in poetic discourse. Tasso employs the form of the *discorso*, with its relative flexibility and informal but still decorous style, because it allows him to resemble "certain scholars at court who, unable to sustain so serious a role, put off the gown and dress in the common fashion" (p. 17). The plainness and shortness of the "gown" that Tasso wears in his work—that is, the modesty, brevity, and concision of his argument—let his discourse take on the look of a work without any claim to authority (for "the role of teacher would be as ill-suited to me," he remarks to Grillo, "as the role of student to you"; p. 17). This common garb of Tasso's, however, is in truth but a masquerade disguising his other aims in writing his theory of dialogue. While it frees him both from the burden of "so serious a role" ("an office that does not suit me"; p. 17) and from the stylistic and procedural constraints of academic discourse, he pursues at the same time his own project for a comprehensive theory of dialogue—which, like Speroni, he calls *l'artificio del bene scrivere* (p. 16)—that is both a summary of all that came before it and a step beyond the ancients and all other moderns.

Modern scholarship has demonstrated beyond reasonable doubt that Tasso's *Discorso dell'arte del dialogo* is a metacritical reading of both Castelvetro's and Sigonio's theories of dialogue.[40] In his brief treatise, Tasso does not mention Castelvetro by name, in a *tralasciamento*—or omission—typical of late Renaissance critical practice in Italy (especially where Castelvetro is concerned). He nonetheless cites verbatim (pp. 19–21) —although without indicating that he is doing so—the long passage from the *"Poetica" d'Aristotele* concerning the staging of dialogue cited earlier in this chapter. Sigonio is not mentioned either, yet many phrases in Tasso's *trattatello* are extremely similar to, if not directly translated from, *De dialogo liber*. It would be irrelevant to engage here in a point-by-point discussion of the specific influence of Castelvetro or Sigonio on Tasso's thought on dialogue; the extent of his intellectual debts to both will emerge in the course of my analysis.[41] What is salient is that the balance of textual evidence points unmistakably to Tasso's participation in the chain of Italian theories of dialogue that extends from Sigonio to Speroni to Castelvetro across the 1560's and 1570's. The intertextual links between Tasso on the one hand and Sigonio and Castelvetro on the other hand confirm that his theory of dialogue represents an attempt to answer the questions raised by the problem of dialogue in the intellectual arena of the late Italian Renaissance. Given Tasso's acute sense of belonging to and participating in the cultural dynamics of the late Cinquecento, and given his ambitious project for a mannerist synthesis of ancient and modern learning, it would be difficult to see it in any other way. By the same token, however, this intertextual relationship indicates that his theory of dialogue is not designed to supply a special interpretive key to his own dialogues; its purpose is not, in other words, to explain the whole of the *Dialoghi* by providing a program for the poetics of Tasso's own dialogical practice, but rather to intervene in the ongoing dialogue on dialogue in Italy.

Until recently, however, an interpretive key to the *Dialoghi* is just what critics have chiefly seen in Tasso's treatise. Since the author's ideas about the writing of dialogue are, or appear to be, so clearly stated in the *Discorso dell'arte del dialogo* (which was first published, after all, together with the collected *Dialoghi* in the 1586 edition of the *Rime e prose*), it has usually been assumed that the *Discorso* reveals Tasso's design in the *Dialoghi* as well.[42] There are good reasons, however, to argue just the opposite. In his theory of dialogue, Tasso mentions his own dialogues only once *en passant*, and the scattered statements concerning the poetics of dialogue found in the *Dialoghi* themselves often tend to go directly against the grain of the argument of the *Discorso dell'arte del dialogo*.[43] Moreover, anyone wishing to collect all of Tasso's disparate statements on dialogue and to form from them a single set of principles with which to interpret the *Dialoghi* would have to overlook the fact that the practice of writing theory is not the same as the practice of writing dialogue (although they may intersect at times, as they do for Speroni). Tasso's theory demands to be analyzed as a part of a practice that is not at all the same as that of the *Dialoghi*. Its theoretical object of analysis is not only the tradition of dialogical texts and the practice of dialogical writing, but also a set of other discourses about dialogue, about literary theory, and so on.[44] Tasso's practice of *systematic* theorizing about dialogue in this sense is, in effect, to be found only in this one work. Any study that wants to treat his theory in all its richly speculative literariness must place it not only in a context of prior ideas concerning dialogue but in a context of prior practices of systematic thinking and writing about dialogue, each with its own specific theoretical procedures, strategies, and subterfuges. Tasso's discourse is a textual site where he cites, and resituates, the different answers to the late Renaissance problem of dialogue while searching for one of his own.[45]

After a brief prologue, in which Tasso modestly denies that he will formulate the "precepts" (*precetti*) and "rules" (*regole*) of a poetics of dialogue (pp. 16, 17), he immediately turns to the definition of mimesis. Tasso's Aristotelianism, unlike that of more than a few of his contemporaries, is anything but a blind repetition of the *Poetics*.[46] He does not limit himself in his discussion of dialogue to the *Poetics*, *Rhetoric*, and *Topics*, the works of Aristotle that seem most relevant to the analysis of dialogue for other sixteenth-century critics, but instead ranges throughout Aristotle's *Organon* from the *On Interpretation* to the *Posterior Analytics* (in fact, Tasso never mentions the *Rhetoric* in the *Discorso dell'arte del dialogo*: Cicero and Demetrius are instead his chief ancient authorities on rhetoric). Tasso exhibits a far greater familiarity with the whole body of Aristotle's work than either Sigonio or Castelvetro. Yet in his investigation of dialogue, while never entirely exiting from the methodological framework of the *Poetics* and Aristotelian thought, Tasso also displays the syncretic and original nature of his cultural project for a recovery and defense of dialogical writing. He is willing to consider a wide spectrum of ideas on literature, from Plato to Demetrius to Longinus, and to break away from the constraints of contemporary critical orthodoxy in his reading of the *Poetics* whenever it suits the purposes of his argument. Unlike both Sigonio and Castelvetro, Tasso feels no need to explain the text of the *Poetics* itself in writing his theory of dialogue, blithely ignoring the passages in the *Poetics* and in *On Poets* that seem so important to his predecessors. By 1585, the sense of urgency surrounding the interpretation of the *Poetics* was already long gone from criticism and theory in Italy.

Controversies and quarrels between critics and theorists, however, were just as much the order of the day in the 1580's as they were earlier in the *secondo* Cinquecento. Tasso could hardly be called a stranger to the literary battlefields of his time, standing as he did at the very center of the dispute over the relative merits (or demerits) of the *Gerusalemme liberata* in comparison to those of Ariosto's *Orlando furioso*.[47] The critical and theoretical discourse of Tasso's age is distinguished by this sense of insuperable difference and by the need to take a polemical position for or against a current theory or interpretation; and both this sense of difference and this need for polemic inform the first section of the *Discorso dell'arte del dialogo*. From the outset, Tasso moves in his treatment of the theory of mimesis to subvert Castelvetro's rationalistic argument that dialogue is a contradiction in terms by showing that the contradictions are those of Castelvetro's own theory, not dialogue itself.[48]

Tasso's opening move in his critique of Castelvetro, following the Aristotelian procedure of *diairesis*, is to separate the parts that are mixed together in the *"Poetica" d'Aristotele*. Mimesis, Tasso notes, is divided into "two chief kinds" since there are two principal objects of mimesis, namely "deeds" (*azioni*) and "discourses" (*parole*; pp. 18, 19). Since all mimesis imitates human experience, this twofold division also translates into a dichotomy between "active men" (*gli attivi*) and "speculative men" (*gli speculativi*; pp. 18, 19), between those who act and those who speak and reason.[49] Where Castelvetro takes dialogue to task because it is unsuited for the stage (and yet must, by virtue of its nonnarrative form, be performed on stage), Tasso contends that this confuses the object of one kind of mimesis with that of another kind of mimesis (that "of speeches and men who reason"; p. 19).[50] Castelvetro complains that dialogue does not successfully represent events and actions, although its mode—especially in Platonic dialogue—is most often that of tragedy and comedy; Tasso responds that dialogue does not principally imitate action at all, but rather "discourse," while freely admitting that "few deeds are performed without words and few discourses without activity, at least of the intellect" (p. 19).[51] And if discourse is the principal object of its representation, then dialogue can never be expected to represent the chance events of the world for its audience, as Castelvetro affirms that it should do, but only "scientific or artistic disputes" between those who are skilled in the arts of discourse. To expect dialogue to have the same object of representation as tragedy is to misunderstand the fundamental difference between the two kinds of literary writing, Tasso implies, since "the things represented on the stage are actions or acts . . . [whereas] in a dialogue the principal object of imitation is a discussion, which needs no stage" (p. 23).[52] Tasso's

154 The Reasons for Asking

first goal is to steer dialogue away from the conceptual trap that Castelvetro has laid out for it by maneuvering his theory back onto the ground of an Aristotelianism integrating means, mode, and object of representation. Throughout the first part of his work, Tasso employs his critical acumen to seek out and destroy the (pseudo-)logic underlying the argument of the "*Poetica*" *d'Aristotele*, mainly by turning it back on itself. Referring obliquely to Castelvetro (one of the "modern writers," *tra' moderni*; pp. 18, 19) for the first and only time in his text, Tasso proceeds to cite almost word for word the tripartite division of the modes of dialogical representation formulated by Castelvetro (see the first section of this chapter for the passage in question).[53] He does so, however, only in order to contest the conclusions that *il Grammaticuccio* draws from that classification. Castelvetro argues that mimetic dialogue "may be set on stage and may be called 'dramatic,' since characters are introduced into it in order to discourse *dramatikos*, that is, in action, as is commonly done in tragedies and comedies." Since the mimetic mode is common to tragedy, comedy, and this kind of dialogue and since there is action in the latter insofar as the characters speak *in atto* without the open intervention of a narrator, Castelvetro deduces that such dialogues may also be staged, like tragedies and comedies, and in fact achieve perfection only in this way.[54] For Tasso, however, this mistakes the mode of mimesis for the object of mimesis; the entire thrust of his critique of Castelvetro is based on the premise that human action is found in dialogue only as a (secondary) object of representation, never *in* the design of the representation itself (which is a text and not an act), as Castelvetro claims. "Presentation on stage seems inappropriate [*non si conviene*] for any dialogue," he objects, "since things represented on stage are actions or acts, and are therefore called plays or dramatic representations" (p. 23), whereas—as we have already seen—all dialogue represents primarily what is not an action or an act in this sense, but rather a scene of speaking.[55]

Castelvetro concludes from his analysis of the dialogical modes that dialogue is a fundamentally flawed form of literary discourse and should become either tragedy or comedy instead.

Tasso turns the tables on his opponent by returning once again to his initial hypothesis of a division between the "two chief kinds" of mimesis. Although it is true that Plato's dialogues may be termed tragic (*Crito, Phaedo*), comic (*Symposium*), or tragicomic (*Menexenus*), Tasso admits, they are still dialogues rather than tragedies or comedies; their tragic or comic aspect is a part of their semantic mode, rather than their generic affiliation. "The fact remains that dialogues are called tragic or comic only by analogy; tragedies and comedies, properly understood, imitate actions, but dialogues imitate discussions and participate in the tragic and the comic only insofar as they deal with actions" (p. 21).[56] Such actions might include, say, Socrates drinking the bowl of hemlock at the end of the *Phaedo* or the rowdy behavior of the drunken Alcibiades in the *Symposium* (p. 21). Castelvetro's classificatory logic likens dialogue to drama by virtue of their common mode of non-narrative mimesis and mutual affinity for action; Tasso reverses it by differentiating the mode from the object of the dialogical representation and then leading his analysis back to the original binary opposition between "discourse" and "action" put forward at the beginning of his discussion of the problem. Although agreeing with Castelvetro that dialogue imitates both action and discourse, Tasso insists that action is always at most a supplement to discourse in dialogue and can never supplant it as the principal object of representation, for the reasons that he has already outlined. In restoring the object of mimesis to a position of central importance in his own analysis of dialogue, Tasso is far closer to the sense of the *Poetics* than is Castelvetro, who chooses to ignore Aristotle's argument that the object of representation is a constituent part of tragedy on which its quality depends (*Poetics* 6, 1450a8–14). Plato's dialogues, and the tradition of philosophical dialogues to which Tasso sees himself an heir, are thus salvaged from Castelvetro's blanket condemnation of the dissonances of dialogical form; and the works of Plato figure prominently in virtually all of Tasso's subsequent theoretical treatment of dialogue.

Tasso's is a deeply organicist notion of dialogue, since for him its form and theme (or object of mimesis) fit together flawlessly in a harmony of the parts of poetic representation. Dialogue imitates/represents a reasoned discussion, just as the figure of dialogism imitates/represents an exchange between speakers. The poetics of dialogue studies the complex but essentially harmonic orchestration of forms of content and discursive strategies that results in an organic and unified textual representation. As we have seen, whatever action there is in dialogue (whether it occurs in description or in narration) "is more or less an adjunct to the discussion" (p. 21). This, Tasso infers, means that "if the action were removed . . . dialogue would not lose its form" (pp. 21, 23).[57] Moreover, what is "essential" rather than "accidental" (p. 23) for dialogue and allows it to assume its true form in the first place are "the things discussed" (*le cose ragionate*; p. 22) in the exchange between speakers, not just its dialogical mode. Sigonio and Castelvetro both tend to privilege strictly formal criteria as far as possible (though very different ones) in making distinctions between dialogues. Tasso, on the other hand, takes the position that "the essential distinctions [*differenze*] between types of dialogue derive from the discussions themselves and from the problems contained within them—from the things discussed, that is, not only from the modes of discussing them" (p. 23).[58] He thus once again shows a more profound understanding of the *Poetics* than Castelvetro, for Aristotle emphasizes above all else the *mimēsis praxeōs* ("imitation of praxis") in the making of fiction.[59]

This form-giving *ousia*, or essence, of all dialogue is always a proposition (*quistione*), Tasso remarks, an idea derived from Sigonio's *De dialogo liber*. However—and this same gesture is repeated a number of times in the *Discorso dell'arte del dialogo*—Tasso reverses a key part of Sigonio's argument by adding that "the subject of debate can be infinite [*la quistione infinita*] . . . or finite [*la finita*]—[like] the question of what Socrates should do once he has been condemned to death" (p. 23).[60] Discussions in dialogue may be directed either toward "speculative" or "contemplative" questions, which are nearly always infinite, on the one hand, or problems of "civil and moral" (*civili e costumati*) action, which may be either finite or infinite, on the other hand.[61] Dialogues may, in other words, investigate either ethical or epistemological questions: "If they are directed toward actions, they deal with choosing and avoiding, if toward contemplative matters, with knowledge [*la scienza*] and truth [*la verità*]" (p. 23).[62] Whereas Sigonio insists that the proposition of a dialogue must always be necessarily infinite or indefinite, rather than topical or casuistic, Tasso counters that dialectical dialogue can discuss either kind of proposition, and thus he allows a far greater spectrum of subjects than Sigonio is willing to. This is the first hint of the more radically open design for dialogue, and for dialectic as well, that Tasso has in mind for his theory.

Tasso's notion of the "two species" (*le due spezie;* pp. 25, 26) of dialogue demonstrates that he is no more immune than his contemporaries to the late Renaissance cultural myth of a calculus of rules (governing literary classifications, the codification of *comportamento,* and the like). That is not its only significance, however. By making the ethical or epistemological drift of the discussion ("the problems contained within them") the basis of classifying all dialogues, Tasso implicitly argues that there is no other fundamental difference between the various forms of dialogue. All structural differences are (unlike semantic ones) accidental, and all dialogues share the same invariable textual structure of question and answer. Tasso is far less interested in rationalizing the formal properties of mimetic and diegetic dialogue than are Speroni and, to a lesser degree, Castelvetro and Sigonio. All dialogues are in his view grounded in speculative problems or ethical cases, and the most urgent task for theory is to define dialogue's approach to those problems and cases. For Tasso, dialogues always possess a definite philosophical dignity, even if they treat opinion instead of truth (Lucian, for example, is mentioned only briefly in the text of the *Discorso dell'arte del dialogo,* and comic and satirical dialogues are never discussed). Although he insists that dialogues are works of fiction subject to the laws of poetics and are not to be confused with philosophy itself, they nevertheless originate in a confrontation with the epistemological or ethical dimensions of a given problem or a given case. Dialogues are fictional texts that are inextricably entangled and compromised with what is paradoxically *not* fictional.[63] How Tasso tries to develop this insight into a theory of dialogue as a flexible instrument of investigation, without ignoring the fictional nature of the dialogical text, can be understood only by a closer look at what he defines as the thought-content of dialogue.

One of Tasso's continuing concerns as a literary theorist and critic, from his first theoretical works to the composition of the *Discorso dell'arte del dialogo* in 1585, is the concept of *mythos* or "plot." For Tasso, as for most others of his age who tried to interpret the *Poetics*, the key to the success or failure of a given work of literary mimesis is found in the degree of unity of its *mythos*.[64] When he remarks in the *Discorsi* that "by 'plot' [*favola*] I mean the form of the poem, which can be defined as the interweaving or composition of its events,"[65] Tasso means that the form of the poem constitutes a single unified action composed of a sequence of different events. Removal of any event, however, would destroy the unity of the *mythos*: every segment of the plot is necessary to the overall esthetic effect of the work.[66] Here the same question arises that Sigonio faces in *De dialogo liber*: How can unity be established in dialogue, which—although it is a representation of thought and experience (moral and mental life) —is not a tragedy and does not have a plot except in the most abstract possible sense? How can all the narrative segments of dialogue be interwoven into a single organic tissue if what is imitated is only discourse and not action? Tasso, following Sigonio's lead and paraphrasing Aristotle in the *Poetics*, proposes the following solution: "What the plot is to a poem, moreover, the subject of debate [*quistione*] is to a dialogue: its form and, as it were, its soul. And just as a plot must possess unity, so, too, must the subject about which questions [*problemi*] are raised in a dialogue" (p. 25).[67] Like Sigonio, Tasso understands the proposition or *quistione* to function as the equivalent of the plot of dialogue (that is, as its form-giving *ousia*). If dialogue is to succeed as a work of mimesis, in his eyes, it cannot represent a random process of slippage from one topic to the next: the discussion must be ordered and organized by the proposition that it first takes up, rather than simply by the rhetorical figure of dialogism (question and response).

The form (the "soul") of any given dialogue derives chiefly from the *quistione* that it contains; the only structural differences between dialogues are based on the individual configuration of the proposition, which always serves as a center for the dialogical web of words.[68] *Inventio* takes priority over *dispositio* in the writing of dialogue, since the ordering of the actions in a poem is contingent on the prior choice of appropriate poetic material.[69] The *quistione* is therefore the first and single most important of the four parts of the dialogical imitation to be treated in the *Discorso dell'arte del dialogo*. Given his general esthetic principles of order and harmony, Tasso's theoretical concern in his analysis of the *quistione* as the central structuring component of dialogue is the unity and integrity of the *quistione*, which it is in turn to impart to the whole of the text. Disputation concerning the *quistione* begins in difference, which generally takes the form of an affirmation followed by the contrapuntal positing of doubt; this in turn results—if the speakers in the dialogical scene are willing to cooperate—in a series of questions and answers. Doubt in dialogue, as Tasso understands it, is not systematic (unlike Cartesian doubt) but simply a condition of its discursive operation: "In every debate, some points are conceded, whereas about others doubts are raised that lead to a disputation in the form of questions and answers" (p. 25).[70] And when something can be or is doubted by speakers, the question of truth is necessarily introduced into the discussion. The asking of questions, which is the basis of the writing of the scene of speaking, always has a specifically cognitive dimension, given that, as Tasso has already established, this kind of questioning occurs in the context of extraordinary rather than ordinary conversations, or specialized "disputations" (*dispute*) rather than "discussions" (*ragionamenti*).

The kind of writer who deals most of all with the art of asking questions, whether they lead to further doubts or (eventually) to probabilities, Tasso observes, is the dialectician: "Because questioning is the particular business of the dialectician, it seems that he is the one who ought to undertake to write dialogues" (p. 25).[71] As for Sigonio, dialogue is the province (or *impresa*) of the dialectician, who explores a given *quistione* for a probable opinion in the form of a syllogism. Dialogue, "since questioning is properly the activity of the dialectician" (p. 27), is dramatically different from all works of mimesis in verse (for syllogisms and inductions, the tools of the dialectician, cannot be suitably expressed in verse, Tasso notes).[72] Furthermore, although all dialogue in general can be said to be a representation of a *ragionamento*, or discussion, dialectical dialogue is alone "an imitation of a dialectical disputation" (p. 29), and the dialectician uses the strategies of mimesis without ever abandoning the art of dialectic for a pure poetic discourse of tropes and figures.[73]

Questions may be asked in dialogue, however, only if they produce "unity in the affirmation or denial" (p. 25). If a question asks "one thing about several subjects or several things about one subject" (p. 25), the unity of the dialogical structure would be threatened by the plurality of possible responses.[74] The procedure of dialogical questioning, if it were to be opened up into a quodlibet, would—as Tasso observes elsewhere—"produce indeterminacy" and destroy the organic form of the work.[75] As long as the *quistione* itself is a unified proposition, this problem is avoidable, since "about a thing that does . . . form a unity . . . there can be . . . [only] a single answer or question" (p. 27). "A dialectical question, then," he notes, "is a request for an answer [*una dimanda della risposta*], an answer that either affirms a proposition or contradicts it" (p. 27).[76] One does not speak carelessly or casually in dialogue, but carefully and cunningly instead; 'to dialogue' means to think while talking, and to do so as astutely as possible (Tasso's theory, in this respect, is the opposite of Bembo's concept of dialogue as a discontinuous *asolare*). The key to the art of dialogue consists in questioning, not in answering, insofar as the question—when formulated in a fully dialectical way—presupposes that a certain answer or certain answers must follow: all true questions, in dialogue, must be *answerable* ones. The highest degree of rigor in questioning in dialogue, and thus the highest degree of organic unity in its representation, is found in dialectical dialogue (which imitates a *disputa* rather than a *ragionamento*).[77]

Tasso's argument in the *Discorso dell'arte del dialogo* concerning dialectical questioning is heavily indebted to Aristotle's ideas on dialectic, in particular in the *Prior Analytics* and the *Posterior Analytics*.[78] Yet—and again this is typical of Tasso's procedure in his treatise—he combines his essentially Aristotelian notion of dialectic with the Platonic device of Socratic questioning as if there were an established and unproblematic continuity between the two.[79] The art of dialectical questioning, Tasso asserts, "consists principally in the kind of questioning that Socrates uses so cleverly in the books of Plato" (p. 29), but his treatise on dialogue betrays no anxiety over the sharp divergence between Plato's and Aristotle's approaches to the system of dialectic.[80] Such a discontinuity between the twin pillars of ancient philosophy is outside Tasso's cultural horizon, with its presuppositions of syncresis and organicity, and so goes unnoticed by him. For him the integrity and authority of the Greek tradition function as a guarantee—although by no means the only one—of the correctness of contemporary Renaissance esthetic theory, and that tradition must therefore be understood as an organic whole in its own right. As a result, after both Speroni and Castelvetro have downgraded Plato's dialogues in different ways, Tasso restores Plato to a place alongside Aristotle in the philosophical pantheon. In assimilating Platonic dialectic to Aristotelian dialectic, Tasso demonstrates his sense of the culture of antiquity as a fixed repertoire of texts and images that do not stand in a truly dynamic, or differential, relationship to each other. They are not situated in a historical process of becoming (where Aristotle's works might be read as a critique of Platonic philosophy); rather, they serve the synthesizing mind of the late Renaissance theorist as a potentially infinite *combinatoire* of more or less equally valid, noncontradictory, and authoritative arguments.[81]

The power to pose questions about knowledge distinguishes dialogue from the demonstrative treatise favored by so many philosophers and scientists. For Tasso, "the proposition to be discussed in a dialogue is one side of a contradiction" (p. 27), just as it is in a demonstration. Whereas demonstrative logic affirms this proposition ("one who is conducting a demonstration does not ask but rather asserts"; p. 27) as the correct side of a contradiction, the "dialectical proposition treats a contradiction *as a question*" (p. 27; my italics).[82] Demonstration (*apodeixis*) asserts rather than doubts; dialogue questions but does not prove; but both are, Tasso implies, equally legitimate forms of discoursing about knowledge. Even if philosophy and analytic are superior to dialectic itself as epistemological procedures, the treatise does not rank higher than dialogue in the hierarchy of late Renaissance kinds of writing. And once this is acknowledged, Tasso is able to make a far-reaching claim—in the form of a syllogism—for dialogue: "If a syllogistic question is the same as a proposition and if propositions figure in every kind of knowledge, then *every kind of knowledge must admit questions*" (p. 27; my italics).[83] Whatever may be treated by demonstration may also be treated by dialogue (that is, by dialectic), even if the end results are not always the same, since both have the same right to consider and discuss propositions. Unlike Sigonio or Castelvetro, Tasso understands dialogue to be a legitimate mode of investigation of any and every kind of knowledge, free of all constraint, even if it always poses doubts and questions about what it examines. According to him, all branches of knowledge are inscribed in the logic of syllogistic propositions and the questions that can be asked about them, and hence all admit the possibility of contradiction; there is no art, no science, no discipline of thought, whose premises cannot be probed in a scene of speaking. The chance that error as well as truth will emerge in this process of interrogation does not concern Tasso in the least, for dialogue is not a search for absolute truths as much as it is a testing of opinions and arguments or, in other words, *forms* of reasoning.[84]

Tasso's project for late Renaissance dialogue in the *Discorso dell'arte del dialogo* is that of restoring literary and philosophical prestige to the activity of questioning (and doubting). The ultimate goal of this project is to prevent dialectic—with its great classical and humanist heritage—from becoming separated and isolated, in the waning years of the sixteenth century in Italy, from the principal discursive modes of inquiry concerning knowledge. His theory maps out a defense of the value of dialectic, and of the fictional and rhetorical arts that accompany it, by exalting the role of dialogue in the production and articulation of probable knowledge.[85] In order to achieve this end, dialectic has to be reintegrated into the art of dialogue, whose origins in ancient philosophy and literature legitimate such a synthesis:

Dialogues can be written about arithmetic, geometry, music, and astronomy, as well as about moral, natural, and divine philosophy; in all the arts and in every kind of knowledge questions can be asked and consequently dialogues can be written. Of this, perhaps, there would be no doubt at all if the dialogues written by Aristotle were extant today, but if we read those of Plato, which are full of propositions touching every kind of knowledge, we shall be able to grasp the same point clearly enough. (p. 27)[86]

With this sweeping claim (verified by Plato's and Aristotle's own respective dialogical practices that treat "every kind of knowledge"), Tasso elevates dialogue—and, together with it, the project of questioning, doubting, asking, and interrogating—to a central position among the possible modes of human cognition. He can do so because for him dialogue occupies a position at the intersection of mimesis and dialectic that makes it, although still a fiction, something more than a search for verisimilitude and decorum and that protects it from ever being cut off completely from its cognitive function (for "in all the arts and in every kind of knowledge questions may be asked and consequently dialogues may be written").[87] Although reminiscent to a degree of Sigonio's *De dialogo liber*, Tasso's strategic defense of the merger of the literary and dialectical arts has a more radical aim, and a more intricate design, than that of his former teacher.

Although acknowledging that "writing dialogues is more appropriate for [the dialectician] . . . than for anyone else" (p. 27), such as natural scientists or mathematicians who deal directly with truth itself, Tasso never backs down from this exaltation of the position of dialogue in the *Discorso dell'arte del dialogo*. He points out that mathematics is, for example, not really a suitable subject for dialogue at all, since mathematical and dialogical propositions differ fundamentally in their convertibility. If the true (*il vero*) could be derived only from the true, and the false (*il falso*) only from the false, then "propositions and their consequences would necessarily be convertible" (p. 29), and all dialectic in dialogue would be relegated to the purely ornamental role of providing the intellectual pleasure that comes from a scene of speaking.[88] But mathematics alone tends to work in this way, Tasso argues, since its propositions "exclude accidents and therefore differ from the propositions in dialogues" (p. 29).[89] The accidental quality of dialogical propositions denies them the kind of absolute logical coherence possessed by mathematical propositions (the possibility of noncontradiction), yet this hardly strikes Tasso as a major flaw in dialectical dialogue. On the contrary, what appeals to him in *i parlari dialettici*, or dialogues, is the intellectual challenge posed by the difficulty of discovering the most probable resolution of a contradiction, while creating a unified textual representation. He notes that, as Aristotle says in the *Posterior Analytics*, it would be "easy" (*facile*; p. 28) to do so if it were impossible to derive the true from the false. Since, however, this is not the case in dialogical propositions, we should appreciate as challenging, but no less legitimate than other kinds of discourse, dialectical dialogue's search for the resolution of a contradiction, whether in "moral, natural, or divine philosophy" (p. 27), while encountering numerous obstacles and "accidents" along the way.

In a sense, one advantage of dialogue is that it is more open in recognizing the problematic elements of the process of cognition than is logical demonstration (which asserts but does not ask questions).[90] A high degree of difficulty is inherent in the kind of dialogue that imitates a dialectical disputation (and not just a discussion), since it must discover, out of a multiplicity of possible statements and responses, the tightly dialectical unity of both the *quistione* and the sequence of questions and answers concerning it. Dialectic is therefore not an ornament in dialectical dialogue, Tasso contends, but rather a basic condition for its textual representation and for the success of its cognitive project. The writing of a truly dialectical dialogue tries the skill of the dialectician, the philosopher, or the poet in the testing and discovery of true syllogisms through the composing of questions: good writing, in Tasso's view, always has its origins in sound and systematic thinking. The intrinsic challenge to writers found in both its *inventio* and *dispositio* makes dialogue, in Tasso's eyes, a litmus test for the truly complete intellectual, who must master both the techniques of dialectical thinking and dialogical writing (*l'artificio del bene scrivere*).

Tasso observes that, even if there are only two possible kinds of subjects (*quistioni*) for dialogue, there are in fact four kinds of disputation that can be represented in dialogue: didactic, dialectical, probative, and contentious (p. 29).[91] Plato certainly uses all four kinds of dialogue, and Aristotle may well have done the same in the lost *logoi exōterikoi* (p. 29). Since "the dialectical is not the only kind of disputation that can be imitated in dialogues" (p. 29), it follows that Plato is not just a dialectician but a dialogist as well, for he writes in different *generi* (p. 28) or *maniere* (p. 28) of dialogical imitation.[92] Tasso hastens to add that the device of Socratic questioning, whether didactic (maiuetic) or dialectical (peirastic), distinguishes the most praiseworthy kinds of dialogue, such as the *Hipparchus*. He shows practically no interest in the other two non-dialectical kinds of dialogue in the *Discorso dell'arte del dialogo* and never mentions them again in the rest of the work. Furthermore, he criticizes Cicero's use of the opposite device in the *Partitiones oratoriae*, where the questioning comes from "the learner rather than the teacher" (p. 31).[93] Tasso decides (going against the evidence of what is known of Aristotle's role in his exoteric dialogues, in order to maintain a full continuity between Plato and Aristotle) that this is the telling distinction between the Greek and Latin styles of dialogue: "It appears that the device of having the learner do the questioning, which Possevino and other Peripatetics use, *perhaps because it is easier*, derives from Cicero and is properly Roman. It is not as [praiseworthy] as the other device, however, and was not, as far as I can remember, used by the ancients [the Greeks]" (p. 31; my italics).[94] The chief difference between these modes of questioning is, then, as Tasso himself says, that the latter is "easier" (*più facile*) than the former.

   This marks another turn in the *Discorso dell'arte del dialogo* away from Sigonio's theory of dialogue, which favors didactic *expositio* over other modes of questioning.[95] Tasso values the difficult nature of the device of Socratic questioning over the didactic mode of the *Partitiones oratoriae* because the former is a greater test for the *ingegno* of the dialogist and also is an integral part of Greek philosophical culture, which in his view is superior to Roman rhetorical culture.[96] Cicero, the greatest of the Latin dialogists, comes closest to the "art of the Greeks" in works such as the *Tusculanae disputationes*, in which he "raises questions in the manner of the Greeks" and uses "the old Socratic method of disputing another person's opinion" (pp. 31, 33)—in other words, in those dialogues in which he imitates Plato, not those in which his style is overtly *scolastico* (p. 30).[97] Tasso is skeptical of the utilitarian value of expository dialogue, where doctrine is divulged to the reader in a manner meant to make it easier to understand. On the contrary, true dialogue is always Socratic dialogue: the unity of its questioning is something that is to be carefully created in the course of the dispute by whoever assumes the role of Socrates, not apparently left to chance by letting the naive and undisciplined interlocutor carry out the questioning. Only in this way can dialogue challenge the reader to rise to the level of Socrates's (or his equivalent's) understanding. Socratic dialogue corresponds in the *Discorso dell'arte del dialogo* to a literary and esthetic ideal of *acutezza*, of which affirming by questioning (*l'affermare domandando*) is one of the highest and most creative modes of textual expression.[98] The ghost that lingers in expository dialogue—the ritual catechistic rhetoric of the scholastic *quaestio*—is thus completely exorcised in Tasso's theory of dialogue, which subordinates all dialogical writing to the technique of Socratic irony.[99]

Tasso concludes his discussion of the *quistione* with a brief description, derived largely from Sigonio's treatise, of the history of the genre of dialogue. At the pinnacle of Greek dialogue, which stands above all Latin and vernacular dialogue, Tasso sets Plato: "Of all the Greek dialogues those of Plato are the most worthy of praise, for they surpass the others in art, subtlety, insight, elegance and variety of conceit, and verbal ornament" (p. 33).[100] Although his version of the history of dialogue is wholly conventional, this list of the qualities of Plato's dialogues signals a transition to the final phase of Tasso's theory. The superiority of Plato's dialogues over all others results not merely from their dialectical structure of argumentation, or the ironic/demonic role played by Socrates in the scene of speaking, or the doctrines of ethics, metaphysics, politics, and so forth that the characters expound in them. The true measure of their excellence is found in their "elegance," "variety of conceit," and "verbal ornament," as well as in the "subtlety" and "insight" of Socrates's arguments; their excellence lies, in other words, as much in their specifically literary traits as in the dialectical unity of their subject matter. With the addition of these literary criteria to his theory, Tasso arrives at his famous description of the writer of dialogue: "The writer of a dialogue must be an imitator no less than the poet; he occupies a middle ground between poet and dialectician. No one performs this imitation or expresses the art of . . . dialogue better than Plato" (*lo scrittore del dialogo deve imitarlo non altramente che faccia il poeta; perch'egli è quasi mezzo fra 'l poeta e 'l dialettico. E niun meglio l'imitò e meglio l'espresse di Platone;* pp. 32, 33). Tasso's figure for the position of the dialogist—*quasi mezzo fra 'l poeta e 'l dialettico*—captures the conceptual tension running through the *Discorso dell'arte del dialogo* and brings it into focus.[101] Nor is this choice of figure by any means accidental or casual. In his *Discorsi del poema eroico* (published in 1594, although composed over a long period of time), Tasso remarks that "we are advised [by Demetrius] to change dangerous metaphors into images, as we easily can by adding the particle *quasi* [as if]."[102] The danger of which Tasso speaks is that of the too daring or farfetched metaphor; if the metaphor is transmuted into a simile by adding *quasi*, its daring metaleptic quality may safely be diminished.

The question that this raises for our reading of the *Discorso dell'arte del dialogo* is Why does Tasso consider the phrase *lo scrittore del dialogo è* . . . *mezzo fra 'l poeta e 'l dialettico* to be daring or even perilous? What risk would he run by positioning dialogue directly between dialectic and mimesis, and why does he feel compelled to use a simile to guard against taking such a risk and to keep the position of dialogue deliberately ambiguous? If the writer of dialogue is neither exactly a poet nor exactly a dialectician, but *quasi mezzo fra 'l poeta e 'l dialettico*, then the terrain of the theory of dialogue is this potentially dangerous middle ground between fictional and dialectical discourse.[103] Tasso first must explain in detail the nature and function of the kind of literary language that Plato and his followers use in dialogue, however, if his theory is to define the borders of this no-man's-land where the figural and the dialectical cross over into each other's domain.

Lexis is not the only other qualitative part of dialogue besides *mythos*, Tasso acknowledges, but he evinces practically no interest of his own in discussing either *dianoia* (thought) or *ethos* (character), brushing both aside with the remark "those who are involved in discussing and disputing will [necessarily] reveal both their opinions and their character" (p. 33).[104] Tasso's cursory treatment of thought and character in dialogue at first appears puzzling; the *Poetics*, after all, analyzes at least the latter at some length (in chapter 15), although Aristotle does no more than refer his readers to the *Rhetoric* for an analysis of *dianoia* as "all the effects to be produced by the language [*logos*]" (*Poetics* 19, 1456a36–37). Sigonio in *De dialogo liber*, moreover, gives considerable attention to the role played by *ethos* (or decorum) in dialogue. Although recognizing the necessary existence of *dianoia* and *ethos*,[105] Tasso argues—against Sigonio and, to a certain degree, even against Aristotle—that neither one is truly theorizable in terms of a poetics of dialogue. In the *Discorso dell'arte del dialogo*, both may instead be subsumed under either *mythos* or *lexis*. Usually a part of rhetoric, thought (proof, refutation, solving problems, magnifying, diminishing, and the like) becomes, in Tasso's theory, a subcategory of the dialogical equivalent of the plot—namely, the *quistione*—out of which it develops, since the problem posed in dialogue is logically prior to the discussion of it. Character becomes, in his theory, an effect of both the *quistione* (which forces character to reveal itself in its choices) and the language (*lexis*) of the text.

Both *dianoia* and *ethos* are too contingent on the specific configuration of the *quistione* and the literary diction of a given dialogical text to be assigned universally valid rules and precepts of their own, apart from the general laws of mimesis. To define the rules for forming character and thought at any greater length would mean to risk rigidifying dialogue into an overly stylized, repetitive, and essentially unpoetic form, since the individual writer's power of invention of concrete verisimilar detail would be severely curtailed.[106] Tasso's theory of dialogue consistently defends dialogical writing against overcodification at the lexical and semantic levels, just as it defends the creative power of the dialogist against the contemporary tendency to prescribe specific norms for every aspect of the literary work. And this creative power, to which the production of both thought and character belong, presents itself in dialogue chiefly at the level of plot and diction. Alongside *mythos*, with its dialectical unity, Tasso elevates poetic *lexis* (*elocuzione*; p. 34) to a privileged position at the very center of his theory of dialogue, for "the writer of dialogue ought to resemble the poets in his expression and in his effort to make us see the things he describes" (p. 37).[107]

Tasso finds himself alone in his treatment of *lexis*, able to confront the ancients on the question without the mediation of other Renaissance theorists of dialogue.[108] Sigonio, after all, has little to say about dialogical *elocutio*, and neither Castelvetro nor Speroni devotes any substantial analysis to it. Yet the characters in dialectical dialogue both ask questions (*erotan*) and speak (*eirein*), and a complete theory of dialogue needs to take into account not only its mode of dialogism but also its mode of elocution.[109] Nor are these two separate issues for Tasso. The figural nature of dialogue is tied to the *quistione* and its dialectical exposition since there can be no dialectic without questions and answers, and there are no true dialectical questions (or answers) without insight and subtlety, which can in turn be expressed only through elegance, variety of conceit, and verbal ornament. A continual textual play of keen words and subtle wits is required so that dialectic may unfold in dialogue. Tasso does not, in short, consider style as something extrinsic to dialogical mimesis; *elocutio* is an organic part of the same unity that binds together dialectic and dialogue, giving the text its peculiarly literary density. Tasso's insight—that the figural is an irreducible component of all dialogues, even dialectical ones—leads him to treat dialogical *elocuzione*, or style, quite differently from all previous theorists of dialogue. If dialogue, as Plato and Cicero establish, imitates "the better kind of men" (p. 35), then it follows that in dialogue "the characters and everything else ought to be magnified rather than diminished" (pp. 35, 37).[110] Dialogical language should seek a stylistic grandeur (*grandezza*; p. 36) and magnificence that enhances the search for probable opinions and subtle truths. In imitating the kinds of discussions in which Socrates takes part, the dialogist ought to amplify (*auxesis*) or magnify (*accrescere*; p. 36) both characters and discourses rather than diminish them (*meiōsis*).

Taking Demetrius as his principal authority, Tasso argues that Plato's work is the outstanding example of the search for grandeur in the *lexis* of dialogue: no one else "occupies [the] middle ground between poet and dialectician" better than he. The poetic force of the Platonic style of *grandezza* is described by Tasso in the following terms:

> In his periods as in every [other part] . . . Plato strives for a greater eleva-
> tion than is sought by Xenophon and the other Greeks. Thus Xenophon
> uses images, but Plato audaciously [*pericolosamente*] employs metaphors
> instead. Plato resembles a man taking a walk through a dangerously
> slippery place; he pleases himself while at the same time exhibiting
> such daring as befits a sublime nature. It is said of him that he raises
> himself far above the pedestrian manner of speaking, that his speech is
> neither entirely like verse nor entirely like prose, and that he uses his
> wit as kings use power. In short, Plato seems to have eschewed no ver-
> bal ornament, no color of rhetoric, and no device of oratorical emphasis.
> (p. 37)[111]

Platonic dialogue is a balancing act on a slippery tightrope stretched between fiction and dialectic (*usa le metafore pericolosa-mente in luogo delle imagini . . . e somiglia colui il quale camina in luogo dove è pericolo di sdrucciolare*).[112] With the audacity and daring of their *elocutio*, Plato's dialogues continually violate the boundaries between conventional categories and classifications, so that they are "neither entirely like verse nor entirely like prose," but stand instead on a middle ground of their own making.[113] This is what accounts for their high degree of stylistic intensification, which is the attribute that makes them in Tasso's eyes such a unique kind of prose poetry.

   Here, as elsewhere, we find a notable divergence between Sigonio's and Tasso's theories of dialogue, approaches to lit-erature in general, and revaluation of classical literature in particular (Greek versus Roman). Tasso makes its high degree of stylistic (figural) intensification an essential component of the literariness of dialogue, whereas for Sigonio its organic form is already proof enough of its literary perfection. Tasso seeks to un-lock the secrets of dialogue as prose poetry: Sigonio limits him-self to the discovery and defense of dialogue's mimetic status. Although Plato neglects no *ornamento di parole*, no *color retorico*, and no *lume d'oratore* in the elaboration of his dialogues, his sty-listic bravura is neither merely decorative nor simply a demon-stration of his own *ingegno* (p. 36); nor is it part of an aimless textual play of tropes. Plato's poetic grandeur, his elevated style (or *hypsos*), his variety of conceit, his metaphors, and his use of rhetorical colors and lights all serve one particular purpose in his dialogues, which is "to make us see the things he describes" (*por le cose inanzi a gli occhi*; pp. 36, 37). The key to understanding the literary quality not only of Plato's dialogues but of all dialogue, and its interdependency with dialectic, is to be found here for Tasso, in the question of the visual power of its writing. The search for a greatly intensified figural language of dialogue is a search, in other words, for the figure of *enargeia*.[114]

Turning to Plato's *Protagoras*, Tasso comments that "when he tells us . . . that Hippocrates blushed in the dark, Plato adds, 'Day was already appearing, so the color in his cheeks could be seen.' Here the clarity—which Latin writers call 'evidence' [*evidenza*]—comes from the care [*cura*] used in expression" (pp. 37, 39).[115] *Evidentia* is a figure of accumulation that in classical and Renaissance rhetorical theory is often synonymous with the figure of *enargeia*, which for the Greeks meant "clarity" or "brightness." In both figures, a description of a person, place, or event is so vividly drawn, and so powerfully simulated, that the reader seems to see the thing described as if it were actually present. In its production of visual and sensual evidence, the figure of *evidentia* or *enargeia* is a kind of textual reconstruction of our experience of the world, similar to *hypotyposis* or *ekphrasis*.[116] Demetrius describes it as arising "from an exact narration overlooking no detail and cutting out nothing . . . no detail which usually occurs and then occurred is omitted" (*On Style* 4.209–10).[117] Tasso's own notion of the figure seems to derive in particular from the Ciceronian dictum *ponite ante oculos* (*por le cose inanzi a gli occhi*), one of the most enduring rhetorical commonplaces of all of sixteenth-century literature.[118]

Over and over again Tasso returns, in his treatment of dialogical *lexis*, to the power of visualization—developed through the use of figures of accumulation—that is found in Plato's dialogues.[119] Tasso lists a series of passages from Plato's works that contain figures of *enargeia* and thus amplify the vivid quality of the texts, such as the descriptions of Hippias on his throne, the eunuch slamming the door in Socrates's face (*Protagoras*), or Crito coming to the prison before daybreak to wait for the condemned

Socrates to wake up (p. 39). The persons, events, and objects in the works are set before the reader's eyes through the use of *enargeia* not just to capture the attention of the reader by dazzling and delighting with their brightness. *Enargeia*, in sixteenth-century Italian literary theory, is generally associated as well with the Aristotelian concept of the "concrete universal." [120] It is a figure of mimesis through particularization and through the creation of detailed concrete images. [121] *Enargeia* in dialogue is a poetic imitation of human experience, not just a textual ornament or embellishment. It therefore functions as an integral part of dialogical representation, according to Tasso's theory, and helps to explain why "the writer of dialogue must be an imitator no less than the poet." *Enargeia* serves in the *Discorso dell'arte del dialogo* as the equivalent of Sigonio's decorum (a term Tasso carefully avoids), but differs from it fundamentally in its lack of normative and prescriptive purpose.

As Tasso describes the consummate skill with which Plato employs *enargeia* in his dialogues, a pattern emerges in his own critical rhetoric: "And in the same dialogue we read with *marvelous delight*"; "and we read with *incredible pleasure*"; "nothing could fill us with more compassion and *wonder*"; "the description of this scene is also *marvelous*"; "such are the truly *marvelous* perfections of Plato" (pp. 39, 41; my italics). [122] Readers familiar with Tasso's other theoretical and critical writings may at first be misled by the language of this passage. For the marvelous, in Tasso's usual usage, "derives from actions that exceed human power," as in Canto 18 of the *Gerusalemme liberata* (the episode of Rinaldo and the *selva incantata*). [123] Although the marvelous (*il maraviglioso*) is an essential part of Tasso's own epic poetry and poetics, in the *Discorso dell'arte del dialogo* the term denotes a sense of imaginative wonder instead. The passages from Plato's dialogues depicting Socrates toying with the locks of Phaedo's hair and Charmides sitting with his friends that Tasso cites with such admiration and ardor are marvelous not because they derive from actions that exceed human power, but because Plato's descriptive skill and the verisimilitude that it produces provoke a sense of *admiratio* in the reader. What Tasso finds to be marvelous in Plato's works is their vivid, lifelike quality as verbal visual images, which, when combined with the *grandezza* of Plato's stylistic technique, produces a magnified sense of delight akin to wonder in the reader (wonder being simply the greatest degree of delight for Tasso). Although he uses the term *sublime* only once in the *Discorso dell'arte del dialogo* (in discussing Plato's "sublime nature"; p. 37), his interest in the affective and elocutionary force of Plato's language and the terms that he uses to describe it (*maraviglioso diletto, piacer incredibile*) suggest that concepts of both elevation and sublimity—rather than the epic marvelous —are the basis of his notion of the esthetic effect of this sense of wonder.[124] Although Tasso, throughout the final part of his argument here, clearly owes his greatest debt to Demetrius's *On Style* (available to him in Vettori's translation)—in which the elevated style (2.36–127) is treated at length—there are suggestions in the treatise of a reading of Longinus as well. Dialogue must be not only a suitable intellectual experience for the reader, Tasso contends, but also a moving imaginative experience, and it is the evocative visual quality of *enargeia* that moves the reader to wonder and powerfully enhances the credibility of the work.[125]

Up to this point, Tasso has set his theory of dialogue largely within the structural limits of Aristotelian poetics, without recourse to concepts of the "reader" or the "audience" of the work (either in general or in particular), concepts that openly intersect with epideictic rhetoric. However, his treatment of *enargeia* closely resembles a theory of description, that is, epideictic rhetoric, operating in the sphere of quality instead of quantity (as it does in *De dialogo liber*).[126] Since *enargeia* serves not just to indicate objects, but to delight the reader by making them visible, Tasso's theory must attempt to account for the reader's pleasure and delight as a product of the elevated style of Plato's dialogues. This turn in his argument would seem, at first glance, to lead him one step closer to the more rhetorically oriented theories of his precursors. As it turns out, however, Tasso does not understand the reader's pleasure as an instrumental end of dialogue in the Horatian sense of *utile dulci*. Rather, like Castelvetro (and Aristotle), he sees it as an end in and of itself: the pleasure that figural language in dialogue produces in the mind of the reader has no specific utility.[127] Even if Plato's figures are at times truly sublime and deeply moving, they are present in his dialogues because *enargeia* is a requisite organic part of dialogical poetics, not because it has a strategic persuasive function to perform, Tasso explains. Since dialogue is a representation of "the better kind of men" (*i migliori*), it is only logical that this representation must "be magnified rather than diminished" (p. 37) by the figural language of the work.[128] The complete or perfect work of literary mimesis produces a noninstrumental esthetic pleasure of its own, and the grandeur of *enargeia* is what completes dialogue and thus makes it perfect by supplying us with that sense of pleasure. Tasso designates, in his theory of dialogue, a specific role for both the imagination and the *technē* of the poet, in addition to the skill of the dialectician. The text of any dialogue is a locus of affect, as well as of intellect, and must bear a double linguistic burden.

This theory of *enargeia* in dialogue might at first seem to contradict Tasso's assertion that dialogue imitates discourse rather than deeds. The passages from Plato's works mentioned in the final pages of the *Discorso dell'arte del dialogo* are by all appearances not images of discourse alone, since in one of them Socrates is depicted scratching his leg and in another one Protagoras is shown strolling about. There is, however, no contradiction between these two parts of Tasso's theory insofar as dialogue only principally (but not exclusively) takes discourse as its object of mimesis. Dialogue must always also represent the *costume* and the *sentenza* of the speakers if its mimesis is to be complete, and it may peripherally represent actions as well (since every dialogue is written in a tragic, comic, or tragicomic mode). The true contradiction in Tasso's theory of dialogue emerges, rather, in his efforts to discover and define a middle ground between dialectic (which is itself neither logic nor rhetoric) and fiction. In his pursuit of the unity of dialogue, Tasso makes it amply clear that dialogue is most appropriate for the dialectician and that the heart and soul of dialectical dialogue is a dialectical proposition concerning knowledge of any single kind. Without this dialectical content, philosophical dialogue is deprived of its most essential component and loses its organicity. Tasso repeatedly states, however, that all dialogue is a representation (mimesis) of a discussion or a disputation and that "we should have no more doubts about the view that the writer of dialogues is an imitator" (p. 41).[129] Furthermore, the search for stylistic grandeur and sublimity through figures of *enargeia* requires the writer of dialogue to employ both technical and imaginative resources of the highest literary order. Where, then, does this leave dialogue? In what discursive space and order is it inscribed if it is *quasi mezzo* between dialectic and poetic fiction? Aristotle's theories of dialectic and poetry hold them to be distinctly different arts of discourse: dialectic is a faculty of furnishing arguments and discovering probabilities, and its instruments are syllogism and induction (both real and apparent); poetry is instead mimesis, and its means of representation are rhythm and language and tune. Given the formidable differences between dialectic and mimesis, can dialogue be said to be (almost) equidistant from both of them?

One critic has recently argued that, in the terms of Tasso's own theory, dialogue is strictly a species of literary mimesis, no more and no less than is any other kind of fiction.[130] Tasso himself, however, steadfastly refuses to admit this in the *Discorso dell'arte del dialogo*. Although it is unthinkable for him that the middle ground that he seeks might not be in the middle at all and that in dialogue dialectical discourse might be impossible to distinguish from fictional discourse, his original simile—*quasi mezzo*—reveals an acute awareness of the problematic nature of his search. If dialogue is to be placed in the middle ground between dialectic and fiction, its use of *enargeia*, Tasso argues, must be restrained so that the dialectical quality of dialogue may fully emerge into view, without being disfigured by the presence of tropes and figures; at the same time, the predominantly fictional nature of dialogue as a scene of speaking must also be maintained in spite of its equally dialectical function. Tasso is in difficulty here, as the ambiguities of his language indicate. And although he does recognize the problem, he evades its full implications for his theory of dialogue. His dilemma—to explain how dialogue is to develop stylistic magnificence and grandeur, but in a way that does not interfere with its cognitive function— haunts the final pages of the treatise and accounts for the position of dialogue in his theory.

The following passage, better than any other, conveys the full dimensions of Tasso's dilemma: "If there is some part of . . .

dialogue to which the advice of Demetrius might be applied, however, it is the conduct of the disputation itself; there a purity and simplicity of style are fitting, for excessive ornamentation impedes argument and blunts, so to speak, insight and subtlety. But the other parts should be diligently ornamented" (p. 37).[131] It would not be too much to say that these words of Tasso's take us to the heart of the problem of dialogue for sixteenth-century Italian poetics. The advice of Demetrius—who is nothing if not a theorist of rhetoric—to which Tasso refers is that dialogue ought to have a simpler and far less periodic style than either oratory or history (p. 37). Tasso objects that neither Plato nor Cicero employs such a style in their own dialogues; they instead seek to achieve differing degrees of stylistic *grandezza* in their writings, as he has already shown. However, he adds, if there is a part of dialogue that should indeed have a "purity and simplicity of style," such as Demetrius advises, it is "the conduct of the disputation itself" (*quella [parte] nella qual si disputa*; p. 36), presumably meaning the part that he has elsewhere called the *quistione*.

Sigonio makes substantially the same argument in *De dialogo liber*, but he proposes a sequential arrangement of quantitative parts of dialogue in order to sustain a clear division between its figural and dialectical elements. Tasso never postulates such a dialogical *dispositio*, yet he follows Sigonio in proposing that the dialectical language of the disputation be kept free of figural elements that might interfere with the insight and subtlety of the statements by the speakers. The danger of having tropes and figures in the disputation, Tasso contends, is that the dialectical insight (*acume*) and subtlety (*sottilità*) of the speakers' statements may be "blunted," "dulled," "restrained," or even "repressed" (*rintuzzare*) by them. Figural language is both superfluous (*soverchio*) for the dialectical part of dialogue and an obstacle that "impedes" the development of the dialectical disputation. Dialogue, in short, should show that it is a middle ground between dialectic and mimesis, but as a site where both of them enhance— rather than interfere with—each other. However, Tasso's desire to limit the role of *enargeia* and to confine it to certain segments of the text conflicts with his equally strong desire to avoid any suggestion of a prescriptive, codified poetics based on a single ideal structure of writing. These two contrasting impulses define a double bind for Tasso that cannot be resolved within his theory without definitively advocating either the exclusively cognitive or the exclusively mimetic function of dialogue, something he is unable to bring himself to do.

Tasso's plight at the end of the *Discorso dell'arte del dialogo* is, for him, a dramatic one. In the *Poetics* (6, 1449b24–31), Aristotle makes it clear that the poet is to imitate by means of "language enriched with all kinds of ornament," each kind of which is to be used separately in the different parts of the work. In saying that some parts of dialogue "should be diligently ornamented" whereas others should not, Tasso would appear to follow the *Poetics* closely, at least, that is, until we realize that Aristotle speaks in terms of the need to ornament the different *quantitative* parts or narrative segments of the work (prologue, and so forth). Tasso instead seems to apply this same idea to the different *qualitative* parts of the work, for he always treats the *quistione* as the equivalent of plot in dialogue. This, however, makes little sense and would constitute a gross misunderstanding of the *Poetics* (something of which Tasso is rarely guilty).[132] If, on the other hand, he does mean that there are quantitative parts of dialogue, one of which is "the conduct of the disputation itself," he never says what they are or what sort of sequence they might constitute.

This is hard to construe as a simple error of omission rather than commission, given the skill with which Tasso constructs the rest of his theory. Perhaps he does not want to put forward a hard-and-fast structure of quantitative parts for his theory of dialogue either because Plato himself—who serves as Tasso's exemplum throughout—does not use a universal sequential narrative order of this sort or because Tasso is aware of Sigonio's indebtedness to ancient theories of public oratory in his own efforts to define such a structure, an indebtedness Tasso wants to avoid. At the same time, he finds himself—in his own theory of dialogue—without an effective means to fence off *enargeia* from the dialectical language of the scene of the speakers' agon. The net result would seem to be that he ends up making recourse in a backhanded way to the same strategy used by his teacher Sigonio in *De dialogo liber* in an attempt to keep dialectic and figuration apart, although Tasso's use of the term *parte* in the text of the *Discorso dell'arte del dialogo* makes it difficult to determine with precision what he is trying to argue. For he speaks not only of "some parts of the dialogue" (p. 37) and "the other parts" (p. 37) but concludes at the end of his treatise that in dialogue "one employs a style that is [in some parts] highly ornamented and [in others] very pure, as befits the *materia*" (p. 41).[133] What or where these parts are, however, is left entirely up to the reader to intuit. Tasso's uncharacteristically awkward attempt to elide the core problem of the theory of dialogue in this way is symptomatic of the quandary of a poetics of philosophical dialogue in late-sixteenth-century Italy.

Figures (*ornamenti*) repress and disrupt the dialectical subtlety and insight of the speakers' statements in the dialogical scene, for the latter always require great purity in their stylistic vehicle. Aristotle warns in the *Poetics* against using an overly elaborate *lexis* in the parts of the poem that reveal *ethos* or *dianoia*, for "too brilliant diction frustrates its own object by diverting attention from the portrayal of character and thought."[134] Tasso seems to transfer this observation about the ornamentation of character and thought to the plot of dialogue. As his repeated use of the term *purità* to describe the dialectical style suggests, *enargeia* is an obstacle to the transparency and purity of dialectic insofar as dialectic is contaminated by any contact with the intricacies of figure. Yet in spite of this, he also argues that *enargeia* is an essential element of all dialogue. The language of the dialectician is, in his eyes, one of simplicity and purity that cannot sustain metaphor; figural language is a linguistic detour standing in the way of the unveiling of the probable truth to be uttered in dialogue, but at the same time there can be no dialogical mimesis without the sense of delight and wonder produced by figures of evidence. Yet he refuses to prescribe point by point a narrative structure for dialogue, just as he refuses to codify its decorum, for he perceives the errors of reading the *Poetics* too literally in this regard and thus rejects any preset or prefixed order of parts except for the organizing nucleus provided by the plot itself. Tasso seeks a guarantee in his theory that dialectic will not become just another ornament or decoration in dialogue, caught up in a continuum of figures of *enargeia*, but this can be accomplished only by theorizing a fundamental binary division between a discourse of statements and a discourse of figures.[135] This would, obviously enough, place the notion of a hybrid dialogical middle ground in question. His theory of dialogue must therefore struggle to keep dialectical statement and *enargeia* from collapsing into each other because for him it is axiomatic that they belong to separate arts of discourse that yet, paradoxically, come together and complement each other in the dialogical text.[136]

This breakdown in Tasso's theory reflects more than the problems caused by his attempt to adhere to the Aristotelian system of arts and sciences in the late Renaissance. It points directly to the source of his dilemma over dialogue; namely, that this difference between statement and figure is what is put in question by dialogical representation. His hesitancy to define in his theory a figural frame surrounding dialectic speaks volumes about the difficulty of establishing the ground of difference between dialectical statement and figure in dialogue. The dialogist must write in a double register, using both the zero degree of dialectical style and magnificent figures of *enargeia*, but without confusing or conflating the two. Rather than explain how each could be kept from interfering with the other in the dialogical text, however, Tasso exalts the roles of dialectic and *enargeia* as if it were obvious to all that the art of *argutezza* and the *lexis* of the visible could not (as well as should not) coincide or collide in dialogue. That this is not so simple as it would seem is obvious from the inconsistencies in his argument, but he cannot face the problem in any other way. Thus, at last, the strategy behind Tasso's selection of a simile rather than a metaphor to describe the position of the dialogist—*è quasi mezzo tra 'l poeta e 'l dialettico*—begins to appear more clearly. The danger involved in trying to position dialogue between dialectic and figural language is that, in the process, there may emerge the groundless ground of dialogue that binds together the terms between which it is supposed to be suspended. The true position and the true space of dialogue must therefore be left hidden in the interstices of Tasso's theory.

Tasso's desire to defend the difference between *kinds of discourse* within the boundaries of the dialogical text and the difficulty into which it leads his theory define the essence of the problem posed by the liminal, or threshold, form of dialogue for all late-sixteenth-century theorists. Dialogue oscillates between dialectic and *enargeia*, *inventio* and *elocutio*, statement and figure, and this movement resists codification and control; Tasso's text shows that dialogue is founded on the reflexivity of these categories—a reflexivity that perpetually threatens to undermine the difference(s) between them.[137] Tasso's project as a late-sixteenth-century theorist of dialogue is to recuperate the heterogeneity of dialectic and description, or statement and figure, out of the hybrid textuality of dialogue. Such categories must stand in a relation of mutual exteriority within the syncretic dialogical text if his cultural program for the late sixteenth century is to be kept intact and if dialogue is to be an effective instrument for that program. Yet the text of the *Discorso dell'arte del dialogo* reveals —against the very claims that Tasso has staked out for dialogue —the illusory basis of this project. His initial insight that the figural is an irreducible component of all dialogues, even dialectical ones, leads his text to the second insight that the figural cannot be reduced to the other of dialectical statement, but instead necessarily coincides with it. Unlike Sigonio, however, Tasso can invent no fiction of structure to block out the disruptive effects of this second insight. The conceptual fissures in the *Discorso dell'arte del dialogo* indicate the precarious nature of any attempt to establish—within the constraints of late Renaissance literary theory—this relation of exteriority in dialogue between kinds of discourse and the categories on which they rely: Tasso's theory thus rehearses the crisis of sixteenth-century poetics in confronting dialogue and takes its answer to the very limits of that century's critical thought and desire.

FIVE

Illusions of Difference: The Poetics and Pragmatics of Dialogue After Tasso

> It has been remarked, my dear Hermippus, that though the ancient philosophers conveyed most of their instruction in the form of dialogue, this method of composition has been little practiced in later ages, and has seldom succeeded in the hands of those who have attempted it. . . . To deliver a system in conversation scarcely seems natural.
>
> David Hume,
> *Dialogues Concerning Natural Religion*

The theorists participating in the sixteenth-century problematization of dialogue in Italy offer competing versions of Renaissance dialogical writing but no one authoritative interpretive key to it. Moreover, such a key is unlikely to be discovered within the framework of late Renaissance poetics and esthetics. My readings of these works have attempted to show that it would be a self-deluded enterprise today to try to extract an ideal model of dialogue in sixteenth-century Italy from the texts produced in the problematization process: this is not, however, an indictment of that process itself. Although the aim of each text is to produce a certain kind of knowledge about dialogue in the form of a general theory of dialogical writing, its discoveries are inseparable from the positionality and figurality of its own theoretical discourse, and they cannot be used today in order to interpret the corpus of sixteenth-century philosophical dialogues without taking this fact into account as well.

A brief review of the past several chapters brings the defining traits of the Cinquecento dialogue on dialogue clearly to light. In *De dialogo liber*, Sigonio sought to limit the interference between the figural and the cognitive dimensions of dialogue in order to maintain a privileged dialectical function for the latter as a means of support for philosophy. In the *Apologia dei Dialoghi*, Speroni described dialogue as a fiction devoid of all philosophical claims, a "delightful garden" of error and eros where the writer—like an invisible and powerful demiurge—puts actors into play in the dialogical scene of speaking without taking sides in the exchange of views. In *La "Poetica" d'Aristotele vulgarizzata et sposta*, Castelvetro expelled dialogue outright from his theory of literature, for he found its position at the crossroads of fiction and dialectic to be hopelessly self-contradictory and illogical; dialogue must become either philosophy or poetry, but it cannot be both. By mandating a pure dialectical language in the dialogical scene, but with no means—short of prescribing a rigidly codified and mechanical narrative sequence (which he rejected)—to protect it from contamination by poetic figures, Tasso found himself caught in the end between his conflicting claims in the *Discorso dell'arte del dialogo* for dialogue as a legitimate genre both of fiction and of dialectical philosophy. This final chapter examines the solution offered by Baroque theorists in Italy to that impasse, a solution that resolves the problem of dialogue by ending the quest for an art of questioning, while bringing better into focus for us the contours of late Italian Renaissance literary theory and esthetics.

Following the death of Tasso, interest in Italy in the theory of dialogue—and in Aristotelian-oriented poetics in general—diminished but did not disappear entirely. The effervescent polemical climate of the second half of the sixteenth century generally gave way at the outset of the seventeenth century to a renewed emphasis on practical criticism of individual texts, leading away from the theoretical perspectives of the late Renaissance (the last major commentary on the *Poetics* in Italy was Paolo Beni's *In Aristotelis poeticam commentarii*, 1613). By the middle decades of the Seicento, theoretical concerns were once again uppermost in the minds of many Italian *letterati*, but these concerns were—as we shall see in the case of the theory of dialogue—quite different from those of the waning phase of the Renaissance. As a reinterpretation of the *Poetics* and as the systematic study of the basic textual units and relations of literary representation, poetics was displaced in seventeenth-century Italy on two related fronts. First and perhaps most obviously, the Baroque revival of the theory of tropes and figures restored rhetoric to its former position of preeminence among the arts of discourse, pushing the concerns of poetics into the background. Second, the concepts of system and method that the theorists and critics of the late Italian Renaissance found so compelling were dismissed—for reasons too complicated to be dealt with adequately here—from the field of literary theory and eventually came to be confined to the study of philosophy, the natural sciences, and mathematics.[1]

These events help to account, in the broadest cultural terms, for the declining sense of urgency about understanding dialogue's position between literature and philosophy that informed seventeenth-century literary theory in Italy. The problematization of dialogue, and the texts produced in that process, undeniably had an effect on subsequent Italian thinking about the form, but the history of a sustained and systematic answer to the problem of dialogue, in the sense defined in this book, ended with Tasso. Just as Petrarch's work did for the Renaissance, Tasso's opus served as the basic point of reference for the Baroque literary culture that followed (John Milton, for instance, is Tasso's most legitimate literary heir). Yet although seventeenth-century theorists of dialogue took his work as a common point of departure, they turned away from his insights as quickly as possible, opting for a quite different approach to dialogical writing—if a far less original one, from today's perspective. During this period, Italy itself was gradually relegated to a secondary role in the making of European culture, and neoclassical France emerged as the center of esthetic research in Europe into the representation of literary conversation, *entretien*, and so on—but that is another story, and another scene.

To see the conclusion of the problematization process in Italy in greater depth than such a broad overview can provide, however, the specific grounds of difference between the theorists of dialogue of the Cinquecento and those of the Seicento need to be defined. It would be beside the point to reconstruct here the entire chain of causes behind the disappearance of the Renaissance tradition of literary theory and criticism discussed in the previous chapters. Such a reconstruction would have to be either grossly synthetic or immensely encyclopedic in scope.[2] What follows is instead intended to serve as a *postilla* to the main body of this book; in it the closure of the question of dialogue, and the end of one particular version of Renaissance literary esthetics, is described through readings of the two major texts on dialogue produced in Baroque Italy. For my purposes, it is enough to bring out into the open the striking contrast between the sixteenth-century theorists of dialogue and their Baroque successors by confronting them directly with each other. This contrast is sharp and vivid, like the *chiaroscuro* effect of an early Seicento painting, and speaks eloquently about the shift in the overall direction of theoretical discourse in Italy, even though it says little that bears directly on the cultural, political, and socioeconomic transformations that provoked this shift. My aim in the following pages is to set these two contrasting groups of theories in a dialogical relationship of their own, in which the respective definitions of dialogue—when placed in direct competition with each other—struggle for mastery of the same terrain.

It would be convenient, but inaccurate, to suppose that the theory of dialogue took this new direction because the possibility of dialogue itself underwent a crisis in Italy in the seventeenth century due to the increasingly stifling cultural controls over writing exercised by Counter-Reformation authorities.[3] Granted, certain kinds of dialogue that figured prominently in the sixteenth century, such as philosophical dialogue, no longer held the same importance in either literary or philosophical circles. Outside the confines of "high" literature and philosophy, however, dialogue was still attractive to various groups of writers during the Seicento in Italy, as it was in other parts of Europe. The humanists who had revived dialogue and renewed the fame of the form had all but vanished by the beginning of the seventeenth century, but a significant number of Italian scientists chose to continue to write in dialogue form. Galileo's *Dialogo sopra i due massimi sistemi del mondo* is perhaps the outstanding example of this tendency, but many other such scientific dialogues were produced over the course of the century.[4] One need only look to other marginally literary modes of writing in Italy, such as the literature of libertinism (for example, Ferrante Pallavicino), or the *trattatistica* of such applied arts as fortification and irrigation, or travel narratives, for further confirmation of the survival of dialogical writing in the Seicento.[5]

The theories of dialogue that did appear in the first half of the seventeenth century—Giambattista Manso's *Del dialogo* (1628) and Pietro Sforza Pallavicino's *Trattato dello stile e del dialogo* (1646; revised edition, 1662)—make it clear that the crisis in the discourse on dialogue in Italy was related primarily to other factors. Both Manso and Pallavicino vigorously defended the practical value and esthetic nobility of dialogical writing in the Baroque age; indeed, they insisted that it should have far fewer restrictions than those assigned to it by the sixteenth-century theorists, and that it should thus play an even greater role in contemporary seventeenth-century Italian culture. However, although both Manso and Pallavicino referred to the *Discorso dell'arte del dialogo* and deferred to Tasso's authority, they broke sharply with the basic premises of Tasso's poetics and with those of his predecessors. Their quarrel was not with dialogue itself; rather, it was with the sixteenth-century way of thinking not only about the problem of dialogue but also about the very function and nature of literature. Why this occurred, however, can be fathomed only through a close look at the seventeenth-century theories and the new stakes for dialogue that they sought to define.

G. B. Manso on the Benefit of Dialogue

Giambattista Manso (ca. 1560–1645) was a wealthy nobleman and a prominent patron of the arts and letters in Naples during the late sixteenth century and the first half of the seventeenth century.[6] In his youth he fought in the service of both the Savoia dynasty and the Spanish viceroyalty, but he eventually withdrew from military life to lead a patrician's existence in his villa overlooking the Bay of Naples. By the beginning of the Seicento, Manso was probably the single most influential and powerful figure in his native city after the resident Spanish viceroy himself. He founded the Accademia degli Oziosi in Naples in 1611, and he actively promoted the establishment of the Collegio de' Nobili for the education—under the direction of the Jesuits—of young Neapolitan aristocrats. He was the author of a book of poems (*Poesie Nomiche*, 1635), two collections of dialogues (*I paradossi, ovvero dell'amore*, 1608, and *Erocallia, ovvero dell'amore e della bellezza*, 1628), and a number of other prose works, of which the best-known today is the *Vita di Torquato Tasso* (1619), the first biography of the poet. This *coltissimo cavaliere*— as the eighteenth-century literary historian Girolamo Tiraboschi called him—knew a great many of the leading Italian *letterati* of the age. He numbered among his acquaintances Paolo Beni (the influential literary critic and theorist), Giambattista Della Porta, Antonio Bruni, Tommaso Campanella, Torquato Accetto, Galileo Galilei, and many other writers, artists, and philosophers up and down the peninsula; and his circle in Naples itself included practically all major figures of the city's literary life.[7] He was, moreover, the friend and benefactor of both Torquato Tasso and Giambattista Marino, perhaps the two most important Italian poets of Manso's lifetime.

Manso befriended Tasso during the poet's troubled period of wandering after his release from confinement in Ferrara; a grateful Tasso dedicated a dialogue on friendship, entitled *Il Manso ovvero dell'amicizia* (1594), to him. One of Tasso's nineteenth-century biographers, Angelo Solerti, found Manso's account of their relationship in the *Vita di Torquato Tasso* to be often "not very credible," but he did not doubt the sincerity of Manso's admiration for Tasso.[8] Manso repeatedly rescued Marino from personal and legal problems, even helping Marino to flee to Rome in order to escape the threat of a death sentence from the viceroy of Naples following a daring attempt to rescue a friend from prison. Later, Manso had Marino personally supervise the republication of *Il Manso* and worked on a biography of Marino after the latter's death in 1625. By late 1638, when John Milton visited Manso in Naples, his aging host had become "a living symbol of Italian literature," one whose life was widely seen to be "identified at many points with the course of Italian literature through the preceding half-century, and more especially with the intellectual interests of Southern Italy in its condition as a Spanish province."[9] Milton, before leaving the city, wrote his Latin poem *Mansus* and presented it to the marquis as a farewell gift; a Latin distich written by Manso for Milton was published by the poet in England in 1645, together with four other Italian tributes. Manso's friendship with Tasso in the twilight of Tasso's career was the pretext for his own *Del dialogo: Trattato del Marchese della Villa* (On dialogue: a treatise by the Marquis della Villa), which includes a conversation on dialogue between Manso and Tasso.[10] And, given his lifelong devotion to the cult of the poet, perhaps no one else of his age was better suited than Manso to restate Tasso's thought on dialogue for seventeenth-century readers. Yet although *Del dialogo* takes Tasso's work as its own dialogical partner, it necessarily reframes it in the vastly transformed context of Baroque literary esthetics and poetics and, in the process, wanders far from the premises on which Tasso's theory depends.

Tasso appears as the protagonist of Manso's *I paradossi*, and the twelve dialogues that make up the *Erocallia* refer widely to Tasso and to his works. Not surprisingly, then, *Del dialogo* begins as a narrative in which Manso reports that when Tasso was a guest at his villa in Naples, sometime in the late 1580's or early 1590's, the two passed their evenings by engaging in pleasant conversation, often concerning Tasso's own poetry and prose.[11] One evening the conversation turned to the topic of dialogue, and although deeply respectful of the older man's ideas, Manso eventually put forward his own theory in the course of a lengthy discussion. He tells readers that his treatise on "the composition of dialogues" was written down "many years ago" (p. 1045), presumably soon after this conversation (otherwise Manso's detailed recollection of Tasso's words would seem "not very credible" indeed).[12] The fact that its origin lies in this conversation, Manso further suggests, means that the work is really not his alone, but rather is a composite (*composto*; p. 1043) of his own arguments and those of Tasso that evening. Both of these claims are profoundly misleading, however, in ways that will become clearer in a moment.[13]

Despite its fictional prologue, *Del dialogo* follows the fairly standard procedure for literary *trattatistica* of starting from universal questions and descending to particular ones; it begins with a general theory of mimesis and concludes with a detailed discussion of each of the parts of dialogue. Arranged in 36 numbered sections, the treatise contains Manso's opening narrative, an ensuing dialogue between himself and Tasso, a long excursus by Tasso on mimesis, and, finally, Manso's own theory of dialogue. Interestingly enough, however, in it Manso never mentions the *Discorso dell'arte del dialogo*,[14] even though he blatantly appropriates the key phrase of Tasso's text for his own argument: "It follows that [the dialogist] ought to resemble the poet in terms of the genus of dialogue and should follow the dialectician in terms of its difference, and is almost in the middle of the two" (p. 1048); at another point, he states that "for this reason we said that the writer of dialogues is in between the poet and the dialectician" (p. 1059).[15] Although *Del dialogo* borrows freely if silently from Tasso's theory of dialogue at a number of points (as, for instance, when Manso argues that the "ornate style" is appropriate for dialogue, or that the *questione* is central for dialogical mimesis),[16] it also ignores many of his most fundamental insights, as it does those of the sixteenth-century problematization of dialogue as a whole. Manso even complains that "this subject [dialogue], although of the greatest importance, has not been sufficiently written about" (p. 1045), as if to emphasize the low regard in which he holds preceding theories of dialogue (apart, of course, from Tasso's).[17] This silence is perhaps best explained by the fact that although Manso appropriates many elements of Tasso's theory, the design and purpose of his own theory diverge radically from it. Manso uses the fiction of a dialogue on dialogue with Tasso chiefly to gain a greater measure of authority for his own arguments (and, secondarily, to commemorate the deceased poet); Tasso's presence in this dialogue is meant to constitute an endorsement of Manso's own ideas, at a time when Tasso's prestige throughout Italy and Europe was great.[18] Manso notes, furthermore, that "it was not at the time [of composition of *Del dialogo*] my idea to put forward any teachings, from which one could know how to fashion dialogues well, but rather to show clearly to others how marvellously well they have been fashioned by Tasso" (p. 1064).[19] Yet although he does in fact refer extensively to Tasso's dialogues in *Del dialogo*, Manso pays virtually no attention at all to how Tasso fashioned dialogues; rather, his aim is to show how marvellously well they correspond to—and thus validate—his own theory of dialogue.

Tasso, Manso tells his readers, argued on that evening many

years ago that the dialogist is an imitator no more and no less than the poet is, although the two have distinctly different reasons for writing fiction; whereas the poet aims to "delight while benefiting," the dialogist instead seeks to "teach while delighting" (p. 1034).[20] Yet Tasso said nothing of the kind in the *Discorso dell'arte del dialogo*, and the evidence of the *Dialoghi* gives little if any support to such an interpretation of Tasso's practice of dialogical writing. From the very first, then, the argument of *Del dialogo* runs counter to the direction of Tasso's work, even while attempting to incorporate it. The first third of the treatise is devoted to the question of the delight or pleasure produced in the audience or reader by all works of mimesis. The fictional voice of Tasso is predominant in this first part, in which he explains to Manso the reasons why all successful works of fiction offer a balanced blend of "delight and benefit" (*del diletto, e del giovamento*; p. 1041), something that treatises can never do. Once this explanation is completed, Manso becomes the sole speaker and turns his attention to the theory of dialogue itself.

Accepting his revered friend's praise of the powers of mimesis, Manso adds that those arts that most directly (*con minor tramezzamento*) represent nature itself or which "depend immediately on nature" are themselves the most "natural," the most mimetic, and therefore the most "noble" of all the arts (pp. 1041–42).[21] One such art, he contends, is that of dialogue: for dialogical writing imitates "our reasonings much more naturally than treatises do," and this proximity to nature makes all dialogues "more noble than treatises" (p. 1042).[22] Furthermore, since dialogue is a fully legitimate form of mimesis, it follows that it must be as delightful as any other such kind of fiction: "Since dialogue contains the imitation of those who speak in a much more lifelike way than in any other manner of representational writing, consequently it follows that dialogue is not only more delightful than treatises, but is just as delightful as any other form of writing" (pp. 1042–43).[23] Dialogue is just as literary as any poem or tragedy, even though its argumentative structure is directly derived from dialectic, and therefore it is just as pleasurable an experience for the reader as a play by Sophocles or a sonnet by Petrarch. There can be no question, then, of dialogue being closer to philosophy than to poetry; it belongs entirely to the literary system, and its rules test the writer's skill and *ingegno* as much as do the requirements of the tragic unities or of poetic metrics.

The "benefit" (*il giovamento*) of dialogue consists, however, not only in the delight that it gives us as a kind of mimesis, but also in the "argumentation" (*l'argomentatione*) that the speakers employ in their encounter (p. 1043). Dialogue always adheres to the procedures of dialectic (*ricevendo . . . l'argomentatione dalla Dialettica*; p. 1043) in its scene of speaking, and this—Manso asserts—powerfully enhances both its form and its function. Since the aim of dialogical writing is to "imitate characters who, in discoursing reciprocally, ask questions among themselves" (p. 1043),[24] it must always contain a form-giving dialectical *questione* at its center (just as it must for Tasso) if it is to avoid dissolving into a random conservation. Given that in any work of mimesis "the subject ought to be a single one," the poet always seeks "the unity of the imitation of a single plot, and in the same way . . . the dialectician [seeks] the unity of a single affirmation, or negation, in each disputation" (p. 1048).[25] This very same unity of the subject is therefore a requisite in "any disputation that arises" (p. 1048) in dialogue as well, since dialogue combines the arts of poetry and dialectic. At the same time, Manso points out, dialogue would not exist without *difference* either in opinions themselves or in the search for opinions. For if there were no difference within the scene of speaking (*la differenza della disputatione*; p. 1048), he observes, then the conversation between the speakers would be akin to "one of those choruses that appear in tragedies" (p. 1043), where all chant the same words in unison.[26] Dialogical writing therefore represents speakers who either "narrate each in turn" the same argument, or "are of contrary opinions among themselves," or "have the same opinion [but] prove it with different arguments" (p. 1043), but who in any case never say exactly the same thing at once.[27] The distinguishing trait of any dialogical scene of speaking is that it is "an imitation of a disputation" (p. 1043), for Manso as for Tasso; the speakers in this scene are bound to each other by a relationship of unity-in-difference (that is, even if they are of the same opinion, they use different arguments to affirm it or use different means to make the same argument).

According to *Del dialogo*, every dialogue possesses the same fundamental representational structure of qualitative parts ("subject, speakers, and form") and quantitative parts ("introduction, disputation, and digressions"; p. 1046).[28] Manso posits —as did Sigonio—that the introduction, which occurs first in the dialogical narrative sequence, should "account for the circumstances of the place, time, and persons gathered there" as well as the "reasons or accidents" for their meeting (p. 1052).[29] Besides satisfying the demands of decorum, this deployment of descriptive detail further serves to make the speakers and their setting "seem to be present to whoever is reading" (*a chi legge paia esservi presente*; p. 1052). If this echoes the language of Tasso's *Discorso dell'arte del dialogo*, it is no mere coincidence: once again, however, Manso reverses Tasso's project even as he synthetically absorbs Tasso's language into his own text. He makes little of this notion of the visibility of dialogical writing other than to note that figures of *enargeia* ignite the reader's imagination and should therefore be an integral part of dialogical writing from the outset, inasmuch as the presence of the scene of speaking in the mind's eye helps to convince the reader of the truth of its fiction.

Throughout *Del dialogo*, Manso follows this same procedure of casually picking up ideas from other theorists, and just as casually casting them aside, without ever really confronting their implications for his own argument. We may nevertheless infer here that—at least in Manso's eyes—the function of making visible the speakers in the scene is in turn linked to the other essential function of the introduction. Not only should this part of dialogue help the reader to envision the scene of speaking, which helps to create the desire to read on, but it should also make the reader "attentive to the question that must be disputed" (p. 1055). The introduction performs the double work of stimulating the reader's imagination and then helping to maintain the reader's attention for the duration of the disputation:

The final role of the introduction is to render the reader docile and attentive to the disputation, and this is done by briefly proposing the subject and the difficulties of the things that must be questioned. Thus whoever reads the dialogue, by learning in advance of the subject of the forthcoming discussion, may practically foresee the outcome of it, and consequently take the entire process as his own, and the speaking of the words toward the foreseen end, and thus [the reader] is made more capable of understanding it, and in this encounter the proposed difficulties create in the reader a desire to know the solution to them, from which desire attention is necessarily born. (pp. 1055–56)[30]

The introduction not only includes figures of *enargeia*, then, but always places a dialectical proposition before the reader as well. As it was for Sigonio, the function of the proposition is to keep the subject of the ensuing discussion clear in the reader's mind and so enhance understanding of the work; Manso adds to this, however, the rhetorical element of enigma and the rhetorical aim of producing a "docile" audience.

The reader's curiosity, he observes in the passage above, is inevitably piqued by the "proposed difficulties" that confront the speakers in the introduction. The enigma presented in the opening part of the work concerns not the solution itself (Manso takes it as axiomatic that there is an answer for every question raised in the disputation), but rather the matter of *how*—by what path, over what route—the speakers will eventually discover what they seek to know. The enigma, in other words, always centers around the form of discovery that will be employed in the dialogical scene. Furthermore, Manso reasons, this interdependence of a lack of knowledge and a desire to know impels the reader to follow the text's unfolding of the dialogical agon and ultimately to "take the entire process as his own." The reader's wholehearted participation in, and adoption of, the dialogical process thus makes him/her docile, and makes it easy for the dialogist to persuade the reader of the truth or likelihood of a given argument. The introduction therefore uses enigma as a rhetorical and psychological ploy to break down the reader's resistance to the process of dialogue itself and to the will of the writer that it embodies. Manso's reliance here on a reader-oriented rhetoric of dialogue (both in terms of *enargeia* and enigma) is symptomatic of the direction of his theory of dialogue as a whole. In *Del dialogo*, the vocabulary of the *Poetics*, with its emphasis on the parts and the structure of mimesis, is nearly always present, but it is deprived of its content; Manso assimilates this mode of analysis into his own more properly rhetorical poetics, but only

by transforming it into a kind of ornamental decor or bric-a-brac
for the latter.

The second part of the dialogical sequence—the disputation
itself—contains "all the instruments that belong to the poet and
the dialectician" (pp. 1056–57).[31] The instruments of the poet are
invention (the selection of a mode of asking questions), character, and style, whereas those of the dialectician are opinion,
argument, and style (*elocutio*, in other words, can be either poetical or dialectical in dialogue). Eloquence is not, then, restricted
to the introduction in dialogue; argumentation and figuration
may mix freely in the scene of speaking. But whereas this inter-
mixture threatens the purity of dialectic in dialogue for Tasso and
undermines its validity, Manso sees no danger of interference
between the mimetic and the dialectical functions of dialogue.
Although dialogue is in his view wholly a work of fiction, it must
also by definition employ the techniques and devices of dialectic
in this part. Every dialogue, he notes, offers a "poetic opinion"
(*una sentenza poetica*; p. 1060), which is always expressed by dialectical arguments; these arguments simply serve as the vehicle
of opinion, as the proper argumentative techniques are fitted to
the opinions to be explored. Manso once again breaks sharply
with the sixteenth-century discourse on dialogue in claiming
that *dianoia*, however, can be concerned with either knowledge,
probability, or belief (even though it is always expressed in dialectical terms). This means that dialogue may express "infallible"
truths, and use the "demonstrative" arguments of dialectical reasoning, as well as its inductive or persuasive ones, in the dialogical scene (p. 1059). And this in turn suggests that—contrary
to what Sigonio, Speroni, and even Tasso affirmed—knowledge
of the truth itself can come directly from what is not true (that
is, from a verisimilar fiction).

Yet Manso must still contend with the same question that con-
fronted his late Renaissance predecessors: How is it possible
for fiction to re-present the truth(s) of philosophy without ultimately altering them or contaminating their purity? *Del dialogo*'s
purported solution to the dilemma of the late Renaissance theorists is couched in the vaguest and most general of terms, as if
Manso were well aware of the shaky ground on which his argument stands. Truth can be conveyed by dialogue, he proposes,

despite its status as mimesis, because dialogue can generate any of these three grades of cognition in the mind of the reader, even without representing demonstrative or infallible knowledge directly in the discourse of the speakers. Manso remarks that "opinion [*dianoia*] must also have the aim of generating in the mind of others one of these three kinds of cognition" and that "opinion is therefore the instrument through which knowledge of something is generated in others' minds" (p. 1059).[32] Thus the question is no longer the philosophical status of the dialogical text itself, but rather the philosophical *effect* that it produces through its fictional devices. Manso makes this his central claim for the value of dialogue, but he does nothing to develop it further; he does not consider the possibility of different audiences for dialogue, for instance, nor does he try to describe the rhetorical mechanisms that would produce the desired knowledge in a given reader's mind. On the contrary, he simply assumes (and asks us to do so as well) that "since [dialogue] represents through imitation, in a way that is so immediate and so lively to the intellect, the things that it means to demonstrate to the intellect, that the intellect in an instant and without any real effort learns it, from which ease of learning the benefit—together with the delight—is also born; and since only in dialogue (and not in any other manner of writing) do we find this, it follows that we may derive far greater benefit from dialogue than from any other form of writing" (p. 1044).[33]

This praise of dialogue is certainly as sweeping as any made during the sixteenth century. Yet Manso's answer to the sixteenth century's concerns about dialogue remains entirely at the level of assertion in his treatise; he never, for instance, addresses what this "way that is so immediate and so lively to the intellect" might be, or how it is that learning can take place "in an instant and without any real effort," and these phrases are simply left dangling in the text as metaphorical expressions of what he sees as the supreme power of dialogical writing as a mode of unilateral communication. Dialogue appeals to him as an allegory of the way that all understanding ought to operate. It would doubtless be fair to infer that he is trying to argue that the dual function of dialogue—to allow the reader to acquire knowledge or opinion rapidly and efficiently while delighting and amusing him/her—expresses its essential value as a mode of writing. Yet whereas for Tasso the single most important benefit of dialogue was the delight of mimesis itself,[34] Manso instead thinks of the dialogical scene primarily in terms of the beneficial use to which it can be put by contemporary *letterati*, simply noting en passant that the pleasure of the text is inevitably produced in the reader's encounter with it.

To a greater or lesser extent, most of the Aristotelian critical or theoretical works produced in sixteenth-century Italy emphasized the utility of art (as we saw with *De dialogo liber*), even if Aristotle's position on the subject is not easy to determine. The question of art's utility, however, with its deep ties to the rhetorics of antiquity and to Horace's *Ars poetica*, was given a new impetus in Italy toward the beginning of the Seicento with the return to rhetoric that marked the literary incipit of the Baroque age in theory and criticism.[35] Many Aristotelian critics and theorists in the Cinquecento (such as Vincenzo Maggi and J. C. Scaliger, to name only two) insisted on the traditional moral function of literature, in essential continuity with medieval and humanist precepts, even while exploring ideas of decisive importance for the development of an early modern European esthetics. Manso's theory, despite its evident debts to the sixteenth-century discourse on dialogue, returns to the long tradition of Horatian literary theory and to its traditional moralism, while discarding—except at the most superficial or ornamental level— the major insights of its late Renaissance predecessors that lead in another direction. It is here that Manso's own ties to, and investment in, the cultural program of the Counter-Reformation are most apparent in *Del dialogo*. Even while proclaiming the superior benefit of dialogue over other kinds of prose writing (and hence over any kind of philosophical writing) and acknowledging the force of its mimesis, he insists that the principal task of the dialogical text is to teach while delighting and not simply to delight while benefiting. Although at first this may appear to differ little from the standard Renaissance prescription of profit and delight, for Manso the specifically pedagogical purpose of dialogue is not to be confused with the profit to be had from the moral lesson provided by a given poem or novella. Because dialogue offers its readers instruction on a potentially infinite range of topics, not just moral, ethical, or even philosophical ones, the benefit that it offers has instead to be understood in far different terms.

Manso's concern with the efficiency and effectiveness of dialogue as a means of instruction appears fully consonant with dominant Counter-Reformation rhetorical theory and practice in Italy, in particular that of the Jesuit order (with whom he had definite ties).[36] The principal directive of seventeenth-century Jesuit casuistic rhetoric was, generally speaking, to make discourse into action rather than representation. Such a rhetoric, literary or otherwise, was to be wholly oriented toward enhancing the speaker's persuasive performance, without requiring adherence to any single unifying principle or model (such as a set of rules or laws); such a rhetoric had to be a highly flexible, and radically contingent, mode of argumentation, adaptable to an infinite number of different cases and circumstances.[37] *Del dialogo* assigns a similar function to the dialogical work. For Manso, dialogue is an instrument of persuasion and teaching—and therefore a mode of action (or, in J. L. Austin's terms, a perlocutionary act)—suitable for treating any kind of knowledge or opinion with the greatest of ease and efficiency.[38] Manso's text thus substantially dilutes and weakens the reasons underlying the privileged structural logic of dialogical mimesis, which play such an important role in Tasso's *Discorso dell'arte del dialogo* and in the other sixteenth-century works on dialogue (except for Speroni's).

Although he adopts the Aristotelian system of quantitative and qualitative parts and insists on the organic unity of the dialogical text, Manso makes little effort to connect these elements into a coherent poetics of the sort advocated by Tasso. He merely relies on one of the most tired commonplaces of Renaissance criticism and theory ("to profit and delight") to prop up his argument about the performative and perlocutionary function of dialogue, while implying—although without offering even a shred of textual evidence—that this notion of profit and delight runs parallel to the argument of the *Poetics*.[39] It is this that makes his text often seem to be a mere palimpsest or assemblage of the ideas of other writers from antiquity and the Renaissance, a sort of seventeenth-century literary cabinet with no apparent organizing vision to bind together all of its elements. His theory of dialogue, while attempting to pose as a compromise between a rationalistic poetics and a psychologistic rhetoric, nevertheless leans heavily in the direction of rhetoric and thus seems far closer in spirit and in practice to the work of Pallavicino than to that of Tasso. The nostalgia that Manso expresses in *Del dialogo* for the sixteenth-century poet's thought on dialogue, far from leading to a recovery of Tasso's ideas, indicates instead his own uneasy sense both of the growing distance between the Baroque world and Tasso's and of the impossibility of belatedly overcoming that distance.

When Reading Is Believing: Pietro Sforza Pallavicino

The Marchese Pietro Sforza Pallavicino (1607–67) was born in Rome, the eldest son of a noble and important Parmesan family. Well before his twentieth birthday he was already a protagonist of Roman intellectual life. As a member of the Academy of the Desirous Ones, and later of the Academy of the Lynceans, and a close friend of the poet-scientist Giovanni Ciampoli, Pallavicino was at the forefront of the movement to open up philosophy in Rome to the new intellectual currents of the age (for instance, he defended Galileo in 1624 against the Jesuit accusers of the *Assayer*). When he presented his doctoral thesis on philosophy at the Collegio Romano in September 1625, the pope and twenty cardinals were in attendance, and soon afterward Pallavicino began an ecclesiastical career at the Congregation of Rites in the Roman Curia (he later took, in 1628, a doctorate in theology as well). The wave of reaction accompanying the second Galileo trial in 1632, however, cost Pallavicino dearly (as it did his mentor Ciampoli); his career in Rome crumbled, and he was exiled to the provinces. After serving as governor of various small cities in the Papal States (Iesi, Orvieto, Camerino), Pallavicino—in a dramatic about-face—joined the Jesuit order in 1637 and was immediately allowed to return to Rome. Within two years, Pallavicino was a professor of philosophy at the Collegio Romano, and later he became a professor of theology there (he was one of the Roman theologians who condemned Cornelis Jansen and his "five propositions"). In addition to his works of literary theory, for which he is chiefly remembered today, Pallavicino authored a tragedy, some poems, an apology for the Jesuits, a number of erudite theological works, and a history of the Council of Trent (*Istoria del Concilio di Trento*, 1656–57) designed to counter Paolo Sarpi's earlier and more renowned version of the same events. In 1659, eight years before his death, he was made a cardinal. In many ways Pallavicino had an exemplary seventeenth-century Roman career: as an aristocrat, a prince of the Church, a theorist of Baroque literature, and a Jesuit theologian, he played a key role in the dominant cultural formation of his age.

Franco Croce accurately speaks in this respect of the mid-Seicento period as "perhaps the moment of the greatest 'clericalization' of Italian literature," when those associated with the Church—especially the Jesuits (including Pallavicino himself)—exercised considerable influence over the direction of Italian literary culture.[40] Although he lived and worked during the peak of Baroque culture in Italy, Pallavicino was basically a *barocco moderato*, intrigued by the literary, philosophical, and scientific innovations of his age, but still seeking to reconcile these to the doctrinal Aristotelianism endorsed by Roman political and religious authority. His literary theories, in particular, capture the intellectual tension between the different strains of Baroque rationalism and the prevalent Marinist esthetic of sensualism and *concettismo* of the 1630's and 1640's. The *Trattato dello stile e del dialogo* (A treatise on style and dialogue), first published in 1646 (under a slightly different title) and revised for the final time in 1662, is not Pallavicino's best-known work of literary theory, but it contains—in a separate section at the end—his theory of dialogue.[41] This treatise not only seconds the arguments of *Del dialogo* in favor of dialogue, but goes far beyond Manso's work in developing a theory of dialogue's applications in the Baroque age. Yet, paradoxically enough, the reasons behind Pallavicino's praise of dialogue are the very ones that help to destroy philosophical dialogue—and a certain kind of philosophy itself—in mid-seventeenth-century Italy.

Unlike Manso, who was so strongly swayed by his personal friendship with Tasso, Pallavicino—born more than a decade after the death of the poet—sets the sixteenth-century problematization of dialogue in a more rigorously historical perspective. All the figures involved in it have already receded into what is recognizably the past for him, and they constitute a literary tradition in their own right.[42] In his work on dialogue, Pallavicino displays little or no anxiety about his debts to his predecessors, although he uses any number of their ideas; they are simply authorities to be arrayed as a buttress for his own arguments. The sixteenth century's view of the problem of dialogue is no longer a living concern for him, but rather a component of the tradition itself. Despite this sense of insuperable historical distance, he generally treats the sixteenth-century theorists of dialogue, particularly Tasso and Speroni, with reverence. For instance, he calls Speroni's *Apologia dei Dialoghi* "most learned" (p. 328), and elsewhere lists Speroni, together with Tasso and Bembo, among the great vernacular dialogists of the Cinquecento.[43] Pallavicino contends that these sixteenth-century writers and thinkers, better than any others, have demonstrated how "ideally suited dialogue is for the communication of the most noble disciplines" (p. 326). The "daring pen" of Tasso—the leading poet of the Counter-Reformation and a vocal supporter of the Jesuits—receives the highest praise from Pallavicino, and Tasso's treatise on dialogue is cited approvingly in a marginal gloss that accompanies the text (p. 325). Even Castelvetro—who served as the straw man for so many of his fellow late-sixteenth-century critics—is given dignified mention at another point as "a gentleman who found arguments to criticize [dialogue]" (p. 331).[44] Of all the sixteenth-century theorists of dialogue, only Sigonio is left unmentioned in the *Trattato dello stile e del dialogo*; a late humanist writing in Latin, Sigonio was outside the mainstream of sixteenth-century Italian literature as Pallavicino defines it from his retrospective vantage point. (He simply ignores Manso, whose work belongs to the Seicento.)

These writers' texts offer proof to Pallavicino that his own work is one of the rightful heirs to the great sixteenth-century Italian literary tradition, for they confirm that his theory of dialogue speaks to the same issue addressed by such authorities as Tasso, Speroni, and Castelvetro (whose influence was never greater in Europe than in the Seicento). As Giacomo Leopardi would remark in his *Zibaldone* in 1823, "Sforza Pallavicino in the *Trattato dello stile e del dialogo* . . . gives his decisive and universal, and not relative but absolute, preference to the *writers, style,* and *language* of the sixteenth century (and also to those of the following century in which he wrote)."[45] The writers on dialogue of the late Cinquecento represent Pallavicino's own sense of both affiliation with and divergence from the Renaissance literary tradition, and he is not in the least concerned that these same writers are theorists as well as poets and *letterati.* His treatise has little to say about any specific ancient or Renaissance dialogues, but is deliberately metatheoretical in its approach to the form; Pallavicino's theory is intended to extend the theories of the late Renaissance in a new direction, thus prolonging and further developing the tradition of discoursing about dialogue. Renaissance writing, whether creative or critical, is an inescapable linguistic and literary fact for the seventeenth-century critic, and it need only be revised and brought to perfection in accordance with the agenda of contemporary literary culture.[46] That Pallavicino's theory of dialogue ultimately closes off rather than prolongs the Renaissance tradition only makes his intentions in the *Trattato* appear in an all the more ironic light to us today.

The *Trattato dello stile e del dialogo* is subtitled "A Search for the Idea of Instructional Writing . . . and of the Nature, Imitation, and Utility of Dialogue" (*il cercarsi l'idea dello scrivere insegnativo . . . e della natura, dell'imitazione, e dell'utilità del dialogo*). This descriptive subtitle states outright the thesis of the work, to which Pallavicino will return constantly. His treatise not only studies the idea or system of instructional writing but also seeks to define the literary nature and utility of dialogue as an invaluable part of that same system of instruction. The portion of the *Trattato* devoted to dialogue is a substantial one, although it is dwarfed in size by the rest of Pallavicino's massive inquiry into the problems of literary style. Despite its academic format, replete with an extensive index, marginal glosses, and numbered sections, the treatise is written in prose of considerable elegance, rich in elaborate similes and metaphors, and offers far more to the reader than can reasonably be dealt with here. My discussion is therefore restricted to only a handful of the most relevant points regarding the theory of dialogue; the section of the treatise devoted exclusively to dialogue (pp. 290–368) revisits, in any case, many of the same arguments made by the earlier Renaissance theorists (such as Tasso's theory of *enargeia*). The most original parts of Pallavicino's theory focus on the question of the relationship between scientific/philosophical writing (*la scrittura scientifica*) and dialogical writing. The chief question that Pallavicino seeks to answer is, in essence, Why should knowledge—in the form of truth and its doctrines—have any legitimate need for eloquence and for its literary forms (such as dialogue)? The answer, as readers of the treatise are soon shown, is easily discovered. Although knowledge exists without eloquence in the form of theorems, formulas, equations, propositions, and so on, a certain degree of style in scientific and philosophical writing is still necessary insofar as knowledge must be translated into discourse if it is to be made understandable for more than a handful of others. The wider the audience sought for a particular doctrine, consequently, the greater the need for an appropriate style of writing.

Once this initial point is granted, Pallavicino suggests, we may begin to see the importance of a *theory* of dialogue. Scientists and philosophers who wish to communicate their discoveries and their knowledge to a general audience, or even to a fairly specialized one, must choose between writing treatises and writing dialogues. How can anyone decide, Pallavicino asks, if "it is more appropriate for a teacher of knowledge [science] to use direct narration in his own person or rather indirect narration through speakers" without a theory of dialogue?[47] Only by developing such a theory will we be able to define the technical criteria of instructional writing that may justify the use of dialogue by those who possess knowledge and wish to disseminate it. Throughout the *Trattato*, Pallavicino confronts the need for a theory of dialogue in terms of its pragmatic value as a kind of writing (*questa forma di scrivere*; pp. 325–26) that can serve as a vehicle for the communication of scientific and philosophical knowledge. He does not seek solely to decide a question of intrinsic esthetic quality, as his sixteenth-century precursors generally tended to do. His aim is instead to discover not merely what dialogical representation is and how it functions, but whether contemporary scientists and philosophers should use dialogues to enlighten readers in regard to the truth (there is never any question in his mind of the literary quality of dialogical writing). This emphasis on the chiefly pragmatic and didactic value of dialogue informs every aspect of Pallavicino's theory and indicates the huge difference between his esthetics and Tasso's. Dialogue is no longer to be thought of as a search for probable opinions and intricate forms of reasoning; it is instead, at least primarily, a vehicle of persuasion and even of indoctrination. The *Trattato* is a study in the use of dialogue as an instrument for transmitting preconstituted knowledge, not for testing and challenging the very basis of such knowledge.

Although, Pallavicino remarks, it is possible to write well without knowing any philosophy, "no one can, without the use of philosophy, know and demonstrate the reasons why one's writing is excellent."[48] Poetics is the philosophy of writing, the one conceivable way to analyze literary texts and their operations and "to contemplate diligently the nature and the utility of poetic imitation."[49] What Pallavicino means by poetics is, however, different from what, say, Tasso or Sigonio understood by the same term. Pallavicino certainly considers himself an Aristotelian critic, and his citation in the *Trattato* of a wide selection of Aristotle's works (ranging from the *Rhetoric* to the *Metaphysics* to *On Interpretation*) demonstrates his command of the Greek philosopher's thought. Yet he relies relatively little on the *Poetics* itself, mentioning it only a handful of times in the part of the treatise devoted to dialogue (pp. 322, 328, 334). His philosophy of writing does not take its main impetus from the study of literary mimesis and the problems that dialogue presents for it. There is no longer a sense, in Pallavicino's work, of the poetics of dialogue as an exploration of the difference between the discourses of dialectical philosophy and fiction; indeed, the terms 'dialectic' and 'syllogism' never appear in the part of the *Trattato* devoted to dialogue. Pallavicino calls instead for a kind of poetic writing committed to the analysis of intellectual and moral issues that is as distant from the sensual excesses of contemporary Baroque poetry as it is from the stylistic barbarisms of scholastic treatises. This ideal medium between a language of figures and a language of concepts is, in essence, dialogue. However, the question of dialogue as a kind of writing is—in Pallavicino's perspective—of no intrinsic interest for literary theory. Rather, it is the technical problem of the application of dialogue by knowledgeable instructors that interests him; his theory of dialogue studies how dialogical fiction, in spite of its "highly evident style of writing," is to be placed at the service of philosophy and science for the purpose of enhancing the power of their truths.[50] Although constructed around a series of possible objections to the use of dialogue for this purpose, his treatise serenely answers all of them. The hybrid textuality of dialogue presents no major problem for theory, in Pallavicino's eyes, except at the local and technical level of its application.

Not surprisingly, this theory of dialogue depends on Aristotle's *Rhetoric* rather than on the *Poetics* as its primary authority and point of reference. Although Pallavicino wants to define dialogue specifically in terms of a poetics, his notion of poetics is so closely connected to rhetoric—he speaks, for example, of "the extremely close relationship that links these two arts that dominate the human heart"—as to be virtually inseparable and indistinguishable from it in practice, even though he does point out a number of theoretical differences between the two.[51] And if poetics is in fact unthinkable apart from rhetoric as a system of persuasion, it is because poetics defines the means of dialogue and rhetoric its end. As was the case for Manso, the reason for this is elementary enough. "Dialogues," Pallavicino explains, "have teaching as their first objective; nor do they provide any pleasure unless it seems useful for maintaining the reader's attention, for impressing doctrine in memory, and, in short, for acquiring and increasing knowledge" (pp. 329–30).[52] Dialogical fiction and the system of representation that produces its elegance and eloquence are subordinate to the system of philosophical and scientific cognition, and all dialogical writing is completely geared toward the transmission of knowledge from writer to reader, which means that every element of the text—even its "pleasure" (*il piacer de' lettori*; p. 340)—functions toward that end.

If dialogue is to communicate ideas to readers effectively, however, it has not only to present or re-present the writer's ideas, but to impress those same ideas into memory, where they will become a part of each reader's storehouse of knowledge. For dialogue simply to be read is not enough; if readers do not retain a dialogue's ideas, the writer's efforts to persuade (or indoctrinate) through a dialogical scene of speaking fail to achieve their end. The pleasure of the dialogical text is particularly effective in this regard, Pallavicino notes, for it is precisely what helps the dialogist "to maintain the reader's attention and to impress doctrine into memory." Here as elsewhere we are far indeed from the premises of Tasso's theory of dialogue (to say nothing of Speroni's or Castelvetro's). Granted there can be no reading of any poetic fiction without an accompanying sense of the pleasure of the text, but in Pallavicino's theory the presence of *il piacere* no longer serves as confirmation of the validity of the esthetic structure of the work. Instead, it is a tool whose specific function is to seduce the reader into reading, learning, and remembering the ideas or doctrines conveyed in the scene of speaking.

The dialogist, Pallavicino notes, is first and foremost a "teacher of knowledge," not a poet, and dialogue is, despite the flourishes of its poetic tropes and figures, but a device that works toward this end. Dialogical writing is not a place for the true testing of ideas, then, but rather for the presentation—in the guise of a scene of speaking—of an already formulated doctrine or set of ideas; it is a recovery in the form of a discovery of truth and its *ragioni* (p. 329).[53] Given this orientation toward the achievement of a particular strategic result—namely, the production of a specific intellectual and moral effect in the mind of the reader—it naturally follows that Pallavicino's poetics of dialogue treats this *forma di scrivere* as a rhetorical technique of persuasion. Pallavicino's poetics is inextricably enmeshed with rhetoric, for it uses rhetorical principles to explain dialogical texts in terms of their rhetorical effects; as he notes, "the teacher of knowledge may demonstrate without disadvantage a studious desire not only to be read but also to be *believed*" (p. 41; my italics).[54] And the power of dialogue to sway, to persuade, and to convince the mind of the reader is perfectly legitimate as long as it is employed for this purpose of "making believe."

In short, dialogue is "a most suitable instrument for instilling doctrine with gaiety" (p. 319), Pallavicino concludes, because the power of its fictional devices does not interfere with the writer's desire to instruct; rather, it complements it.[55] These fictional devices are not, however, the same as those found in more purely poetic kinds of literary mimesis. Dialogues, like letters and histories, "contain some mixture of imitation, and yet are not called imitative practices like poetry" (p. 329), he observes, but neither are they purely conceptual discourses.[56] As a prose form, dialogue "is no more difficult to compose than letters, histories, or other prose writings" (p. 329), but it has the great advantage of being more poetic and fictional than either letters or histories.[57] Pallavicino explains that this arises from dialogue's use of "well-proportioned words and speculative but informal speakers" (p. 329) in order to represent a scene of intellectual agon; although it avoids an overly ornate style, for it is chiefly operative rather than decorative in nature, dialogue does not entirely neglect the use of tropes and figures ("well-proportioned words").[58] As always in the *Trattato*, Pallavicino is acutely aware that the dialogical product is an illusion of conceptual discourse, for "even if fiction imitates truth . . . this does not mean that the mode of expression of fiction is an imitation of the mode of expression of truth," and therefore it must always employ a poetic language of illusion.[59]

In contrast to Sigonio and Tasso, for Pallavicino dialogue can never represent an uncontaminated scene of dialectical disputation; every part of the text can potentially be charged with figurality. Nor, as in Speroni's theory, does its production of illusion make dialogue a parody or a travesty of philosophy. Dialogue is instead a *mode of accommodation* of the discourse of truth, which should convince its readers as completely as if it were the truth itself, even though it is but a fiction. The positive power of this illusion is the source of dialogue's value, for it is this same illusion that, in the hands of those with access to the truth and its doctrines, allows the transmission of truth to take place and to have effect. The writer of the dialogical text is not obliged to reproduce the true with absolute fidelity; that is by no means a moral imperative for Pallavicino. The ideas and doctrines that a dialogue conveys are always founded in truth, but are made acceptable and understandable for the reader only through the illusion of the dialogical scene. This process of translation does not lead readers astray into a world of deception and error, however, for dialogue's *elocutio* is entirely subject to its *inventio*; topic controls trope, and scientific and philosophical knowledge completely commands the fiction that expresses it.

Even the most apparently poetic elements of dialogical writing—its figures of evidence or *enargeia*—are motivated by the same rhetorical rationale that governs the rest of the text. *Enargeia* signifies for Pallavicino "this artifice of making words seem almost visible through the lively narration of most elegant facts" (p. 342).[60] Readers of Tasso's *Discorso dell'arte del dialogo*—and Pallavicino is one of them—are familiar with such figures of "visible speech" as integral elements of dialogical writing (although Tasso, unlike Pallavicino, never actually used the term *enargeia* in his treatise). The dialogist exploits the descriptive details included in the text—its garland of greetings, witty exchanges, digressions—in order to enhance its verisimilitude and thus to amplify the "force" (*forza*; p. 339) of its pleasure. Employing a language of vision and embodiment, dialogical description operates as a seductive repetition of the seen, that constant source of intellectual and sensual delight. The function of verisimilitude in dialogue unequivocally stands at the center of Pallavicino's illusionist esthetic of *argutezza*.[61] The convincingly realistic appearance of the dialogical text (its version of the seen) generates, in the hands of the skilled dialogist, an illusion of a probable reality in the mind of the reader; this effect helps to convince readers of the reality and—ultimately—the truth of a given scene of speaking, unlike that produced by what is unfamiliar or marvelous. The *fatti* and *descrizioni*, which give variety and color to the dialogical narrative and amplify the reader's delight, therefore play an important role in its textual system of persuasion.

In point of fact, Pallavicino notes, description and *enargeia* serve as poetic "frames" (*cornici*; p. 340) for the philosophical disputation at the heart of the work: "Although those facts that dialogue reports would not in themselves deserve the praise of narration, nevertheless, in the function of frames, they confer upon the imitated discussions that grace and that *enargeia* which minute and credible details give to the poem for the same reason" (pp. 340–41).[62] Yet, unlike Tasso and Sigonio, Pallavicino defines no "inside" or "outside" of the philosophical content of dialogue. Although he speaks of figures in terms of frames for the "imitated discussions" of the speakers, there is in fact in his eyes nothing completely outside figural language in dialogue, for such language is intermingled to a greater or lesser extent everywhere in the text with the imitated discussions. What differs in the parts of a given dialogue is rather the *degree* of figural and stylistic intensification. Where the facts and descriptive details of the dialogical work are predominant, we find the highest degree of figurality, and where the imitated discussions are predominant, we find the lowest degree; nowhere, however, is figurality absent in dialogue. Figures of *enargeia* in dialogical writing are like a false frame painted around the edge of a canvas; there is an illusion of difference, but in fact the frame is continuous with what it contains.

"Grace" and *enargeia* are necessary not only to confer credibility on the conversation, but to make it—and this leads back once again to the rhetorical foundations of Pallavicino's theory —more memorable than the unadorned logic of abstract arguments. The eye—the organ of vision—is, for the human subject, the locus not only of pleasure but also of cognition and recognition, according to Pallavicino's Baroque esthetics.[63] "Aristotle," he notes, "profoundly observed that we love our eyes above all our other senses because we learn more from them than from all our other senses" (p. 343).[64] The function of description (*enargeia*) is to sustain the "vivacity" (*vivacità*; p. 354) of dialogue, making it visible and living and unforgettable, for the purpose of enhancing the delight of the reader's eye and the strength of the reader's cognition. Figures of *enargeia* in dialogue are therefore, Pallavicino says, like "so many blows of the hammer that deeply sculpt the images of the things taught in the minds of those who learn" (p. 354).[65] This operation of inscription on the *tabula* of the reader's consciousness alone ultimately justifies the choice of dialogue, as a strategy of writing, over the treatise or the summa; in this, as in so many other aspects of the *Trattato*, Pallavicino shows no interest in a primarily esthetic justification either for the inclusion of *enargeia* in dialogue or for dialogue itself. Since the human body, he remarks, is not nourished by quintessences (food purified of all that cannot be consumed), there must always be some surplus or excess generated in the corporeal economy (just as sunlight is inevitably accompanied by shadow): Does not the same thing hold for the study of the truth?[66] Yet, in dialogue, even such figural excess is functional.[67] Although philosophical and scientific discourse can effectively exist without figures of *enargeia* because the truth is already fully formed and fully available to the writer, the writer's pragmatic purpose cannot be achieved without them in the writing of a dialogical work.

Even the introduction of speakers into the dialogical scene is part of this same overall design. The monological *maniera insegnativa* of treatises, Pallavicino points out, leaves readers feeling defenseless against the writer's arguments, which loom as all the more authoritative because no effective counterarguments are offered in the work. Treatise writing has its advantages, especially for mathematical and geometrical subjects, which require the development of long and complex formulas and equations that would be disrupted by objections or digressions. The general reader, however, who has no practical means of measuring and judging the truth of the claims advanced in a philosophical treatise is far less likely to accept those claims at face value and far more inclined to doubt the authority of its doctrine. If knowledge is to be divulged in a convincing manner to a general audience, then dialogue should be considered superior to treatise writing because "it contains both a fountain to sprinkle its discourses with that pleasure and a forge to manufacture shields with this strength" (p. 357).[68] "That pleasure" is the delight of verisimilitude, developed through the writer's judicious use of figures of *enargeia*; "this strength" is dialogue's two-voiced mode of argumentation through the deployment of characters in the scene of speaking, which offers the reader two or more differing perspectives on the topic under discussion. Unlike a treatise, which provides—in its monological framework—only one point of view, dialogue has shields that give readers a sense of protection against being blindly led into error by the writer, by virtue of its staging of the process through which a truth is discovered. The arguments and counterarguments presented in dialogue dramatize how one frees oneself from doubt and refutes error, Pallavicino contends; and the text forms the stage for this particular kind of scene. The drama of the dialogical discovery of truth offers an exemplum for the reader, demonstrating how to defend or shield oneself successfully—like the winner in the dialogical agon—against the persuasive but deceptive rhetoric of those opposed to the truth.

This theatricalization of the process of cognitive discovery in dialogue may, however, persuade readers that truth has been attained by the speaker-actors in the dialogical scene only by the unconditional defeat of "false opinion": "Since the field may be entered by the supporter of false opinion, who contrives to persuade with it by using all the most deceptive practices of eloquence, the teacher of truth should openly reveal the fraud of those proofs, which appear to be giants but in reality are but clouds of air, and break the spells with which the magic of emotion made the unwary reader err" (p. 357).[69] As part of this inherent textual theatricality, the dialogist ("the teacher of truth" —*l'insegnatore del vero*) deliberately introduces error into the debate and even allows its proponents in the scene of speaking to try as best they can to persuade the reader of its validity. This rhetoric of error is, however, only a precondition for the dialogist's frontal assault on falsehood (*falsa opinione*); it is only a preliminary phase, or stage, in the enactment of the dialogical process of discovery. There can be no question of the supporter of a false opinion holding his/her own ground for long: through the dialogical agon and its eventual resolution, the reader is always shown the fraudulent nature of such opinions and the superiority of the truth that opposes them.

Readers of dialogue ought never to be left, Pallavicino notes (agreeing with Sigonio), "either in the darkness of doubt or in danger of deception" (p. 320).[70] The works of Plato and Cicero are therefore "flawed for teaching, although through no fault of their own" (p. 345) because their style is not didactic enough and their own ideas not always clearly stated.[71] On the contrary, in authentic instructional dialogue—which is the only kind of any interest to Pallavicino—"the writer's opinion and its foundation shine forth with great clarity" (p. 346), something that would be anathema for Speroni.[72] Dialogue is a mise-en-scène of the struggle between truth and falsehood, and its happy ending.[73] Although both treatises and dialogues may in the end provide the reader with an equally valid measure of truth, the dialogical method alone portrays all the many facets of the process of arriving at that truth, through an encounter with the errors scattered in its path.[74] Pallavicino's theory of dialogue is far from describing the kind of dialogical contest proposed by Tasso, in which an agonistic structure of speaking is desirable principally because it is more stylistically demanding and complex. Dialogue—while still a fiction—is instead to be understood as an enthusiastic affirmation of the truth of the doctrines of philosophy and science and an instructive refutation of error, falsehood, and deception.

Dialogue emerges in the *Trattato dello stile e del dialogo* as far more than an extrinsic ornament or a decorative veil stretched over the blinding truth of the text. Consistent with Pallavicino's stance as a moderate Baroque theorist, and as an apologist for the Jesuit view of literature, his notion of dialogue goes beyond a mere reiteration of a formal *humanitas* typical of the later phases of the Counter-Reformation in Italy.[75] The literariness of dialogue is instead one fundamental condition for the communication and dissemination of new cognitions and established doctrines to a wider public; although not required by any specific logic, it is an essential tool for the seventeenth-century writer who seeks to convince readers to open themselves up to the evidence of truth. Pallavicino revels in the power of this literary rhetoric and its concrete, varied, vivid imagery, even though he equally insists that it not challenge the primacy of the cognitive discourses of philosophy and science. Rooted in affective psychology (the passions and pleasures of readers and reading), Pallavicino's thought on dialogue incorporates the experiential realm of visible and tangible circumstances into the philosophical and scientific discourse of truth, in a far more self-consistent way than that of any of his sixteenth-century predecessors. At the same time, his theory has lost almost all points of contact with the original problem of dialogue. He strips dialogue of the privileges accorded it by Tasso and Sigonio as a uniquely philosophical fiction, although, unlike Castelvetro, he bears no animus against it. The *Trattato* simply presupposes that knowledge (ideas or doctrines) can and should be made understandable at a more general level and that dialogue is the most suitable means for effecting such understanding in the mind of the general reading public. The transfer of knowledge accomplished in dialogue —its "translation" into dialogue, or, in other words, its being made legible for all—thus establishes a continuity between the age-old Western literary tradition and the new cognitions, discoveries, and doctrines of the Seicento. Dialogue, with its distinguished line of descent from the great philosophers and rhetors of classical Athens itself, forges a bond between tradition and the present and legitimates the latter in the process.

Paradoxically, then, Pallavicino sees his theory of dialogue as a natural outgrowth of Renaissance literary culture, even as he celebrates that culture's closure. Dialogue is the ultimate literary proof of the principle that there is no well-written text without well-organized thoughts, no rhetoric that is not—or should not be—controlled by philosophy. The will and intellect of "the writer about knowledge" who seeks to operate on language (and on those who use language) wholly determine the dialogical "art of composition" (*arte di comporre*; p. 368). There must be, behind every dialogical text, a mind that creates its "reasons," controls them, and exploits them for its own ends; Pallavicino's theory is an eminently rationalist one that seeks in dialogical writing a logic that the mind can decipher and discipline.[76] The theory of dialogue is no longer an exploration of difference, a probing of the boundaries between the discourses of philosophy (science) and fiction in the representational structure of the text, as it was for the critics of the late Renaissance, but rather a search for ways to harness dialogical writing in the interests of what is already known with certainty and affirmed as doctrine. In this, as in so many other aspects of Pallavicino's theory glossed over here, the prevailing concern with conviction and with "making believe," with the struggle for the hearts and minds of readers (like his own agon with the work of Paolo Sarpi), marks a merger of Counter-Reformation ideology and literary esthetics.[77]

In its every statement about dialogue, the *Trattato dello stile e del dialogo* openly announces the end of the Renaissance problematization of the relationship between writing and the scene of speaking. Discarding all previous answers in favor of a rhetoric of theatricality and illusion, Pallavicino's theory defines the *techne* of dialogical writing as a method of persuasion rather than as a structure of literary representation, thus making the very value of dialogue, and of the discursive arts in general, profoundly different for him than it was for Tasso or Sigonio or Castelvetro. In part this is because the value of rhetoric in relation to philosophy is sharply different for him as well; rhetoric is but an ancilla of philosophy, and literature but a subgenre of rhetoric. Dialogue therefore loses its urgency as a problem for literary theory, for its position within the universe of genres of discourse is always already determined in advance; simply put, the problem is no longer what dialogue is, or where it is, but what its use is. There is no question that dialogue belongs to literature, not philosophy or even dialectic, and that it lacks the technical resources of dialectic; yet, even in its essential figurality, dialogue remains forever bound to the service of philosophy and science (and the power on whose side they stand). Since Pallavicino denies that true dialogical writing could interfere with the cognitions that it conveys, he neutralizes its textuality, but at the cost of converting it into a wholly didactic rhetorical device far removed from the ground traversed by Tasso, Sigonio, and the others. Dialogue is not altogether a simple form in this theory, because it still challenges the *ingegno* and the skill of the seventeenth-century writer; appropriate arguments and figures must always be invented, not automatically drawn from a storehouse of commonplaces. Nevertheless, in the *Trattato*, the problem of dialogue as it was defined in the sixteenth century no longer exists as a major theoretical concern.

Mikhail Bakhtin points out that "when the genre of the Socratic dialogue entered the service of the established, dogmatic worldviews of various philosophical schools and religious doctrines, it lost all connection with a carnival sense of the world and was transformed into a simple form for expounding already found, ready-made irrefutable truth; ultimately, it degenerated completely into a question-and-answer form for training neophytes (catechism)."[78] Bakhtin's account of the decline of Socratic dialogue between classical and late antiquity describes a process closely resembling the change that occurs in the history of the theory of dialogue between Tasso and Pallavicino. With Pallavicino's treatise, discourse on dialogue in Italy can be said to have come full circle from Sigonio, who first sought to define it as a fully empowered figural equivalent (or image) of dialectic. But dialectic itself can no longer be considered a discursive option for Pallavicino, whose notion of the univocality of doctrine rigorously excludes the kind of "traveling" (p. 365) done in a genuine dialectical excursus. Dialogue is not, in Pallavicino's theory, a truly philosophical or dialectical fiction, despite its double-voiced design; it is instead primarily a textual strategy for passively reflecting and translating doctrinal truths—not opinions—that may be new but have always been authorized in advance. And as long as dialogue is but a shadow play with no claim of its own to the privileged domain of dialectic or demonstration (except in a highly refracted form), his theory is able to remain intact. This by no means slight achievement, however, cannot offset the fact that, in the passage from opinion to doctrine and from a syncretic system of systems to a didactic rhetorical device, the single most recognizable element of dialogue as defined by the sixteenth-century Italian theorists—namely, the art of questioning, doubting, exploring the lateral paths and possibilities of thought—is definitively banished from the scene of speaking and is at last lost to sight.

Reference Matter

Notes

Complete authors' names, titles, and publication data are given in the Selected List of Works Consulted, pp. 281–92.

Chapter 1

1. Mesnard, p. 16, argues that the years 1580–1630 mark the passage from the Renaissance to modernity in France; in Italy this movement out of the Renaissance began even earlier. See also Cochrane; and Braudel.

2. Writers on dialogue such as Suydenham, Shaftesbury, Diderot (who has an interesting article on "La philosophie socratique" in the *Encyclopédie*), and De Maistre are Enlightenment or post-Enlightenment thinkers and fall outside of the scope of this inquiry.

3. Saint-Mard, p. 3: "La Nature du Dialogue n'a jamais été éclaircie. C'est la Destinée des choses simples."

4. Throughout this book, I refer to the approximate dates of composition of these works, rather than to their respective dates of publication. Armstrong, pp. 38–39, points out that Agricola, *De inventione dialectica*, Book 2, ed. I. M. Phrissemius (Paris, 1534), 424 ff—under the heading "Quomodo oblectandus oratione auditor"—and Sturm, *Partitionum dialecticarum libri quatuor* (Strasbourg, 1549), Book 3, discuss dialogue in terms of dialectic, but are indifferent to the literary problem of dialogue that is explored in the present work.

5. The most ambitious study of the genre of dialogue is still Hirzel. He gives short shrift to the Renaissance, though, in this mammoth *Gattungsgeschichte*.

6. Deakins, p. 6.   7. Kahn, p. 388.
8. Brooks, p. x.   9. Brooks, p. xi.

10. I use the term 'hermeneutics' loosely here, since the discipline itself had, of course, not yet come into being in the Renaissance. Allegorical, mythological, and Biblical interpretation are among the various Renaissance forerunners of modern hermeneutics.

11. Todorov, p. xxvi. Brooks, pp. ix–x, adds that "it is in structuralist thought that poetics has found the strongest impulse to its reformulation since perhaps the Renaissance."

12. Todorov, p. xxiv.

13. Todorov, p. xxvi.

14. B. Croce, *Poeti*, 2: 123–24. Croce remarks that "one would need to theorize the dialogue as the representation of the life of thought, of the making of truth out of conflict and subsequent trials and sketches and errors, distinguishing it from the representation of a lovely and already-found, definitive and static, truth" ("bisognerebbe teorizzare il dialogo come la rappresentazione della vita del pensiero, del farsi della verità tra contrasti e tentativi successivi ed abbozzi ed errori, distinguendola dalla rappresentazione della verità bella e trovata, definitiva e statica"). Saint-Mard, p. 4, points out that "dialogue is the oldest kind of writing. . . . Having discovered the means of rendering their ideas by the use of words, men began to converse; and I can hardly doubt that, given their tendency to imitate, they gave their writings the form of conversation, or dialogue, as it likely should have presented itself to them" ("le Dialogue est le genre d'écrire le plus Ancien. . . . Les Hommes ayant trouvé le moyen de rendre leurs Idées par l'usage des Mots, lièrent des Conversations; et je ne doute presque point, qu'avec le penchant qu'ils ont à l'Imitation, ils n'aient donné à leurs Écrits la Forme de Conversation, ou de Dialogue, qui devoit vraisemblablement se présenter à eux"). He adds that for the ancients "this manner of writing was natural" ("cette Manière d'écrire étoit Naturelle"). Dupriez, p. 152, makes the similar observation that "the dialogue is the most natural mode of speech when it attains the state of an exchange" ("le dialogue est le mode le plus naturel de la parole lorsqu'elle accède au stade de l'échange").

15. Baldwin, *Renaissance Literary Theory*, p. 43: "[Dialogue's] vogue was evidently stimulated by the increasing availability of Plato in both translation and Greek text; but its method is not often his."

16. Ibid., pp. 42–43.

17. Galilei, *Dialogue*, p. 6.

18. Foucault, "Discourse and Truth," pp. 115–16, defines "problematization" as "an 'answer' to a concrete situation. . . . A given problematization is not an effect or consequence of a historical context or situation, but is an answer given by definite individuals (although you may find this same answer given in a series of texts, and at a certain point the answer may become so general that it also becomes anonymous). . . . The fact that an answer is neither a representation nor an effect of a situation does not mean that it answers to nothing. . . . A problematization is always a kind of creation; but a creation in the sense that, given

a certain situation, you cannot infer that this kind of problematization will follow. . . . I think that it is possible to give an analysis of a given problematization as the history of an answer—the original, specific, and singular answer of thought—to a certain situation."

19. Weinberg, *History*, 1: 431.

20. Gadamer, *Truth and Method*, p. 333.

21. Foucault, "Discourse and Truth," p. 116.

22. Marsh, p. 16: "By the early sixteenth century, only an exceptional genius like Erasmus, for whom Latin was a living language, could preserve the connection between spoken and written word which makes the dialogue a vital form of expression. The future of the dialogue lay, quite logically, in the realm of the vernacular, and the dialogues of the Cinquecento deal from the outset with the problems of the *volgare* and its proper role in a new and emerging culture."

23. A complete history of literary criticism and theory in the Italian Renaissance has yet to be written and is perhaps beyond the scope of any single study. The most important surveys of the field are still Weinberg, *History*; and Hathaway, *Age*. Weinberg, *Trattati*, provides an important collection of texts.

24. De Certeau, *Heterologies*, p. 192.

25. Ibid.

26. Kahn, p. 389: "Theory has for too long been associated with . . . the subordination of practice to a speculative model of the truth. . . . The aim of the dialectical critic, however, is to formulate theory as a 'metapractice,' or 'practice about practice,' one that is necessarily bound up with desires, interests, intentions to persuade."

27. Nietzsche, *Birth of Tragedy*, pp. 90–91, describes the literary nature of Plato's dialogues as follows: Dialogue "may be described as an infinitely enhanced Aesopian fable, in which poetry holds the same rank in relation to dialectical philosophy as this same philosophy held for many centuries in relation to theology; namely the rank of *ancilla*. This was the new position into which Plato, under the pressure of the demonic Socrates, forced poetry. Here *philosophic* thought overgrows art and compels it to cling close to the trunk of dialectic. . . . Socrates, the dialectical hero of the Platonic drama, reminds us of the kindred nature of the Euripidean hero who must defend his action with arguments and counterarguments and in the process often risks the loss of our tragic pity; for who could mistake the *optimistic* element in the nature of dialectic, which celebrates a triumph with every conclusion and can breathe only in cool clarity and consciousness."

28. Deakins, p. 6, is only partly correct in arguing that "it was the introduction of printing, with its potential for mass audiences for books

and pamphlets, that forced the humanists to spell out the laws by which dialogues were to be written and read."

29. Hathaway, *Marvels and Commonplaces*, p. 93: "Poetry was preeminently an intimate union of philosophy and eloquence and . . . in this union it was the duty of eloquence somehow to render dry abstractions in a concrete form that would incorporate the passions and make present and vivid . . . the materials presented, beliefs that are all derived from rhetorical theory."

30. Rosello's treatise is found in his *Due dialoghi*. A careful comparison of these theories and early seventeenth-century theories of dissimulation, such as Torquato Accetto's *Della dissimulazione onesta*, Scipione Ammirato's *Della segretezza* (in *Opuscoli*, 1: 313–53), or Giovanni Bonifacio's *L'arte de' cenni*, has yet to be made. See Rosa.

31. Compare Floriani, pp. 29–30, on the relationship between the theory of dialogue and the genre of dialogue in the sixteenth century. Mulas, p. 251, adds that "for all sixteenth-century men of letters, awareness of the simulation of the poetic text is too high for the principle of imitation to be conceived of in the hyper-realistic terms of 'reproduction'" ("in ogni letterato del '500, troppo alta è la coscienza della simulazione del testo poetico, perché il principio dell'imitazione possa essere concepito nei termini iperrealistici di riproduzione").

32. Weinberg, *History*, 1: 39.

33. For instance, Quondam, p. 11, makes the all-too-typical remark that "the characteristic trait of literature on literature that is peculiar to mannerism can be traced to a market that is exhausted and closed up, that no longer offers exchanges and adapts itself to living on what it has, even at the level of intellectual experiences" ("la caratteristica della letteratura sulla letteratura, propria del Manierismo, è riferibile a un mercato che si esaurisce, che si chiude, che non conosce più lo scambio e si adatta a vivere di quello che ha, anche sul piano delle esperienze intellettuali").

34. In Italy, some of the most interesting work in this area is currently being performed at the Istituto di Studi Rinascimentali di Ferrara, in association with the Centro di Studi sulle Società di Antico Regime "Europa delle corti": see the series Biblioteca del Cinquecento published in Rome under the auspices of the latter.

35. Kristeller, *Renaissance Thought: The Classic, Scholastic and Humanist Strains*, p. 36. Concerning Paduan Aristotelianism in particular, see Giard, "L'Aristotélisme padouan," to which this entire passage is deeply indebted. See also Giard's "Histoire de l'Université."

36. The phrase "resistance to theory" is from Paul de Man, "Resistance."

37. Weinberg, *History*, 1: 39.

38. Greene, *Light in Troy*, pp. 28–53, discusses this at length.

39. Mack, p. 189, remarks that "there is no systematic or comprehensive ancient analysis of dialogue."

40. Foucault, "Nietzsche, Genealogy, History," in his *Language, Memory, Counter-Practice*, pp. 146–52, discusses the notions of genealogy, affiliation, and descent in this perspective.

41. Marsh, pp. 1–23, presents a strong case that Cicero is the dominant ancient authority on dialogue for the fifteenth century, not Plato.

42. Baldwin, *Renaissance Literary Theory*, p. 43.

43. Wilson, "Continuity," pp. 23–27. See also Ong, p. 37.

44. Plato, in his youth, was a student of the Eleatic doctrines, and Diogenes Laertius (3.48; trans. Hicks, p. 319) states that "they say that Zeno the Eleatic was the first to write dialogues." In the first book of the lost *On Poets*, Aristotle remarks that Alexamenos of Styra or Teos was the first to write dialogues; Atheneaus (505B–C) notes that both Nicias of Nicaea and Sotion testify to the truth of Aristotle's claim (= Rose 72, in Aristotle, *Works*, ed. Ross, 12: 73).

45. According to the testimony of Diogenes Laertius (3.24; trans. Hicks, p. 299), Plato was "the first who in philosophical discussion employed . . . [the term] 'dialectic.'" See also Sichirollo, p. 14.

46. Xenophon, *Memorabilia* 4.5.12; in Plato and Xenophon, *Socratic Discourses*, trans. J. S. Watson, p. 141—I have altered the translation somewhat. Sichirollo, p. 15, notes that the term *dialegesthai* itself is not original to Socrates, but is already to be found in the writings of Homer, Archilocus, and Sappho: it generally means "to discuss [something] with reciprocal understanding and satisfaction . . . [i.e.] to converse." Scaliger remarks, in his *Poetices libri septem* (1.3), that "a second mode of poetry is conversation, such as is employed in comedies. The original Greek term for this was *dialogetikos* (*conversational*), and the word was most accurately employed, for it was usage that yielded the derived meaning of disputation. In fact, *dialektos* has no other meaning than conversation. . . . In line with this, the loose discourses which reproduce the conversation of a group of men—not of two only, as the grammarians falsely assert—were called dialogues" (trans. Padelford, p. 19).

47. In the *Protagoras* alone, for instance, this verb appears 33 times (Sichirollo, p. 43).

48. Vernant, pp. 47–57, 132–33. Bakhtin, *Dostoyevsky's Poetics*, p. 108, remarks: "The genres of the serio-comical [e.g., dialogue] do not rely on *legend* and do not sanctify themselves through it, they *consciously* rely on *experience* . . . and on *free invention*; their relationship to legend

is in most cases deeply critical, and at times even resembles a cynical exposé. . . . This is a complete revolution in the history of the literary image."

49. Hirzel, 1: 413. He adds that "Plato is, moreover, for us the first to pronounce an opinion on written dialogue" ("Platon ist ausserdem für uns der Erste, der ein Urteil über geschriebene Dialoge . . . ausspricht").

50. Trans. Grube, pp. 63–65.

51. In Plato, *Republic*, trans. Bloom, p. 359.

52. See ibid., p. 358, for a summary of Socrates's reasons.

53. Plato's authorship of the *Letters* is generally considered doubtful today, although as early as Thrasyllus they were included in the corpus of Platonic writings. See Bury, in Plato, *Epistles*, p. 385.

54. Plato, *Epistles*, trans. Bury, p. 417.

55. Ibid., p. 531. For an illuminating discussion of Platonic writing, see Berger.

56. Bakhtin, *Dostoyevsky's Poetics*, p. 109: "Originally the genre of the Socratic dialogue—already at the literary stage of its development—was almost a memoir genre; it consisted of reminiscences of actual conversations that Socrates had conducted, transcriptions of remembered conversations framed by a brief story. But very soon a freely creative attitude toward the material liberated the genre almost completely from the limitations of history and memoir."

57. Cf. de Certeau, *Heterologies*, p. 70.

58. Russell, pp. 56–57.

59. Weinberg, *History*, 1: 349: "There is no doubt that the signal event in the history of literary criticism in the Italian Renaissance was the discovery of Aristotle's *Poetics* and its incorporation into the critical tradition."

60. For a more complete listing of sixteenth-century editions, see Cranz; and Cooper and Gudeman. For a more detailed discussion of Barbaro, Poliziano, and the *Poetics*, see Branca.

61. Herrick, *Fusion*, treats this at length.

62. Weinberg, *History*, 1: 38.

63. A wide variety of ancient writers remarked on Aristotle's dialogues (see the *testimonia* in the Rose fragments, in Aristotle, *Works*, ed. Ross, 12: 1–6); besides Cicero and Quintilian, one would have to mention at least Ammonius, Saint Basil, and Elias.

64. Ross, in Aristotle, *Works*, 12: vii–ix. Diogenes Laertius and Heyschius also testify to this. Ross, p. ix, observes that "it seems probable that Aristotle began with short dialogues called (on the Platonic model) by one-word names (three of which are actually identical with the names of Platonic dialogues), that from these he proceeded to works

which were still dialogues but began to have something of the character of treatises and are therefore still distinguished as 'on' so-and-so, and later still went on to the large works containing more than one book."

65. Trans. Fyfe, p. 7.

66. Else, *Aristotle's "Poetics,"* p. 40. See also Else, *Plato and Aristotle,* pp. 75–80. Lodovico Castelvetro was one of many Renaissance editors to make this conjecture; in all fairness it should be noted that the modern text of the *Poetics* is not the same one available in the Renaissance and has been greatly emended and improved by the work of nineteenth- and twentieth-century textual scholarship.

67. Hathaway, *Age,* p. 89.

68. Trans. Fyfe, p. 9.

69. "The plot then is the first principle and as it were the soul of tragedy" (*Poetics* 6, 1450a37–38; trans. Fyfe, p. 27).

70. The notion of the difference between speech and writing is obviously already present in Plato's work, but his understanding of this difference is altogether opposed to Aristotle's attempt in the *Poetics* to theorize the *lex operis* of fiction.

71. As cited by Athenaeus, 505B–C; trans. Ross, in Aristotle, *Works,* 12: 73.

72. Compare Ricoeur, 1: 45, who comments: "If we continue to translate mimesis by 'imitation,' we have to understand something completely contrary to a copy of some pre-existing reality and speak instead of a creative imitation. And if we translate mimesis by 'representation' . . . we must not understand by this word some redoubling of presence, as we could still do for Platonic mimesis, but rather the break that opens the space for fiction. Artisans who work with words produce not things but quasi-things; they invent the as-if. And in this sense, the Aristotelian mimesis is the emblem of the shift [*décrochage*] that . . . produces the 'literariness' of the work of literature."

73. Diogenes Laertius, 3.37; trans. Hicks, p. 311.

74. Trimpi, *Muses,* p. 132n.

75. See, for instance, the debate between G. B. Pigna and G. Giraldi Cinthio in the 1550's in Ferrara over Ariosto and the nature of the romance and the epic: Giraldi Cinthio, 2: 153–66. See also Stanesco, pp. 170–79.

76. Weinberg, *History,* 1: 475.

77. The most important of these are Quintilian, *Institutio oratoria* (5.14.27–28; 10.5.15), and Demetrius, 1.21.

78. One of the most original and interesting of the critical texts on Plato is an anonymous "Introduction to Plato" of late Neoplatonic origin

(chaps. 14–15), in Russell, pp. 178–80. The author of this text enumerates seven possible reasons, ranging from the rhetorical to the metaphysical, for Plato's decision to write dialogues.

79. Cicero testifies that his *De oratore* is written in the "Aristotelian manner," or "at least that is what I wanted to do" (*Letters to His Friends* 1.9.23; trans. Williams, 1: 83). See other *testimonia* on Aristotle's dialogues in the *Letters to Atticus* (4.16.2; 13.19.3–4). In the *De oratore* (3.21.80), Cicero remarks that "if there has ever really been a person who was able in Aristotelian fashion to speak on both sides about every subject, and by means of knowing Aristotle's rules to reel off two speeches on opposite sides on every case . . . and who to that method adds the experience and practice in speaking indicated, he would be the one and only true and perfect orator" (trans. Rackham, p. 65).

80. Baldwin, *Renaissance Literary Theory*, p. 43.

81. Grube, p. 191.

82. Harry Caplan reports a remark by Julius Rufinianus regarding the rhetorical figure of dialogism: "*Dialogismos* occurs when someone discusses with himself and ponders what he is doing or what he thinks ought to be done" (Caplan, in Cicero, *Ad Herennium*, p. 366*n*).

83. Trans. Hubbell, p. 353.

84. Grube, p. 176.

85. Lucian, trans. Harmon, vol. 3, esp. pp. 135–51. All citations of *The Double Indictment* in the text include the section numbers of Harmon's translation. I am indebted to Trimpi, *Muses*, pp. 21–24, for his discussion of this work.

Chapter 2

1. All biographical data about Sigonio are from Muratori, i–xx; Tiraboschi, *Biblioteca*, 5: 76–119; Tiraboschi, *Storia*, 3: 1206–31; and Maier. As for the publication date of *De dialogo liber*, the frontispiece of the Venetian *editio princeps* states 1562, and the text concludes with the date 1562. However, Muratori dates *De dialogo liber* to 1561 instead ("feriebant postrema ista verba Sigonium, qui praecedente Anno 1561 Librum *de Dialogo* scripserat, atque evulgarat"; p. vii), and both Tiraboschi and Maier concur with this judgment.

2. Solerti, 1: 62.

3. Dionisotti, *Geografia*, p. 199: "A history of Italian humanism, it seems to me, may with greater certainty be brought to a close with the era and the names of Vettori and Sigonio, rather than with those of Bruno and Galileo" ("Una storia dell'Umanesimo italiano pare a me si possa con più sicura coscienza arrestare all'età e ai nomi di Vettori e Sigonio, che non a quella e a quelli di Bruno e Galileo").

4. Schmitt, *Aristotelian Tradition*, provides a number of excellent essays on this topic.

5. Tiraboschi, *Storia*, 3: 1228–29: "On February 13 and March 6, 1562, Robortello published a challenge to Sigonio. He posted at the schools two notices: in one he boasted of wanting to put forward an entirely new method for teaching Latin, and in the other of wanting to treat the art of writing dialogues *longe secus ac inepti et indocti quidam, quos refellere non erit alienum a me, ut discant posthac cautius scribere.* These words made it perfectly clear to all that Robortello was taking aim at Sigonio (although without naming him), who the year before had published his book *De dialogo*" ("Robortello a' 13 di febbraio e a' 6 di marzo del 1562 pubblicò un cartello di sfida contro il Sigonio, affiggendo alle pubbliche scuole due cedole, in una delle quali vantavasi di voler proporre un metodo del tutto nuovo per insegnare la lingua latina; nell'altra di voler trattar dell'arte di scriver dialoghi *longe secus ac inepti et indocti quidam, quos refellere non erit alienum a me, ut discant posthac cautius scribere;* parole, colle quali non v'era chi non vedesse ch'ei prendeva di mira, benchè senza nominarlo, il Sigonio, che l'anno precedente stampato avea il suo libro *De dialogo*"). See also Tiraboschi's source, Muratori, vii.

6. Scarpati, p. 165.

7. Scarpati, p. 157: "Gli *studia humanitatis* . . . quasi acquistano, nel progetto epistemologico di Sigonio, in continuità piena con le tesi dell'umanesimo quattrocentesco, il carattere di fondamento unitario di ogni costruzione conoscitiva."

8. Mulas, p. 246*n*, provides a partial list of brief comments on dialogue made by sixteenth-century Italian critic-theorists, including Maggi and Lombardi, pp. 51–54; Robortello, pp. 11–13; Vettori, pp. 13–14; Alessandro Piccolomini, pp. 22–23. The dialogue is also treated as a mode of representation by Scaliger, 1: 6, and B. Varchi, *Della Poetica* (1553), printed in his *Lezzioni* (1590), pp. 580–82. For an essentially rhetorical approach to dialogue by an early sixteenth-century humanist, see Becichemo.

9. The two standard reference works for the history of Italian Renaissance literary criticism remain Weinberg, *History;* and Hathaway, *Age*.

10. As Hathaway, *Marvels and Commonplaces*, p. 22, remarks: "The development of a body of critical theory that was the characteristic innovation in philosophy in the sixteenth century, especially in Italy, was a university phenomenon."

11. Sigonio, *De dialogo liber*, 1r: "Quod in primis divinum hominem facere solitum Aristotelem intelligimus." See also 9r. All references are to the Venetian *editio princeps* (1561). In each case, the Latin text appears in the note, and the leaf number (plus notation for *recto* or *verso*)

is included in the text in parentheses. No attempt has been made to modernize Sigonio's punctuation or orthography. Unless otherwise indicated, all translations are my own.

12. "Quae caussae philosophos impulerint ad doctrinam in dialogo tradendam."

13. His references to classical writers are not always uncritical. Sigonio finds Diogenes Laertius's definition of dialogue "lacking" (9*v*) in substance, criticizes Plato for violating the laws of decorum in his dialogues (34*r*), and notes that the *Poetics* itself is "obscure" (12*r*) at times. On the whole, Cicero is the most perfect of all the ancients for Sigonio —a reflection of Cicero's strong influence on all of Sigonio's thought and work.

14. Compare Weinberg, "Robortello," pp. 320, 348. Sigonio published a commentary on Aristotle's *Rhetoric* a few years later (1565); it is included in the *Opera omnia*, 6: 559–658, under the title *Aristotelis "De Arte Rhetorica"* . . . *C. Sigonio Interprete*.

15. "Mihi vero in hanc rem diligentius intuenti ea ad dialogi investigandam definitionem praeclara via est visa, quam in libro de arte poetarum Aristoteles indicavit."

16. Compare Weinberg, *History*, 1: 474. Weinberg, 1: 247, points out that "thinking about literature in terms of the rules or precepts for specific genres had, of course, long been a standard approach. Some of it is already found in Horace, its tendencies are accentuated in the earliest commentators, and during the Middle Ages it produces such schematizations as the 'wheel of Virgil,' in which each of the genres involved a specific kind of subject matter, a type of personage, and a style."

17. "Nihil esse debere impedimento puto, quin quam illi ceteris in rebus rationem, eandem nos quoque eorum imitatione adducti ad dialogi doctrinam, atque artem conficiendam adhibeamus."

18. "Quae tradenda sunt de antiquo dialogi more praecepta."

19. On mannerism, see the detailed and useful bibliography in Mirollo.

20. "Therefore . . . we should dispute, by means of further discussion, more about these parts, if we want to form a perfect dialogue, such as that ancient form of dialogue [was]" ("de his igitur partibus res admonet, ut pluribus disputemus, si perfectum, qualis antiquus ille fuit, informare dialogum volumus"; 18*r*). This leaf is misnumbered in the text of the *editio princeps* as leaf 1, but its signature (F2) confirms that it is actually leaf 18.

21. The critical literature on the humanist practice of *imitatio* is immense. One useful recent work is Greene, *Light in Troy*; for an older but still useful survey of the topic, see Gmelin.

22. "Hoc genus omni priscarum litterarum subsidio, atque instrumento nudatum ita esse reperiet."

23. "Sin autem nihil me dicam, quod ab antiquorum consuetudine disciplinae abhorreat, allaturum, sed ex praeclaris eorum monumentis, tanquam ex uberrimis quibusdam fontibus omnes huius quaestionis rivulos deducturum."

24. For a dissenting sixteenth-century opinion, see Erasmus, *Ciceronianus*, where he scoffs at the prevailing Ciceronianism of the Italian humanists and their theory of *imitatio*. The Pico-Barbaro debate also offers an alternative point of view on Italian Ciceronianism.

25. Kahn, p. 379: "Examples in humanist and humanist-influenced texts are resistant to theory because they call for judgment and use rather than naive or slavish imitation . . . they are problematizing rather than illustrative or problem solving." Cf. Greene, *Light in Troy*, p. 177.

26. Mulas, p. 253, observes that "for Sigonio all reference to a code of orality appears absent, if not to that ideal and regulated orality of the 'best [men]' " ("per Sigonio . . . appare assente qualunque richiamo ad un codice dell'oralità, se non di quella ideale e regolata 'de' migliori' ").

27. Cf. 9*v*–10*r*: "Mihi vero in hanc rem diligentius intuenti ea ad dialogi investigandam definitionem praeclara via est visa, quam in libro de arte poetarum Aristoteles indicavit . . . ille enim cum ad singulas poeseos partes definitione aperiendas fundamenta iaceret, universum earum genus imitationem, generis autem eius differentias tripartitas esse constituit, a rebus, ab instrumentis, a modis." It is outside the scope of the present study to discuss fully the imposing and complex history of the term 'imitation' or 'mimesis.' For some basic approaches to the problem, see McKeon, "Literary Criticism"; Russell; and, again, the standard works of Weinberg and Hathaway.

28. "Ne multa, sic statuo, nihil tam certum videri, quam imitationem in dialogum convenire."

29. "Quae igitur ratio doctissimos homines, ut de ceteris rebus et remota, et adiuncta imitatione scriberent, movit, eadem ut ad eas etiam, quae in philosophia differerentur, utrunque hoc adhiberent instrumentum, adduxit. quam vero cum imitatione coniunctam esse voluerunt, dialogum appellarunt. in quem haud fecus, ac in poesim imitationis nomen convenire, post planius indicabo."

30. In 1*r* Sigonio uses Ammonius's phrase "the very nature of the dialogical writings" (*auta prosōpa, kai dialogika sungrammata*) as support for his argument. The *sungramma*—from Plato to the late Hellenistic rhetors—signifies a style appropriate to literary texts (Russell, pp. 156–57). Sigonio remarks that, in dialogical imitation, "as in tragedy, comedy and epic, these related conversations are brought into being by the char-

acters" ("atque in tragoedia, comoedia, et epopoeia sermones confingi moribus refertos animadvertat"; 10r).

31. A century and a half later, Saint-Mard, pp. 29–30, comments: "Enemy of the pompous, the dialogue cannot tolerate daring figures. It is necessary to take the tone of conversation, which is simple" ("Ennemi du Pompeux, le Dialogue ne souffre point les Figures hardies. . . . Il faut prendre le Ton de la Conversation, qui est simple").

32. "Haec autem sunt, quae iidem illi *auta prosōpa, kai dialogika sungrammata* nominarunt. quorum eam fuisse vim Ammonio placet, ut in iis officium omne disputationis auctor ipse doctrinae subiret, in his aliena inducenda persona sibi subsidium compararet. id quod quia assequi sine aliqua alieni sermonis simulatione non posset, propterea ad imitationem, quasi quidam poeta confugeret."

33. See, e.g., Rimmon-Kenan, pp. 106–8; and Genette, pp. 128–33. Cf. Aristotle, *Poetics* 3, 1448a19–24 ("A third difference in these arts is the manner in which one may represent each of these objects. For in representing the same objects by the same means it is possible to proceed either partly by narrative and partly by assuming a character other than your own—this is Homer's method—or by remaining yourself without such change, or else to represent the characters as carrying out the whole action themselves"; trans. Fyfe, p. 11); and *De dialogo liber*, 3r.

34. Hutton, in Aristotle, *Poetics*, p. 82, points out that "since imitation is essential, Aristotle sometimes prefers to speak of the poet's 'imitation' instead of his 'poem,' and he generally uses the verb 'to imitate' as meaning, not 'to copy,' but 'to give an imitation'—e.g., 'to give an imitation of men in action.' In this meaning it is often convenient to translate it as 'represent.' "

35. McKeon, "Literary Criticism," p. 161. See also Hathaway, *Age*, p. 35.

36. McKeon, "Literary Criticism," p. 163.

37. Ibid., p. 149, notes that "the word 'imitation,' as Plato uses it, is at no time established in a literal meaning or delimited to a specific subject matter."

38. Weinberg, *History*, 1: 250–96.

39. Compare these two passages from *De dialogo liber*: "If Aristotle thought dialogue was imitation in *On Poets*, would he have thought otherwise in the *Poetics*? I think not" ("An vero si dialogum in libro de poetis imitationem esse censuit Aristoteles, secus in libro de poetarum artificio existimavit? non, arbitror"; 10v); and "Plato [was called] 'most mimetic' because he created the most suitable characters for the

individual personae that he brought in" ("Platonem ipsum omnium *mimētikotaton* appellavit, quod singulis, quas induxisset, personis, mores aptissimos affinxisset"; 11*r*).

40. The sixteenth-century critic Francesco Patrizi remarked that whereas Aristotle makes narration one of the specific modes of mimesis, Plato makes mimesis one of the specific modes of narration; quoted in Hathaway, *Age*, p. 51.

41. "Cur dialogus a philosophis sit inventus."

42. "Itaque de diis, de natura, de virtute, de republica, de re familiari tractanda duo extiterunt genera scriptorum, quorum alterum praecipue ab Aristotele celebratum est, alterum a Platone."

43. Agamben, p. 75.

44. "Itaque quoniam disputatio, quaedam est disquisitio rationis, quae inter eruditos homines percontando, et respondendo versatur, quod graece *dialegesthai* dicitur, ea de re dialogum antiqui tradiderunt ex interrogatione, et responsione compositum, dialecticae nimirum ipsius spectantes potestatem, quam constat inveniendorum esse facultatem argumentorum, quibus confirmemus, vel refellamus quid, adversario ita interrogationibus impellendo, ut ei optionem relinquamus, utram velit repugnantium partem, accipiendi."

45. "Quarum artium subsidiis dialogus sustineatur."

46. "Tres enim sunt artes, quarum praeceptis, ac institutis dialogus informatur, nempe poetarum, oratorum, et dialecticorum. poetarum, quia eadem, quae in poesim, in dialogum imitatio cadit: oratorum, quia soluta, non numeris vincta oratione scribitur." Compare Aristotle's definition of prose, *Rhetoric* 3.9 (1409b), as "what is poured forth promiscuously in flowing, unfettered language" (trans. Freese, p. 388*n*).

47. Aristotle, *Rhetoric* 1.1 (1354a).

48. Michel, "L'Influence," p. 12.

49. Trimpi, "Ancient Hypothesis," p. 15. See also Aristotle, *Rhetoric* 1.1 (1355b) and 1.2 (1356a). In the second passage, he remarks of rhetoric and dialectic that "neither of them is a science that deals with the nature of any definite subject, but they are merely faculties of furnishing arguments" (trans. Freese, p. 19).

50. "Sic perfectam dialogi speciem tum poeticis, tum oratoriis institutis absolvi, poeticis ad imitationem cum personarum decoro suscipiendam, oratoriis ad orationem eloquentiae luminibus illustrandam. Quanquam ne hoc quidem est satis. dialectica suppellex adiungatur necesse est, sine qua nec acutum, ac difficile disputationis munus praeclari scriptor dialogi sustinere, nec idoneam poscendae, aut ponendae quaestionis consuetudinem, aut probabilia quae sint, ex rebus eliciendi,

aut adversarii urgendi, aut ex eius forte insidiis, tanquam ex laqueis elabendi, quae omnia ut dialecticae, sic dialogorum sunt instrumenta, rationem cognoscere poterit."

51. Compare *Poetics* 6, 1449b24–31: "Tragedy is, then, a representation of an action that is heroic and complete and of a certain magnitude —by means of language enriched with all kinds of ornament, each used separately in the different parts of the play . . . by 'the kinds separately' I mean that some effects are produced by verse alone and some again by song" (trans. Fyfe, p. 23).

52. Mulas, p. 254.

53. Aristotle, *Poetics* 12, 1452b14–18: "We have already spoken of the constituent parts to be used as ingredients of tragedy. The separable members into which it is quantitatively divided are these: Prologue, Episode, Exode, Choral Song, the last being divided into Parode and Stasimon. These are common to all tragedies" (trans. Fyfe, p. 43).

54. Aristotle, *Poetics* 8, 1451a31–32; trans. Fyfe, pp. 33, 35.

55. "Praeparatio, quam Graeci *kataskeuē* vocant, est sermo ille universus, qui in principio dialogi ad communiendum propositae contentioni aditum adhibetur." Sigonio has little use for the Horatian dictum *in mediis rebus*.

56. Aristotle, *Rhetoric* 3.14 (1414b): "The exordium is the beginning of a speech, as the prologue in poetry and the prelude in flute-playing; for all these are beginnings, and as it were a paving the way for what follows" (trans. Freese, p. 427). Sigonio notes that "this part has the same role in dialogue as the prologue does in tragedy and comedy" ("haec pars idem valet in dialogo, quod in tragoedia, atque comoedia prologus"; 18r).

57. "Ut in ipso quasi vestibulo qui, et quales sint, quos induxerit, et quo tempore, et quo in loco, et qua ratione ad eam disputationem pervenerint, planum faciat."

58. "Iam vero mores . . . non minori effingere cura conabimur, quam sententiam expresserimus."

59. Verisimilitude, Sigonio notes, was called *eidos* by the Greeks (18v), a term that generally indicates argumentation by recourse to probability. It seems more than likely, however, that Sigonio derives the criteria of the five elements of decorum from a reading of Proclus's *Commentary on the "Republic"* 1.3 (16.26–19.25; trans. Festugière, 1: 32–34), which discusses the "external circumstances" of Plato's *Republic* in terms of time, place, and character. In *De dialogo liber*, Sigonio refers to Proclus's reading of the *Republic* in 3r and again in 18v, toward the beginning of the section that discusses decorum.

60. "Quippe quae decoro in primis, et verisimilitudini serviant, qui-

bus tuendis officiis nihil in omnibus artibus fuit unquam vel doctissi-
morum hominum judicio difficilius"; trans. Weinberg, *History*, 1: 484.
Compare *De dialogo liber*, 19*v* (misnumbered "16" in the text): "Ut in
vita, sic in oratione nihil difficilius est, quam quod deceat, *prepon* appellant Graeci, nos appellemus sane decorum" (paraphrasing Cicero in the
Orator 21: "Nothing is more difficult than to see what is becoming. The
Greeks call this *prepon*, we call it *decorum*"). See also Aristotle, *Rhetoric*
3.7 (1408a).

61. "Imitatio omnis verisimilitudinis, et decori officio tuendo perfici-
tur."

62. Weinberg, *History*, 1: 484. Deakins, p. 11; and Wilson, *Incomplete
Fictions*, p. 13, essentially agree with this judgment.

63. "Quid igitur hoc de genere praecipiendum est aliud, nisi utrunque in personarum, temporum, locorum, et caussarum consideratione,
atque animadversione esse positum?"; trans. Weinberg, *History*, 1: 484.

64. Trimpi, *Muses*, pp. 84–85; see also Patterson, pp. 8–15.

65. "De genere personarum . . . de officio personarum . . . de loco
et tempore colloquiis idoneo . . . quibus ex locis dialogi praeparatio
deducatur." Cf. Cicero, *De oratore* 1.7.24–29.

66. "Iam vero decorum poeticum cum in imitandis moribus hominum, tum in convenienti affingenda oratione versatur."

67. "Et quoniam actio nulla est nisi in tempore, et loco, propterea
quod in re est, id etiam oratione exprimatur necesse est"; trans. Weinberg, *History*, 1: 485. *Dianoia*, or "all the effects produced by language,"
is explained by rhetorical rather than poetic theory, as Aristotle notes
in chap. 19 of the *Poetics*.

68. Cf. Ong, pp. 212–13: "Decorum had always involved a complex
notion of adaptation, with a certain personalist valence, since the choice
of style depended not merely upon some mechanically conceived ad-
justment but upon *ethos* or character." See also Kushner, "Le dialogue
en France de 1550 à 1560," p. 158. Weinberg, *History*, 1: 394–95, points
out that in the theory of decorum each character is assigned "a complex
of traits . . . in accordance with the circumstances surrounding" that
character. See also Aristotle, *Rhetoric* 2, where a general theory of types
is presented, and *Rhetoric* 3.16 (1417a) ("Mathematical treatises have no
moral character, because neither have they moral purpose; for they have
no moral end. But the Socratic dialogues have; for they discuss such
questions. Other ethical indications are the accompanying peculiarities
of each individual character"; trans. Freese, p. 447).

69. Manley, p. 154, contends that external places "provided argumentative means for adapting . . . to new social and historical contin-
gencies. Arguments for adaptation tended to cohere around [among

other things] . . . the categories of time, place, circumstance, and comparison, all of which underlined differences in social settings." Weinberg, *History*, 1: 476, adds that in the Renaissance "the insistence upon decorum . . . leads increasingly to an emphasis upon social distinctions where Aristotle had made ethical distinctions, and upon ethical distinctions which derive rather from tradition than from the needs of a particular poem." Cf. Kushner, "Le dialogue de 1580 à 1630," p. 163.

70. "Neque enim satis decorum, aut consonum foret, principes reip. viros, et in maximis eius curis, et negotiis occupatos aut quocunque die, aut quencunque in locum ventitare, ut de iis subtilius rebus disputando exquirerent, quae in arte, et scientia aliqua versarentur"; trans. Deakins, p. 12.

71. "Quod Ciceronem inprimis fecisse animadvertimus, cum homines in maximis potius reipublicae rebus, quam in studiis litterarum exercitatos induceret."

72. See *De dialogo liber*, 28v–29r.

73. "Haec ego non nego, quin mirifica quadam sint suavitate condita omnia, sed ratio personarum fecit, quae non generis, sed vitae, non rerum gestarum, sed doctrinae nobilitate sunt commendatae, ut quanto plus habent iucunditatis, tanta magnificentiae minus"; trans. Deakins, p. 14.

74. See *De dialogo liber*, 23r–23v.

75. "In moribus haec quatuor spectari oportere censet Aristoteles in libro de arte poetarum, ut sint boni, convenientes, similes et aequabiles. boni quidem, quia virtutum nos decet esse imitatores, non vitiorum; congruentes autem sunt, qui cuique aetati, sexui, nationi, et conditioni conveniunt, ut fortitudo viro, mulieri mollicies, non contra. atque ita in ceteris; similes autem effinget, si cum aliis poetis in virtute alicuius exprimenda non discrepabit, in quod vitium incurret"; trans. Deakins, p. 12. Cf. Aristotle, *Poetics* 15, 1454a16–24, and *Rhetoric* 3.7 (1408a), as well as Horace, *Ars poetica* 119.

76. Aristotle, *Poetics* 25, 1460b14–15; trans. Fyfe, p. 101.

77. Samuel, Introduction, in Tasso, *Discourses on the Heroic Poem*, p. xxix, makes this point in regard to Tasso's theory of decorum, but it is equally applicable to Sigonio's.

78. Trimpi, "Quality of Fiction," p. 22.

79. "Neque vero minus de tempore, aut loco est laborandum, ut quo anno, quo mense, et, si fieri possit, quo die, et quo in loco ea sit disputatio instituta, in ipso dialogi vestibulo patefaciamus." Hamon, p. 3, observes that this idea of decorum is "part principally of the epideictic genre that requires systematic description, especially in the form of praise of certain individuals, places, times of the year, [and] socially privileged monuments or objects."

80. Manley, p. 154.

81. "Huius enim praeteritio officii incredibile est, quantum ei sermoni adimat auctoritatis, et fidei, ut cum ea legas, quae nec temporis, nec loci habeant commemorationem, prorsus ut sunt, falsa, et ficta esse existimes. sin autem rem cum personis, locis, temporibus consentire intelligas, mirabiliter omnibus iis, quae dicantur, quaeque agantur, assentiaris."

82. See note 70 above for Latin text.

83. "Quae pars quia mirificum quendam ingenii leporem, et quandam quasi morum festivitatem desiderat."

84. Saint-Mard, p. 11, adds: "What is also noteworthy in Cicero's dialogues is the choice that he makes of his interlocutors and the attention that he devotes to making them reason according to their characters" ("Ce qu'il y a encore de remarquable dans les Dialogues de Cicéron, c'est le choix, qu'il fait de ses Interlocuteurs; et l'Attention, qu'il a à les faire raisonner dans leur Caractère").

85. Kahn, p. 377. Cf. Marsh, p. 11.

86. "Hoc autem poeticum eius est potestatis, atque naturae, ut cum adest, efficiat, ne res, ut est ficta, sic videatur. ficta autem videbitur, quae a vero longe abhorrebit, nec veritatis ullam similitudinem consequetur, id est, quae cum personis, temporibus, et locis discrepabit, et caussas nullas, cur ita factum sit, aut certe non probabiles continebit"; trans. Weinberg, *History*, 1: 484–85.

87. Grube, p. 177.

88. "Contentio, qui *agōn* graece dicitur, est quidquid verborum de re ad disputandum proposita vel confirmandi vel refellendi gratia sit."

89. "Est enim locus, qui dialogum vi, ac potestate sua totum amplectitur."

90. "Si dialogum disputationem quandam esse dialecticam ponimus. omnino enim si propriam, et a veteribus nobilissimis auctoribus celebratam vim dialogorum exquirimus, eadem sit dialogo, quae dialecticae subiecta materia, necesse est."

91. "Haec autem pars ut tota in rei contemplatione est posita, ita in duo quasi membra discerpitur, rei propositionem, et probationem."

92. "Ita sit hoc genus argumentandi tripartitum. prima pars constat ex similitudine una, pluribusve; altera ex eo, quod concedi volumus, cuius caussa similitudines adhibitae sunt. *tertia ex conclusione*, quae aut confirmat concessionem, aut quod ex ea conficiatur, ostendit" (my italics).

93. Cicero, *De partitione oratoria* 18.61 (in *De oratore*, trans. Rackham, p. 357); Quintilian, 3.5.5. Trimpi, *Muses*, pp. 25–72, provides an excellent discussion of thesis and hypothesis. An alternative translation for the term *propositio* might be "declarative statement."

94. Trans. Butler, 1: 399.

95. "Quis est enim locus de Deo, de natura, de animis nostris, de virtutibus, de republica, de re domestica, de ratione, de scientia, de oratorum."

96. "Itaque hoc potissimum philosophus a dialectico differre putatur, quod ille perpetuam, aeternamque materiam, quam tractet, propositam habeat, hic quancunque, ille rationibus necessariis, hic probabilibus, ille a sola rei natura, aut iis, quae illam necessario consequuntur, hic et hinc, et undecunque argumenta, et quidem non ad constituendam scientiam, sed ad inserendam opinionem eliciat."

97. "Ut aut in primis verbis, quod saepe factum ostendi, aut non ita multo post, extet, atque appareat" (34*v*); "est enim propositio nihil aliud, quam conclusio probationis" (36*r*). Aristotle, *Poetics* 7, 1450b27–32, makes it clear that this structure of beginning, middle, and end is necessary to the organicity of the poetic text: "A whole is what has a beginning and middle and end. A beginning is that which is not a necessary consequent of anything else but after which something else exists or happens as a natural result. An end on the contrary is that which is inevitably or, as a rule, the natural result of something else but from which nothing else follows; a middle follows something else and something follows from it" (trans. Fyfe, p. 31).

98. Rhetoric, in one of the senses defined by Sigonio in *De dialogo liber*, is omnipresent in dialogue as prose or *oratio soluta*; it serves as the linguistic continuum of dialogue. Rhetoric, in this restricted sense, is closer to the daily use of speech than to verse, inasmuch as prose is closer to speech than verse is. Sigonio points out that for dialogue "prose [*oratio soluta*] is, however, its instrument, not closely attached by meter in the manner of poetry; this very thing . . . brings back the daily use of speech" ("quarum quae proxima est, ab instrumento ducitur imitandi. instrumentum autem est oratio soluta, non numeris poetico more devincta, eademque, quia quotidianam quandam refert sermonis consuetudinem"; 14*r*). In the pages that follow, however, I refer to rhetoric in a second sense—as a system of description and persuasion—that has to be distinguished from the dialectical language of statement.

99. Aristotle, *Rhetoric*, 3.13 (1414a): "A speech has two parts. It is necessary to state the subject, and then to prove it. Wherefore it is impossible to make a statement without proving it, or to prove it without first putting it forward; for both he who proves proves something, and he who puts something forward does so in order to prove it. The first of these parts is the statement of the case, the second the proof, a similar division to that of problem and demonstration" (trans. Freese, p. 425).

100. "Ut in eo haec etiam tria exprimi statuamus, *actionem in ipsa*

eorum, qui colloquuntur, sermonis communicatione, sententiam in eorundem argumentatione, mores in instituto, et electione" (my italics).

101. "Est igitur ita haec quasi dialogi fabula constituenda."

102. Wilson, "Continuity," p. 36. Saint-Mard, p. 27, comments that "the dialogue, in order to be perfect, must contain a single idea within itself. When it is alone, the idea is much better perceived" ("le Dialogue, pour être parfait, doit renfermer une Idée . . . unique. Quand elle est seule, elle est bien mieux apperçue").

103. "Unam expositionis, alteram inquisitionis, mistam tertiam."

104. "Expositionem appello, cum qui praecipiendi partes habet, ut fere apud eum Socrates, alieno, ut sit, rogatu, aperte quid de proposita sentiat quaestione, demonstrat." Tasso, in his *Discorso dell'arte del dialogo,* p. 29, argues instead that this is a Ciceronian mode of questioning; Socrates, in his most didactic dialogues, still asks the majority of the questions himself. Kushner, "Le dialogue de 1580 à 1630," p. 149, contends that dialogue is in fact always reducible to a handful of basic narrative situations and is thus a restricted model of all literary communication.

105. Sigonio calls this mode "maieutic" (42*v*): "Obstetricium enim dialogum, sive, ut Graeco verbo utar, *maieutikon* Graeci appellant. in quo Socrates ita disputat."

106. "Inquisitionem vero, cum idem, ille interrogandis aliis, aliquanto obscurius intimum animi sui sensum patefacit."

107. Compare Wilson, *Incomplete Fictions,* p. 49.

108. "Deinceps sequuntur tentativi. sic enim libet vertere, quos Graeci *peirastikos* appellarunt" (47*r*).

109. Wilson, *Incomplete Fictions,* p. 50. Buckley, p. 148, notes that for Cicero "philosophizing lies precisely in this ongoing conversation, the clash of statements and judgments, and the value of the method emerges precisely in this discrimination of perspectives and the differentiation of frames of reference. . . . The claim of the author is simply, 'I place in your midst the opinions (*sententiae*) of the philosophers.' The truth emerges from the methodological testing of the arguments by submitting these statements to the differing perspectives."

110. Dupriez, p. 154.

111. "Quam laudem quibus potissimum instrumentis assequeremur, Aristoteles in dialecticis indicavit."

112. Compare Aristotle, *Rhetoric* 1.1 (1354a–56b).

113. "His ergo instrumentorum generibus sancientur omnia, aut revellentur, argumentis ex iis sedibus eruendis, quae nobis ars dialecticorum ostendit."

114. Buckley, p. 144.

115. "Neque enim in omnibus rebus eadem subtilitas veritatis exquiritur, verum in plerisque satis habetur, si probabilia proferantur."

116. "Itaque definitiones quidem, et caussas, et effecta, ut dialecticorum sic dialogorum afferet consuetudo, sed non quae reciprocentur omnino, ac necessitatem scientiae, sed quandam opinionis probabilitatem inducant."

117. "Si dialogum disputationem quandam esse dialecticam ponimus" (13*r*); "dialogus quaedam est dialecticae disputationis imago" (14*v*); *imago* could also be translated here as "likeness" or "semblance." See Aristotle, *Rhetoric* 1.1 (1354a).

118. Aristotle, *Rhetoric* 1.2 (1356a).

119. Grube, p. 92.

120. For a fuller treatment of this topic, see Armstrong.

121. "Nam probabilia sunt, quae aut omnium, aut plurimorum, aut certe sapientum opinione probantur, persuasibilia, quibus rudis, et imperita multitudo plerunque assentitur. Nam iniuriam accipere, quam facere praestantius esse, quod multis philosophis placuit, in dialectica disputatione, ut probabile concedetur, in concione, ut parum persuasibile, totius fortasse populi iudicio explodetur"; trans. Deakins, pp. 13–14. "Probability," or "resting on opinion," is defined by Aristotle (*Topics* 1.1) as "things generally admitted by all, or by most men, or by the wise, or by all or most of these, or by the most notable and esteemed" (as quoted by Freese, in Aristotle, *Rhetoric*, p. 10*n*).

122. Armstrong, p. 43.

123. Kristeller, *Renaissance Thought and Its Sources*, p. 253.

124. "Ne diu lectoris animus in argumento percipiendo aberret."

125. "Sed diu sententiae, et controversiae, quae inter eos verse[n]tur, qui loquuntur, incertus, mente vageris et fluctues." Saint-Mard, p. 8, sees this in the opposite way: "The ancients did not trouble themselves with going toward the truth by the shortest possible route. They reserved for themselves the pleasure of looking for it for a long time. Plato is one of the most prolix writers that antiquity produced. A small idea, often banal, furnishes him with a very long dialogue; and what we learn from it always is well worthwhile" ("Les Anciens ne se picquoient point d'aller à la Vérité par le chemin le plus court. Ils se ménageoient le Plaisir de la chercher longtemps. Platon est un des plus diffus qu'ait produit l'Antiquité. Une petite Idée, souvent commune, lui fournit un Dialogue très long; et ce qu'on y apprend se fait toujours bien payer").

126. See 14*v*. The vestibule, in this perspective, is also determined to a considerable degree by a psychology of reading (the factors of distraction or concentration, for instance, in description), just as the art of rhetoric is, for Aristotle, a kind of psychology.

127. Ferraro, p. 40.

128. Weinberg, *History*, 1: 485, remarks that "Sigonio still writes at a time when the implications of Aristotle's method are not clear, when it is easy to pass from one critical context to another, when there is no notion at all of methodological rigor."

129. McKeon, "Literary Criticism," p. 171, notes that Aristotle instead distinguishes "the two disciplines sharply: only two of the six [qualitative] 'parts' of tragedy—thought and diction—are properly treated in rhetoric; and only one of them—thought—receives the same treatment in Aristotle's *Rhetoric* and *Poetics.*"

130. Herrick, *Fusion*, pp. 39–47.

131. Trans. Caplan, p. 107. Cf. Cicero, *De inventione* 1.37.67.

132. Trimpi, "Quality of Fiction," pp. 57–59. In *De dialogo liber*, the *complexio* is implicitly understood to be attached to the *probatio*, insofar as dialogues ought never to be aporetic in Sigonio's view. See also Aristotle, *Rhetoric* 3.13 (1414b): "So the necessary parts of a speech are the statement of the case and proof. These divisions are appropriate to every speech, and at the most the parts are four in number—exordium, statement, proof and epilogue" (trans. Freese, p. 427).

133. Trimpi, "Quality of Fiction," p. 57. Weinberg, *History*, 1: 197, observes that "thinking . . . in terms of rhetorical ends was bound to lead to thinking in terms of rhetorical means, and hence we have a growing desire to speak of such parts of a poem as the proposition, the narration, the exordium."

134. Doueihi, p. 77. Greene, *Vulnerable Text*, p. xii, warns in this regard that "part of the [Renaissance] text's vulnerability lies in its dependence on secondhand signifiers, a vulnerability aggravated in a culture which does not yet fetishize originality."

135. Michel, "L'Influence," p. 12.

136. Compare Rice and Schafer, p. xi.

137. "Et eiusmodi alia, quae plurima incredibilis illa ad omnia tum Platonici, tum Tulliani ingenii facultas." Recall that Cicero, unlike Plato, is present in his own dialogues as a speaker: Sigonio favors, on the whole, the Ciceronian model of dialogue, but includes in it the Platonic fiction of a figure like Socrates to control the disputation.

138. Sigonio, of course, claims the contrary: "I will offer nothing that is averse to the practice of the discipline of the ancients, but instead I will draw out from their noble monuments all the rivers of this question" ([iir]). See note 23 for the Latin text.

139. Scarpati, p. 165.

140. See Rosmarin, p. 49, for an examination of history versus system in genre theory.

141. Rosmarin, p. 50.

142. Lucian was widely read and admired in the fifteenth century and the first half of the sixteenth century in Italy, especially in Florence. Lucian's *Opuscola*, in the translation by More and Erasmus, was published in Venice in 1516 by Aldo Manuzio. Sapegno, p. 966*n*, points out that after Leon Battista Alberti—in his *Momus*—published Latin dialogues in the style of Lucian, Lucian's fame spread gradually across Europe. See also Dionisotti, *Machiavellerie*, pp. 212, 214. For a survey of some little-known Italian Renaissance dialogues of this kind (by Antonio Vignali and others), see Borsellino.

143. "Postremo a Luciano ad deos, ad mortuos, et ad meretrices risus, ut ipse confessus est, captandi gratia temere translatam esse, animadvertimus."

144. "Hanc ergo consuetudinem ab omnibus antesancte custoditam, primus etiam, ut dixi, Lucianus depravavit, atque corrupit, cum de rebus ridiculis, de amoribus, ac fallaciis meretriciis dialogum loqui coegerit." The collected works of Lucian were placed on the *Index librorum prohibitorum* in 1554/55, some six years before the completion of the treatise. Although Paul IV's 1559 Index instead banned only two of Lucian's dialogues, this Index appears to have been suppressed in Venice after Paul IV's death on August 18, 1559, because of its overall severity. See Grendler, p. 126.

145. "Quibus tamen parce tanquam sale . . . utemur, ne studium, operamque in captando risu ponere videamur."

146. Cf. Bakhtin, *Rabelais*, pp. 69–70, and all of Bakhtin's discussion of "carnivalization"; also Bakhtin, "Characteristics of Genre and Plot Composition in Dostoyevsky's Works," in idem, *Dostoyevsky's Poetics*, pp. 101–80.

147. Sigonio, *De latinae lingua usu retinendo* (1556), in *Opera omnia*, 6: 529–36. Cf. also Dionisotti, *Geografia*, pp. 163–78, 179–200, 227–54.

148. Floriani, pp. 29–30, 33–49.

Chapter 3

1. Hathaway, *Age*, p. viii, remarks that "any list of the great critical theorists of the Renaissance, if not of the whole modern world, should include Sperone Speroni, Robortello, Francesco Patrizi, Lodovico Castelvetro, Tasso, Giacopo Mazzoni, Francesco Buonamici, and Paolo Beni, but of these only Tasso and Castelvetro have received the attention they deserve."

2. All biographical data on Speroni are from the following sources: Fano, chap. 2; and Pozzi, 1: 472–74, 692*n*. Information on Speroni's life may also be found in Cammarosano.

3. Cf. Pozzi, 1: 503*n*, 723*n*.

4. Two dialogues appeared in French in 1546 (Lyon, 1546), and a complete translation of the *Dialoghi* appeared five years later (Paris, 1551).

5. All references to the *Apologia dei Dialoghi* are to the 1740 edition, *Opere di M. Sperone Speroni degli Alvarotti*, ed. dalle Laste and Forcellini, 1: 266–425, and are included in the text in parentheses. The only modern edition, in Pozzi, 1: 683–724, is of Part 1 only, and so is of limited use. I have not modernized Speroni's orthography or punctuation anywhere in this essay except for the titles of his work on dialogue and his *Dialogues*. All translations from the *Apologia dei Dialoghi* are my own and are accompanied by the original Italian text either in the notes or in the body of the chapter. Speroni refers to the anonymous "gentiluomo" on p. 266.

The *Apologia dei Dialoghi* presents several difficulties of a textological nature. The treatise was not published in the author's own lifetime. The first edition (Venice, 1596) was posthumously published, together with the *Dialoghi*, by G. Alberti, without the supervision of Speroni's literary executor, his grandson Ingolfo de' Conti. The eighteenth-century editors of Speroni's collected works, Natal dalle Laste and Marco Forcellini, attacked the 1596 edition of the *Dialoghi* as "monstrous," adding that "with the addition of eight other dialogues, along with the defenses, it should have been the most perfect [edition]" but instead Alberti "foully dishonored our author" (in *Opere* 1: xii). The 1740 edition of the *Opere* by dalle Laste and Forcellini is based for the most part on "the original manuscripts" of Speroni, which were in the possession of the de' Conti family until the middle of the eighteenth century. Following the preparation and publication of the *Opere*, the manuscripts were donated to the Biblioteca del Seminario Vescovile in Padua, where they remain to this day in seventeen carefully organized codices (E 13/1–17); the manuscript of the *Apologia dei Dialoghi* is found in Cod. E 13/1, and fragments of various drafts of the treatise are found in Cod. E 13/2. Mario Pozzi, the only modern editor of the *Apologia dei Dialoghi*, states that the 1740 edition is "good" and "still fundamental" (p. 503) and bases his own edition of Part 1 of the text on it. Pozzi does not point out, however, that some sections of the original manuscripts are much damaged, and that any critical reading of Parts 2–4 would have to be based largely on conjecture since to a considerable degree the manuscript for these parts is now illegible and appears to have been so since at least the early eighteenth century. It seems probable that the copy used by dalle Laste and Forcellini in preparing their edition of Parts 2–4 was an apographic manuscript, presumably made for circulation among Speroni's friends in Padua and elsewhere soon after the completion of the *Apologia dei*

Dialoghi in 1574. This copy is perhaps the one now in the Biblioteca Marciana in Venice (Cl. VIII, Cod. ital. XIV, 6200).

6. Pozzi, 1: 684*n*. This denunciation could have had many other possible purposes at the time: see Fano for a fuller account of Speroni's life in the intrigue-riddled Rome of the 1560's and 1570's. On the topic of censorship and the Roman Inquisition in the late sixteenth century, see also Longo.

7. "Il quale (cioè amore) vero signore e vero Dio di ogni nostra operazione"; "quei dolci nomi d'innamorato e innamorata derivati da amore, sciocamente in due strani e odiosi vocaboli moglie e marito di convertire deliberarono"; "così l'anima delle donne è composta di sentimento e di amore, Dio massimo ed ottimo." Speroni lists these and other controversial passages from the *Dialoghi* on p. 296.

8. Tedeschi, p. 131, observes that "according to Roman censorship practice, total prohibition was generally reserved for the *opera omnia* of arch-heretics and for the religious writings of lesser heretics. Books by Protestant authors on subjects of a non-controversial nature might be temporarily suspended and then permitted to circulate after expurgation, which normally took the form of crude pen and ink erasures applied to the text by officials attached to the Congregation of the Index in Rome and the local tribunals of the Holy Office. It is difficult to estimate how many titles passed through the censorship process in practice, because there were mountains of them to be dealt with, and the personnel to perform the task few, and perhaps not always willing."

9. "Quando il reverendo Padre Maestro cominciò a leggermi alcuni luoghi nei miei dialogi; tutto che piano li mi legesse e in voce piena di carità; io nondimeno alla sua lettura, non altrimenti che se da folgore o da bombarda venisse il suono delle parole, rimasi in guisa intronato."

10. Speroni, *Opere*, 5: 209.

11. Speroni, *Opere*, 5: 210: "non m'inganno a dirvi che la vedrete conditissima, ma di condizione non più avvertita, benchè insegnata già mille ottocento anni: la vedrete in uno stile non più veduto, e con tale arte formata, che voi direte: ella è sua."

12. Pozzi, 1: 485.

13. Fano, 1: 113, adds: "He revised and corrected the dialogues from his youth, in accordance with the criticisms that had been made of them, because he wanted to reprint them in Rome" ("Rivide anche e corresse i dialoghi giovanili, secondo le imposizioni che gli venivan fatte, perchè in Roma si voleva ristamparli").

14. Rosa, p. 318.

15. "Se ciò non si potrà; son contento che mondi il fuoco le macchie

loro." At another level, this statement would seem to refer to the precedent set by Plato in burning his poetry when he turned to philosophy; Speroni implies here that he, too, would consider burning the works of his errant youth.

16. Pallavicino, *Trattato*, p. 355. See Chapter 5 for further details of Pallavicino's attitude toward Speroni.

17. Kelly(-Gadol).

18. "Il precetto della esercitazione oratoria, tanto lodato da Cicerone; onde io difesi li miei dialogi."

19. Ferguson, p. 11, remarks that "the defense is a signal instance of the Renaissance capacity to create mixed or even 'monstruous' genres which contain imitations of various classical forms and bear family resemblances to 'new-old' forms like the Erasmian mock-encomium and the *paragone*."

20. Speroni also speaks of "the authority of the holy men" ("l'autorità de' santi uomini"; p. 290) and of "the reason of the wise" ("la ragione dei sapienti"; p. 290), for instance.

21. "I miei dialogi innocentissimi, quanto ai precetti della loro arte particolare . . . non possono essere condannati."

22. Ferguson, pp. 2, 137.

23. "Renderò conto particolare della bontà e malizia de' miei dialogi giovenili: alli quali per avventura secondo l'uso delle commedie, io padre e vecchio oltre ad ogni altro sarò severo. Che se innocenti si trovaranno, senza alcun dubbio l'altrui giudicio benignamente li accoglierà ed assolverà: il che del mio non prometto. . . . Sanarò bene, o che io spero! con lo artificio del bene scrivere anticamente insegnato, e purgarò le sue note (chiamo inferma quella innocenzia, la quale è ancora dubbiosa)."

24. "The good father laughed sometimes as I defended myself in that way; and I dare believe that he was not mocking me with his laughter, for, as soon as I fell silent, with a gentle look he began to speak to me like this: 'If I acted alone in forbidding your dialogues, I will not be alone in ending that ban. Willingly will I discuss this case with my colleagues and superiors'" ("Ridea talora il buon Padre, mentre in tal modo mi difendeva; ed oso creder che quel suo riso non mi schernisse: perciocchè subito che io mi tacqui, con dolce vista così mi prese a parlare. Se io fui solo al divieto de' tuoi dialogi, non sarò solo al fermarlo. Volentieri con i miei compagni e signori di questo fatto ragionarò"; pp. 269–70).

25. *Apologia dei Dialoghi*, pp. 361–91. Speroni uses a similar "dialogue within a dialogue" in his *Dialogo delle lingue* as well.

26. This relationship mirrors in reverse the one described by Dostoy-

evsky in the Grand Inquisitor segment of *The Brothers Karamazov*, where the accused (Christ) is silent and the Grand Inquisitor alone speaks.

27. The father inquisitor, during a formal trial, generally belonged to a tribunal that included at least two other ecclesiastical authorities: the inquisitor led the questioning, and took part in the deliberations leading to a verdict. See, for instance, Grendler, pp. 48–53.

28. "Although I am certain that I am saying nothing that you do not know, I will say it anyway. You, who are listening out of courtesy and fairness, will be an example (to whomever does not do so) of what it means to be careful when it is a question of another person's honor, and to teach, if nothing else, the patience to listen" ("Benchè io sia certo di non dir cosa che non sappiate, io nondimeno la pur dirò. Voi ascoltando per cortesia e per giustizia, farete esemplo a chi manco fa, di star attento quando si tratta dell'altrui onore, ed imparare se non altro la pazienza dello ascoltare"; p. 267). "Yet there is someone who murmurs I know not what; no, on the contrary, I know what it is, and I will say it myself. But I only ask each person, since I freely speak the accusations that have been made against my dialogues, to deign please to listen courteously to, and to understand well, my defenses" ("Pur è chi mormori non so che; anzi il so io, e dirollo: ma sia pregato ciascuno, che siccome io liberamente dico le accuse che date sono alli miei dialogi, così allo 'ncontro alcun altro degni di udire cortesemente e bene intender le mie difese"; p. 290). "Someone will venture to say, already guessing from that beginning what is to be the means and the scope of my *Apologia*, which is unwillingly listened to by those who do not wish me well: 'This good man speaks too much of the manner of his dialogues; why doesn't he come to the point?' Surely keeping silent when it is time to do so is no less excellent than defending an accused person. . . . Nor will I say such vulgar things, even though I do not speak Greek or Latin, nor things that are so irrelevant to my argument, that this discourse should be taken out of my mouth and broken off at the halfway point. So anyone who would interrupt me should keep silent instead, or go and look for someone else—certainly not me—who wants to talk incessantly, and accuse innocent people without listening to them or giving them space to defend themselves" ("Dirà alcuno per avventura, già indovinando da tal principio, qual sia per essere il mezzo e il fine di questa mia Apologia, mal volentieri ascoltata da chi mi vuol poco bene: troppo parla questo buono uomo delle maniere de' suoi dialogi; non ne vuole egli venire a capo una volta? Certo il tacersi quando egli è tempo, non è men bello, che sia il difendere uno accusato . . . nè cose dico così volgari, benchè io non parli latino o greco, nè alla mia causa sì impertinenti, che 'l cominciato ragionamento mi debba esser di bocca tolto, e rotto

appunto in sul mezzo. Però taccia chi mi interrompe, o trovi altro uomo, che io non sono io, chi vuol parlar sempremai, ed accusar gli innocenti senza ascoltarli, nè dar loro spazio a difendersi"; pp. 275–76).

29. Cf. *Phaedrus* 257C–278B.

30. "Le ragioni più generali, che a tali farli mi indussero."

31. "Ora io non parlo specialmente de' miei dialogi; parlo ben della *idea* dei miei dialogi e degli altrui" (my italics).

32. I take the term and the notion of "writerly" from the now-classic work of Barthes, *S/Z*, p. 4.

33. "Ogni dialogo sente non poco della commedia" (p. 267); "i dialogi son commedie" (p. 334). Cf. Saint Basil's letter (135) to Diodorus, in which Plato is highly praised for his dialogues in this regard. Speroni refers to this letter later on in Part 1 (pp. 292–93). The same letter is cited by Sigonio in *De dialogo liber* as well, while Saint-Mard, p. 30, notes: "Comedy is a species of dialogue where the rules—in my opinion— have been best observed" ("La Comédie est une espèce de Dialogue, où les Règles, à mon gré, ont été le mieux observées").

34. "È poema il dialogo" (p. 285); "la poetica o dialogica finzione" (p. 286). Curiously, elsewhere Speroni *defends* the position that poetry is limited to verse forms; see *Giudizio sopra la tragedia di Canace e Macareo*, in *Opere*, 4: 117–19; and *Sopra Virgilio*, in *Opere*, 4: 534 (see also Hathaway, *Age*, p. 92*n*). Speroni is in many ways a critical chameleon, since the arguments that he employs in his critical writings are chosen as much for the rhetorical effect that they produce as for their insight into contemporary literary issues. It is often extremely misleading to cite Speroni out of context; i.e., outside of the particular argument that he is making in a particular work aimed at achieving a particular effect.

35. "Comicamente, cioè in stil basso e non molto netto."

36. Speroni lists, among the elements of comic dialogue, "irony" ("l'ironia"), "cunning disguised by foolishness" ("l'astuzia mascherata da sciocchezza"), "amphibological speech" ("l'amfibologico parlamento"), and "deception generally done to the deceiver" ("lo 'nganno fatto generalmente allo 'ngannatore") (pp. 278–79). On the comic in general, see Herrick, *Comic Theory*, who provides useful synopses of the comic theories of Robortello, Giraldi Cinthio, Minturno, Trissino, Scaliger, and Castelvetro, together with a translation of Robortello's 1548 treatise *On Comedy*. Vincenzo Maggi's *De ridiculis* (1550) and Bernardo Pino da Cagli's *Breve considerazione intorno al componimento de la comedia de' nostri tempi* (1572) can be found in Weinberg, *Trattati*, 2: 91–125, 629–49, along with a number of other Cinquecento works on comedy.

37. "Parla ognuno da quel che egli è, o pare essere."

38. Speroni speaks explicitly of "the decorum of the characters, good

and bad, who enter into conversation" ("il decoro delle persone buone e cattive, che si riducono a parlamento"; p. 278).

39. "E non è onore a Platone, che sia commedia il dialogo: che se di tragico che era prima, quasi sdegnando si fe filosofo; qual ragione doveva indurlo, poichè era tale, a dover scrivere comicamente . . . la gentilezza de' suoi degni ed alti concetti?"

40. Speroni speaks, for instance, of "well-formed dialogue, such as Plato's" ("il dialogo ben formato, siccome è quel di Platone"; p. 267). Later on, in Part 2, he states that his own model for dialogue is none other than Plato: "but imitating Plato, who makes his Socrates speak, I . . ." ("ma imitando Platone che fa parlare il suo Socrate, io . . ."; p. 314).

41. "Ha molti e varii interlocutori, che tal ragionano, quale è il costume e la vita, che ciascun d'essi ci rappresenta."

42. Andrieu, pp. 304–5, lists these, together with other instances where the two-speaker structure emerges after an opening scene with more than two speakers in it, as in the *Lesser Hippias* or the *Cratylus*.

43. Andrieu, p. 307, points out that "in Plato one never finds a diegetic dialogue that has only two characters, as is instead the case in Xenophon" ("on ne trouve jamais chez Platon un dialogue en récit ne comportant que deux personnages, comme c'est le cas du Hiéron de Xénophon").

44. This identification has some basis in the textual tradition, as Andrieu, p. 283, remarks: "Philosophical papyri, when compared to theatrical ones, show that there is but a single published form for two different literary genres" ("Les papyrus philosophiques, comparés à ceux du théâtre, montrent qu'il n'y a qu'une seule forme d'édition pour deux genres littéraires distincts").

45. "Di far parlare probabilmente di ogni materia uomini e donne, di varii gradi e costumi, e disputare a lor modo." Scaliger, in his influential *Poetices libri septem* (1.2), remarks: "Why does Horace question whether or not comedy is poetry? Because it is humble, must it be denied title of poetry? Surely an unfortunate ruling! So far from comedy not being poetry, I would almost consider it the first and truest of all poetry, for comedy employs every kind of invention, and seeks for all kinds of material." Trans. Padelford, p. 17.

46. Weinberg, *History*, 1: 342, points out that this is a common feature of Speroni's later critical writings: discussing the *Discorso dell'arte, della natura, e di Dio*, he notes that "it is difficult to say whether his doctrine is primarily Platonic or Aristotelian, as elements from both seem to be intermingled."

47. Ong, pp. 61, 176. See Hermann, p. 4, for a list of all of Plato's statements on dialectic. For Aristotle's idea of dialectic, see Chapter 2 above.

48. "Gli oratori e gli filosofici fussero seme del nascimento de' miei dialogi" (p. 272); "Danna ancora eloquentemente la filosofia e la rettorica, che fur sue proprie professioni; senza le quali nulla sarebbe della sua gloria" (p. 269).

49. "La dialettica e la rettorica sono due arti atte a provare e persuadere il vero e il falso, il sì e il no d'ogni cosa." He adds at another point that "in truth no man knew more about this art than Plato, nor taught it like Aristotle did" ("e nel vero mai non fu uomo, che di questa arte sapesse più di Platone; nè la insegnasse come Aristotile"; p. 343).

50. "Ma guastarebbe generalmente l'arte e la forma d'ogni dialogo."

51. "L'uomo molte fiate in dialogo le buone cose suol biasimare, e laudar le non buone."

52. "Parla anche in vano il dialogo, mentre che egli erra di giuoco in giuoco senza appressare alla verità; ma il vaneggiar in tal modo non è cosa empia nè disonesta." See also p. 422.

53. Eco, p. 358.

54. Matthews, pp. 17–22.

55. "E così come non è commedia, la qual non sia amorosa . . . così il parlar dello amore . . . non è disdetto al dialogo."

56. "Son dunque specchi d'innamorati li miei dialogi."

57. "Chiamo piacevole labirinto, non già lo amar per amore ed intricarsi ne' suoi diletti, ma ragionar delli innamorati, ed imitarli senza lo affetto nelle parole."

58. "Di adulazione, di gelosia, di stupidezza e di vanità di chi ama."

59. Barthes, "Rhétorique ancienne," p. 177, writes: "Platonic rhetoric rejects writing and seeks a personal interlocutor, *l'adhominatio*; the fundamental modality of discourse is dialogue as it occurs between teacher and pupil, united by inspired love. 'To think together' might be the motto of dialectic. Rhetoric is a dialogue of love" ("La rhétorique platonicienne écarte l'écrit et recherche l'interlocution personnelle, *l'adhominatio*; le mode fondamental du discours est le dialogue entre le maître et l'élève, unis par l'amour inspiré. *Penser en commun*, telle pourrait être la devise de la dialectique. La rhétorique est un dialogue d'amour").

60. "Dipinture e commedie a giuoco."

61. Speroni contends, in one of his innumerable throwaway lines of defense that are left undeveloped, that this mirror function has a moral utility for the reader who is also a lover: "It may also be that what was a delight to me, while I was writing my dialogues, may have been not only delight, but also sagacity and advice for those who read them. In them, one reads of how lovers are foolish in the midst of their delights . . . [and] how they stupidly err in every act and word. My dialogues are therefore mirrors of lovers, in which some of them, sometimes, may with luck see themselves reflected; and they will not

be able, in recognizing the state in which they are, to do otherwise than to be ashamed of themselves" ("E può anche esser, che quel che in me fu diletto, mentre io scriveva li miei dialogi, sia stato in quelli che letti gli hanno, non pur diletto, ma accorgimento e consiglio. Quivi si legge come nel mezzo de' lor diletti sono insensati gli amanti . . . [e] come vaneggino scioccamente in ogni atto e parola. Son dunque specchi d'innamorati li miei dialogi: nelli quali quantunque volte alcun d'essi, sua bona sorte, si specchierà; altrettante del proprio stato accorgendosi non potrà fare, che di se stesso non si vergogni"; p. 289).

62. "E perciocchè questo è il punto, onde deriva la mia difesa, come da centro circunferenzia"; "Or tai parole, se scritte sono ne' miei dialogi . . . non solamente non fanno empio il dialogo, ma intiero lo fanno e perfetto."

63. He speaks of "the roses of my dialogues and others' dialogues" ("le rose de' miei dialogi e delli altrui"; pp. 290–91).

64. "Ma se si dice di voler sceglier le spine sole e stirparle"; "se solamente di stecchi e spine sa ragionare?"

65. Greene, *Light in Troy*, p. 6.

66. "Nè vaglia a dire, che la puntura di queste spine desta in chi legge li miei dialogi molti pensieri non ragionevoli . . . anzi vaglia a provare, che delle spine, non che de' fiori de' miei dialogi si possa trar molto pro." Hathaway, *Age*, p. 69, adds that "here he [Speroni] absolved the writer of poetry from all responsibility for the soundness of the ideas he projects but defended the poet's use of ideas."

67. On the notion of "unfinalizability," see Bakhtin, *Dostoyevsky's Poetics*, p. 166.

68. "Varii dico quanto alle cose di cui si parla, e quanto al modo di favellare."

69. "L'uno è quando l'autore istesso cortesemente, quasi loro oste, par che le meni con esso seco nel suo dialogo."

70. "E però scrive, il tal disse ed il tal rispose."

71. "Perciocchè pura non è, ma è meschiata delle persone e dello scrittore, il qual non imita se medesimo." Lacoue-Labarthe and Nancy, "Genre," p. 6, speak of "the complexity of the structure of something like the *Symposium*: that is to say . . . of a story including, or recalling, a dialogue, which in turn contains intercalated discourses. We know that, since antiquity, this type of structure has been the reason for the true originality of the Platonic mode of writing. It is this structure as well that we in fact find in varying degrees of complexity in most of the major dialogues of Plato, from the *Republic* to the *Sophist*, and including the *Theaetetus*. We know too that this structure was . . . 'reflected on' and condemned by Plato in the *Republic*." Lacoue-Labarthe and Nancy

call this an "auto-critique" on Plato's part. My discussion of Speroni's treatment of Plato is indebted throughout to the work of these two critics in *L'Absolu littéraire*.

72. "L'altro è il modo imitante li nostri alterni ragionamenti, non introdotti nè interotti dallo scrittore, ma alla maniera delle commedie: la qual forma piacque a Platone ed a Luciano, e non dispiacque a Plutarco."

73. "L'autor del dialogo messa in silenzio la sola e propria sua voce, riempie quelli di varii nomi e costumi, e novi e varii ragionamenti."

74. "Nei dialogi di Platone non parla Socrate, nè Alcibiade, nè Gorgia, ma alli lor nomi, che vi son scritti e dipinti, si fa parlare a quel modo, che si teneva da tutti tre nel contendere."

75. "E come i servi, e le meretrici, e li roffiani, e li parasiti, e li soldati, e li pedagogi, se le parole da essi usate imitando son convenevoli à lor costumi fastidiosi, sono e 'l diletto e la bellezza delle commedie; così qualora in alcun dialogo uno sciocco, uno empio, uno innamorato, uno adulatore, o alcun sofista arrogante, sono ritratti dal naturale." Bernardo Pino da Cagli, in his *Breve considerazione intorno al componimento de la comedia de' nostri tempi* (1572), makes a number of observations about comedy that closely resemble Speroni's. However, he adamantly insists that all the characters in the Counter-Reformation comedy ought to be "good" (*buoni*), and that parasites, thieves, seducers, and so on should be banished altogether from it. See Weinberg, *Trattati*, 2: 629–49, for the text of Pino da Cagli's treatise.

76. Compare Aristotle, *Poetics* 4, 1448b4–19.

77. "Che così come non di ogni fatto si scrive istoria, ma solamente di quel che è degno e notevole; così l'autor del dialogo quei soli detti delle persone da lui condotte dee riferire, che gli sia onore il parlarne e dee tacer tutti gli altri."

78. "Chi conchiudesse, che'l buon Platone fusse ignorante e reo uomo, o mala cosa li suoi dialogi, per avventura farebbe invalido sillogismo, e mostrarebbe di non sapere che cosa fusse dialogizzare. E ciò sia detto generalmente quanto alla forma di tutti quanti i dialogi."

79. "Se poema è il dialogo, ed è il poeta il dialogista, e se sa poco il poeta, quantunque paja di saper molto, imitando; seguentemente si può concludere, che poco sappia chi si dà a scriver dialogi." See also Plato, *Apology* 22B–C.

80. "Platone scrisse i dialogi e fu grandissimo sapiente: anzi pare che perchè fu sapiente, negasse egli di essere autore della dottrina de' suoi dialogi."

81. "Del buono parlo, quale era quel di Platone."

82. Hirzel, 1: 292, remarks that "among writers of dialogue Aristotle is the first, so it seems, to have ventured to introduce himself,

through the use of 'I said,' into his works, and thereby to state openly the identity of one of the speaking characters with the dialogist" ("Aristoteles ist, wie es scheint, unter den Dialogenschreibern der Erste, der es gewagt hat mit einem 'Ich sagte' sich selber redend einzuführen und dadurch die Identität einer Gesprächsperson mit dem Verfasser ganz offen auszusprechen").

83. Gadamer, *Dialogue*, p. 105.

84. "Con sue sole due parolette queta il rumore, che ne può nascere; scrivendo in fine di una sua lettera, che la dottrina piena di liti e contenzioni nei suoi dialogi dispensate, non era sua opinione."

85. Trans. Bury, p. 417. Speroni accepts this possibly apocryphal statement as "what he [Plato] said about himself" ("quel che dicesse di se medesimo"; p. 269).

86. "Lo autore del dialogo dette e provate le opinioni delle persone introdotte, rade volte sopra esse vuol dar sentenzia finale; ma resta sempre intra due." It is worth noting in this regard that all anonymous works published after 1518 were banned by the 1559 Index of Paul IV (Grendler, p. 117). Dialogue would then be—from Speroni's point of view—the next best thing for an author seeking to express his/her ideas without fear of reprisal.

87. "Ciascun de' favellatori possa vantarsi di aver ragione nella vittoria, ed appagarsi del suo sapere."

88. Tasso, *Prose diverse*, 2: 227, letter to Torquato Rangone. This does not, however, accurately describe Tasso's theory of dialogue in the *Discorso dell'arte del dialogo* (see Chapter 4).

89. "Vegna a mutarsi infelicemente, non in cicala una volta sola, come Titone, ma molte e molte, come Tiresia." Elsewhere Speroni remarks of Plato that "he is, in rhetoric, Tiresias: all others are empty shadows compared to him" ("è Tiresia nella rettorica: tutti li altri sono ombre vane rispetto a lui"; p. 343).

90. Trans. Fowler, p. 207.

91. Diogenes Laertius, 3.37, trans. Hicks, p. 311. The *Apology* is, of course, *not* a dialogue. Plato refers to himself as a "tragedian" in the *Laws* 817A–B.

92. Trans. Bury, p. 17 (my italics).

93. Cf. the Platonic polemic against writing in the *Phaedrus* and the question of how writing is to defend itself in the absence of the author. Two essays by Jacques Derrida also address this question: see "Plato's Pharmacy," pp. 61–172, and "The Double Session," pp. 173–285, in *Dissemination*.

94. Compare Brun, *Socrate*, p. 49: "A book does not begin a true dialogue; one cannot question a text as one questions a living being, and

writing is finally an obstacle between living men and women" ("Un livre n'amorce pas un dialogue véritable, on n'interroge pas un texte comme on interroge un être vivant et l'écriture est finalement un obstacle qui vient s'interposer entre les vivants").

95. Speroni points out that Socrates knew how "to mock the sophists, when he seemed to be honoring them, and to trick them with their own sophistries" ("dileggiar li sofisti, quando pareva che li onorasse, ed ingannarli con le lor proprie sofisterie"; p. 279).

96. There is a precedent in Socrates's argument in the *Republic* 3.392C–403C: Bloom (Plato, *Republic*, p. 360) points out that "the poet is unable to imitate the best kind of man, the philosopher. The philosopher would ruin a tragedy; and although he might appear in a comedy, only certain effects of his activity, and not that activity itself, could be shown. A ruler can be shown ruling on the stage; and most other human types can also be shown as they are. But it is impossible to show a philosopher philosophizing."

97. Michel, "L'Influence," p. 14.

98. Richetti, p. 22. It is worth noting here that Plato, in the *Laws* (816D-E), considers comedy in an essentially negative light. Grube, pp. 64–65, neatly summarizes this passage as follows: "To know what is serious one should know what is laughable, if only so that one should not inadvertently say or do something ridiculous. However, acting in comedies, and probably writing them also, will be a task for foreigners and slaves, no citizen should be seen to learn comedy, and it should remain, for our citizens, something unfamiliar."

99. Cf. Lacoue-Labarthe and Nancy, "Genre," pp. 5–7.

100. Speroni remarks in *Della imitazione*, in *Opere*, 5: 559, that "Aristotle's way of writing cannot be imitated. One can certainly write as he does, but by the use of reason, not by imitating him. Plato was no less wise, but he wrote in a probable rather than in a scientific way, except perhaps when dividing and defining; in all else he was an orator, or at most a dialectician" ("il modo tenuto da Aristotile nello scrivere non è imitabile. Si può bene scriver come ello fa, ma non già imitando lui, ma con ragion procedendo. . . . Platone . . . non fu men di lui sapiente, ma non ne scrisse scientemente, ma probabilmente; se non forse quando divide e diffinisce: nel resto è oratore, o al più dialettico"). It is impossible to imitate Aristotle's style, in other words, since *he has no style* to imitate; he stands at the zero degree of style. There is nothing to imitate, in this sense, except for the Aristotelian *methodos*—but that practice will lead to new works of philosophy rather than literature.

101. As it is in the *Poetics*, where dialogue is treated as a member of the set of previously unclassifiable literary works.

102. Saint-Mard, p. 20: "Ne diroit-on pas que les Héros des Romans sont des Substances pensantes, à qui l'on n'a ajouté un Corps, que par manière d'acquit, et pour ne servir de rien à leurs Plaisirs?"

103. Compare Bakhtin, "Epic and Novel," in idem, *Dialogic Imagination*, p. 22.

104. Pozzi, 1: 699*n*. See also Aristotle, *Poetics* 25, 1460b8–11.

105. Hathaway, *Age*, pp. 81–86, notes that this was a commonly used metaphor for sixteenth-century commentators on the *Poetics* (although some, such as Castelvetro, sharply criticized this same metaphor). Guillaume de Brebeuf, *La Pharsale de Lucien* (1683), notes that "writing is art: / To paint speech and to speak to the eyes, / And through the varied aspects of the traced figures, / To give color and body to thoughts" (quoted and trans. in Oechslin, p. 97).

106. "Ci colorisca la verità"; "certo di queste cotai pitture una è la prosa de' miei dialogi." Significantly enough, Speroni identifies Lucian as another such "painter" in dialogue (p. 304).

107. "In alcun dialogo uno sciocco, uno empio, uno innamorato, uno adulatore o alcun sofista arrogante, sono ritratti dal naturale; tal dipintura di nomi e verbi, e d'altre parti d'orazione non dee men cara istimarsi, che la volgare delli colori."

108. "Vuol ragione che lo scrittore debba esser vago dello esser letto; nè ello è letto di bona voglia, se non insegna o diletta. Per l'uno e l'altro di questi fini si legge Socrate e Senofonte, Virgilio, Omero, Livio, Tucidide, Cicerone, e tutti quanti i filosofi. Ma me e gli altri, che poco fanno rime, romanzi, e sì fatte cose, non è chi legga se non per scherzo e per dilettarsi. Or non è dubbio che tai scrittori son molto simili ai dipintori: onde in quel modo ci suol piacer la scrittura, che la pittura ci è dilettevole."

109. "Le parole sono le imagini delle cose"; "segni, spettri, ed imagini, e similitudini delle cose."

110. "Che così come il pittore di tutto l'uomo null'altra cosa ci fa mostrare, che la sua ultima superficie, con tali linee e tai colori, onde il pittore sia il bagatella della natura; così l'autore del dialogo non va sì dentro alla cosa scritta, che possa giungere alla sua essenza; ma le va intorno, quasi ballando, sì fattamente, che nulla insegna giammai: che chi non sa non insegna, ma par che sappia ed insegni."

111. Weinberg, *History*, 1: 345, accurately observes that "during the last thirty years of the Cinquecento . . . there is much less direct reference to the texts of Plato themselves, to the point that it is sometimes difficult to distinguish whether a critic actually has a Platonic basis for his point of view or whether he starts from vague and anonymous positions of heterogeneous origin. By this late date there comes to be a *koinē*

of Platonic ideas, present universally but unspecifically in the minds of men; it is to this common fund that reference is made by critics rather than to the dialogues themselves. Such references remain fragmentary and scattered . . . because of the fundamentally unsystematic attitude of the critics. That is, Plato remains a collection of passages concerning the poetic art—passages extracted from many dialogues—rather than a philosopher having a total system in the light of which his various ideas on poetry were developed."

112. Imitation is therefore at once "a metaphysical and esthetic problem" for Speroni: see Weinberg, *History*, 1: 426.

113. "La imitazion nel dialogo è cosa comica e poesia senza versi. È dunque giuoco e diletto, ed è diletto ozioso."

114. For a more detailed theory of painting, see Speroni's *Discorso in lode della pittura*, in *Opere*, 3: 441–46.

115. "È scherzo la sua scrittura, perchè dipinge, ma non incarna le cose."

116. "Dunque altrettanto dee esser licito alla imitazion del dialogo il disputarsi probabilmente d'ogni materia tra le persone introdotte, quanto al poeta ed al dipintore lo effigiarla e rappresentarla."

117. "Può fare intero il ragionamento della imitazion del dialogo."

118. "La cosa è questa, che nel dialogo non pur si imitano le persone, che sono in esso introdotte; ma nelle cose, che vi si dicono disputando, la vera e certa scienzia, che si può d'esse acquistare, non è espressa in effetto quale è nel metodo Aristotelico, ma è imitata e ritratta."

119. Mulas, p. 258, remarks that in the *Apologia dei Dialoghi* "in essence, rhetoric, dialectic, and logic are more a parody of each other than three degrees of approximation to knowledge" ("in sostanza, retorica, dialettica e logica, più che tre gradi di approssimazione alla conoscenza, sarebbero l'una parodia dell'altra").

120. Weinberg, *History*, 1: 1–2.

121. "Ecco adunque tre belle schiere ordinate di varie nostre imitazioni e cognizioni" (p. 281); "o è scienzia, quale Aristotile ha definita, o opinione, o persuasione" (p. 386).

122. "Quella prima cognizione, la qual è certa ed invariabile, è veramente scienzia, ed è chiamata dimostrativa; perchè è fattura del sillogismo dimostrativo."

123. Demonstrative "knowledge," Speroni comments, "is quite close to mathematics, with some part of natural science, the cognition of which is rather more certain than that of the civil 'sciences' [dialectic and rhetoric] and less certain than mathematics" ("la prima è intorno alle matematiche con qualche parte della natura, la cognizion della quale è assai più certa della civile; e meno assai della matematica"; p. 386).

124. "E questo genera opinione" (p. 280); "la opinione per sillogismo ed induzione" (p. 386).

125. "Altre cose non certamente sapute" (p. 280); "Platone, Socrate, e Senofonte con argomenti dialettici ci dà probabile opinione del nostro viver civile" (p. 281).

126. "La persuasione per entimema od esempio."

127. The entire passage is "Vuole in somma Aristotile, che la persuasione e l'opinione, quantunque buone e diritte, siano sofistiche conoscenze. Son dunque tali non per inganno . . . ma per difetto della certezza" (p. 386).

128. "E se egli trova (e trovarà senza fallo) che l'entimema oratorio sia quasi effigie imperfetta del sillogismo probabile, ed il probabile sillogismo esser imagine della perfetta dimostrazione, non altrimenti che sia la scimia dello uomo in certi atti della persona, e il pappagallo nelle parole; per qual cagione non dee poter inferire, che la persuasione rettorica sia dipintura ed imitazion della opinione, e la opinione della scienzia . . . ?"

129. Just as for Plato, all art is "three degrees removed from the truth" (*Republic* 10.599A). Scarpati, p. 192, observes that this passage from the *Republic*, so essential to Speroni's theory of dialogue, is the "crucial point of the entire sixteenth-century rethinking of esthetics, the incandescent nucleus (even if not always clearly formulated) of the debates over poetics, rhetoric, and the philosophy of language between Florence, Padua, and Ferrara, from Speroni to Varchi to Tomitano to Patrizi" ("punto cruciale di tutto il ripensamento estetico cinquecentesco, nucleo incandescente, anche se non sempre chiaramente formulato, delle dispute di poetica, retorica, di filosofia del linguaggio tra Firenze, Padova e Ferrara, dallo Speroni al Varchi al Tomitano al Patrizi").

130. "Tale è dunque nelle scienzie e nelle arti la strada utile Aristotelica, la quale conduce al sapere."

131. "E se imitare è giuocare, giuoco è dunque la opinione, la qual si genera nel dialogo."

132. "Io se di quello che ci si tratta, avessi avuto certa scienzia, non ne faceva dialogi; ma avrei scritto ogni cosa alla maniera Aristotelica."

133. Compare generic statements such as "and Aristotle generated true knowledge for us with demonstrative syllogisms concerning these" ("e di queste Aristotile con sillogismi dimostrativi vera scienzia ci ha generato"; p. 281); or "I can say yet again . . .that we acquire true and perfect knowledge through demonstration" ("posso ancor farmi per dir . . . che la scienzia certa e perfetta per la dimostrazione acquistiamo"; p. 386).

134. It could also be argued that Speroni does not incorporate the

traits of official post-Tridentine philosophical discourse into his argument in order to avoid running the risk of subjecting the *Apologia dei Dialoghi* to attack for its possible misrepresentation of doctrine.

135. Hathaway, *Age*, p. 68, comments dryly that "quite possibly, Speroni, who was defending himself before the Inquisition in this argument in defense of his dialogues, did not wish to be understood perfectly."

Chapter 4

1. All biographical information on Castelvetro is from Marchetti and Patrizi, which also offers an extensive bibliography of works by and on Castelvetro.

2. Tedeschi, p. 129. See also Mazzacurati, "Aristotele a corte," p. 283.

3. Weinberg, "Castelvetro's Theory," pp. 349–50.

4. Raimondi, *Poesia*, pp. 20–21, touches on the Protestantism underlying Castelvetro's ideas.

5. Lodovico Muratori, "Vita Caroli Sigonii," in *Opera omnia*, 1: iv–v.

6. Marchetti and Patrizi, p. 20, add that "from Tasso to Gravina to the theorists of French classicism to Vico, many [thinkers] later understood the implicit overtures in Castelvetro's thought" ("molti, successivamente, da Tasso a Gravina, ai teorici del classicismo francese, a Vico, compresero le aperture implicite nel pensiero del Castelvetro"). Scarpati, p. 179, calls Castelvetro's treatise "the most ambitious book of the 1570's" ("il libro più ambizioso degli anni Settanta").

7. Cf. Letter 38 (1575) and Letter 82 (1576), in Tasso, *Lettere*; also Tasso, *Prose diverse*, 1: 279–95 ("Estratti dalla *Poetica* di Castelvetro"). Tasso, in fact, was so interested in Castelvetro's theories (even if he ultimately viewed them as wrong) that he read works by Castelvetro that circulated exclusively in manuscript form during Tasso's own lifetime. At the very beginning of Book 4 of his *Discourses on the Heroic Poem* (1587) Tasso unequivocally shows that he had read an important *disputatio* of Castelvetro's—*Parere sopra l'aiuto che domandano i poeti alle Muse* (An opinion concerning the help that poets ask from the muses)—that was published for the first time only in 1727 (Lodovico Muratori, ed., *Opere varie critiche di Lodovico Castelvetro*, Bern, 1727). See *Discourses on the Heroic Poem*, pp. 111–13 (= *Prose*, pp. 626–27).

8. Castelvetro, *"Poetica" d'Aristotele*, Parte prima principale, 4 (1447a28–1447b24); ed. Romani, 1: 30–48. The page numbers of all references to this edition of Castelvetro's treatise are included in the text in parentheses; the original Italian text is provided in a note in each instance. Castelvetro's text was first published by G. Stainhofer in Vienna in 1570; a revised edition was published by Pietro Perna ("Pietro de

Sedabonis") in Basel in 1576. An abridged English translation is *Castelvetro on the Art of Poetry*, ed. and trans. Bongiorno; see pp. 10–16 for the comments on dialogue. Although Bongiorno's translation is generally accurate, I have preferred to use my own translations in some cases in the pages that follow, chiefly for the sake of terminological consistency with the other chapters of this book. A brief English-language summary of Castelvetro's overall theory of literature can be found in Weinberg, "Castelvetro's Theory." A much longer and more detailed one may be found in Bongiorno, pp. xiii–xlviii.

9. "Questo testo è reputato alquanto oscuro."

10. In his dedication to the work (1: 2), Castelvetro confesses that "I was [not] able to alleviate all the difficulties and smooth out all the rough passages" in the *Poetics* ("confesso . . . che io [non] abbia potuto agevolare tutte le difficultà e appianare tutti i passi forti"; my translation). In the passage from the *Poetics* under examination—undoubtedly one of the most difficult for all Renaissance textual critics of Aristotle (see Hathaway, *Age*, pp. 87–117)—Castelvetro's efforts to smooth out Aristotle's text result in a reading that, though appropriate to his own interpretive aims, is obviously incongruous with much of the rest of the argument of the *Poetics*. Many other Renaissance critics who puzzled over the same passage (Varchi, Robortello, Maggi, Piccolomini, Antonio Minturno) did not arrive at the same conclusions as Castelvetro. It should be recognized, however, that Aristotle's text was available to him only in a mutilated version containing serious lacunae and *passi forti*, despite the efforts of previous sixteenth-century editors. At the same time, there is no denying that Castelvetro (for a number of different reasons) often flagrantly bends his interpretation of the *Poetics* to suit the requirements of his own idiosyncratic esthetic theory. As Daria Perocco, pp. 545–46, points out, Castelvetro's commentary "does not seek out its object, but uses it and bends it at will; it makes the commentary the tool and expression of radical dissent in regard to Renaissance court culture and its adherents. It represents programmatic dissent from inside a structure—whether a gloss or a commentary— that has been emptied of its traditional value as the extension of the text. The voice of dissent arms itself with the sole implement that its age allows, namely the commentary, used as a vehicle for its own ideas. Castelvetro does not suffer from an Oedipal complex; and his metatext is conceived solely in terms of the destruction of the text that generated it" ("essa non tanto mira all'oggetto, ma se ne serve, lo piega e ne fa strumento ed espressione di un dissenso radicale nei riguardi della cultura cortigiana rinascimentale e dei suoi esecutori. Dissenso programmatico dall'interno di una struttura, dunque, chiose o commento che siano,

svuotata del suo valore tradizionale di prolungamento del testo. La voce del dissenso si arma dell'unico strumento che le consente l'epoca sua, il commento, usato come veicolo per le sue idee. Il Castelvetro non soffre di problemi edipici; ed il suo metatesto è concepito solo in funzione della distruzione del testo che l'ha generato").

11. "Li quali (*sc.* dialoghi) avendo soggetto di poesia, cioè rassomiglianza (*sc.* mimesi), sono distesi in prosa e non in verso." Here as elsewhere I have chosen to translate *rassomiglianza* (literally "resemblance") as "mimesis," since Castelvetro never uses the term *imitazione* ("imitation") in this sense in the *"Poetica" d'Aristotele.* As Werther Romani points out ("Nota Critico-Filologica," in Castelvetro, *"Poetica" d'Aristotele,* 2: 381), *rassomiglianza* contains two markedly different semantic components, since it suggests an imitative purpose, on the one hand, and an inventive one, on the other hand. *Rassomigliare* means at once "to represent through verisimilitude" and also "to discover"/"to invent," and thus is similar to the Aristotelian concept of mimesis.

12. "S'era detto che Platone aveva, scrivendo i suoi *Ragionamenti,* fatta cosa contraria agli ammaestramenti dati da lui al suo Comune, fuori del quale egli scaccia e bandisce Omero e le rappresentazioni"; trans. Bongiorno, p. 11. I have altered his translation of *rappresentazioni* from "imitative" to "mimetic" poetry. It would also arguably be possible, in this context, to translate the term as "dramatic performances."

13. "Ora, per provare che i *Ragionamenti* platonici sieno rappresentazioni, s'adduce l'autorità d'Aristotele del libro *De' poeti"*; trans. Bongiorno, p. 11.

14. "Parleremo in generale di tutti que' ragionamenti che sono dinomati da' greci *dialogoi"*; cf. Bongiorno, p. 13.

15. "Simili ragionamenti adunque sono di tre maniere, l'una delle quali può montare in palco e si può nominare rappresentativa, perciochè in essi vi sono persone introdotte a ragionare *dramatikos,* cioè in atto, come è usanza di farsi nelle tragedie e nelle comedie; e simile maniera è tenuta da Platone ne' suoi *Ragionamenti* e da Luciano ne' suoi per lo più. Ma un'altra ce n'è che non può montare in palco, perciochè, conservando l'autore la sua persona, come istorico narra quello che disse il tale e il cotale: e questi ragionamenti si possono dinomare istorici o narrativi, e tali sono per lo più que' di Cicerone. E ci è ancora la terza maniera, e è di quelli che sono mescolati della prima e della seconda maniera, conservando l'autore da prima la sua persona e narrando come istorico, e poi introducendo le persone a favellare *dramatikos,* come s'usa pur di fare nelle tragedie e nelle comedie, in guisa che questa ultima maniera può e non può montare in palco: cioè non può montarvi in quanto l'autore conserva da prima la sua persona e è come istorico, e

può montarvi in quanto s'introducono le persone rappresentativamente a favellare; e Cicerone fece alcun ragionamento così fatto"; cf. Bongiorno, p. 13; my translation here differs substantially from his.

16. "Ora queste maniere di ragionamenti hanno o possono avere alcuni *difetti* che sono communi a tutte e tre loro" (my italics); trans. Bongiorno, p. 13.

17. "Se adunque montano o possono montare in palco, sì come fanno i primi in tutto e i terzi in parte, seguita di necessità che abbiano il commune popolo per veditore e per ascoltatore, per cagione del quale commune popolo e per diletto solo della moltitudine rozza è stato trovato il palco e la maniera rappresentativa . . . seguita medesimamente di necessità che il soggetto sia tal quale si richiede al popolo e alla moltitudine, il quale e la quale non sono né possono essere capaci e intendenti di dispute di scienze né d'arte, ma solamente sono atti a comprendere gli avenimenti fortunosi del mondo"; I have modified somewhat Bongiorno, p. 13.

18. Marchetti and Patrizi, p. 19.

19. "Conciosia cosa che la poesia sia stata trovata solamente per dilettare e per ricreare; io dico per dilettare e per ricreare gli animi della rozza moltitudine e del commune popolo, il quale non intende le ragioni né le divisioni né gli argomenti sottili e lontani dall'uso degl'idioti, quali adoperano i filosofi in investigare la verità delle cose e gli artisti in ordinare le arti; e non gli 'ntendendo, conviene, quando altri ne favella, che egli ne senta noia e dispiacere" (p. 46); trans. Bongiorno, p. 19.

20. Trans. Bongiorno, p. 13. Castelvetro requires, for different reasons, the narrative and mixed modes of dialogue to have a "popolesco" subject as well: "Insofar as they are historical wholly or in part they should not properly treat subjects unsuited to a popular audience" ("Ma ancora negl'istorici e ne' mescolati, li quali, in quanto sono o in tutto istorici o in parte, non deono potere avere soggetto non popolesco, sì come materia non convenevole a loro"; p. 36), trans. Bongiorno, p. 13.

21. Mulas, p. 249.

22. "Contiene materia della quale ciascuno idiota e simplice uomo è capace"; cf. Bongiorno, p. 15.

23. "L'altro difetto, che è o può essere comune a tutte e tre le maniere, s'è che i predetti ragionamenti sono tessuti in prosa, la qual prosa non si conviene a' ragionamenti di soggetto rassomigliativo e trovato dallo 'ngegno dello scrittore e che in verità non sia mai stato tenuto da quelle persone che sono introdotte a ragionare, sì come non sono mai stati in verità tenuti i ragionamenti degli autori di sopra nominati; conciosia cosa che sì come il verso è fermissimo argomento a darci ad intendere che il soggetto compreso in lui è imaginato e non vero . . .

così la prosa debba essere non meno fermo argomento a dimostrare che il soggetto a lei sottoposto sia verità, e non cosa imaginata"; my translation differs considerably from Bongiorno, pp. 13–14.

24. Castelvetro also offers a number of other arguments against each of the different kinds of dialogue, but these are secondary to the two main arguments against dialogue already mentioned (cf. pp. 37–40).

25. "La poesia ha sua materia trovata e imaginata dallo 'ngegno del poeta, e ha le parole non tali quali s'usano ragionando, perciochè non s'usa tra gli uomini di ragionare in versi, ma le ha composte in misurati versi per l'opera dello 'ngegno del poeta" (p. 44); trans. Bongiorno, p. 18 ("But the matter of poetry is invented and imagined by the poet's genius, and its language is not that of ordinary discourse, since men do not address one another in verse, but is ordered metrically by the poet").

26. Actually one kind of dialogue is more acceptable to Castelvetro than the others. This is allegorical dialogue between animals, plants, or "other inanimate beings." See Bongiorno, p. 15, for Castelvetro's full explanation.

27. Romani (in Castelvetro, *"Poetica" d'Aristotele*, 2: 380) notes that Castelvetro's entire system is "configurato come una specie di grande sillogismo."

28. Raimondi, *Poesia*, pp. 20–21; see also Ong, chap. 11.

29. Ong, p. 230. Mazzacurati, in "Aristotele a corte," provides a superb analysis of Castelvetro's importance in the development of late-sixteenth-century Italian culture.

30. Weinberg, *History*, 1: 511, describes the "essentially rhetorical character" of Castelvetro's system.

31. Hathaway, *Age*, p. 413.

32. Solerti, 1: 397*n*.

33. "Voi mi pregate, Padre Molto Reverendo, nelle vostre lettere, ch'io voglia darvi alcun ammaestramento; e 'l chiedete, se non m'inganno, de lo scrivere i dialogi"; p. 16; in Tasso, *Dialogues*, trans. Lord and Trafton, p. 17. All further references to Tasso's treatise are to this bilingual edition, and the page number for each reference appears in parentheses. The original Italian text accompanies the translation in each case, either in a note or in the body of the chapter. Any changes or additions made by me to this translation are noted, with the following exception: Lord and Trafton's translation of *disputa* as "dispute" has been altered to "disputation" in every instance. Tasso's treatise was originally published by G. Vasalini in Venice in 1586 in *Delle rime e prose del sig. Torquato Tasso, parte quarta*.

34. Trans. by Lord and Trafton in their introduction, p. 9.

35. Ettore Mazzali, in his edition of the *Discorso dell'arte del dialogo*, does not even mention Castelvetro in the textual apparatus, for example; see Tasso, *Prose*, ed. Mazzali, pp. 333–35.

36. As Mazzacurati observes in "Aristotele a corte," p. 267, "as perhaps never again (except possibly in our own time), the masters of *dispositio* and *elocutio*, the critics, the interpreters of great institutional messages were privileged by the century. Beginning in those years (starting, for instance, with Speroni's *Canace*) and for many decades to follow, until Tasso and even beyond him, the practice of forms often appeared as a *mise-en-scène* or figural execution for theoretical models that had already been elaborated. Never before or after was the critic closer to the artist, never were their roles more frequently interchanged, never did the critic more rigidly oversee the artistic work in the making while gazing over the artist's shoulder, in order to ensure that the work would adhere to the critic's own manifestos and exegetical proposals" ("il nuovo secolo privilegiava, come mai più è accaduto prima o dopo (fuorché, forse, nel nostro tempo) i maestri della *dispositio* e della *elocutio*, i critici, gli interpreti dei grandi messaggi istituzionali. A partire da quegli anni (a partire, ad esempio, dalla *Canace* dello Speroni) e per molti decenni, fino al Tasso ed oltre, la pratica delle forme assunse spesso il volto di una messa in scena o di una esecuzione figurale per modelli teorici elaborati in anticipo: mai, prima o dopo, il critico fu più vicino all'artista, mai i ruoli furono più frequentemente scambiati, mai con tanto irrigidita vicenda il critico sorvegliò l'opera nel suo farsi, *par-dessus l'épaule*, perché risultasse del tutto aderente ai propri manifesti, alle proprie proposte esegetiche").

37. Baldassari, "Il discorso," pp. 93–94.

38. Cf. Mazzali, in Tasso, *Prose*, p. xxxv: "The truest and most congenial literary expressions of Tasso's 'perfect' culture are the conceptual dialogue, the discourse on various philosophical and literary issues, and theological or programmatically heroic poetry" ("La più vera e congeniale espressione letteraria della cultura 'perfetta' del Tasso è il dialogo concettuale, il discorso di varia filosofia e letteratura, la poesia teologica o programmaticamente eroica").

39. "Perchè niuna cosa debbo tenervi celata, la qual possa giovar a gli altri, o pur a me stesso" (p. 16). Tasso adds that "the role of teacher would be as ill-suited to me as the role of student to you. Nor do I fear that in refusing this role I shall be blamed as Giotto was; he rejected an appropriate honor, while I am refusing an office that does not suit me. Perhaps the rules of writing are rather like laws; just as the Genoese have laws that are different from those of the Venetians or the Ragusans, so the precepts in the art of good writing may vary. But I do not

want to give such a title to what follows, nor should you advertise it as such. The rules that I have collected in this very brief work resemble certain scholars at court who, unable to sustain so serious a role, put off the gown and dress in the common fashion" ("tanto a me disdicevol sarebbe la persona di maestro quanto a voi quella di scolare; nè rifiutandola io temo di poterne esser biasimato, come Giotto; perch'egli ricusò convenevole onore, io non accetto ufficio non conveniente. . . . E se delle regole aviene quel che delle leggi; sì come altre leggi hanno i Genovesi diverse da quelle de' Viniziani o de' Ragusei; così potrebbono avere altri precetti nell'artificio del bene scrivere. Ma io non gli voglio dare questo nome, nè voi gliele scrivete in fronte; perciochè io l'ho raccolte in una operetta assai breve per assomigliar alcuni dottori cortegiani, i quali non potendo sostener persona così grave vestono di corto"; pp. 16, 17).

40. Baldassari, "L'arte," p. 14, remarks that "in his *Discorso dell'arte del dialogo* Tasso rejected, point for point, the theses put forward by Castelvetro in the '*Poetica*'" ("Tasso rigetteva punto per punto, nel suo discorso *Dell'arte del dialogo*, le tesi avanzate dal Castelvetro nella '*Poetica*'"); he also notes that "it would seem impossible to doubt that Tasso knew *De dialogo liber.* An examination of the points of contact between Sigonio's and Tasso's respective theories will be able to assure us of this" ("che Torquato Tasso conoscesse il *De dialogo liber,* non sembra possa venir messo in dubbio. Un esame dei punti di contatto fra la teoria del Sigonio e quella tassiana ce ne potrà assicurare"; p. 11). See the notes to Baldassari's edition of Tasso's treatise on dialogue, "Il discorso," for a point-by-point comparison of the relevant passages from Castelvetro and Sigonio.

41. Lord and Trafton, p. 246*n*, observe that "Tasso's *Discourse* seems to borrow heavily from the treatise by Sigonio, his former teacher, as well as from Castelvetro's commentary on the *Poetics.* Nevertheless, the *Discourse* as a whole amounts to a personal and original statement."

42. Lord and Trafton, p. 246*n*, call the *Discorso* a statement of "Tasso's aims and practice as a writer of dialogues," for instance. Yet Baldassari, "L'arte," p. 45, acutely points out that "it is particularly clear that the *Discorso dell'arte del dialogo* is infinitely less complex than the reasons that combine to provide the support justifying the composition and the concrete reality of Tasso's *Dialogues*" ("è particolarmente chiaro come il discorso *Dell'arte del dialogo* sia infinitamente meno complesso dei motivi che s'intrecciano a formare il supporto che giustifica la composizione e la concreta realtà dei *Dialoghi* tassiani"). He also warns (p. 17) that "from a study limited to the *Discorso dell'arte del dialogo* we should not expect an interpretive canon for understanding Tasso's dialogical output" ("dallo studio ristretto del discorso *Dell'arte del dialogo* non bisogna attendersi

un canone interpretativo già pronto per comprendere la produzione dialogica tassiana").

43. Baldassari, "L'arte," p. 45.

44. Here I disagree, for precisely this reason, with Ferguson's claim (p. 215*n*) that "Tasso's theory and practice of dialogue are deeply influenced by the fact that he was writing while imprisoned and ill with a disease that involved, among other symptoms, hearing voices he sometimes defines as products of his own imagination and, at other times, as demons invading his mind from outside." Although Tasso did suffer from hallucinations while in Sant'Anna, there is no trace of this in the *Discorso dell'arte del dialogo*, which participates in a quite different textual problematic.

45. Foucault, *Birth*, p. xix: "What counts in the things said by men is not so much what they may have thought or the extent to which these things represent their thoughts, as that which systematizes them from the outset, thus making them thereafter endlessly accessible to new discourses and open to the task of transforming them."

46. Scarpati, p. 179, observes: "It seems ever clearer that Tasso's Aristotelianism was not born with the characteristics of scholastic doctrine, and that its sources are to be found in the most up-to-date fields of thought in which the highest kind of humanistic philology was joined together with open and wide-ranging discussion" ("Sempre più chiaramente risulta che l'aristotelismo tassiano non nasce con i caratteri di una dottrina scolastica, e che le sue fonti si trovano nei più aggiornati laboratori ove la grande filologia umanistica si salda con una discussione mobile e aperta").

47. Tasso published an apology entitled *Difesa della sua "Gerusalemme liberata"* in 1585, following an attack on the poem by the Accademia della Crusca; he also wrote a number of other treatises, letters, and the like in the 1580's in defense of his epic poem and the revisions that he had undertaken while in Sant'Anna.

48. Tasso follows the same procedure in the *Discorsi del poema eroico* (1587), repeatedly attacking Castelvetro without naming him: see Samuel, Introduction, in Tasso, *Discourses on the Heroic Poem*, pp. xxxii–xxxiii.

49. This is not Aristotle's argument in the *Poetics*; there, "character and experiences and actions" (1, 1447a28) or men doing or experiencing something (2, 1448a1) are the objects of mimesis, which are then categorized in terms of ethical differences.

50. "Due saran dunque i primi generi dell'imitazione; l'un dell'azione, nel qual son rassomigliati gli operanti; l'altro delle parole, nel quale sono introdotti i ragionanti" (p. 18).

51. "E quantunque poche operazioni si facciano alla mutola, e pochi

discorsi senza operazione, almeno dell'intelletto, nondimeno assai diverse giudico quelle da questi" (p. 18).

52. "Avegnachè nella scena si rappresenti l'azione, o atto, dal quale son denominate le favole e le rappresentazioni drammatice. Ma nel dialogo principalmente s'imita il ragionamento, il qual non ha bisogno di palco" (p. 22).

53. Lord and Trafton, p. 246n, do not fully accept Baldassari's attribution to Castelvetro's "Poetica" of the long passage on the three dialogical modes (pp. 18, 20), although they follow his edition in enclosing this passage in quotation marks in the Discorso dell'arte del dialogo. They remark that "Tasso's sources are often difficult to determine, especially in his works of literary theory"; yet the passage in question is virtually identical to the one in Castelvetro's treatise, with but a few slight changes in wording.

54. Compare Tasso's "Estratti," Prose diverse, p. 279, where he summarizes Castelvetro's argument as follows: "Plato and Cicero err gravely in writing dialogues on philosophical or artistic subjects; because dialogue, being dramatic and having the stage as its end, must be about a popular subject" ("Platone e Cicerone peccano gravemente a scrivere in dialoghi di materia filosofica o d'arte; perchè il dialogo, essendo drammatico, ed avendo per fine il palco, deve essere di materia popolare").

55. "Anzi più tosto non si conviene ad alcun dialogo" (p. 22): see note 52 for the rest of this passage.

56. "Nondimeno i dialoghi sono stati detti tragici e comici per similitudine, perchè le tragedie e le comedie propriamente sono l'imitazioni dell'azioni" (p. 20).

57. "Ma ne' dialogi l'azione è quasi per giunta de' ragionamenti; e s'altri la rimovesse il dialogo non perderebbe la sua forma" (p. 20). Cf. Aristotle, Poetics 8, 1451a35–36: "for if the presence or absence of a thing makes no visible difference, then it is not an integral part of the whole" (trans. Fyfe, p. 35).

58. "Ma le proprie (sc. differenze) si toranno dal ragionamento istesso, e da' problemi in lui contenuti, ciò è dalle cose ragionate, non sol dal modo di ragionare" (p. 22).

59. Ricoeur, 1: 34.

60. "Laonde alcuni dialoghi debbono esser detti civili e costumati, altri speculativi: e 'l soggetto de gli uni e de gli altri o sarà la quistione infinita: come la virtù si possa insegnare; o la finita: che debba far Socrate condennato alla morte" (p. 22).

61. B. Croce, Poeti, 2: 122, notes that in the Discorso dell'arte del dialogo "Tasso recognizes that dialogue equally embraces infinite propositions (universal and theoretical ones) and finite propositions (particular, his-

torical and practical ones)" ("il Tasso riconosce che il dialogo abbraccia del pari le questioni infinite [universali e teoriche] e quelle finite [particolari, storiche e pratiche]").

62. "E ne gli uni sono i problemi intenti all'elezione ed alla fuga; ne gli altri quelli che risguardano la scienza e la verità" (p. 22). At the end of the *Discorso*, Tasso repeats this same claim: "Furthermore, there are two kinds of dialogue: one deals with choosing and avoiding; the other is speculative and takes for the subjects of its debates matters that touch on truth and knowledge" ("E che due sian le specie; l'una, nel soggetto della quale sono i problemi che risguardano l'elezione e la fuga; l'altra speculativa, la qual prende per subietto quistione ch'appertiene alla verità ed alla scienza"; pp. 40, 41).

63. This is Tasso's final polemical point in his thinly veiled quarrel with Castelvetro. Whereas Castelvetro argues that the subject of dialogue is not historically true, but must instead always be imaginary, Tasso counters that the subject of dialogue is (among other things) the truth. And whereas Castelvetro concludes that dialogue, since it is a work of the imagination, should be written in verse, Tasso responds that "as others have said [e.g., Sigonio], dialogues should not be written in verse; they should be in prose, which is the form of speech that suits both the speculative man and the civil man who reasons about duties and virtues" (pp. 23, 25), which is not the work of the imagination per se. As he points out, "syllogisms, inductions, and enthymemes and examples could not be suitably formulated in verse" (p. 24; my translation—Lord and Trafton do not translate this sentence), and yet they are essential to dialogue.

64. Compare *Discourses on the Heroic Poem*, pp. 62–63 (Italian text in *Prose*, pp. 568–69): "The plot is to be whole or entire because it is to be perfect, and nothing can be perfect that is not entire. Perfection and integrity will be found in the plot if it possesses a beginning, a middle, and an end. . . . I call a plot 'whole' if it contains in itself everything necessary to its intelligibility, sets forth the causes and origin of the deed that it undertakes to treat, and leads by due means to an end that leaves nothing inadequately concluded or resolved." (I have modified Cavalchini and Samuel's translation somewhat.)

65. Tasso, *Discourses on the Heroic Poem*, p. 62 (I have modified the translation): "Favola chiamo la forma del poema che difinir si può testura o composizione de gli avvenimenti o de le cose" (= *Prose*, p. 568). See also Günsberg, pp. 154–55.

66. *Poetics* 8, 1451a15–36.

67. "E quale è la favola nel poema, tale è nel dialogo la quistione; e dico la sua forma e quasi l'anima. Però s'una è la favola, uno dovrebbe

esser il soggetto del quale si propongono i problemi" (p. 24). Cf. *Poetics* 6, 1450a37–38: "The plot is the first principle and as it were the soul of tragedy" (trans. Fyfe, p. 27).

68. See Tasso's letter (1587) to Filippo Spinelli: "I do not send you the dialogue, because the subject of every dialogue ought to be some disputed proposition; and the argument that you wrote down for me is simple narration, which could not be reduced to this form of composition. Perhaps you are of a different opinion, and think that dialogue needs only to alternate speakers without a contest or diversity of opinions" ("Non le mando il dialogo, perch'il soggetto d'ogni dialogo dovrebbe esser qualche questione disputata; e ne l'argomento che mi lasciò scritto, è una semplice narrazione, la qual non si potrebbe ridurre in questa forma di componimento. . . . Forse ella porta contraria opinione, che basti al dialogo un ragionamento vicendevole, senza contesa o diversità di pareri"; *Lettere*, 4: no. 944: as quoted in Baldassari, "L'arte," pp. 28–29).

69. The lingering influence of Ciceronian rhetorical theory on Tasso's poetics of dialogue is perhaps most clearly visible here: cf. Günsberg, p. 156.

70. "Dico adunque ch'in ogni questione si concede alcuna cosa e d'alcuna si dubita: e intorno a quella di cui si dubita nasce la disputa, la qual si forma della dimanda e della risposta" (p. 24).

71. "E perchè 'l dimandare s'appartiene particolarmente al dialettico, par che lo scrivere il dialogo sia impresa di lui" (p. 24).

72. "Sì come il dimandare è proprio al dialettico" (p. 26); "nè gli conviene ancora il verso, come hanno detto, ma la prosa, perciochè la prosa è parlar conveniente allo speculativo" (pp. 22, 24).

73. "Il dialogo sarà imitazione di una disputa dialettica" (p. 28). Cf. Sigonio, *De dialogo liber* (14*v*): "dialogus quedam est dialecticae disputationis imago."

74. "Ma il dialettico non dee richieder più cose d'uno, o pur una cosa di molti; perchè s'altri rispondesse non sarebbe una l'affirmazione o la negazione" (p. 24). Tasso gives an example of what he means by this: "When I speak of one thing, moreover, I do not mean whatever has a single name, unless its parts actually form a unity. A man, for example, is an animal, a biped, and tame, and all these qualities form a unity. On the other hand, as Aristotle pointed out, white, being a man, and walking do not combine into a unity, and if someone were to affirm something about them it would not constitute a single affirmation but rather a single statement containing many affirmations" ("E non chiamo una cosa quella c'ha un nome solo, se non si fa una cosa di quelle; come l'uomo è animal con due piedi e mansueto; ma di tutte queste si fa una

sola cosa: ma dell'esser bianco, e dell'esser uomo, e del caminare, come dice Aristotele, non se ne fa uno; però s'alcuno affermasse qualche cosa, non sarebbe una affermazione ma una voce, e molte l'affermazioni"; pp. 24–27). See Aristotle, *On Interpretation* 20b12–26, in *"Categories" and "Propositions,"* trans. Apostle, pp. 39–40.

75. Tasso, *Discourses on the Heroic Poem*, p. 67 (= *Prose*, p. 574): "I add that multiplicity produces indeterminacy, and this process could go on *ad infinitum*, unless art fixed and prescribed limits" (I have modified the translation).

76. "Se dunque l'interrogazione dialettica è una dimanda della risposta, o vero della proposizione, o vero dell'altra parte della contradizione" (p. 26).

77. "Il dialogo è imitazione del ragionamento, e 'l dialogo dialettico imitazione della disputa" (p. 32).

78. See the notes to Baldassari's edition of the *Discorso dell'arte del dialogo*, "Il discorso," pp. 125–27.

79. In the *Discorso dell'arte del dialogo*, Tasso has little use for Platonic dialectic itself, although this is certainly not the case in the *Dialoghi*.

80. "L'artificio della quale consiste principalmente nella dimanda usata con molto artificio da Socrate ne' libri di Platone" (p. 28).

81. Mazzali, in Tasso, *Prose*, p. 356: "At the institutional level of culture, the great writers—especially philosophers—represent syntheses" for Tasso ("Sul piano istituzionale della cultura, i grandi scrittori, soprattutto i filosofi, rappresentano delle sintesi"). In the *Discorso dell'arte del dialogo*, for example, Tasso argues that the different kinds of dialogue derive from Plato and that "whoever wants to write dialogues according to the doctrine of Aristotle and enrich the Peripatetic schools by this ornament can work in all four kinds" ("ma chi volesse scriver dialogi secondo la dottrina de Aristotele, ed arrichir di questo ornamento le scuole peripatetiche, potrebbe scriverli in tutte quattro le maniere"; pp. 28, 29).

82. "La demonstrativa prende l'altra parte della contradizione; perciochè colui il qual dimostra non dimanda, ma piglia; ma la dialettica è dimanda della contradizione" (p. 26).

83. "S'è il medesimo l'interrogazione sillogistica e la proposizione, e le proposizioni si fanno in ciascuna scienza, in ciascuna scienza ancora si posson fare le dimande" (p. 26).

84. It goes almost without saying that Tasso's poetics of dialogue represents a complete reversal of Speroni's theory in the *Apologia dei Dialoghi*.

85. Tasso reaches substantially different conclusions about dialogue elsewhere in his work. In the *Risposta*, for example, he states that "in dia-

logues as in poetry, one does not necessarily seek the truth, but rather verisimilitude and decorum" (trans. Ferguson, p. 81). Saint-Mard, pp. 12–13, comments that "when we have considered an object, we have the presumption to judge it. We have (we say) turned it in all directions; we have seen all its sides. Yet who really knows? Could it not be that something of it has escaped our understanding? Who knows if this object does not have some sides that still remain to be perceived? The pleasure of examination ought to be enough for our reason. Shadowy and limited as it is, it is poorly suited to deciding" ("quand on a considéré un Objet, on se donne l'Audace d'en juger. On l'a, dit-on, tourné en tous les Sens; on en a bien vu toutes les Faces. Qui le sçait? Et ne se peut-il pas qu'il en soit échappé à l'Esprit? Qui sçait encore si cet Objet n'a pas des Faces, qui ne lui ont point été données, pour être apperçues? Le Plaisir de l'Examen devroit suffire à notre Raison. Ténébreuse et bornée, comme elle est, il lui sied mal de décider").

86. "Laonde io raccolgo che si possan fare i dialoghi nell'aritmetica, nella geometria, nella musica e nell'astronomia, e nella morale e nella naturale e nella divina filosofia; ed in tutte l'arti ed in tutte le scienze si posson far le richieste e conseguentemente i dialogi. E s'oggi fossero in luce i dialogi scritti d'Aristotele, non ce ne sarebbe per aventura dubbio alcuno. Ma leggendo que' di Platone, i quali son pieni di proposizioni appertenenti a tutte le scienze, potremo chiaramente conoscere l'istesso" (p. 26).

87. Tasso observes that dialogues can be written "according to the doctrine of Aristotle" in order to "enrich the Peripatetic schools" (p. 29). The form of the treatise is not, then, the only appropriate form of Aristotelian discourse, as it is for Sigonio and Speroni.

88. "Se fosse impossibile mostrar dal falso il vero, sarebbe facile il risolvere, perchè si convertirebbono di necessità" (p. 28). Dialogue itself is an "ornamento" (p. 28) of doctrine in the sense that it is an artifice or device, but the role of dialectic in dialogue is not an ornamental one.

89. "Perchè non ricevono alcuno accidente; e 'n ciò son differenti da quelle che son ne' dialogi" (p. 28).

90. Pallavicino was later to develop this point at length in his *Trattato*.

91. Tasso also admits—although he does not concede the point to Sigonio—that in *De dialogo liber* "the four kinds are not distinguished in this way," since it only describes "three kinds": "in one, Socrates exhorts young men; in another, he censures the Sophists; and the third is a mixture of the first two and is no doubt more delightful for that reason" ("nondimeno questi quattro generi non sono così partitamente distinti dagli interpreti di Platone, i quali pongono tre maniere de' dialogi: l'una, nella quale Socrate essorta i giovanetti, nell'altra riprova i Sofisti; la

terza è mescolata dell'una e dell'altra, la qual senza dubbio è più soave per la mescolanza"; pp. 28, 29).

92. "Ma perchè quattro sono i generi delle dispute, il dottrinale, il dialettico, il tentativo e il contenzioso; l'altre dispute ancora si possono imitare ne' dialogi" (p. 28). Tasso's classificatory scheme produces a total of 36 different possible subspecies of dialogue out of his initial division of dialogue into four kinds on the basis of Plato's writings (didactic = *Phaedrus, Phaedo*, etc.; dialectical = *Parmenides*; probative = *Greater Hippias, Gorgias*; contentious = *Euthydemus*).

93. "Pone la dimanda in bocca non di quel ch'insegna ma di colui ch'impara" (p. 30).

94. "Laonde pare che la dimanda fatta dal discepolo sia derivata da Cicerone, e l'artificio sia proprio de' Romani, il quale s'usò dal Possevino e da altri nella dottrina peripatetica perchè forse è più facile; ma non è così lodevole, nè fu, ch'io mi ricordi, usata da gli antichi" (p. 30).

95. This passage on Cicero seems to have been drafted out of a direct confrontation with *De dialogo liber*: the passages that Tasso refers to here are the same ones that Sigonio cites, but Tasso's conclusions are markedly different from his teacher's.

96. "There is no one else among the Latin authors who approaches his [Cicero's] excellence or who can be compared to the Greeks" ("Ma nel secondo luogo non so chi se gli avicini, o chi si possa paragonare a' Greci"; pp. 32, 33). Cf. Horace, *Ars poetica* 268–69.

97. "La quale è vecchia e socratica ragione da disputar contra l'altrui opinione; tuttavolta il por la conclusione ha dello scolastico" (p. 30). Tasso admits Sigonio's point that the "decorum" required of a Roman senator does not allow this sort of questioning to occur in a work like *De oratore*, "and therefore he introduces Crassus and Anthony in a different manner" ("ma non si dimenticò ne' libri dell'*Oratore* di quel ch'era convenevole a' Romani senatori; laonde Crasso ed Antonio in altra maniera introduce a favellare"; pp. 32, 33).

98. Mulas, p. 261, calls this a mannerist ideal. Saint-Mard, pp. 24–25, adds that "if we examine the charms of the language, we will find that their most important source lies in certain oppositions that throw the mind into a sort of confusion that it always takes satisfaction in straightening out. What is contrary in what we say and what we feel carries with it something that excites us. It is the destiny of all oppositions that we put into language to have a pleasant effect on the mind" ("si l'on examine les agréments du langage, on trouvera que la source la plus considérable en est dans de certaines Oppositions, qui jettent l'esprit dans une sorte d'embarras, qu'il a toujours de l'honneur à démêler. . . . Ce qu'il y a de Contraire dans ce qu'on dit et ce qu'on sent, porte avec

soi quelque chose qui pique. C'est la destinée de toutes les Oppositions qu'on met dans le Langage, de faire sur l'Esprit un effet agréable").

99. For instance, Tasso notes that "Cicero stands first among the Latin writers, which makes him a kind of parallel to Plato," but is in fact at times not so much a dialogist as an orator: "His manner of debating and disputing is sometimes closer to the orators than to the dialecticians" ("Ma Cicerone è primo fra' Latini, il quale volle forse assomigliarsi a Platone; nondimeno nelle quistioni e nelle dispute alcuna volta è più simile a gli oratori ch'a' dialettici"; pp. 32, 33).

100. "Ma fra tutti dialogi greci lodevolissimi son que' di Platone, perciochè superano gli altri d'arte, di sottilità, d'acume, d'eleganza, e di varietà di concetti e d'ornamento di parole" (p. 32).

101. One modern editor, Mazzali, argues that "the passage is corrupt" ("il passo è corrotto"; *Prose*, p. 342*n*), but no textual evidence supports this. Instead of judging the passage corrupt, we may see it as pointing to a problematic moment in the unfolding of Tasso's theory of dialogue.

102. Tasso, *Discourses on the Heroic Poem*, p. 126 (= *Prose*, p. 644).

103. Tasso, *Lettere*, 2: 478, no. 456: "Know, then, that that dialogue was written by me many years ago in obedience to the suggestion of a prince, who perhaps was not ill-intentioned; nor did I consider it a great flaw or danger to treat this subject almost poetically" ("Sappiate che quel dialogo fu da me fatto molti anni sono per ubidire al cenno di un principe, il qual forse non aveva cattiva intenzione; nè io stimava gran fallo o pericolo trattar questa materia quasi poeticamente"); quoted in Baldassari, "L'arte," p. 24.

104. "È necessario ch'i ragionanti e disputanti abbiano qualche opinione delle cose disputate e qualche costume, il qual si manifesta alcuna volta nel disputare" (p. 32).

105. As Aristotle comments in the *Poetics* (19, 1456b7–8), the effects to be produced in language (i.e., *dianoia*) must be the result of the specific activity of speaking and thus of using language by human beings: "For what would be the use of a speaker, if the required effect were likely to be felt without the aid of the speeches?" (trans. Fyfe, p. 73).

106. In the same nonprogrammatic way, dialogues ought to admit digressions into their *dispositio* as well, which serve—like the episodes in a poem—to bring variety to the plot without destroying its unity: "Besides those parts," Tasso notes, "there are digressions in dialogues just as there are episodes in poems. The story of Eacus, Minos, and Rhadamanthus in the *Gorgias* constitutes such a digression, as do the stories of Thoth, the daimon of the Egyptians, in the *Phaedrus*, and of Er the Pamphylian in the *Republic*" ("Ci sono le digressioni, come nel

poema gli episodi: e tale è quella d'Eaco e di Minos e di Radamanto nel *Gorgia*; e quella di Teut demone de gli Egizii nel *Fedro*; e d'Ero Pamfilio ne' dialogi della *Republica*"; pp. 34, 35). Tasso's theory of the unity of the *quistione* leads him to interpret the Platonic myths as digressions from the true dialogical *mythos*.

107. "E dovendo lo scrittor del dialogo assomigliare i poeti nell'espressione e nel por le cose inanzi a gli occhi" (p. 36).

108. Even Baldassari ("Il discorso," pp. 130–34) can find only two brief references to *De dialogo liber* in Tasso's long discussion of the fourth part of dialogue, and none at all to Castelvetro.

109. Brun, p. 88.

110. "E nell'imitazioni sì fatte le persone e le cose imitate debbono più tosto accrescere che diminuire" (pp. 34, 36). Cf. *Poetics* 15, 1454b8–11: "Since tragedy is a representation of men better than ourselves we must copy the good portrait-painters who, while rendering the distinctive form and making a likeness, yet paint people better than they are" (trans. Fyfe, p. 57).

111. "Perch'egli così nel periodo com'in ciascun'altra parte ricercò la grandezza più di Senofonte e de gli altri; laonde usa le metafore pericolosamente in luogo delle imagini, che sono usate da Senofonte; e somiglia colui il quale camina in luogo dove è pericolo di sdrucciolare, compiacendo a sé medesimo ed avendo molto ardire, sì come è proprio delle nature sublimi. Talchè fu detto di lui ch'egli molto s'inalzava sovra il parlar pedestre; e ch'il suo parlare non era in tutto simile al verso, nè 'n tutto simile alla prosa, e ch'egli usava l'ingegno non altramente ch'i re facciano la podestà. Ed in somma niun ornamento di parole, niun color retorico, niun lume d'oratore par che sia rifiutato da Platone" (p. 36).

112. The language employed by Tasso here is directly derived from Demetrius, *On Style* 2.80 ("In this way we obtain a simile and a less risky expression, in the other way metaphor and greater danger. Plato's employment of metaphors rather than similes is, therefore, to be regarded as a risky feature of his style"; trans. Roberts, pp. 353, 355). Longinus notes, in *On the Sublime* (32.2–4), that "Aristotle and Theophrastus say that bold metaphors are softened by inserting 'as if' or 'as it were' or 'if one may say so' or 'if one may risk the expression.' The apology, they say, mitigates the audacity of the language. I accept this, but at the same time, as I said in speaking of 'figures,' the proper antidote for a multitude of daring metaphors is strong and timely emotion and genuine sublimity. These by their nature sweep everything along in the forward surge of their current, or rather they positively demand bold imagery as essential to their effect, and do not give the hearer time to examine how many metaphors there are, because he shares the excitement of the speaker" (trans. Fyfe, in Aristotle, *Poetics*, p. 213).

113. This approach to Plato, which is by no means exclusive to Tasso —cf. Longinus, *On the Sublime* 32.5–8 (197*v*–198*v*); Quintilian, *Institutio oratoria* 10.1.81; Aelius Aristides, *Oratio platonica secunda*; and (especially) Demetrius, *On Style* 2.37 (229*r*)—is common to many of his writings. A list of related passages in which Tasso discusses Plato's metaphorical language may be found in Baldassari, "Il discorso," pp. 131–32*n*.

114. Tasso never simply parrots the ancient authorities that he uses in the *Discorso dell'arte del dialogo*. Demetrius, 4.208–20, defines *enargeia* as a component of the plain style, for instance, not the elevated style; Tasso reverses this. See also Quintilian, *Institutio oratoria* 8.3.61–71.

115. "Il quale nel *Protagora*, parlando d'Ippocrate che s'era arrosito essendo ancora di notte, soggiunge: 'Già appariva la luce, onde il color poteva esser veduto'; e la chiarezza, ch'evidenza è chiamata da' Latini, nasce dalla cura usata nel parlare" (pp. 36, 38). See *Protagoras* 312A. This passage from Plato appears to have been taken directly from Demetrius, *On Style* 4.218, near the end of the discussion of *enargeia*. See Baldassari, "Il discorso," p. 132*n*. Tasso's treatment of *elocutio* in the *Discourses on the Heroic Poem* is similarly derived from the work of Demetrius; see Raimondi, *Poesia*, pp. 25–70.

116. Lausberg, p. 118. See also Demetrius, *On Style* 4.217–20. Tasso states in the *Discourses on the Heroic Poem*, p. 189 (= *Prose*, p. 709), that "what the lowly style requires above all else is likelihood and what the Latins called *evidentia*, the Greeks energy, which we might no less properly call clarity or expressiveness. This is the power that makes us almost behold the things narrated; it comes from a minutely attentive narration that omits nothing." See also the *Discorsi dell'arte poetica*, in *Prose*, p. 401.

117. Trans. Roberts, pp. 429, 431.

118. It also occurs in the works of Horace, Quintilian, and numerous other ancient rhetoricians and critics. Saint-Mard, pp. 5–6, remarks in this regard: "Rich in description, the dialogist always chooses pleasant objects to paint, and paints them with force: the most abstract reasonings acquire a certain gracefulness by passing through his imagination, which is extremely colorful; and the quality of being a philosopher, to which he professes, in no way makes him renounce the language of the poet" ("Riche dans ses Descriptions, il choisit toujours, pour peindre, des Objets agréables, et les peint avec Force: les Raisonnemens les plus abstraits acquièrent quelque chose de gracieux, en passant par son Imagination, qui est extrèmement fleurie; et la Qualité de Philosophe, dont il se pique, ne le fait point renoncer au Langage de Poète").

119. "Platone meglio di ciascuno ce le (*sc. le cose*) fa quasi *vedere*"; "e ci par di *vedere*"; "e quasi *veggiamo*"; "ci par di *vedere* e ascoltare quel che leggiamo" (pp. 36, 38, 40; my italics). Cf. Demetrius, *On Style*

4.217: "Vividness [*enargeia*] may also be produced by mentioning the accompanying circumstances of any action" (trans. Roberts, p. 435).

120. Hathaway, *Age*, pp. 11–12: "It is important to call attention to the fact that several of the literary critics of sixteenth-century Italy dealt at more or less length with *enargeia*. . . . Some of the outstanding treatments of *enargeia* are to be found in Pigna, Giraldi Cinthio, Cavalcanti's *Retorica*, Muzio, Tasso, Mazzoni, and Beni." See also Castelvetro, "*Poetica*" *d'Aristotele*, 1: 366–73. Tasso's tendency to confuse *enargeia* with *energeia* (energy, vigor) in other critical works of his, such as in Book 6 of the *Discourses on the Heroic Poem*, p. 189 (= *Prose*, p. 709), is of little consequence for his theory of clarity or evidence in the *Discorso dell'arte del dialogo*. See also Patterson, pp. 131–33.

121. Tasso, *Discourses on the Heroic Poem*, p. 191 (= *Prose*, p. 711): "Every imitation involves *evidentia*."

122. "E 'n quella d'Alcibiade, di Fedro e di Carmide i costumi de' nobili giovani son descritti maravigliosamente"; "nel medesimo dialogo leggiamo con maraviglioso diletto"; "e con piacer incredibile leggiamo"; "ma sopra tutte le cose c'empie di compassione e di maraviglia"; "e nella descrizione parimente è maraviglioso"; "queste son le perfezioni di Platone, veramente maravigliose" (pp. 34, 38, 40).

123. Montgomery, p. 160.

124. Longinus, *On the Sublime* 15.1–2 (187*v*): "Weight, grandeur and energy in writing are very largely produced . . . by the use of 'images.' . . . For the term Imagination [*phantasia*] is applied in general to an idea which enters the mind from any source and engenders speech, but the word now has come to be used predominantly of passages where, inspired by strong emotion, *you seem to see what you describe and bring it vividly before the eyes of your audience*. . . . The object of poetry is to enthrall, of prose writing to present things vividly [*enargeia*], though both indeed aim at this latter and at excited feeling" (trans. Fyfe, in Aristotle, *Poetics*, p. 171; my italics). See also *On the Sublime* 1.3–4 (179*r*) and 8.1 (182*v*).

125. Montgomery, pp. 159–60. Burke, p. 78, points out that the concern with imagination in the classical theories of rhetoric "was often treated in terms of 'actualization' (*energeia*, the use of words that suggest purposive movement) and 'vividness' (*enargeia*)."

126. Marmontel, "Description," *Encyclopédie*, as quoted by Hamon, p. 3: "Description is a figure of thought by development which, instead of simply indicating an object, makes it somehow visible, by the lively and animated exposition of its most interesting properties and circumstances."

127. This is one way in which Tasso's notion of the *maraviglioso* is

distinguished from Longinus's notion of the sublime proper, which is much more closely tied to its rhetorical effects.

128. "Nell'imitazioni sì fatte le persone e le cose imitate debbono più tosto accrescere che diminuire" (pp. 34, 36). Cf. *Poetics* 2, 1448a1–5: "Since living persons are the objects of representation, there must necessarily be either good men or inferior [ones] . . . that is to say, either better than ourselves or worse or much what we are" (trans. Fyfe, p. 9).

129. "Non ci rimarrà dubbio alcuno che lo scrittor del dialogo non sia imitatore o quasi mezzo fra 'l poeta e 'l dialettico" (p. 40).

130. Baldassari, "L'arte," p. 24.

131. "Ma s'in alcuna parte del dialogo debbiamo aver risguardo a gli avvertimenti di Demetrio, è in quella nella qual si disputa; perch'in lei si conviene la purità e la simplicità dell'elocuzione, e 'l soverchio ornamento par ch'impedisca gli argomenti, e che rintuzzi, per così dire, l'acume e la sottilità. Ma l'altre parti debbono esser ornate con maggior diligenza" (p. 36).

132. Samuel, p. xxvi, in her introduction to Tasso, *Discourses on the Heroic Poem*, points out that in his first discourse Tasso transforms some of the qualitative elements of the Aristotelian plot (such as *peripeteia* and *pathos*) into quantitative parts of the poem.

133. "Alcuna parte del dialogo"; "l'altre parti"; "con elocuzioni in alcune parti piene di ornamento, in altre di purità, come par che si convenga alla materia" (pp. 36, 40). Lord and Trafton translate *materia* as "subject," but that is not precisely what Tasso means here; "object of mimesis" is closer to the sense of the Italian term. I have also altered their rendering of *in alcune parti* from "sometimes" to "in some parts" and *in altre* [*parti*] from "sometimes" to "in others."

134. *Poetics* 24, 1460b4–5; trans. Fyfe, p. 101.

135. Compare Howell, p. 32, who discusses the "literature of statement" as "the writings produced according to the Aristotelian theories of rhetoric and dialectic."

136. In the *Discourses on the Heroic Poem*, p. 29 (= *Prose*, p. 525), Tasso argues that "poetry surely belongs under dialectic along with rhetoric, which, as Aristotle says, is the other child of the dialectical faculty."

137. De Man, "Epistemology," p. 13: "Metaphors, tropes, and figural language in general have been a perennial problem and, at times, a recognized source of embarrassment for philosophical discourse and, by extension, for all discursive uses of language including historiography and literary analysis. It appears that philosophy either has to give up its own constitutive claim to rigor in order to come to terms with the figurality of its own language or that it has to free itself from figuration altogether. And if the latter is considered impossible, philosophy could

at least learn to control figuration by keeping it, so to speak, in its place, by delimiting the boundaries of its influence and thus restricting the epistemological damage that it may cause."

Chapter 5

1. This corresponds, as Walter Ong (p. 290) has pointed out, to a wider epistemic shift at the end of the Renaissance to "a logic of individual inquiry into issues thought of as existing *outside* a framework of discourse or dialectic rather than a logic of discourse" (my italics). See also Gilbert, pp. 221–31.

2. See Battistini and Raimondi for a recent synoptic overview of the question.

3. Among the symptoms of this would be the stricter application of the rules of the Index of Forbidden Books (Clement VIII's new 1596 Index set the tone) and the hegemonic role played by the Inquisition in that process; the continual confiscation and destruction of books; the precarious, even dangerous, position of publishers; and the suppression of deviant political theories and philosophies (Giordano Bruno's death at the stake in the Campo de' Fiori in Rome in 1600 is emblematic in this regard, but a number of others paid only a slightly smaller price for their unorthodoxy). It is doubtless true that there was inevitably an impoverishment of Italian religious, spiritual, and cultural life and a greater degree of isolation of Italian culture in regard to the models and currents of thought from beyond the Alps in the final years of the sixteenth century and in the first third of the seventeenth century; see Rosa, pp. 318–19.

4. Biagi, pp. 920–23. Biagi quotes Tommaso Cornelio, *Progymnasmata* (1663), as follows: "According to what others have written, in scientific subjects the style should not be dissimilar from that which men of letters usually use when they discuss among themselves, for which reason the form of dialogue was esteemed for such subjects by the great men [of the past]" ("Nelle materie scientifiche, dee lo stile per quanto n'ha altri lasciato scritto, esser non dissimile da quello, che gli huomini letterati sogliono usare, quando tra di essi ragionano, che però da gli huomini grandi è stata stimata a proposito per tali materie la forma de' Dialoghi"). Biagi (pp. 918–30) supplies a number of examples of such works, ranging from Tommaso Cornelio to Giuseppe Ferroni to A. Vallisneri and Filippo Buonanini.

5. For example, the vast and largely unknown travel literature of the seventeenth century (which survives largely in manuscript form) from the city of Venice offers numerous prose dialogues: see the documentation provided by Donazzolo.

6. All information on the life of Manso is from Masson, 1: 807–20; Parker, 1: 174, 2: 827; and Tiraboschi, *Storia*, 8.1: 52–54. Other works on Manso include A. Borzelli, G. B. *Manso, Marchese di Villa* (Naples, 1916); and M. Manfredi, G. B. *Manso nella vita e nelle opere* (Naples, 1919).

7. Tiraboschi, *Storia*, 8.1: 52–53.

8. Solerti, 1: 882.

9. Quoted in Parker, 1: 174; Masson, 1: 811.

10. Manso's treatise on dialogue was published as an appendix to the *Erocallia, ovvero dell'amore e della bellezza* (Venice, 1628), pp. 1033–64. All future references are to this edition of *Del dialogo* and are included in the text in parentheses. All translations are my own; the original Italian text is included in each case in an accompanying note (no attempt has been made to modernize Manso's Italian prose).

11. "Il quale nel tempo ch'honorò della sua presenza la casa mia, solendo le sere con esso meco favellare, e le più volte de' suoi Poemi, e delle Prose" (p. 1034).

12. "Laonde volentieri Signor Principe ubbedisco a quel che hier m'imponeste mandandovi di presente queste brevissime regole ch'io doversi osservare intorno alla composition de' Dialoghi scrissi è già molti anni, negli argomenti da me fatti sopra quelli del medesimo Tasso." Despite this passage, it seems certain that *Del dialogo* was composed at least twenty years after the death of Tasso, if not more.

13. Solerti (1: 397), for instance, notes that, regarding Tasso's theory of dialogue, Manso only "pretended to report his ideas" ("finse di riferirne le idee") in *Del dialogo*.

14. He simply remarks at one point that maiuetic dialogue, in particular, was "praised and imitated more by Tasso" ("fu più lodato e imitato dal Tasso"; p. 1058), without citing a source.

15. "Ne siegue, che quanto al genere debba rassomigliarsi al Poeta, e quanto alla differenza conformarsi al Dialettico, e quasi un mezzo fra amendue" (p. 1048); "ma percioche dicemmo lo scrittor de' Dialoghi esser un certo, che di mezzo tra 'l Poeta e 'l Dialettico" (p. 1059).

16. He observes that "the examples of Plato and Cicero teach us to use the ornate style" ("gli esempi di Platone, e di Cicerone n'insegnano d'usare l'ornata"; p. 1061), in a direct paraphrase of the *Discorso dell'arte del dialogo*.

17. "Le quali cose tutte hanno bisogno di regole particolari, non pure malagevoli ad osservarsi, ma anche a determinarsi, percioche di questa materia quantunque importantissima non è però stato scritto, a sofficienza." Unlike Pallavicino, Manso never acknowledges his sources in *Del dialogo*.

18. Despite this conspicuous silence in Manso's text, Tasso's dia-

logues nonetheless serve as one of the touchstones for the argument that Manso makes in *Del dialogo*. Manso takes the *Dialoghi* to be representative of the entire Italian vernacular tradition of dialogue, and he repeatedly compares them favorably with Plato's and Cicero's dialogues, or, in other words, with the greatest works of the dialogical tradition of antiquity. One of the dialogues by Tasso that Manso mentions most frequently and most enthusiastically is, not surprisingly, *Il Manso*.

19. "Non fu all'hor mio pensiero di proporre ammaestramenti, onde si sappiano i Dialoghi ben formare, ma più tosto di dare altrui a divedere, come stati siano maravigliosamente bene dal nostro Tasso formati."

20. "Mi disse che l'imitatione era al Poeta, e allo scrittore de' Dialoghi parimente commune; perche l'uno imitava l'humane attioni, e l'altro i ragionamenti: con questa differenza però, che quegli imita à fin di dilettare giovando, e questi d'insegnar dilettando."

21. "Essendo la Natura più antica dell'arte, quell'arte sara certamente fra tutte l'altre più antica che dalla Natura stessa immediatamente dipende, ma l'arti, che maggiormente imitano del naturale dipendono con minor tramezzamento dalla Natura . . . adunque esser deono parimente le più antiche."

22. "Il perche imitando il Dialogo molto più del naturale i nostri ragionamenti, che non fanno i Trattati, siegue che l'invention del Dialogo esser dovesse di quella de' Trattati più antica. . . . Dunque a ragione deono i Dialoghi e per origine più antica, e per unione più prossima alla Natura esser più nobili de' Trattati."

23. "Essendo nel Dialogo l'imitation di coloro, che favellano molto più vivamente, ch'in niun' altra maniera di scrittura rappresentata, per conseguente ne viene, ch'esso non che più de' Trattati, ma di qualunque altra forma di scrivere parimente sia dilettevole."

24. "È insiememente nella sua propria spetie costituito, che è d'imitare le persone, che scambievolmente ragionando, fra di lor questionano"; Manso also defines dialogue as "un'imitation di ragionamento fra persone, che intorno alcuna questione disputino" (p. 1046).

25. "Il soggetto dee esser uno: percioche essendo il Dialogo costituito come habbiam detto, sotto 'l genere dell'imitatione, è l'imitato per la differenza della disputatione . . . essendo richiesto . . . al Dialettico l'unità d'una semplice affermatione, o negatione in ciascuna disputatione."

26. "Se tutti confermassero le medesime cose, e nel medesimo modo all'uno non rimarebbe, che rispondere all'altro, onde non sarebbe Dialogo, ma più tosto un di que' chori, che si rappresentano nelle tragedie."

27. Manso lists "color ch' a vicenda favellano, o sono fra sé di contra-

rij pareri, per gli quali disputano, o se pur tutti hanno una medesima opinione la provano con diversi argomenti."

28. "Ma in ciascun Dialogo (io favellava de que' del Tasso) andaremo sette principali parti considerando: primieramente il titolo da cui viene tutto 'l ragionamento dinominato, secondariamente il soggetto, i favellatori, e la forma, che sono le tre parti, che riguardano la qualità, e ultimamente l'Introdottione, la Questione, e le Digressioni, che sono l'altre, e tre alla quantità appartenenti." The title, which Manso considers separately, distinguishes each dialogue from all others so that it can be recognized at first glance by the reader; since it always precedes the rest of the text and thus belongs to a specific narrative order, the title would seem to be a quantitative part as well (although Manso himself does not say this).

29. "Primieramente di dar contezza delle circostanze del luogo, del tempo, e delle persone ragunate a favellare. Appresso esporre la cagione, o gli accidenti, per gli quali elleno si sono ragunate." Manso would appear to be deeply indebted here to Sigonio, although he makes no mention of *De dialogo liber*.

30. "L'ultimo officio dell'introdottione [è] di render docile, e attento il lettore alla question e si compie col proporre brievemente il soggetto e le difficoltà delle cose che si deono questionare. Conciosia cosa che il risapersi la materia del futuro ragionamento faccia, a chi legge antiveder presso a poco la riuscita di quello, e per coseguente addottar tutto il processo, e 'l discorrimento delle parole al preveduto fine, ond'egli più capevole se ne rende, e allo 'ncontro le proposte difficoltà accendono nel lettore vaghezza di sapere la solution di essa, dalqual desiderio necessariamente nasce l'attentione." This is reminiscent of the language of Book 4 of Tasso's *Discourses on the Heroic Poem*, p. 116 (= *Prose*, p. 631): "If the proposition is virtually the poet's proem, it is to my mind highly appropriate to move the reader's expectation and make him attentive at that point."

31. "La disputatione imita nel Dialogo com'ella è la maggiore, e principal parte di essi, così e più d'ogn' altra capace di tutti gli stormenti, che sono al Poeta e al Dialettico appartenenti."

32. "La sentenza adonque percioche, è istromento per lo cui mezzo si genera nella mente altrui conoscimento d'alcuna cosa, e percioche questa contezza non può essere se non di tre sorti, di scienza, di opinione, o di fede, quindi siegue, che la sentenza etiandio debba haver per fine di generare nell'altrui mente una di queste tre conoscenze."

33. "Percioche egli con l'imitatione rappresenta per modo così pronto, e così vivace allo 'ntelletto le cose che dimostrargli intende,

ch'egli incontanente, e senza veruna fatica l'apprende, onde dall'agevo-
lezza dell'apprendere nasce unito col diletto etiandio il giovamento, e
percioche nel Dialogo solo propriamente cotal modo, e non in altra
maniera di scrivere si ritrova, quindi siegue, che da esso molto maggior
giovamento, che da qualunque sia forma di scrittura possiamo trarre."

34. Tasso remarks, in Book 1 of the *Discourses on the Heroic Poem*, p. 11
(= *Prose*, pp. 499–500) that "hence perhaps the purpose of pleasure (as
Fracastoro held in his *Dialogue on Poetry*) is not to be scorned; on the
contrary, to aim at pleasure is nobler than to aim at profit, since enjoy-
ment is sought for itself, and other things for its sake. In this respect it
is like happiness, which is man's goal as citizen; indeed, nothing can
be found more like happiness. . . . The useful is not sought for itself but
for something else; this is why it is a less noble purpose than pleasure
and has less resemblance to the final purpose."

35. Barilli, pp. 89–94.

36. For a brief summary of seventeenth-century Jesuit literary ideology, see Battistini and Raimondi, 3.1: 119–20.

37. These comments are indebted to the work of Michel de Certeau,
in particular *La fable mystique* and "Le dix-septième français."

38. Austin, p. 101. Manso does point out that dialogue is "hard for
the writer, whose business it is to deal with many more things, and
more difficult ones, than others do" ("malagevole allo scrittore, cui fa
mestiero d'haver a molte più cose riguardo, e molte più difficile, a com-
piere, che gli altri non hanno"; p. 1044). He adds that although didactic
dialogue is "easier, and more convenient, for explaining mental concepts" ("più facile, e più comodo, a spiegare i concetti della mente"),
Tasso praised and imitated maiuetic dialogue—Socratic questioning—
for being "much more artful and wandering" ("come molto più artifi-
cioso, e pellegrino"; p. 1058). Although Manso displays a certain interest
in the challenge of writing dialogues in a deliberately artful and wandering style, however, this interest is always subordinate to the main
function of dialogical writing—instruction.

39. Weinberg, *History*, 1: 201–49, points out that this is a common
procedure among Italian critics and theorists in the late Renaissance.

40. F. Croce, "Critica," p. 494. All biographical information on Pallavicino is from Scotti, "Sforza Pallavicino," pp. 747–49; Raimondi, *Trattatisti*, pp. 193–96; and principally from the excellent documentation in
Redondi, pp. 73–74, 100–101, 200–202, 264–65, 288–89, to whom I am
much indebted here.

41. Pallavicino, *Trattato*. The title of the *editio princeps* is *Considerazioni
sopra l'arte dello stile e del dialogo* (Rome, 1646). All references are to the
1662 edition of the *Trattato* and are included in the text in parentheses.

All translations are my own; the original Italian text is included in each case in an accompanying note.

42. F. Croce, "Critica," p. 493, speaks of "seventeenth-century culture's general coming to an awareness of its separation from the Renaissance" ("la generale presa di coscienza da parte della cultura secentesca del suo stacco dal Rinascimento").

43. "Lo Speroni in quella sua dottissima *Apologia de' Dialoghi*" (p. 328); Pallavicino further compliments Speroni later, noting that "in which [undertaking] we will be briefer if we pass over many things that in the aforementioned *Apology* by Speroni our reader will have ventured to have seen" ("nel che faremo più brevi per tralasciar molte cose che nella mentovata Apologia dello Sperone havrà per avventura vedute il nostro lettore"; p. 395). Regarding the sixteenth-century tradition represented by Speroni and Tasso, Pallavicino observes that "Cardinal Bembo, Sperone Speroni, Cesare Bargagli, and many others, but principally the daring pen of Torquato Tasso, show with their most fortunate example just how ideally suited dialogue is for the communication of the most noble disciplines" ("il Cardinal Bembo, Sperone Speroni, Cesare Bargagli, ed altri assaissimi, ma . . . principalmente l'avventurosa penna di Torquato Tasso, fanno vedere con la loro felicità dell'esempio loro quanto il Dialogo sia idoneo alla comunicazione delle più nobili discipline"; p. 326).

44. "Un valenthuomo che . . . colse gli argomenti per biasimarla."

45. Leopardi, 2: 29.

46. F. Croce, *Tre momenti*, pp. 191–92.

47. "Nel disputare se all'insegnator di scienzia più si convenga la favella diritta in persona propria, o vero l'obliqua per introdotti parlatori" (unnumbered p. of preface).

48. "Non potrà già veruno senza filosofia conoscere e dimostrare onde avvenga che la sua composizione sia eccellente" (unnumbered p. of preface).

49. "Contemplar diligentemente la natura e l'utilità della poetica imitazione" (unnumbered p. of preface).

50. F. Croce, *Tre momenti*, p. 178.

51. "La strettissima parentela onde son legate queste due Arti dominatrici del cuore umano" (unnumbered p. of preface).

52. "I Dialoghi vogliono come primo lor obietto l'insegnamento; nè vi aspergono il piacere se non quanto il conoscono profittevole à mantener l'attenzione, ad imprimer la dottrina nella memoria, ed in breve, all'acquisto e all'aumento della scienza."

53. "Nella testura del Dialogo l'industria più operosa è tutta impiegata nel ritrovamento della verità e delle ragioni."

54. "Non solo può l'Insegnator di scienze dimostrare senza disavvantaggio uno studioso desiderio d'esser letto, ma d'esser creduto."

55. "Ordigno attissimo per istillarvi con giocondità la dottrina" (p. 319); "un'altra assai meglio insegnativa maniera d'accoppiar la dottrina all'imitazione s'è ritrovata: ed è la composizione del Dialogo" (p. 325).

56. "Nelle quali tutte contiensi qualche mescolamento d'imitazione; e pure non diconsi professioni imitatrici, come la Poesia."

57. "Essendo poi non più malagevole . . . di quel che sia il dettare ò lettere, ò istorie, ò altra scrittura di prosa."

58. "Parole proporzionate à parlatori familiari e specolativi."

59. Pallavicino, *Del bene* (1644), p. 462; as quoted in F. Croce, *Tre momenti*, p. 171.

60. "Quest'artifizio di render quasi visibili le parole col vivace racconto di graziosissimi fatti." Barilli, p. 93, notes that the production of visual and sensual evidence is a textual reconstruction of experience itself.

61. F. Croce, *Tre momenti*, p. 166, notes that Pallavicino's is a "love of the verisimilar, not because of a will to truth, but because of a commitment to wittily exact constructs—a love of the verisimilar that is also a taste for illusion" ("amor di verisimile, non per una volontà di verità, ma per un impegno di costruzioni argutamente esatte, amor di verisimile che è insieme gusto illusionistico").

62. "Pertanto quei fatti che il Dialogo riferisce, benchè per sè soli non meriterebbono il pregio della narrazione; tuttavia come cornici degl'imitati ragionamenti danno lor quella grazia e quella *enargeia* che le minute e verisimili particolarità aggiungono per la stessa ragione al Poema."

63. Mulas (p. 262) remarks that "pleasure acts in this case as what activates and strengthens memory, since those small and most graceful facts are the *loci* to which memory will connect the words uttered by the interlocutors, in order to find them more easily [later on]" ("il diletto agisce in questo caso come attivatore e potenziatore della memoria, poichè quei piccoli e graziosissimi fatti sono i *loci* ai quali la memoria collegherà, per ritrovarle più agevolmente, le parole pronunciate degli interlocutori").

64. "Molto significò Aristotile quando disse, che noi amiamo i nostri occhi sopra tutti gli altri sensi, peròche impariamo da essi più che da tutti gli altri sensi."

65. "Sono tante martellate che scolpiscono altamente le immagini delle cose insegnate nell'animo de' discepoli."

66. "Così nè lo studiare sol per via di Compendij e di Somme" (p. 351)? Mulas (p. 262) observes that "according to Pallavicino, in nature as

in learning, excess is always functional" ("secondo Pallavicino, così in natura . . . come nell'apprendimento, l'eccedente è sempre funzionale").

67. Compare Mulas, p. 260: "It is always, in the last analysis, the written word that has the power to ignite the mind of the reader, and it is reading, not listening, that allows a well-trained intellect to grasp a clue to the truth that lies beneath the literary game" ("È sempre, in ultima analisi, la parola scritta che ha il potere di accendere la mente del lettore, ed è la lettura, non l'ascolto, che consente ad un intelletto ben esercitato di cogliere un indizio di verità sotto il gioco letterario").

68. "Il dialogo contiene insieme e una fontana per ispruzzare i discorsi di quel piacere; e una fucina per fabricar le rotelle di questa tempra."

69. "Potendosi porre in campo il sostenitore della falsa opinione, il quale con tutte l'industrie più ingannevoli dell'eloquenza s'insegni di persuaderla; indi far che l'insegnatore del vero con maniera schietta palesi la fraude di quelle prove, Giganti nell'apparenza, mà nuvole d'aria nell'esistenza; e disfaccia quegl'incanti con cui la magia dell'affetto facea travedere il mal accorto lettore."

70. "O nell'oscurità del dubbio, o nel pericolo dell'inganno."

71. "Senza fallo son difettuose per insegnare."

72. "Peròche in essi con gran chiarezza riluce l'opinione dello Scrittore e 'l suo fondamento."

73. Mulas, p. 263.

74. Compare Mulas, pp. 262–63: "But above all dialogue differs from scientific discourse because of its ability to make possession of the truth less uncertain in the mind of the reader" ("Ma soprattutto il dialogo differisce dal discorso scientifico per la sua capacità di rendere meno incerto nel lettore il possesso della verità").

75. Garin, La filosofia, 2: 222.

76. Costanzo, 2: 159.

77. Nietzsche, Daybreak, trans. Hollingdale, 5.535 (p. 212), observes that "in itself truth is no power at all. . . . It has, rather, to draw power over to its side, or go over to the side of power, or it will perish again and again." Pallavicino mandates instead that truth and power should be inseparable in every aspect of Italian social and cultural life in the mid-seventeenth century, including dialogue, which works exclusively for the benefit of both.

78. Bakhtin, Dostoyevsky's Poetics, p. 110.

Selected List of Works Consulted

Accetto, Torquato. *Della dissimulazione onesta*. Ed. Salvatore S. Nigro. Genoa, 1983.

Agamben, Giorgio. "Le philosophe et la muse." Trans. Gérard Macé. *Commerce* 62/63 (Autumn 1985): 73–90.

Andrieu, J. *Le dialogue antique: structure et présentation*. Collection d'Études Latines, Série Scientifique 29. Paris, 1954.

Ammirato, Scipione. *Opuscoli*. Florence, 1640.

Aristotle. *"Art" of Rhetoric*. Trans. J. H. Freese. Cambridge, Mass., and London, 1982 [1926].

———. *"Categories" and "Propositions."* Trans. Hippocrates G. Apostle. Grinnell, Iowa, 1980.

———. *Poetics*. Trans. W. Hamilton Fyfe. Cambridge, Mass., and London, 1973 [rev. ed. 1932].

———. *Poetics*. Trans. James Hutton. New York and London, 1982.

———. *Posterior Analytics*. Trans. Hippocrates G. Apostle. Grinnell, Iowa, 1981.

———. *Works*. Vol. 12. Ed. David Ross. Oxford, 1952.

Armstrong, C.J.R. "The Dialectical Road to Truth: The Dialogue." In *French Renaissance Studies, 1540–70: Humanism and the Encyclopedia*. Ed. Peter Sharatt. Edinburgh, 1976, pp. 36–51.

Asor Rosa, Alberto, ed. *Letteratura italiana*. 7 vols. to date. Turin, 1982– .

Atkins, J.W.H. *Literary Criticism in Antiquity*. London, 1952.

Austin, J.L. *How to Do Things with Words*. Ed. J.O. Urmson and Marina Sbisà. 2d ed. Cambridge, Mass., 1975.

Bakhtin, Mikhail M. *The Dialogic Imagination: Four Essays*. Ed. Michael Holquist. Trans. Michael Holquist and Caryl Emerson. Texas Slavic Series 1. Austin, Tex., 1981.

———. *Problems of Dostoyevsky's Poetics*. Ed. and trans. Caryl Emerson. Theory and History of Literature 8. Minneapolis, 1984.

282   *Selected List of Works Consulted*

------. *Rabelais and His World*. Trans. Helene Iswolsky. Bloomington, Ind., 1984 [1968].

Baldassari, Guido. "L'arte del dialogo in Torquato Tasso." *Studi tassiani* 20 (1970): 5–46.

------. "Il discorso tassiano 'Dell'arte del dialogo.' " *Rassegna della letteratura italiana*, 7th series, 75, nos. 1–2 (Jan.–Aug. 1971): 93–134.

Baldwin, Charles Sears. *Ancient Rhetoric and Poetics Interpreted from Representative Works*. Gloucester, Mass., 1959 [1924].

------. *Renaissance Literary Theory and Practice: Classicism in the Rhetoric and Poetic of Italy, France and England, 1400–1600*. Ed. Donald L. Clark. New York, 1939.

Barilli, Renato. *La retorica*. Milan, 1979.

Barthes, Roland. "L'Ancienne rhétorique: aide-mémoire." *Communications* 16 (1970): 172–229.

------. *S/Z*. Trans. Richard Miller. New York, 1974.

Battistini, Andrea, and Ezio Raimondi. "Retoriche e poetiche dominanti." In *Letteratura italiana*. Vol. 3.1. Ed. Alberto Asor Rosa. Turin, 1984, pp. 82–125.

Becichemo, Mar. *Panegyricus, con epistolicarum quaestionum: centuria prima*. Brescia, 1505.

Beni, Paolo. *In Aristotelis poeticam commentarii*. Padua, 1613.

Bénoius, Mustapha Kemal. *Le dialogue philosophique dans la littérature française du seizième siècle*. The Hague, 1976.

Berger, Harry, Jr. "Facing Sophists: Socrates' Charismatic Bondage in *Protagoras*." *Representations* 5 (Winter 1984): 66–89.

Biagi, Maria Luisa Altieri. "Forme della comunicazione scientifica." In *Letteratura italiana*. Vol. 3.2. Ed. Alberto Asor Rosa. Turin, 1984, pp. 891–947.

Bonfantini, Massimo, and Augusto Ponzio. "Dialogo sui dialoghi." *Versus* 34 (Jan.–Apr. 1983): 79–111.

Bonifacio, Giovanni. *L'arte de' cenni*. Vicenza, 1616.

Borsellino, Nino. "Morfologie del dialogo osceno: 'La cazzaria' dell'Arsiccio Intronato." In *Il dialogo: scambi e passaggi della parola*. Ed. Giulio Ferroni. Palermo, 1985, pp. 110–23.

Branca, Vittore. *Poliziano e l'umanesimo della parola*. Turin, 1983.

Braudel, Fernand. *Il secondo Rinascimento: due secoli e tre Italie*. Trans. Corrado Vivanti. Turin, 1986 [1974].

Bray, Bernard. "Le dialogue comme forme littéraire au XVIIème siècle." *Cahiers de l'Association internationale des études françaises* 24 (May 1972): 9–29.

Brooks, Peter. Introduction. In *Introduction to Poetics*. By Tzvetan Todorov. Trans. Richard Howard. Theory and History of Literature 1. Minneapolis, 1981, pp. vii–xix.

Brun, Jean. *Socrate*. Paris, 1982 [1960].

Buckley, Michael J. "Philosophic Method in Cicero." *Journal of the History of Philosophy* 8 (1970): 143–54.

Burke, Kenneth. *A Rhetoric of Motives*. Berkeley, Calif., 1969 [1950].

Cammarosano, Francesco. *La vita e le opere di Sperone Speroni*. Empoli, 1920.

Castelvetro, Lodovico. *On the Art of Poetry*. Ed. and trans. Andrew Bongiorno. MRTS 29. Binghamton, N.Y., 1984.

———. *Opere varie critiche*. Poetiken des Cinquecento 11. Munich, 1969 [Bern, 1727].

———. *"Poetica" d'Aristotele vulgarizzata et sposta*. Ed. Werther Romani. Scrittori d'Italia 264–65. 2 vols. Bari, 1978–79.

Certeau, Michel de. "Le dix-septième français et ses langages spirituels." In *Dictionnaire de spiritualité*. Paris, 1974.

———. *La fable mystique, XVIe–XVIIe siècles*. Paris, 1975.

———. *Heterologies: Discourses on the Other*. Trans. Brian Massumi. Theory and History of Literature 17. Minneapolis, 1986.

Cicero. *Brutus. Orator*. Trans. G. L. Hendrickson and H. M. Hubbell. Cambridge, Mass., and London, 1952 [1939].

———. *De inventione*. Trans. H. M. Hubbell. Cambridge, Mass., and London, 1976 [1949].

———. *De oratore*. Trans. H. Rackham. 2 vols. Cambridge, Mass., and London, 1982 [1942].

———. *Letters to His Friends*. Trans. W. Glynn Williams. 3 vols. London and New York, 1927–29.

(Cicero). *Rhetorica ad C. Herennium*. Trans. Harry Caplan. Cambridge, Mass., and London, 1954.

Cochrane, Eric, ed. *The Late Italian Renaissance, 1525–1630*. New York, 1970.

Colie, Rosalie. *Paradoxia Epidemica: The Renaissance Tradition of Paradox*. Princeton, N.J., 1966.

Cooper, Lane, and Alfred Gudeman. *A Bibliography of the "Poetics" of Aristotle*. New Haven, Conn., 1928.

Costanzo, Mario. *Critica e poetica del primo Seicento*. 2 vols. Rome, 1971.

Cranz, F. Edward. *A Bibliography of Aristotle Editions, 1501–1600*. Revised by Charles B. Schmitt. Baden-Baden, 1984.

Croce, Benedetto. *Poeti e scrittori del pieno e del tardo Rinascimento*. Scritti di storia letteraria e politica 36. 3 vols. Bari, 1945.

———. *Problemi di estetica e contributi alla storia dell'estetica italiana*. Bari, 1954.

———. *Storia dell'età barocca in Italia*. Bari, 1929.

Croce, Franco. "Critica e trattatistica del barocco." In *Storia della letteratura italiana*. Vol. 5. Milan, 1967, pp. 473–518.

———. "Le poetiche del barocco in Italia." In *Momenti e problemi di storia dell'estetica*. Vol. 1. Milan, 1959, pp. 547–75.

———. *Tre momenti del barocco letterario italiano*. Florence, 1966.

Deakins, Roger. "The Tudor Prose Dialogue: Genre and Anti-genre." *Studies in English Literature, 1500–1900*. 20.1 (Winter 1983): 5–23.

Demetrius. *On Style*. Trans. W. Rhys Roberts. In Aristotle, *Poetics*, et al. Cambridge, Mass., and London, 1973 [rev. ed. 1932].

Derrida, Jacques. *Dissemination*. Trans. Barbara Johnson. Chicago, 1981.

Diogenes Laertius. *Lives of the Eminent Philosophers*. Trans. R. D. Hicks. Cambridge, Mass., and London, 1966 [1925].

Dionisotti, Carlo. *Geografia e storia della letteratura italiana*. Turin, 1980 [1967].

———. *Machiavellerie*. Turin, 1980.

Donazzolo, Pietro. *I viaggiatori veneti minori—Studio bio-bibliografico*. Rome, 1927.

Douehi, Milad. "Traps of Representation." Review of *Le portrait du roi*, by Louis Marin, and *Money, Language and Thought*, by Marc Shell. *Diacritics*, Spring 1984, pp. 66–77.

Dupriez, Bernard. *Gradus: les procédés littéraires*. Paris, 1984.

Eco, Umberto. *Sugli specchi e altri saggi*. Milan, 1985.

Else, Gerald F. *Aristotle's "Poetics": The Argument*. Cambridge, Mass., 1967.

———. *Plato and Aristotle on Poetry*. Ed. Peter Burian. Chapel Hill, N.C., 1986.

Erasmus, Desiderius. *Ciceronianus, or a Dialogue on the Best Style of Speaking*. Trans. Izora Scott. New York, 1972 [1908].

Fano, Amelia. *Sperone Speroni (1500–1588): saggio sulla vita e sulle opere*. Padua, 1909.

Ferguson, Margaret. *Trials of Desire: Renaissance Defenses of Poetry*. New Haven, Conn., 1983.

Ferraro, Rose Mary. *Giudizi critici e criteri estetici nei "Poetices Libri Septem" di Giulio Cesare Scaligero rispetto alla teoria letteraria del Rinascimento*. UNC Studies in Comparative Literature 52. Chapel Hill, N.C., 1971.

Ferroni, Giulio, ed. *Il dialogo: scambi e passaggi della parola*. Palermo, 1985.

Floriani, Piero. *I gentiluomini letterati: studi sul dibattito culturale nel primo Cinquecento*. Le Forme del Significato 29. Naples, 1981.

Foucault, Michel. *The Birth of the Clinic: An Archaeology of Medical Perception*. Trans. A. M. Sheridan Smith. New York, 1973.

———. "Discourse and Truth: The Problematization of *Parrhēsia*." Fall 1983 Seminar, University of California, Berkeley. Unpublished lecture summary.

———. *Language, Memory, Counter-Practice*. Ed. Donald F. Bouchard.

Trans. Donald F. Bouchard and Sherry Simon. Ithaca, N.Y., 1980
[1977].

Gadamer, Hans-Georg. *Dialogue and Dialectic: Eight Hermeneutical Studies on Plato*. Trans. P. Christopher Smith. New Haven, Conn., 1980.

———. *Truth and Method*. Ed. Garrett Barden and John Cumming. New York, 1984 [1975].

Galilei, Galileo. *La prosa*. Ed. Isidoro del Lungo and Antonio Favaro. Florence, 1984 [1957].

———. *Dialogue Concerning the Two Chief World Systems—Ptolemaic and Copernican*. Trans. Stillman Drake. 2d ed. Berkeley, Calif., 1967.

Garin, Eugenio. *La cultura filosofica del Rinascimento italiano*. Florence, 1961.

———. *La filosofia*. 2 vols. Milan, 1947.

Genette, Gérard. *Figures of Literary Discourse*. Trans. Alan Sheridan. New York, 1982.

Giard, Luce. "L'Aristotélisme padouan: histoire et historiographie." *Les études philosophiques* 3 (1986): 281–307.

———. "Histoire de l'université et histoire du savoir: Padoue (XIVᵉ–XVIᵉ siècle)." *Revue de synthèse* 104 (1983): 139–69; 105 (1984): 259–98; 106 (1985): 419–42.

Gilbert, Neal W. *Renaissance Concepts of Method*. New York, 1960.

Giraldi Cinthio, G. B. *On Romances*. Ed. and trans. Henry L. Snuggs. Lexington, Ky., 1968.

———. *Scritti estetici*. 2 vols. Ed. Giulio Antimaco. Biblioteca Rara 52–53. Milan, 1864.

Gmelin, Hermann. "Das Prinzip der Imitatio in den romanischen Literaturen der Renaissance." *Romanische Forschungen* 46 (1932): 83–360.

Grassi, Ernesto. *Rhetoric as Philosophy: The Humanist Tradition*. University Park, Pa., 1980.

Greene, Thomas. *The Light in Troy: Imitation and Discovery in Renaissance Poetry*. Elizabethan Club Series 7. New Haven, Conn., 1982.

———. *The Vulnerable Text: Essays on Renaissance Literature*. New York, 1986.

Grendler, Paul F. *The Roman Inquisition and the Venetian Press, 1540–1605*. Princeton, N.J., 1977.

Grube, G.M.A. *The Greek and Roman Critics*. London, 1965.

Guasti, Cesare. *Le prose diverse di Torquato Tasso*. Florence, 1875.

Günsberg, Maggie. "Tasso's *Materia-Favola* Distinction and the Formalist Notion of *Fabula* and *Sjužet*." *Romance Philology* 37.2 (Nov. 1983): 151–64.

Hall, Vernon, Jr. *Renaissance Literary Criticism: A Study of Its Social Content*. Gloucester, Mass., 1959 [1945].

Hamon, Philippe. "The Rhetorical Status of the Descriptive." Trans. Patricia Baudoin. *Yale French Studies* 61 (1981): 1–26.

Hathaway, Baxter. *The Age of Criticism: The Late Renaissance in Italy.* Ithaca, N.Y., 1962.

———. *Marvels and Commonplaces: Renaissance Literary Criticism.* New York, 1968.

Hermann, Gundert. *Dialog und Dialektik: zur Struktur des platonischen Dialogs.* Amsterdam, 1971.

Herrick, Marvin. *Comic Theory in the Sixteenth Century.* Urbana, Ill., 1950.

———. *The Fusion of Horatian and Aristotelian Literary Criticism, 1531–1555.* Urbana, Ill., 1946.

Hirzel, Rudolph. *Der Dialog: Ein literarhistorischer Versuch.* 2 vols. Hildesheim, 1963 [1895].

Howell, Wilbur Samuel. *Poetics, Rhetoric and Logic: Studies in the Basic Disciplines of Criticism.* Ithaca, N.Y., 1975.

Hume, David. *Dialogues Concerning Natural Religion.* Ed. Richard A. Popkin. Indianapolis, 1980.

Hyland, Drew. "Why Plato Wrote Dialogues." *Philosophy and Rhetoric* 1 (1968): 38–50.

Jacques, Francis. *Dialogiques: recherches logiques sur le dialogue.* Paris, 1979.

Jones-Davies, M. T., ed. *Le dialogue au temps de la Renaissance.* Centre de Recherches sur la Renaissance 9. Paris, 1984.

Kahn, Victoria. "Humanism and the Resistance to Theory." In *Literary Theory / Renaissance Texts.* Ed. Patricia Parker and David Quint. Baltimore, 1986, pp. 373–96.

Kelly(-Gadol), Joan. "Tommaso Campanella: The Agony of Political Theory in the Counter-Reformation." In *Philosophy and Humanism: Renaissance Essays in Honor of Paul Oskar Kristeller.* Ed. Edward P. Mahoney. New York, 1976, pp. 164–89.

Krentz, Arthur A. "Dramatic Form and Philosophical Content in Plato's Dialogues." *Philosophy and Literature* 7.1 (Apr. 1983): 32–47.

Kristeller, Paul Oskar. *Eight Philosophers of the Italian Renaissance.* Stanford, Calif., 1964.

———. *Renaissance Thought and Its Sources.* Ed. Michael Mooney. New York, 1979.

———. *Renaissance Thought: The Classic, Scholastic and Humanist Strains.* New York, 1961.

Kushner, Eva. "Le dialogue de 1580 à 1630: articulations et fonctions." In *L'Automne de la Renaissance.* Ed. Jean Lafond and André Stegmann. Paris, 1981, pp. 149–62.

———. "Le dialogue en France à la Renaissance: quelques critères génologiques." *Revue canadienne de littérature comparée*, Spring 1978, pp. 142–53.

———. "Le dialogue en France de 1550 à 1560." In *Le dialogue au temps de la Renaissance.* Ed. M. T. Jones-Davies. Paris, 1984, pp. 151–67.

———. "The Dialogue of the French Renaissance: Work of Art or Instrument of Inquiry?" *Zagadnienia Rodzajòw Literackich* 20.2 (1977): 23–35.

———. "Réflexions sur le dialogue en France au XVIème siècle." *Revue des sciences humaines* 148 (Oct.–Dec. 1972): 485–501.

———. "Vers une poétique du dialogue de la Renaissance." In *Essays Presented to C. M. Vajda on his Seventieth Birthday.* Szeged, 1983, pp. 131–36.

Lacoue-Labarthe, Philippe, and Jean-Luc Nancy. *L'Absolu littéraire: théorie de la littérature du romantisme allemand.* Paris, 1978.

———. "Le dialogue des genres." *Poétique* 6.21 (1975): 148–75.

———. "Genre." Trans. Lawrence R. Schehr. *Glyph* 7 (1980): 1–14.

Lafond, Jean, and André Stegmann, eds. *L'Automne de la Renaissance, 1580–1630.* Paris, 1981.

Lausberg, Heinrich. *Elemente der literarischen Rhetorik.* Abr. ed. Munich, 1971 [1963].

Leopardi, Giacomo. *Zibaldone di pensieri.* 2 vols. Ed. Francesco Flora. Milan, 1961 [1937].

Levi, Albert William. "Philosophy as Literature: The Dialogue." *Philosophy and Rhetoric* 9.1 (Winter 1976): 1–20.

Levine, Philip. "Cicero and the Literary Dialogue." *Classical Journal* 53 (1957): 146–51.

Longinus. *On the Sublime.* Trans. W. Hamilton Fyfe. In Aristotle, *Poetics,* et al. Cambridge, Mass., and London, 1973 [rev. ed. 1932].

Longo, Nicola. "La letteratura proibita." In *Letteratura italiana.* Vol. 5. Ed. Alberto Asor Rosa. Turin, 1985, pp. 965–87.

Lucian. *Collected Works.* 8 vols. Trans. A. M. Harmon. Cambridge, Mass., and London, 1969.

Mack, Peter. "The Dialogue in English Education of the Sixteenth Century." In *Le dialogue au temps de la Renaissance.* Ed. M. T. Jones-Davies. Paris, 1984, pp. 189–212.

Maggi, Vincenzo, and Bartolomeo Lombardi. *In Aristotelis librum de Poetica communes explanationes.* Venice, 1550.

Maier, Bruno. "Carlo Sigonio." In *Dizionario critico della letteratura italiana.* Vol. 3. Turin, 1974, pp. 399–401.

Man, Paul de. "Dialogue and Dialogism." *Poetics Today* 4.1 (1983): 99–107.

———. "The Epistemology of Metaphor." *Critical Inquiry* 5.1 (Autumn 1978): 13–30. Reprinted in *On Metaphor.* Ed. Sheldon Sacks. Chicago, 1979, pp. 11–28.

———. "The Resistance to Theory." *The Pedagogical Imperative.* Ed. Barbara Johnson. *Yale French Studies* 63 (1982): 3–20. Reprinted in Paul de

Man, *The Resistance to Theory*. Ed. Wlad Godzich. Minneapolis, 1986, pp. 3–20.

Manley, Lawrence. *Convention, 1500–1750*. Cambridge, Mass., 1980.

Manso, G. B. *Del dialogo*. In *Erocallia, ovvero dell'amore e della bellezza*. Venice, 1628.

Marchetti, V., and G. Patrizi. "Lodovico Castelvetro." In *Dizionario biografico degli italiani*. Vol. 22. Rome, 1979, pp. 8–21.

Marsh, David. *The Quattrocento Dialogue: Classical Tradition and Humanist Innovation*. Cambridge, Mass., 1980.

Masson, David. *The Life of John Milton*. New York, 1946 [1881].

Matthews, W. H. *Mazes and Labyrinths: Their History and Development*. New York, 1970 [1922].

Mazzacurati, Giancarlo. "Aristotele a corte: il piacere e le regole (Castelvetro e l'edonismo)." In *Culture et société en Italie du Moyen-Age à la Renaissance*. Centre Interuniversitaire de Recherche sur la Renaissance Italienne 13. Paris, 1985, pp. 265–83.

――――. *Conflitti di culture nel Cinquecento*. Naples, 1977.

――――. *Il Rinascimento dei moderni: la crisi culturale del XVI° secolo e la negazione delle origini*. Bologna, 1985.

McKeon, Richard. "Literary Criticism and the Concept of Imitation in Antiquity." In *Critics and Criticism: Ancient and Modern*. Ed. R. S. Crane. Chicago, 1952, pp. 147–75.

――――. "Rhetoric and Poetic in the Philosophy of Aristotle." In *Aristotle's "Poetics" and English Literature: A Collection of Critical Essays*. Ed. Elder Olson. Chicago, 1965, pp. 207–36.

Mesnard, Jean. "Genèse d'une modernité." In *L'Automne de la Renaissance, 1580–1630*. Ed. Jean Lafond and André Stegmann. Paris, 1981, pp. 5–16.

Michel, Alain. "L'Influence du dialogue cicéronien sur la tradition philosophique et littéraire." In *Le dialogue au temps de la Renaissance*. Ed. M. T. Jones-Davies. Paris, 1984, pp. 9–24.

――――. *La parole et la beauté: rhétorique et esthétique dans la tradition occidentale*. Paris, 1982.

――――. *Rhétorique et philosophie chez Cicéron; essais sur les fondements philosophiques de l'art de persuader*. Paris, 1960.

Mirollo, James V. *Mannerism and Renaissance Poetry: Concept, Mode, Inner Design*. New Haven, Conn., 1984.

Montgomery, Robert L. *The Reader's Eye: Studies in Didactic Literary Theory from Dante to Tasso*. Berkeley, Calif., 1979.

Mulas, Luisa. "La scrittura del dialogo: teorie del dialogo tra Cinque e Seicento." In *Oralità e scrittura nel sistema letterario*. Ed. Giovanna Cerina, Cristina Lavinio, and Luisa Mulas. Rome, 1982, pp. 245–64.

Muratori, Lodovico Antonio. "Vita Caroli Sigonii Mutinensis." In Carlo Sigonio, *Opera omnia*. Vol. 1. Ed. Lodovico Antonio Muratori. Milan, 1732, pp. i–xx.

Murphy, James J., ed. *Renaissance Eloquence: Studies in the Theory and Practice of Renaissance Rhetoric*. Berkeley, Calif., 1983.

Nietzsche, Friedrich. *The Birth of Tragedy / The Case of Wagner*. Trans. Walter Kaufmann. New York, 1967.

———. *Daybreak: Thoughts on the Prejudices of Morality*. Trans. R. J. Hollingdale. Cambridge, Eng., 1982.

Oechslin, Werner. "Architecture and Alphabet." Trans. Carol A. Brévart, *Via* 8 (1986): 97–125.

Ong, Walter J. *Ramus, Method, and the Decay of Dialogue: From the Art of Discourse to the Art of Reason*. Cambridge, Mass., 1983 [1958].

Orsini, G. N. Giordano. *Organic Unity in Ancient and Later Poetics*. Carbondale, Ill., 1975.

Padelford, F. M., ed. and trans. *Select Translations from Scaliger's "Poetics."* Yale Studies in English 26. New York, 1905.

Pallavicino, Pietro Sforza. *Del bene libri quattro*. Rome, 1644.

———. *Trattato dello stile e del dialogo*. Rome, 1662 [1646].

Parker, William Riley. *Milton: A Biography*. Oxford, 1968.

Patterson, Annabel M. *Hermogenes and the Renaissance: Seven Ideas of Style*. Princeton, N.J., 1970.

Perocco, Daria. "Lodovico Castelvetro traduttore di Melantone (Vat. Lat. 7755)." *Giornale storico della letteratura italiana* 156 (1979): 541–47.

Piccolomini, Alessandro. *Annotazioni nel libro della Poetica d'Aristotele*. Venice, 1575 [1572].

Plato. *Phaedo*. Trans. H. N. Fowler. Cambridge, Mass., and London, 1982 [1914].

———. *Republic*. Trans. Allan Bloom. New York, 1968.

———. *Republic*. Trans. G.M.A. Grube. Indianapolis, Ind., 1974.

———. *Sophist*. Trans. H. N. Fowler. Cambridge, Mass., and London, 1977 [1921].

———. *Timaeus, Critias, Cleitophon, Menexenus, Epistles*. Trans. R. G. Bury. Cambridge, Mass., and London, 1981 [1929].

Plato and Xenophon. *Socratic Discourses*. Everyman Library 457. London and New York, 1947 [1910].

Le pouvoir et la plume: incitation, contrôle et répression dans l'Italie du XVIème siècle. Paris, 1982.

Pozzi, Mario. *Trattatisti del Cinquecento*. 2 vols. Milan and Naples, 1978.

Proclus Diadochus. *Commentaires sur la "République."* 3 vols. Trans. A. J. Festugière. Paris, 1970.

Quintilian. *Institutio oratoria*. 4 vols. Trans. H. E. Butler. Cambridge, Mass., and London, 1969 [1920].

Quondam, Amedeo. *La parola nel labirinto: società e scrittura del manierismo a Napoli.* Bari, 1975.

Raimondi, Ezio. *Anatomie secentesche.* Pisa, 1966.

————. *Poesia come retorica.* Florence, 1980.

————. *Rinascimento inquieto.* Palermo, 1966.

————, ed. *Trattatisti e narratori del Seicento.* Milan and Naples, 1960.

Redondi, Pietro. *Galileo Heretic.* Trans. Raymond Rosenthal. Princeton, N.J., 1987.

Riccoboni, Antonio. *Aristotelis "Liber de Poetica."* Venice, 1584.

Rice, Donald, and Peter Schafer. *Rhetorical Poetics: Theory and Practice of Figural and Symbolic Reading in Modern French Literature.* Madison, Wisc., 1983.

Richetti, John J. *Philosophical Writing: Locke, Berkeley, Hume.* Cambridge, Mass., 1983.

Ricoeur, Paul. *Time and Narrative.* Vol. 1. Trans. Kathleen McGlaughlin and David Pellauer. Chicago, 1984.

Rimmon-Kenan, Shlomith. *Narrative Fiction: Contemporary Poetics.* London, 1983.

Robortello, Francesco. *In librum Aristotelis de arte poetica explicationes.* Basel, 1555 [1548].

Roelens, Maurice. "Le dialogue philosophique, genre impossible? L'opinion des siècles classiques." *Cahiers de l'Association internationale des études françaises* 24 (May 1972): 43–58.

Rosa, Mario. "La chiesa e gli stati regionali nell'età dell'assolutismo." In *Letteratura italiana.* Vol. 1. Ed. Alberto Asor Rosa. Turin, 1982, pp. 257–389.

Rosello, Lucio Paolo. *Due dialoghi.* Venice, 1549.

Rosmarin, Adena. *The Power of Genre.* Minneapolis, 1985.

Ruch, Michel. *Le préambule dans les oeuvres philosophiques de Cicéron: essai sur la genèse et l'art du dialogue.* Paris, 1958.

Russell, D. A. *Criticism in Antiquity.* Berkeley, Calif., 1981.

Russell, D. A. and M. Winterbottom, eds. *Ancient Literary Criticism.* Oxford, 1972.

Saint-Mard, Rémond de. *Nouveaux dialogues des dieux, ou réflexions sur les passions, avec un discours sur la nature du dialogue.* Cologne, 1713.

Sapegno, Maria Serena. "Il trattato politico e utopico." In *Letteratura italiana.* Vol. 3.2. Ed. Alberto Asor Rosa. Turin, 1984, pp. 949–1010.

Scaliger, J. C. *Poetices libri septem.* Stuttgart, 1964 [1561]. (See also Padelford.)

Scarpati, Claudio. *Studi sul Cinquecento italiano.* Milan, 1982.

Schmitt, Charles. *The Aristotelian Tradition and Renaissance Universities.* London, 1984.

————. *Aristotle and the Renaissance.* Cambridge, Mass., 1983.

Scotti, Mario. "Sforza Pallavicino." In *Dizionario critico della letteratura italiana.* Vol. 2. Turin, 1974, pp. 747–49.

————, ed. *"Storia del Concilio di Trento" ed altri scritti di Sforza Pallavicino.* Turin, 1962.

Scrivano, Riccardo. *La norma e lo scarto: proposte per il Cinquecento letterario italiano.* Rome, 1980.

Seigel, Jerrold E. *Rhetoric and Philosophy in Renaissance Humanism: The Union of Eloquence and Wisdom, Petrarch to Valla.* Princeton, N.J., 1968.

Shaftesbury, Anthony, Earl of. *Characteristics of Men, Manners, Opinions, Times.* Ed. John M. Robertson. Indianapolis, 1964.

Sichirollo, Livio. *La dialettica.* Milan, 1983 [1973].

Sigonio, Carlo. *De dialogo liber.* Venice, 1561.

————. *Opera omnia.* 6 vols. Ed. Lodovico Antonio Muratori. Milan, 1732–38.

Solerti, Angelo. *Vita di Torquato Tasso.* 2 vols. Turin and Rome, 1895.

Speroni, Sperone. *I dialoghi.* Venice, 1542.

————. *Dialoghi.* Venice, 1596.

————. *Les dialogues de Messieur Speron Sperone italien.* Trans. Claude Gruget. Paris, 1551.

————. *Opere.* 5 vols. Ed. Natal dalle Laste and Marco Forcellini. Venice, 1740.

Spingarn, Joel. *A History of Literary Criticism in the Italian Renaissance.* New York, 1963 [1899].

Stanesco, Michel. "Premières théories du roman." *Poétique* 70 (Apr. 1987): 167–80.

Tasso, Torquato. *Dialoghi.* 3 vols. Ed. Ezio Raimondi. Florence, 1958.

————. *Dialogues.* Trans. Carnes Lord and Dain A. Trafton. Berkeley, Calif., 1982.

————. *Discourses on the Heroic Poem.* Trans. Mariella Cavalchini and Irene Samuel. Oxford, 1973.

————. *Lettere.* 5 vols. Ed. Cesare Guasti. Naples, 1857.

————. *Opere colle controversie.* 33 vols. Ed. Giovanni Rosini. Pisa, 1821–32.

————. *Prose.* Ed. Ettore Mazzali. Milan and Naples, 1959.

————. *Prose diverse.* 2 vols. Ed. Cesare Guasti. Florence, 1875.

Tateo, Francesco. *Tradizione e realtà nell'umanesimo italiano.* Bari, 1967.

Tedeschi, John. "The Cultural Contributions of Italian Protestant Reformers in the Late Renaissance." *Schifanoia* 1: 127–51.

Tiraboschi, Girolamo. *Biblioteca modenese.* 6 vols. Modena, 1781–86.

————. *Storia della letteratura italiana.* 18 vols. Florence, 1774–82.

Todorov, Tzvetan. *Introduction to Poetics.* Trans. Richard Howard. Theory and History of Literature 1. Minneapolis, 1981.

Trimpi, Wesley. "The Ancient Hypothesis of Fiction: An Essay on the Origins of Literary Theory." *Traditio* 27 (1971): 1–78.

———. *Muses of One Mind: The Literary Analysis of Experience and Its Continuity.* Princeton, N.J., 1983.

———. *The Quality of Fiction: The Rhetorical Transmission of Literary Theory.* New York, 1974. Reprinted from *Traditio* 30 (1974): 1–118.

Varchi, Benedetto. *Lezzioni di M. Benedetto Varchi Accademico Fiorentino.* Florence, 1590.

Vernant, Jean-Pierre. *Les origines de la pensée grecque.* Paris, 1983 [1962].

Vettori, Pietro. *Commentarii in primum librum Aristotelis de Arte Poetarum.* Florence, 1560.

Volpe, Galvano della. *Poetica del Cinquecento.* Bari, 1954.

Weinberg, Bernard. "Castelvetro's Theory of Poetics." In *Critics and Criticism: Ancient and Modern.* Ed. R. S. Crane. Chicago, 1952, pp. 349–71.

———. *History of Literary Criticism in the Italian Renaissance.* 2 vols. Chicago, 1961.

———. "Robortello on the *Poetics.*" In *Critics and Criticism: Ancient and Modern.* Ed. R. S. Crane. Chicago, 1952, pp. 319–48.

———, ed. *Trattati di poetica e retorica del Cinquecento.* 4 vols. Bari, 1970–74.

Wilson, Kenneth J. "The Continuity of Post-Classical Dialogue." *Cithara* 21 (1981): 23–44.

———. *Incomplete Fictions: The Formation of English Renaissance Dialogue.* Washington, D.C., 1985.

Index

In this index an "f" after a number indicates a separate reference on the next page, and an "ff" indicates separate references on the next two pages. A continuous discussion over two or more pages is indicated by a span of page numbers, e.g., "57–59." *Passim* is used for a cluster of references in close but not consecutive sequence.

Library of Congress Cataloging-in-Publication Data

Snyder, Jon R., 1954–
    Writing the scene of speaking : theories of dialogue in the late
    Italian Renaissance / Jon R. Snyder.
    p.   cm.
    Bibliography: p.
    Includes index.
    ISBN 0-8047-1459-2 (alk. paper) :
    1. Dialogue.   2. Authorship.   3. Italian literature—16th century—
History and criticism.   4. Italian literature—17th century—
History and criticism.   I. Title.
PN1551.S6   1989
808.2—dc 19   88-34254
                                                           CIP